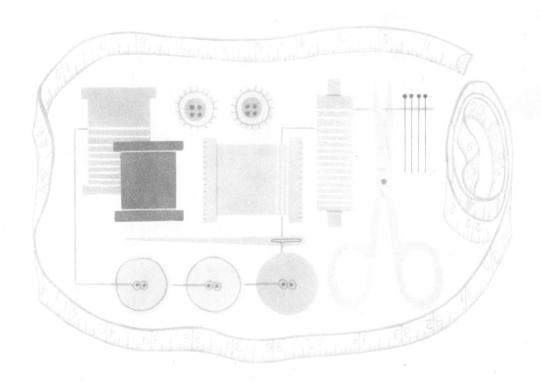

McCall's SEWING

in colour

1 The necessity of moving everything in the middle of dressmaking to lay the table is frustrating. Aim at achieving a well lit comfortable corner where you can carry on where you left off, undisturbed.

Photograph by courtesy of Singer Sewing Machine Company Ltd.

Cover photograph by Denis Hughes-Gilbey. Fabrics by courtesy of the Cotton Board. Sewing basket by courtesy of the General Welfare of the Blind, London. Model by courtesy of John Lewis Partnership, London.

McCall's
SEWING
in colour

HOME DRESSMAKING. TAILORING.
MENDING. SOFT FURNISHINGS

HAMLYN

LONDON · NEW YORK · SYDNEY · TORONTO

First edition published 1964
Eighth impression 1971
THE HAMLYN PUBLISHING GROUP LIMITED
LONDON · NEW YORK · SYDNEY · TORONTO
Hamlyn House · Feltham · Middlesex · England
© Copyright 1963 by McCall Corporation
All rights reserved
Printed in Czechoslovakia by Polygrafia Prague
52004/08
ISBN 0 600 02457 1

CONTENTS

INTRODUCTION

This is a book for the woman who sews—and for the woman who wants to. It explores the art of sewing in all its facets to show you how to transform a piece of fabric into a lovely gown, how to change a dowdy appearance into an attractive, individual one. For just knowing how to sew is not enough. You must know how to select the right pattern for your figure, your personality, your way of life, and then fit it and finish it to give the clothes you make the smart look of good ready-to-wear ones.

This book has been planned to help you do just that. It takes you step by step through the selection of a becoming and appropriate style, the choice of a flattering fabric, and then into construction. Beginners will find outlined the simple construction methods that will let the merest novice turn out a professional-looking garment. And more experienced dressmakers will welcome details on advanced construction techniques, as well as the fact-filled chapters on tailoring and home decoration.

Even the woman who seldom sews will find helpful the information on how to choose the most becoming styles, the instructions for mending and remodelling, the wealth of data on selection and care of fabrics valuable, not only for home dressmaking, but in choosing ready-made clothes as well.

Sewing can be fun, and easy to do if you take it one detail at a time. You can make it a pleasant, satisfying hobby with the added and long-lasting enjoyment of being able to wear the results of your creativity with pride.

CHAPTER 1

BUILDING A NEW YOU

YOUR GOAL — FASHION PERFECTION

The look of fashion is an intangible thing, difficult to analyse, but easier than you think to achieve. There are several ways to earn a place in the list of "best-dressed" women in your town. You can put yourself in the hands of a top couturier and expect for the price you pay to get dresses made just for you, properly fitted, in the right size, in styles which are most becoming to your face and figure, and in colours and fabrics which are flattering. Or, if you are one of the lucky few who is a "perfect" size 10, 12 or 14, you can find, if you search diligently, ready-made garments that you can wear right off the rack.

Realistically, of course, few women have the money it takes to be a full-time patron of the *haute couture*. Even fewer are so perfectly proportioned that any ready-to-wear garment will fit perfectly without some adjustment to individual measurements. They are subject, too, to the curse of mass production—thousands of copies of their dress—any of which is just waiting to be met at a party, a meeting or at the home of a friend.

Thousands of women are finding that there is a practical answer to their desire for clothes that look right, fit right and have the touch of individuality that a ready-made garment can never give them. They are becoming their own couturiers, are making their own clothes and at a fraction of the cost. Like them, you too can always be sure of having the right dress in the right colour. You can free yourself from the whims of manufacturers, from the dictates of fashion whose current decrees may not be the most becoming styles or hues for you. You can create a new you with a wardrobe tailored to fit *your* specifications.

Personal Analysis

Like the beauty of a work of art, which is dependent upon an artist's ability to create pleasing line composition and use colour attractively, fashion perfection is also achieved by correct application of line and colour. However, in the case of a fashion design, you are the canvas. And you are a great deal more complex than a flat cloth surface. So the first step in creating the appearance you want is to analyse yourself and decide exactly how you want to look.

Because it is difficult to see oneself as one really is, don't rely on a mirror. A snapshot or two (one full-face, the other side view), preferably in a bathing suit, will give you a better answer. Flaws never seem quite so realistic in a mirror as they do in a picture, And don't be disheartened. Once you know what's wrong, there's a great deal you can do to correct it.

FIGURE CHECK. First study the general effect you present to the world. Are you short or tall, fat or thin, average in weight and height? How is your posture? Are your shoulders squared and straight, or do they have a tired droop? How about your tummy? Is it flat and tucked in? Is your head held confidently high? Is your waistline clearly defined? Are you well proportioned, or do you bulge in the wrong places? Are you tall enough for your width?

Your body measurements can also be revealing, so make a record of them. Measure around chest, bust, waist, abdomen, upper hip, lower hip, thigh, knee, calf, ankle, upper arm and wrist. And measure your height accurately, without shoes and with the height heel you normally wear. Because the appearance of clothes is improved when placed on a well-proportioned figure, now's the time to begin correcting any irregularities. But whether you try to change your proportions or not, measurements have a disconcerting habit of changing, so keep your record up to date.

FACIAL CHECK. Push back your hair and look into the mirror. The ideal facial shape is an oval. Decide whether your face is oval, round, oblong, square or triangular. By choosing the correct neckline you can often make the shape of the face seem to change.

COLOUR CHECK. Decide which colours are most flattering to your skin, hair and eye colours. Drape fabrics of different colours over your shoulders and see which bring out the highlights in your hair, emphasise the colour of your eyes, make your skin look its glowing best. These are the colours you should stress in your wardrobe planning.

THE EFFECT OF LINE

Since line is a major factor in developing a pleasing appearance, line and the things you can do with it deserve first place in your choice of a style. The total appearance you present to the world contains a profusion of line—not only in the clothes your wear, but in the contours of your face and figure. Notice how lines define the basic body outline, how they separate the form into various areas. Necklines, sleevelines, waistlines and hemlines act as dividers which form shapes and spaces. They make the design interesting and pleasing to the eye. If the direction and spacing of each line is not carefully plotted, the result can be one of confusion.

Line Analysis

In order to use line correctly, it is important to understand that lines have both functional and emotional significance. Although there are only two types of line, straight and curved, they offer infinite variety. Straight lines may follow a vertical, horizontal or diagonal direction; they can be continuous or broken and combined into angles. Curved lines can be round as a full moon or flattened until they appear almost straight. No matter what form a line takes, it has an inherent power to create strong impressions.

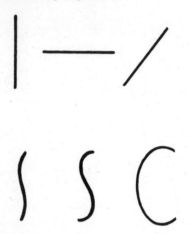

STRAIGHT LINES. The straight line seems stiff and unrelenting to the point of seriousness or sternness. However, the direction it takes can influence the mood of a design. Vertical lines give a feeling of dignity and sophistication, while horizontal lines are calm and gentle. Diagonal lines are a satisfying combination of both. They modify the vertical qualities of dignity and sophistication to give a more relaxed feeling.

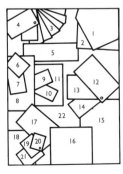

2 There is still no substitute for wool — tartans, tweeds, velours, bouclés, facecloths, jerseys, hopsacks — the weaves and textures are endless.

1 Fancy mid-weight check tweed with **2** Co-ordinate two-tone tweed. **3** Gossamer-light wool crêpes in pink and plum tones. **4** Fancy embossed coating. **5** Check bouclé coating. **6** Medium-weight two-tone shepherd's check with **7** Matching plain. **8** Fancy two-tone woollen. **9** Lightweight two-tone diamond pattern dress weight. **10** Lightweight bouclé woollen. **11** Hopsack. **12** Chunky bouclé coating. **13** Two-tone tweed with brushed surface. **14** Fancy woollen suiting. **15** Thick lacy bouclé tweed. **16** Thick lacy bouclé tweed. **17** Chunky diagonal and check patterned coating. **18** Embossed plain toned check worsted. **19** Brushed woollen. **20** Worsted twill. **21** Nubbly lace tweed. **22** Hopsack background.

Photograph by courtesy of the International Wool Secretariat

3 From the heaviest nubbly tweed through fine worsteds to the most airy woollen lace, wool can be found made up in weights suitable for every possible occasion.

1 Velour. **2** Lightweight tweed in subdued shepherd's check. **3** Bouclé tweed. **4** Thick woollen with pronounced step design. **5** Machine knitted rib fabric. **6** Double jersey. **7** Hopsack. **8** Plain tone tweed. **9** and **9a** Washable afghalaine and washable wool doeskin. **10** Brushed wool tweed. **11** Two-tone fancy tweed. **12** Dice-patterned woollen bouclé. **13** Crêpe. **14** Jacquard jersey. **15** Embroidered lightweight woollen. **16** Co-ordinate plain and check suiting. **17** Heavy, fancy coating tweed. **18** Printed worsted. **19** Lightweight lace. **20** and **21** Bouclé woollen coatings. **22** Crêpe. **23** and **24** Plain and check co-ordinating twill weave tweeds. **25** Check worsted serge. **26** and **27** Saxony wool tartans.

Photograph by courtesy of the International Wool Secretariat

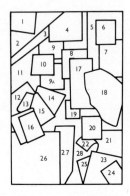

CURVED LINES. The curved line, on the other hand, creates an entirely different mood, and is considered to be more graceful than a straight line. However, curved lines must be controlled if they are to be completely lovely. A full circle can become monotonous. The most graceful curved line is one which takes a diagonal direction. Curved lines can be merry half moons, large luxurious graceful curves, or gay little restless round circles.

DOMINANT LINES. When several lines appear simultaneously, as they do in most dress designs, the eye will follow the strongest line. It is this reaction that makes it possible to emphasise figure assets and minimise faults by attracting the eye to a certain area. If you can keep attention focused on a pretty face, a badly proportioned figure may go unnoticed.

The drawings shown here illustrate various dominant line patterns. Notice the strong horizontal line in each case. A large collar draws attention to a pretty face; pockets and waistline interest emphasise a tiny waist, and a decorative motif atracts the eye to lovely legs.

Tricks with Line

Sometimes it is hard to believe that your eyes don't always tell the truth, but because they don't you can employ fallacies of vision to create a more attractive appearance. To do so, it's important to understand optical illusion and understand how this magic can be put to work to produce the kind of effect you want. Here are some simple examples:

Take the first group of lines, A. You can see immediately that one looks longer than the other although, when you measure them, they are identical in length. Now notice how the vertical lines in B seem to curve. Actually, they are straight. And while the circles superimposed on the pentagon C may seem to flatten out, they are really perfectly round.

Now look at the rectangles in D. Certainly the one divided by the vertical line looks narrower than the one divided by the horizontal line, yet they are identical. The rectangle in E with the narrow panel appears much narrower than the one with the wide panel; they too are alike. As a final example, in F, the rectangle divided by a diagonal which starts at the top line looks narrower than the same rectangle with a diagonal which starts at the side.

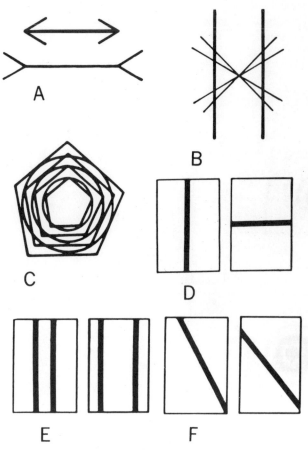

You may wonder how these geometric shapes can apply to dress design. By applying these same principles to your clothes, you can make yourself look taller and thinner—or shorter and wider.

Notice how the diagrams shown here illustrate this.

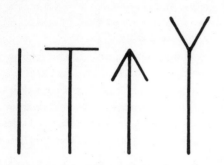

In the first line, there is no opposing force. Therefore the eye continues upward to the end of the line, and an illusion of height is created. Going up the second line, the eye meets the opposing horizontal and starts to travel from side to side, making the vertical line seem shorter. In the third line, the eye is forced downward by the diagonal lines and so this line seems even shorter than the second; in the fourth line, the diagonal lines carry the eye upward so that the vertical line seems even longer than it did in the first diagram.

By analysing line direction in the design when you select a pattern, you can often achieve the effect you wish.

Remember: lines which carry the eye in a vertical direction will make you look taller; those which move in a horizontal direction will give an effect of width; while those that travel diagonally will create an effect of tallness or wideness depending on whether their emphasis is vertical or horizontal.

Tricks with Space

Line is not the only factor to use in creating illusions. Spaces can play tricks too. The manner in which a design is divided into areas by lines influences the appearance. Remember how much wider the rectangle looked when it was divided by a horizontal line? In

dress design the same principle can be followed. A straight hip-length jacket presents the same illusion as the rectangle divided by a horizontal. Conversely, a simple sheath dress with a straight front closing can create the same effect as the rectangle divided by a vertical line. In dividing an area into smaller sections, the reaction of the eye must always be considered. For instance, study again the rectangles divided into panels. The narrow centre panel makes the rectangle appear

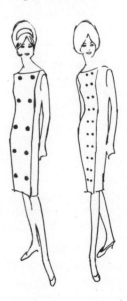

narrower because the eye travels upward between the lines with little attention to the rest of the design. When the wider panel is used, however, the eye moves back and forth between the lines giving an impression of width.

Thus, although the general principle of line is that verticals make an object appear taller while horizontal lines widen, there is always the exception that proves the rule. A reverse effect may occur when pleats, tucks or striped fabrics are used. Notice in this drawing how

much wider the vertical lines make the area look than the horizontal lines do. This is due to the spacing between the stripes, so in planning an arrangement which gives a striped effect, it is important to study the reaction of the eye so that the effect is the one you want to achieve.

Vertical Illusions

One of the best ways to produce a tall slender illusion is to use the tubular silhouette, unbroken by horizontal lines. A straight princess-line sheath is an excellent example of this line. The garment should fit the figure gently, being neither too tight nor too loose. A narrow centre panel, often seen in a princess-line dress, will add height if it is correctly proportioned to the figure. The long lines of surplice openings and full-length coats, or a short bolero jacket with the corresponding long line of a straight skirt, will emphasise the tall

illusion. Tuxedo collars which extend the entire length of a coat can produce the same effect.

If you wish to make your face and throat appear more slender, wear a V-line at the neck. The U-line, particularly a deep U, can produce this effect too, but it will be less pronounced than the V-line. Fairly narrow collars that produce a V-shape, or a coat collar worn open at the throat and high at the back of the neck, will keep the eye moving upward and add length to the face.

Your choice of accessories, too, can help to maintain a vertical illusion. Scarves and hats can add to the upward look. Belts should be narrow with unobtrusive closings and in the same fabric as the dress so that the eye will not be stopped in its vertical movement.

Horizontal Illusions

Generally the bouffant or bell-shaped silhouette will produce a horizontal illusion. However, the impression it creates will depend on the width of the skirt. Wide

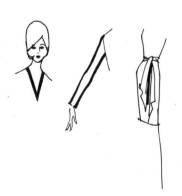

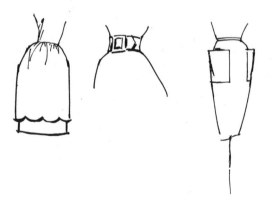

or full sleeves, or sleeves with cuffs that end at the bustline or hipline, will carry the eye across the figure, making it seem wider especially at that spot. Pockets can produce the same effect. Wide belts make the waistline seem broader, and suits, two-piece dresses, short capes, or short jackets which cut the figure in half, or three-quarter-length coats will tend to shorten the figure. Tunics and peplums, particularly if they flare, will have the same effect.

In order to make a thin face seem broader, round, bateau and square necklines can add width. High, close necklines, and round collars such as a Peter Pan, can

create the same illusion of width. Collars with wide revers extending almost to the armhole with the points falling below the shoulder line, or a scarf tied so that the ends extend horizontally, will also keep the eye moving from side to side.

THE EFFECT OF FABRIC DESIGNS

The optical illusions that are accomplished by proper use of line can often be achieved or heightened through the use of patterned fabrics such as stripes or prints. These effects may often be more difficult to accomplish than the ones in which you depend upon line alone, but the figure flattery you can achieve may be well worth the effort.

Tricks with Stripes

Stripes are a perennial favourite, and variations in widths, colours and arrangement give them a new look each year. Not only do stripes produce interesting effects, they can also create flattering illusions. Usually stripes running in a vertical direction will make a person look taller and thinner, but this is not a hard-and-fast rule. There are times when stripes can make the figure appear much wider. The same principle holds true when using stripes horizontally. Although usually stripes moving from side to side make the figure seem stouter and shorter, it is also possible for this direction to make the figure look taller. It all depends on how your eye reacts to the width of the stripes and the distance between them.

If this is hard to believe, notice how the different arrangements of lines shown here seem to create varying illusions. In one the vertical lines keep the eye moving upward, creating a feeling of height, but in the other vertical lines carry the eye from side to side, increasing the apparent width of the area. If you can't quite believe what your eyes are telling you, measure each of the areas to be sure. When the spaces between the stripes are proportioned so that the eye moves easily from one line to the other without stopping, a sideways illusion is created.

Using stripes in a diagonal direction can also create optical illusions. Notice how the diagonals converging at one spot can make two parallel lines seem to bulge.

Therefore, it's very important to analyse a striped fabric before you buy it. Always keep your dress pattern in mind and visualise the direction the stripes will take. Will this have the effect on your figure you desire? Usually, a simple design will give the most pleasing results.

Tricks with Prints

Like stripes, prints also can be used to create desirable effects. However, you should remember that prints

usually make the figure look larger than a plain fabric in the same colour. Usually designs of medium size with close colour contrasts will prove the most flattering to any figure type. Light and bright colours, sharp contrasts and large motifs will tend to increase the apparent size of the wearer; while darker, blurred, all-over patterns will act to decrease size.

Motifs arranged to give a vertical movement to the design seem to add height. When this kind of design is made up of colours that are close in value and the motifs are closely spaced, the print will be flattering to a short figure. Widely spaced, sharply contrasted motifs will call attention to the wearer's size even though the background may be subdued. Circular

motifs give an illusion of roundness and will have a flattering effect if you are thin.

Border prints used at the hemline will have a tendency to attract the eye, particularly if the border is dark and wide. Such a border is ideal if you wish to call attention to pretty legs. However, the strong horizontal illusion makes it impossible to create a feeling of height at the same time, so this type of print is more becoming on a tall slender figure than on a short one.

There is one way to create a lengthening effect with a border print, and that is to use it as the central panel running up and down the dress. Thus the panel creates a path for the eye to follow. This is most successful if the border is a narrow one.

THE EFFECTS OF FABRIC

Fabrics, like lines, can also influence your apparent size. Often a person can select just the right style and lines for figure flattery and then ruin the effect by selecting the wrong fabric. Whether a fabric reflects or absorbs light, is rough or smooth, stiff or clinging will account to some degree for its effect on your appearance.

Light Reflection

Shiny fabrics which reflect a great deal of light will make the figure appear larger, while dull surfaces will tend to minimise size. The illusion created is the same as when an object is placed in a bright clear light, then in a dim diffused light. Naturally, the more light it receives and reflects, the larger the body appears. So the heavy person who selects a design with long, tall vertical lines and then makes the dress in a very shiny satin is defeating her own purpose. She may wonder why she looks so large, yet if she had used a dull silk broadcloth, the gown would have been just as dressy and vastly more flattering.

Some fabrics both reflect and absorb light. Velvet is a good example of this type in which the pile catches light and also casts shadows. As long as the fabric is not a bulky one, it will not noticeably affect the apparent size of the figure.

Rough and Smooth Textures

Rough-textured fabrics tend to appear bulkier than they are, and will increase the size of the figure in proportion to their roughness and bulkiness. Naturally, a pebbly crêpe will not noticeably add pounds, but a very rough, nubbly wool tweed may have a decided effect. Smooth textures will not affect the appearance of the figure as long as they are not shiny.

Stiff Textures

Stiff materials tend to conceal the outline of the figure because they do not follow it. However, although they can hide some figure faults, they usually make the body seem somewhat larger. For example, a person with heavy hips, but with a waistline and bustline in proportion to her height, could wear a stiff fabric to advantage, whereas a person who is heavy all over should avoid it.

Clinging Textures

Fabrics of this type have a double personality. When used for straight, tubular designs, clinging materials outline the figure so completely that they often make it seem larger or thinner than it actually is. However, when they are draped into soft silhouettes, they can be very flattering.

Transparent Textures

Although see-through materials can often be draped in soft, graceful folds, they also reveal the outline of the figure. It is not wise to use transparent fabric if you wish to hide extra folds of flesh or a too thin bony structure.

THE EFFECT OF COLOUR

Lines and textures do not offer the only "bag of tricks" at your disposal for creating optical illusions and enhancing the effects you wish to achieve. Colours can produce illusions, too.

Although there are hundreds and hundreds of different hues, they all come from three basic colours—red, yellow and blue—which are called primary colours. When two primary colours are combined

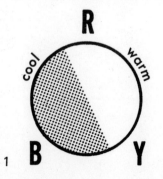

in equal parts, secondary colours—orange, green and purple—are created. This type of combination can continue indefinitely to give us the infinite variety of colours we see all around us (1).

Colours may vary in other ways, too. Depending upon whether they are mixed with white or black, they have qualities of lightness and darkness which are known as

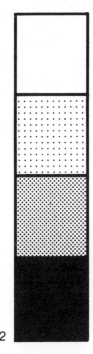

2

values. Colours also have brightness or dullness, which is described as their *intensity* (2). All of these factors can affect the way your eye will react to a colour, so it is important to know just what tricks colour can play.

Tricks with Colour

Colours can make you feel warmer or cooler; they can make you look larger or smaller. Some hues will cause your skin to seem clear and lovely; others may tinge it with unpleasant red or yellow tones.

In terms of comfort, red and orange seem to give an impression of warmth; blue and blue-violet of coolness. Dark colours and black which absorb light also make you feel warmer, while white and light colours which reflect light actually make you feel cooler. Keep these ideas in mind when selecting colours to wear at various times of the year.

As far as size is concerned, hues containing red and yellow are called advancing colours; they make an object seem closer and in turn larger. On the other hand, colours containing blue are receding; they make an

object seem farther away and of course smaller. However, value and intensity also influence the size, so you cannot say that every red dress will make you look larger than every blue dress. A bright crimson may increase size, but dark, grayed red will probably not affect the size of your figure at all. A good way to test this is to look at your feet in white and in black shoes; in shiny patent leather and in suède.

Facial Flattery

Tones of the skin, hair and eyes vary so widely that it is impossible to give definite rules for colour selection that will be flattering to everyone. Probably the best results are obtained by actually testing colours against your face, to find out which hues give the best effect with your individual combination of skin, hair and eyes.

Generally, the skin is considered first when selecting a colour for a costume. Skin tones are composed of varying amounts of red and yellow, and naturally you will want to subdue any predominance of either of these tones. By remembering that colour will be emphasised both by repetition and contrast, you will avoid using complementary colours such as green if your skin is ruddy, or purple if your skin is sallow. You won't choose yellow if there is a predominance of yellow in your skin tone, or red if there is too much red. Usually, dark colours grayed in tone are becoming to a person with a florid complexion but should be avoided if the skin is yellow.

The power of white to reflect light and black to absorb it should be considered when choosing colours to be worn next to your face. Black seems to remove the colour from your skin. This is the reason for wearing a light collar on a dark dress. Although a dark colour can create a dramatic effect if worn by a person with a clear white skin, it is usually better for a person with a pale complexion to avoid it. Large amounts of bright colour will have the same effect. To emphasise the pink tones in your cheeks, wear greens and blue-greens.

If your skin is dark in tone, you will find the blue-greens especially becoming. Grayed medium colours will be more pleasing than the very bright, light or dark.

To emphasise the colour of the hair, you will find that light colours make black and dark brown hair seem darker, whereas dark colours will emphasise the golden lights in blonde hair.

Sometimes a person with lovely eyes wants to enhance their beauty. This can be done by repeating the colour of the eyes in small amounts of a bright colour, large amounts of a grayed one, or by using complementary colours.

Figure Flattery

Although colours are usually chosen to enhance the beauty of the face, their effect on the figure should not be forgotten. Remember how dark, grayed and receding colours make the figure appear smaller, whereas light, bright and advancing colours make it seem larger? Although black makes the figure look smaller, it does clearly define the outline. If you want to camouflage a figure irregularity, such as heavy hips, you will want to avoid the use of black and use instead medium or grayed colours that blend with the background.

The possessor of a tall and well-proportioned figure is fortunate. She can wear all types of colours. She can even introduce strong colour contrasts in her outfit, dividing the costume into definite parts.

The tall, angular figure can also use colour in many ways. Two-colour costumes will be good. They give an illusion of soft roundness, which she needs.

The tall, heavy figure should wear colour carefully. She should avoid colours which will add bulk to her large figure. Grayed medium colours that make the outline indefinite will be best. Sometimes a front panel of a lighter colour will create a slimming illusion.

The short, slender figure will find one-colour costumes most flattering. Designs using two colours, such as a light blouse and dark skirt, should be avoided.

The short, stout figure should also wear one-colour costumes. Dark- or medium-value colours will make the heavy figure appear taller and thinner. Light and bright colours, as well as costumes that have a definite contrast in colour, should be avoided.

When the figure is out of proportion in certain areas, it is best to wear medium grayed colours. Light and bright colours, as well as sharp contrasts, will only emphasise the imperfection.

BECOMING LINES, FABRICS AND COLOURS

All of the factors just outlined have to be put together to get results that will be right for you. As a guide, here are the most important points to remember in relation to your figure type:

Tall and Slender

You're a natural for high fashion and may as well enjoy it. Lines or colour values and intensities shouldn't offer many problems for you. Do avoid lines and colours that make you appear too tall and slender for fear of looking gaunt. Maintain the slenderness without too much height by selecting soft, curved vertical lines. Use bright, vivid colours if they suit your colouring and personality; make good use of striking colour contrasts. Avoid very coarse or heavy fabrics which may overpower the delicacy of your figure.

Tall, Too Thin

The flat, angular look may be right on the pages of fashion magazines, but in real life you're apt to look scrawny. A rounded feminine figure is more pleasing to the eye. Use restrained and slightly full curves in your clothes. Wear bouffant skirts, wide collars, full sleeves. Divide your rectangular figure into spaces to produce a widening effect. Peplums, tunics, hip-length jackets, tiered skirts will do this. If possible, wear bright colours that add a bit of fullness to the figure. Colour contrasts at waist and hip will make your figure seem shorter and fuller. Select medium-weight fabrics which drape nicely and add roundness, stiff fabrics which add fullness, and fairly heavy-weight fabrics with smooth surfaces. Avoid clinging fabrics which reveal the thinness of the figure and too coarse or too heavy fabrics.

Tall, Heavy

Lines for the "Viking" type are a problem. You'll want those which slenderise without adding height. Diagonal lines are the answer; they have the power to be both horizontal and vertical at the same time. Surplice closings, draped effects, gentle flares will be flattering, as long as they are kept simple in design. Softness is what you want, rather than severely tailored or very frilly designs. Grayed colours or those of medium intensity will be more flattering than very light or very dark ones. Select medium-weight fabrics which drape nicely, dull fabrics which have slightly uneven textures, and smooth textures for tailored garments. Avoid large patterns, very crisp and shiny fabrics.

Short and Slender

Usually the short person wants to appear taller, and seeks vertical illusions in her clothes. Coat dresses, princess lines, narrow front panels, surplice closings will all create the tall illusion. Be careful when selecting suits or jackets; keep them fairly short, usually waist-length. A long expanse of skirt will make the figure appear taller. Keep costumes in one colour, matching belts; if contrast is used, keep it high. Select soft fabrics in light or medium weights and small patterned fabrics. Avoid coarse and heavy fabrics which may overpower the figure.

Short and Plump

Vertical is again the general direction for the short and plump figure—not perfectly straight lines, but carefully controlled diagonals and verticals which slenderise. Actually, many of the same lines used for the tall, heavy person can be used here, but in a slightly different manner. The diagonals should be almost vertical in direction. Surplice closings, princess lines, coat dresses with a slight flare will be good choices. Jackets that cut the figure in half are best avoided. One-colour

costumes in medium grayed tones will make the outline of the figure indefinite and will be more flattering. Select dull, soft fabrics, blurry indistinct patterns. Avoid heavy, crisp, coarse and shiny fabrics.

You may be happy with the height of your figure and its size, but have a particular problem which you'd like to camouflage; or maybe you have a lovely feature you would like to emphasise. Line and colour illusion can be used equally effectively for these purposes.

Hip-Heavy

This is the most common problem of all, since women are naturally full-hipped. Keep bodices trim; avoid very straight skirts. Select flattering flares instead and keep skirts smooth fitting over the hips. Place interest high on the costume, using neckline interest to draw attention away from the hipline. Avoid jackets, overblouses and peplums which cut across the hip. Do not use colour contrasts at hipline. However, if you have a tiny waist and well-proportioned bustline, a dark skirt and a light bodice will de-emphasise hips.

Small Bust

If you have a small waist and bust, then look for set-in midriff styles, gathers beneath the bust, slightly bloused bodices. For a large-waisted figure, yokes, soft fullness at the neckline and draped bodices will be more flattering. You can use overblouses if your hips are fairly narrow.

Low, Full Bust

Start with the proper foundation garments, and if possible, have them fitted by a professional. Then select softly draped bodices, with not too much fullness but just a little. Keep interest high on the figure. Avoid very high or low necklines. Do not use bodice colours that are light, bright or shiny, or fabrics that cling.

Thick Rib Cage

Centre the interest away from the rib cage, at neckline or hemline, depending on your best feature. Boxy jackets, bloused bodices, soft draping, overblouses will help de-emphasise this area.

Short-Waisted

Make the waist look longer through low-waisted designs, hip-length jackets, overblouses. Wear one-colour costumes with smooth, uninterrupted lines. Avoid contrasting belts, very full skirts or very slim ones.

Long-Waisted

Wide sashes, contrasting belts, set-in midriffs will give a lift to the waistline. Tunics, peplums and long jackets are equally effective. This figure must be careful, when short, short skirts are the fashion, to avoid looking top-heavy.

Round Shoulders

Bloused bodices will help conceal the curved line, as will necklines with angular rather than curved collars. Try using shoulder pads to raise the shoulder line at the right spot, and placing the shoulder line of a garment behind its normal position will help.

Narrow Shoulders

Set-in sleeves with a small amount of padding to build up the shoulder will best conceal too-narrow shoulders. Avoid kimono sleeves, dolman and raglan styles which only emphasise the narrow line.

Short Neck

Choose necklines no higher than a jewel neckline. Stand-away collars, collarless styles and V- or U-shaped necklines will make the neck seem longer.

Long Neck

The swanlike throat can be enviable, but it can also look plain scrawny. Shorten it with high turtle and mandarin necklines, or large collars and high chokers.

Prominent Abdomen

Start with a good foundation garment and check your posture. Pleats or shirring at sides of the skirt with a straight front panel will be the best camouflage. Wear boxy hip-length jackets. Strive for vertical lines to carry the eye up the figure, thus skimming over the problem area.

Prominent Derrière

Look for flowing lines, especially those which flow at the back. Hip-length boxy jackets will help; box-pleated skirts, flared skirts and shirred waistlines are effective. Fill in the hollow above the derrière with blousing such as a sash or a flying panel.

WARDROBE NEEDS

With the tricks of optical illusion at your disposal and a definite idea of what you want to do to change your appearance, you should consider your wardrobe needs. No matter how carefully you have chosen your design, the effect will be spoiled unless the garment is right for the occasion at which it is worn. This doesn't mean that you need lots and lots of clothes. A few costumes which can be used for different occasions are a wise choice. Usually every woman needs a simple coat, a classic suit, several basic dresses which may be dressed up or down by the use of accessories, a casual dress, skirt, blouse, sweater, sports ensemble and after-five dress. However, when to wear them may be confusing. A few general suggestions are given here for you to consider in planning your wardrobe.

At Home

The homemaker often makes the big mistake of thinking she does not have to look her best when doing her daily chores. Actually, ill-fitting clothes lower her morale and make her less able to cope with everyday trials. This doesn't mean she has to dress up, but it does mean that she should look neat and trim.

If you look well and feel comfortable in slacks or shorts, wear them when working in the home. But be sure you look well in them and that they fit properly.

A simple shirtwaist dress or wrap-around with flared or pleated skirt will often present a much more attractive appearance and be just as comfortable as pants.

For evenings at home a simple dress is always in good taste. But dress up a little bit if you wish. It adds a touch of gaiety or elegance to a family gathering. However, the degree of dressing-up depends on your situation. Fancy pants or long skirts may look ludicrous in one place, marvellous in another.

On the Job

A simple dress, suit, skirt, jacket, and blouse that can be mixed and matched form the basis of this wardrobe. Keep the clothes tailored, uncluttered and easy to care for. Usually a career girl's wardrobe is largely

selected in dark and basic colours, but don't be afraid to include some brighter colours just to add a little pep.

Clothes that are too tight or too revealing are taboo in an office. Dressy, low-cut clothes should be avoided. Casual clothes that look wonderful for informal occasions are out of place in a more sophisticated business atmosphere.

For School

Separates are the answer to the schoolgirl's needs. Skirts, sweaters, jackets and blouses that can mix and match are perfect. A few basic dresses for social occasions such as church, teas, informal gatherings, and a party dress or dressy separates for formal functions will complete the schoolgirl's wardrobe. Of course, a good cover-everything coat is a necessity.

For Sports

Sportswear in our modern sense covers both clothes for sports events and casual clothes in general. Naturally, participating in special sports requires special costumes. What you need for golf is wrong for tennis. And as a spectator at sports events, choose comfortable, sturdy-looking clothes. Separates, simple dresses and classic suits are always appropriate.

For Shopping

By this, we mean shopping in a city department store. Slacks and shorts are taboo. Again, simple dresses and suits are best. A comfortable topcoat which can be worn over suit or dress is most useful.

For Evening Parties

Evening clothes depend entirely on the type of social life you lead. For informal parties, an afternoon or cocktail dress or suit can be used. For formal dances, long or short evening gowns can be worn. The formality of your evening clothes will depend upon the community you live in.

For Travelling

Tailored clothes are always best. Flared skirts are more comfortable to sit in, and give a more pleasing look as well. When you reach your destination, the clothes you need will depend on the locale. Resorts require rather gay, festive clothes; cities more conservative businesslike costumes, while rough country life demands casual, comfortable garments.

For Club Activities

Dressmaker suits, simple dresses, such as the sheath, shirtwaist and coat dress are always appropriate. They may have soft touches, but avoid fussy styles.

CHAPTER 2

KEYSTONE TO FASHION — A PERFECT PATTERN

Without patterns, home-sewing would probably be a lost art, or at best would be relegated to mending and altering ready-to-wear clothes. The fun of sewing would disappear, and with it the satisfaction and enjoyment of creating something lovely and unique to wear. For every one of the hundreds of new patterns which appear each year is destined to make someone look more attractive if that pattern is chosen with discrimination and care.

Naturally, not every pattern style will look equally well on everyone, just as no ready-made garment is the answer for every woman. But unlike ready-to-wear, the garment you plan to make at home cannot be tried on in advance. You have to take a chance, but if you know how to pick the right pattern, your risk can be a very small one. This is not just a matter of flipping through the pages of a pattern catalogue and selecting an appropriate style. It involves finding your correct figure type and size.

Choosing a pattern in the correct figure type and size seems to be a difficult thing for many women to do. They prefer to choose a style and then worry about how to make it fit, whereas if they chose the correct pattern in the first place, it would solve a great many of their problems. It may also make the difference between a smooth, professional look and an amateurish one. Pattern companies divide their catalogues into sections depending upon figure types, so that once you have determined your type, you can turn directly to the section you need.

FIGURE TYPES AND SIZES

If you look around you, you will notice that women are made in a great variety of shapes. You also know that while many women have almost identical measurements, this is where the similarity ends. Their general proportions are so varied, their figures appear to be entirely different. One may seem tall and slender, another fairly plump; yet bust, waist and hip measurements of both are the same.

Figure Types

Because of women's varying shapes, McCall's Patterns

has designed patterns to fit seven different groups of figures with differences in height and contour: Pre-teen, Teen, Junior, Misses', Women's, Junior Petite, and Half-Size. Although these figure type names may seem to refer to age groups, they don't. Generally, a Junior figure belongs to a young girl, but it is just as possible for a woman of forty to have the same measurements and proportions. It is equally possible for a girl of fourteen to require a Misses' pattern.

To illustrate more clearly how these seven figure types differ in proportions, study the chart on page 16. Notice the important differences in height, position of the bustline and thickness of the waist.

Pattern Sizes

Each figure type is made in various sizes. Pre-teen

patterns are available in size 8 to 14; Teen, 10 to 16; Junior, 9 to 15; Misses', 10 to 20; Women's, 40 to 46; Junior Petite, 3 to 11; Half-Size, 12½ to 24½.

Pattern sizes and ready-to-wear sizes are not comparable. There are often vast differences between a Junior dress you buy and one you make. The only accurate way to select your correct pattern size and type is to study your body contours and analyse your measurements.

Figure Measurements

If you haven't checked your measurements, be sure to do it before you purchase a pattern. If possible, have someone help you. Wear the undergarments you expect to wear with the garment you plan to make. Tie a ribbon around your waist. Then stand in a normal-posture position with your feet together and have the person doing the measuring standing behind you.

The essential measurements for determining figure type and size are: height, bust, waist, hip and length of back waist. Measure *height* by standing flat against a wall, lightly marking the position of the top of your head on the wall. Then measure from the floor up and record the actual feet and inches. To measure the *bust*, place the tape over the fullest part of the bust, running

it under the arms and straight across the back. For the *waist* measurement, place the tape snugly around your natural waistline. For the *hip*, measure around

MEASUREMENTS NEEDED TO BUY PATTERN	MEASUREMENTS AND DATE TAKEN			
BUST				
WAIST				
HIPS				
BACK WAIST LENGTH				

FRONT   BACK

3

the fullest part, usually seven inches below the natural waistline. *Back waist length* is measured from the prominent bone at the centre back of the neck to the natural waistline where you have tied the ribbon.

Record these measurements and the date they are taken. Be sure to check your measurements often. It's surprising how they can change in a matter of weeks (3).

With your measurements and your own knowledge of your figure, you should have little difficulty finding your figure type. Check your height and general proportions with the chart (4) showing general silhouettes and characteristics of each figure type. Select the out-

4

	PRE-TEEN	TEEN	JUNIOR	MISSES'	WOMEN'S	JUNIOR PETITE	HALF-SIZE
HEIGHT	about 5'1"	about 5'3"	about 5'5"	about 5'6"	about 5'6"	about 5'1"	about 5'3"
BUST	very small (just beginning to mature)	small high	mature high	mature normal	fully developed	normal	fully developed
WAIST	slightly large for height	slightly large for height	normal	normal	large for height	small	large for height
HIP	slightly large for height	slightly large for height	rounded	full	full	full	full
BACK WAIST LENGTH	short	short	short	normal	long	short	short

line which best corresponds to your figure. If you are not sure whether you are short-waisted or long-waisted, consider a 16-inch back waist length as a standard. The adult figure of less than 16-inch back waist length can be considered short-waisted, and should choose her figure type from the shorter-waisted types: Junior or Half-Size; or if she is very short, the Junior Petite. The normal or longer-waisted figure will look for her type either in the Misses' or Women's types. The young figure will choose from the Pre-teen or Teen types.

After you have determined the figure type your figure most closely resembles, use your measurements to find the right size within that figure type. Compare your bust, waist, hip and back waist length measurements with those shown for the various figure types and sizes on the chart shown (5). Find the set or combination of measurements which most closely corresponds with your own. Remember that bust, waist and hip measurements of sizes in two different figure types may be quite similar, but the back waist length will differ. Be sure you select the size that will best fit you lengthwise as well as around the body.

If you find a set of measurements which exactly matches yours, you are among the lucky ones. Most people have slight variations. If you find your measurements fall between two sizes, select the pattern in the smaller size if you have a small bone structure; in the larger size if your bone structure is very large.

You may find that bust and back waist length in a size are about the same as your measurements, but your waist and hip are either larger or smaller. When this occurs, select the size according to your bust measurement if the pattern is a dress, coat or suit. It is easier to alter waist and hip measurements than the bustline. However, if back waist length, hip and waist all compare but you have a larger-than-average bust, you may want to select the size that fits waist and hip and alter the pattern for the bustline.

5

TEEN

Size	10T	12T	14T	16T
Bust	30	32	34	36
Waist	24	25	26	28
Hip	32	34	36	38
Back Waist Length	$14\frac{3}{4}$	15	$15\frac{1}{4}$	$15\frac{1}{2}$

JUNIOR

Size	9	11	13	15
Bust	$30\frac{1}{2}$	$31\frac{1}{2}$	33	35
Waist	$23\frac{1}{2}$	$24\frac{1}{2}$	$25\frac{1}{2}$	27
Hip	$32\frac{1}{2}$	$33\frac{1}{2}$	35	37
Back Waist Length	15	$15\frac{1}{4}$	$15\frac{1}{2}$	$15\frac{3}{4}$

MISSES'

Size	10	12	14	16	18	20
Bust	31	32	34	36	38	40
Waist	24	25	26	28	30	32
Hip	33	34	36	38	40	42
Back Waist Length	$15\frac{3}{4}$	16	$16\frac{1}{4}$	$16\frac{1}{2}$	$16\frac{3}{4}$	17

WOMEN'S

Size	40	42	44	46
Bust	42	44	46	48
Waist	34	36	$38\frac{1}{2}$	41
Hip	44	46	48	50
Back Waist Length	$17\frac{1}{8}$	$17\frac{1}{4}$	$17\frac{3}{8}$	$17\frac{1}{2}$

JUNIOR PETITE

Size	3JP	5JP	7JP	9JP	11JP
Bust	31	$31\frac{1}{2}$	32	$32\frac{1}{2}$	33
Waist	$22\frac{1}{2}$	23	$23\frac{1}{2}$	24	$24\frac{1}{2}$
Hip	$32\frac{1}{2}$	33	$33\frac{1}{2}$	34	$34\frac{1}{2}$
Back Waist Length	14	$14\frac{1}{4}$	$14\frac{1}{2}$	$14\frac{3}{4}$	15

PRE-TEEN

Size	8PT	10PT	12PT	14PT
Bust	28	29	31	33
Waist	23	24	25	26
Hip	31	32	34	36
Back Waist Length	$13\frac{1}{2}$	$13\frac{3}{4}$	14	$14\frac{1}{4}$

HALF-SIZE

Size	$12\frac{1}{2}$	$14\frac{1}{2}$	$16\frac{1}{2}$	$18\frac{1}{2}$	$20\frac{1}{2}$	$22\frac{1}{2}$	$24\frac{1}{2}$
Bust	33	35	37	39	41	43	45
Waist	27	29	31	33	35	$37\frac{1}{2}$	40
Hip	37	39	41	43	45	47	49
Back Waist Length	$15\frac{1}{4}$	$15\frac{1}{2}$	$15\frac{3}{4}$	16	$16\frac{1}{4}$	$16\frac{1}{2}$	$16\frac{3}{4}$

Generally, dresses, suits and coats are selected according to bust measurements. Skirts are selected by waist measurement unless the hip is two inches larger than the standard hip measurement given for the size. If this is the case, then select skirts for the hip measurement and alter the waist to fit. Full skirts can be bought according to waist measurement, since there is usually enough fullness to take care of the larger hip. Slacks are selected by hip measurement.

Ease Allowance

There is one important thing to keep in mind when determining your size in a pattern. The measurements given for each size are *standard body measurements*, not actual measurements of the pattern pieces. If garment measurements were the same as the figure, the fabric would pull across the figure and probably split with every movement of the body. To ensure that a garment will fit comfortably and smoothly, there has to be a certain amount of ease. McCall's patterns provides this ease in every pattern.

Generally, the ease allowance in McCall's patterns is:

Bust: $3\frac{1}{2}$ inches over the standard bust measurement, in most dresses. Evening bodices which are designed to fit very tightly in the bodice may have less.
Waist: $\frac{1}{2}$ inch.
Hip: Approximately $2\frac{1}{2}$ inches on slim skirts.
Back Waist Length: $\frac{1}{4}$ to $\frac{3}{8}$ inch.

Proportioned Patterns

Many women find that they have normal body proportions for a Misses' or Junior size but the over-all height in the figure type does not correspond to their own. McCall's has a special pattern to meet this need, the proportioned-to-height patterns in the Misses' and Junior figure types. These patterns are designed to fit tall (5′ 8″ to 5′ 10″), medium (5′ 6″ to 5′ 7″) or short (5′ 3″ to 5′ 5″) figures. All construction markings and proportioning details such as darts, crotch lengths, pleats and hemlines are printed on the pattern for tall, medium and short figures.

If none of the pattern types and sizes have back waist length measurements to suit your figure, don't despair. Select the type and size which is closest to your measurements and general contours. You will be able to adjust the pattern using the Easy-Rule Guide for the short- or long-waisted figure, which is another special feature of McCall's Patterns.

Once you have determined your figure type, please don't be tempted to try a different type simply because you like a particular style. And insist on buying the size that fits you best. If the store don't have it, ask them to order it. It will be better to wait a few days for it than to struggle through the great amount of adjusting that is necessary to alter the wrong size.

Sizes for Children

Once you've developed your sewing skill, undoubtedly you'll want to make garments for your family.

Children's, Toddlers', Boys' and Girls' pattern sizes are based on waist and chest measurements. They should never be selected according to the age, height or weight of the child. Compare the child's measurements with (6) standard body measurements for each size shown below. It is easy to lengthen or shorten bodices, skirts or sleeves by using the printed Easy-Rule Guide.

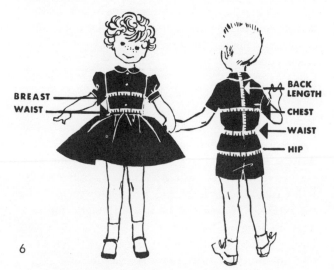

Children's Sizes:

Size	1	2	3	4	5	6	6X
Breast	20	21	22	23	23½	24	25
Waist	19½	20	20½	21	21½	22	22½
Hip					25	26	27
Back Waist Length	8⅛	8½	9	9½	10	10½	11

Toddlers' Sizes:

Size	6 Mos.	1	2	3
Breast	19	20	21	22
Waist	19	19½	20	20½

Children need lots of room in their garments, since they are more active than adults. Patterns provide this ease at the waistline of dress patterns, generally two to three inches over the standard body waist measurement. Skirts, slacks and shorts which must fit snugly at the waist do not have this additional ease allowance.

On many dress patterns, the design features a raised waistline located above the child's normal or natural waistline. When the design does feature this type of waist, you will find the words "high-waisted" in the description of the style on the back of the pattern envelope. If you want a dress which fits the natural waistline, you should select another style.

There is often some confusion about the differences between Toddlers' and Children's sizes. Toddlers' sizes are designed for the non-walking child and are two inches shorter than children's sizes, with the same chest and waist measurements.

Sizes for Men

When sewing for the men in your life, select their shirt patterns according to the neck size, no matter what the chest measurement is. It is almost impossible to alter the neckline of a shirt, but with the pattern's full eight inches of ease through the chest, there is ample allowance for chest girth variations. If you find there is too much ease to suit him, the pattern may be easily altered according to the instructions given in Chapter 6.

Men's shorts, pants and slacks are sized according to waist measurements; sports coats and vests by chest measurements.

Men's Sizes:

Chest	32	34	36	38	40	42	44	46	48
Waist	28	30	32	34	36	38	40	42	44
Neck Base Girth	13½	14	14½	15	15½	16	16½	17	17½
Shirt Sleeve Length	33	33	33	33	34	34	34	35	35

PATTERNS AND SKILL

When you choose a pattern, remember not every seamstress is an expert. Your own prowess should be a determining factor in pattern selection. Don't choose a pattern that is too difficult. It is much better to select something simple and construct it in a professional way than to do an unprofessional job on a more difficult design. As you become more proficient, you can proceed from the easy to the more difficult constructions.

Slim or flared skirts make excellent beginning projects. A blouse with an unmounted sleeve such as kimono and raglan also can be made by the novice. Graduate from blouses and skirts to jumpers and dresses before you attempt a coat or suit.

THE LANGUAGE OF PATTERNS

A beginning seamstress may feel Einstein's theories are as easy to understand as the intricacies of a first pattern. Here again is a place where first steps should be taken slowly. Once you have the basic information that will allow you to read the easy-to-follow directions, when you can decipher the symbols and follow the charts that come with your pattern, you will find using a pattern no more difficult than using a recipe. And, whether you are a beginner or an experienced home-sewer, every pattern should be carefully studied before you lay out your pattern and start to cut.

Each pattern company differs to some extent in the symbols used to mark its patterns and in the sewing methods it recommends. Be sure to choose a pattern from a firm that marks them clearly and accurately and provides adequate directions presented in an easily understandable manner. A McCall's pattern, for example, not only gives complete instructions for constructing the garment, but also suggests the proper fabrics to use and provides basic information on preparing fabric, adjusting the pattern, cutting, marking and sewing techniques. Vital directions are clearly printed on the pattern tissue, and each pattern has an Easy Sewing Guide to lead you through the construction step by step. Once you know how to interpret each symbol and direction correctly, working with a pattern is easy.

The Pattern Envelope

Your study should begin with the pattern envelope before you buy the pattern. The envelope is a storehouse of valuable information. It provides enough data to help you judge how the garment will look and fit your figure, and whether you can easily handle the construction of it. Remember, patterns cannot be returned.

THE FRONT DESIGN. No doubt the sketch of the design on the front of the envelope will catch your eye first. Study it. Be sure the silhouette and design lines are right for you. Check the different views and versions of the design. Decide which one will be most suitable for your needs. Note the fabric and trims illustrated. If the design is a good one for plaids, prints, checks or stripes, the illustration will feature these fabrics. If the designer feels that certain trims will enhance the design, these are also illustrated (7).

TYPE AND SIZE. Double-check the figure type and size of the pattern. Be sure it is the right one for you. Do not accept another size or type even if the one you wish is not readily available. The figure type is listed under the large pattern number, preceding a very brief description of the type of garment. Size is noted on the same line as the large pattern number. The Junior Petite, Pre-teen and Teen patterns will also have an identifying "JP," "PT" or "T" preceding the pattern size.

McCall's PRINTED PATTERN

MISSES' DRESS WITH SLIM OR FULL SKIRT

"EASY TO SEW"

6566

SIZE 12 BUST 32

IN CANADA 60c

EASY
*RECOMMENDED FOR BEGINNERS

2. Special features

1. Type and size

7

SPECIAL FEATURES. Special pattern features such as EASY, INSTANT and Proportioned will be clearly marked on the front of the envelope. The EASY and INSTANT patterns are identified in big red letters which can't be missed. The Proportioned patterns have the word "proportioned" preceding the figure type. Look for these names and use them for quick, easy sewing. Detailed instructions for handling these special patterns are given in Chapter 8.

THE BACK SKETCHES. On the back of the pattern envelope there is quite a bit of information to digest. First check the sketch of the back view of the design to see if it will be flattering. Read the detailed description of the design above the sketch, noting the type of sleeve, collar, skirt and closings used. Decide whether the design features the details you want. Beginners may wish to avoid certain design features such as gussets, long button-front closings, complicated collars, intricate darting. These features may not be clearly shown in the sketch, but will be noted in the description. Use this information to judge whether the construction of the garment is within your level of skill (8).

The sketch of each pattern piece which appears on the back of the envelope is mainly to help you sort the pattern before cutting. Here each piece is sketched to scale and identified as to section. The experienced seamstress can tell a great deal about the construction

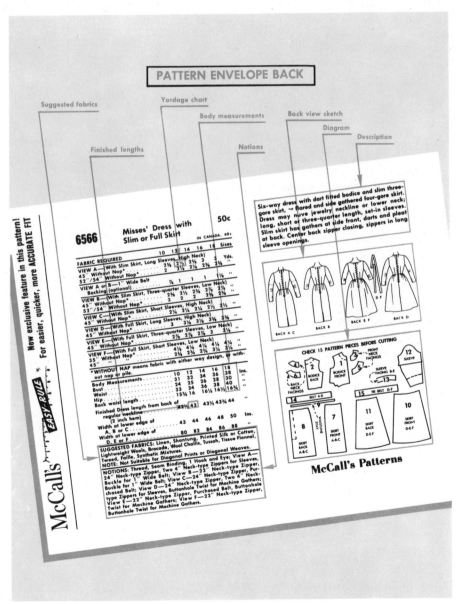

8

of the garment from studying the pieces sketched, and can judge approximately how much time it will take to construct the garment. The beginner should avoid designs made with a great many pieces, since these are usually more time-consuming and more difficult to handle than the simpler styles.

SUGGESTED FABRICS. Perhaps the most important and most neglected section on the back of the pattern envelope is the "Suggested Fabrics" listing. Here the designer notes the fabrics he knows have the proper weight and draping quality for the design. Remember that in discussing fabric for a design in Chapter 1, the importance was stressed of finding a fabric which naturally drapes or falls into the general silhouette and line of the pattern. If you neglect to follow the suggestions given, your fabric may create a silhouette which is entirely different from the one intended.

The pattern on p. 21 gives a sample "Suggested Fabrics" list. All the fabrics indicated are medium-weight materials that have firmness and body. Any of these can be successfully used, or one of comparable weight and body such as a waffle piqué, firm rayon similar to linen, brocade, denim or cotton tweed. A sheer voile, a soft batiste or a heavy-weight fleece would completely alter the look of the design.

If you plan to use a diagonal print or weave or stripes, checks or plaids, read the "Suggested Fabrics" section very carefully. If the design is cut so that these fabrics are unsuitable, a notation "Not Suitable for Diagonal Prints or Diagonal Weaves" will appear in the section. The same notation will be made for stripes, checks and plaids.

YARDAGE CHART. Once you have the type of fabric in mind, refer to the yardage chart to find out how much material you will need for the garment in your size. The yardage chart has been carefully tested to give the exact yardage needed for each size, view and width of fabric when using the layouts given in the pattern instructions. By reading down the column from the size and across from the widths of fabric listed, the exact yardage for size and width of fabric is noted. On proportioned patterns, yardage is given for height as well as size and width of fabric. Be sure to note whether the fabric is listed as "Without Nap" or "With Nap." "Without Nap" refers to any fabric which can be cut with the pattern pieces laid in opposite directions, up and down. "With Nap" means that all pattern pieces must be cut in one direction on the fabric. Among "With Nap" fabrics are one-way designs, prints or weaves; those which reflect light in different ways depending on the up-and-down direction of the weave (satin); all the pile or napped fabrics such as velveteen, velvet, fleece, fake furs; and some flannels and bouclés.

If you do plan to use a napped fabric and the yardage chart doesn't indicate "With Nap" yardage, examine the design sketch carefully to be sure a napped fabric can be used successfully. You'll have to devise your own cutting layout because there will not be one in the pattern instructions, so try a sample layout before purchasing fabric. Lay the pattern pieces out, all going in the same direction, on brown paper folded to the width of the fabric you plan to use. Measure the length needed to lay out the pattern and buy that length of fabric.

When interfacings or other shaping materials are essential to the design, the yardages will be listed. Since shaping materials are becoming increasingly important in garment construction, many patterns are now suggesting linings and underlinings which are optional. You should use them whenever you feel they will help the look and wear of the garment. If you do plan to use a lining or underlining and yardage is not given, work out the proper yardage by laying out the pieces to be lined in a sample layout, and measure the length of fabric needed.

Yardages for belting for fabric belts and for special trims suggested for a design will also be noted in this section.

NOTIONS. While making a list of fabrics and trims needed, check the "Notions" section to see what notions are needed. You will save time by buying everything at one time, and it's easier to match colour of thread, zipper, buttons and trims if they are all purchased at once. Be sure to buy all the notions listed. It's frustrating to have to interrupt a sewing session just to run out and pick up a forgotten item.

BODY MEASUREMENTS. For your convenience, the body measurements of the figure types and sizes available in a particular pattern are listed on the back of the pattern envelope. Although you should be fully aware of your proper type and size before you request a pattern, you may wish to refer to this for a double-check.

FINISHED LENGTHS. When you become familiar with pattern alterations, and know generally whether you need to shorten or lengthen a pattern to suit your figure, you will want to check the finished lengths listed on the pattern envelope. As you sew, become familiar with the length jacket, skirt, blouse, dress you prefer. Compare these to the finished length indicated on the pattern you plan to purchase. You can estimate whether you'll have to shorten or lengthen, and this may affect the yardage needed. Become familiar with the width skirt you find most flattering, and also compare this with the notation on the pattern envelope.

Certainly, with all this information right at your fingertips, it should be an easy decision whether to purchase the pattern or not. If one pattern doesn't suit your specific needs, look for another. The large collection of McCall's Patterns most certainly will include more than one pattern that is a perfect choice for you.

Sewing Guide

A special sheet of instructions is placed in every pattern. Each pattern company prepares this guide in a different manner. McCall's has given the preparation of its Easy Sewing Guide a great deal of thought, making it simple to understand and follow. Directions are presented in step-by-step form. Illustrations are clearly drawn and profusely shown (9).

Before any work is done with your pattern, read the sewing guide carefully. This is important even for the experienced seamstress. Study each step of the construction process. If any part is not clear, find out how it should be handled before you begin to sew.

This sewing book has been written for just that purpose, to provide reference material which will amplify and clarify sewing instructions. Beginners may find that the printed instructions are not as detailed as they might be, because instruction sheets are printed to fit a certain space and sometimes do not include minute details. The pattern company must assume that the customer has certain basic sewing knowledge and understands the sewing language.

In addition to the basic construction information, the Easy Sewing Guide contains helpful suggestions for altering the pattern by the Easy-Rule Guide, preparing the fabric, and general tips on cutting, mark-

9

McCall's
6444

EASY SEWING GUIDE
FOR STEP-BY-STEP, CUTTING AND ASSEMBLING

1. YOUR PATTERN

a. All the pattern pieces included in this design are shown in diagram below. Select the pattern pieces to be used. Place remaining pieces inside the envelope. Press pattern pieces.

b. If pattern adjustments are necessary, they should be made before placing pieces on fabric. NOTE: For complete information regarding pattern adjustments, see "McCall's Easy Sewing Book".

2. CUTTING LAYOUTS

a. Mark a circle around layout to be followed.

b. Pin ALL pattern pieces to fabric before cutting.

3. YOUR FABRIC

IMPORTANT — First be sure that woolens, washable fabrics and interfacings are pre-shrunk.

HOW TO STRAIGHTEN FABRIC

Straighten ends of fabric by tearing across, or if it does not tear well, draw a thread across; then cut on line of drawn thread (sketches A and B).

To straighten fabric (sketch C), stretch fabric on the bias in opposite direction until the crosswise threads are squared with selvages (sketch D).

HOW TO CUT

Cut pattern and fabric through the white center of the double line. Do not cut off the margin before cutting fabric.

The margin falls away as you cut through pattern and fabric.

MARKING WITH TRACING WHEEL

All markings should be made on the WRONG SIDE of fabric. Trace lines of pattern with a tracing wheels. For single thickness, lay one piece of dressmaker's carbon paper FACE UP under the WRONG SIDE of fabric. For doubled fabric, lay one piece of tracing paper, FACE UP, under the fabric; another piece FACE DOWN directly underneath the tissue pattern.

GENERAL DIRECTIONS

STAY-STITCHING

Run a row of machine-stitching a scant 1/8" outside the seam line indicated on pattern to prevent edge from stretching.

BASTE GARMENT TOGETHER and try on for fitting before stitching seams.

TO MAKE DARTS — Fold dart on solid line, having RIGHT SIDES of fabric together; then stitch together along dotted lines to point.

TRIM ENCLOSED SEAMS to about 1/4" from stitching on collars, etc., before turning right side out.

FOR A SEAM HAVING INTERFACING JOINED IN, first trim away seam allowance on interfacing close to stitching (sketch A); then trim remaining seam edges to 1/4" from stitching (sketch B). If heavy fabric is used, grade seam by trimming one edge a little more than the other to prevent a ridge when pressing.

CLIP SEAM EDGES on inward curves and corners when necessary.

SEAM FINISHINGS

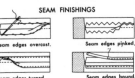

Seam edges overcast.   Seam edges pinked.

Seam edges turned in and stitched.   Seam edges bound.

PRESSING

PRESS SEAMS AND SECTIONS as the work progresses. Press each seam open after stitching unless the directions state otherwise.

ing, sewing and pressing. Even the experienced seamstress will find this worthwhile reading. McCall's staff

sketch of the pieces found on the back of the pattern envelope to make sure the right pieces are included in

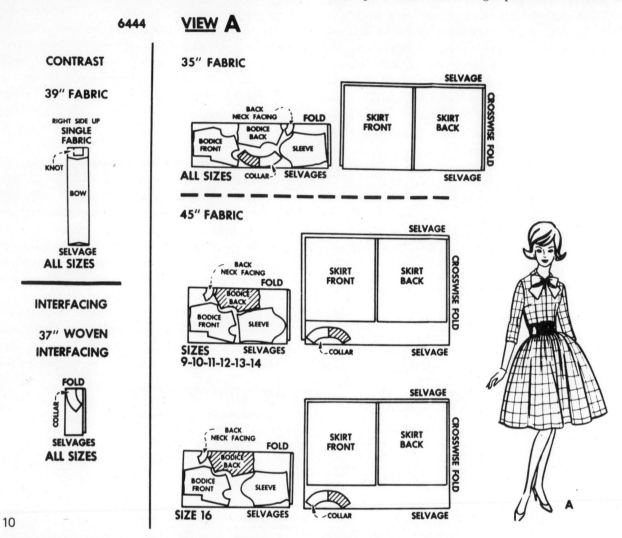

10

of experts constantly experiments to find new and easy methods of sewing. When they do discover better ways of doing things, their findings are included in the Easy Sewing Guide.

One of the most important features of the Easy Sewing Guide is the section which provides pattern layouts for various sizes and widths of fabric (10). Circle the one for your view, size, and width of fabric. You'll be referring to it often when you begin laying the pattern on the fabric. If you plan to use a napped fabric, check to see if a napped layout is provided.

The Pattern

Sort the pattern pieces carefully, selecting only those needed for the version of the garment you're making. Use the layout as a guide for sorting as well as the

the pattern. As you sort, check each piece to see that the correct pattern number and size are printed on it. Patterns are packed by hand, and once in a great while a wrong piece is inserted in the envelope, or a piece is omitted. It rarely occurs, but it's best to double-check. If you do find a mistake in packaging, return the pattern to the pattern company, and they will replace it with the correct pattern.

Each pattern company provides various markings on the printed pattern pieces which help you construct the garment. McCall's prints all markings on the patterns, making construction as easy, accurate and quick as possible. There are markings which aid in quick sorting of the pieces, markings for pattern alterations, markings for proper layout, and the actual construction markings. Outlined here are the various types of markings, and a brief description of each (11).

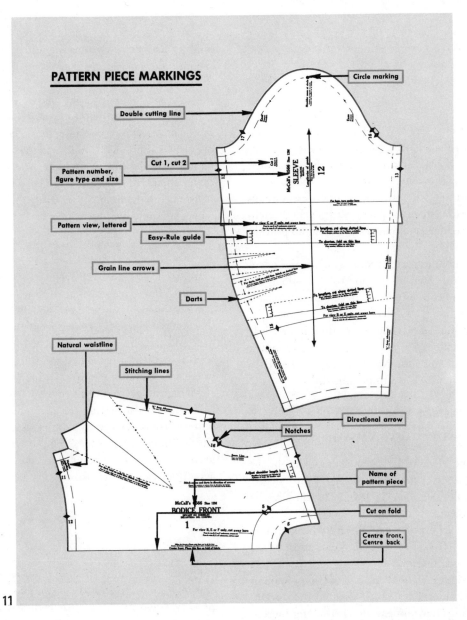

Markings for Sorting Pattern Pieces

□ Pattern number, figure type and size printed in centre of each pattern piece.

□ Pattern view lettered by an identifying *A, B, C, D*. Select only those pieces with the letter symbol for the view you plan to make.

Markings for Pattern Alteration

□ Easy-Rule Guide, a solid and dotted line marking, divided like a ruler, is printed on bodice, sleeve, shoulder and skirt to make shortening and lengthening the pattern piece an easy task.

□ Lines on Proportioned patterns indicating where height adjustments are to be made.

Markings for Correct Layout

□ Arrow line indicates fabric grain line and should be placed along a single yarn of the fabric. Printed along arrow line will be the words "lengthwise [or crosswise] of goods," indicating the direction in which the piece should be laid.

□ Single line at edge of pattern will have "place this line on fold of fabric" printed along the line. This appears at centre back or centre front of a garment.

□ "Cut 1," "Cut 2" or the words "to be faced" printed on the pattern piece indicates the number of fabric pieces to be cut from the one pattern piece.

When "to be faced" appears, a second piece of fabric or facing material is cut from the pattern piece.

Markings for Accurate Cutting

☐ Double cutting lines, an exclusive feature of McCall's Patterns, make cutting more accurate and easier. Cutting is done directly between the two lines.

☐ Direction arrows along the seam line indicate the direction to cut and stitch the fabric in order to maintain proper grain direction. This will prevent stretching the fabric, reduce ravelling of cut edges and prevent any grain distortion.

☐ Notches are used to match seams quickly and accurately and are indicated by diamond shapes along the seamline. Cut notches out from, never into, seam allowance which may be needed for alteration. Cut along the solid line across the top of double or triple notches; it is much easier to cut and as easy to match as separately cut notches. Notches are numbered in the order in which they are to be joined.

Markings for Accurate Sewing and Fitting

☐ Printed name of each pattern piece appears in the centre of the piece. Skirt front, bodice front, sleeve, facing are quickly identified by simply looking for the name on the pieces.

☐ Darts and tucks are marked by short broken lines indicating the stitching line. Stitching lines must be accurately matched; the solid line in the centre of dart and tuck markings is used as a fold line, making matching of stitching lines easier and more accurate.

☐ Circle markings may appear along stitching lines of darts and tucks indicating points to match for accurate stitching. Circles along seam lines may also indicate the beginning and ending of an opening. Stitch the seam only as far as the marked circle.

☐ Seam line stitching lines are long broken lines along the edge of pattern piece, normally $5/8$ inch from the cutting line which is the standard seam allowance.

☐ Pieces for set-in sleeves have large circles at the top of a sleeve-cap seam line to indicate the point on the sleeve that should be matched to the shoulder seam line of the bodice. Notches and small circles on the seam line of the sleeve cap and bodice armhole are matched so fullness or ease may be evenly distributed.

☐ Buttonholes are marked by solid lines with small circles at outer edge which indicate the termination of buttonhole. These markings will be the correct length for the size buttons suggested in the "Notions" section on the pattern envelope. They are also in proper position for the design, unless the pattern piece must be shortened or lengthened.

☐ "Clip" or "slash" will be printed along a solid line on the pattern piece, meaning the piece must be clipped or slashed along that line. Study the guide sheet before clipping or slashing. Sometimes the seam is stitched, then clipped; at other times a slash has to be reinforced before it is cut. Be sure to read the instructions to find which method is required for each particular design.

Markings for Correct Fit

☐ Centre front and back are marked along the fold or stitching line except when button closings are used. On buttoned closings, there will be a separate solid line with the words "centre front" or "centre back" printed along it. Mark these clearly on the garment section with basting. These markings indicate width of lap and emphasise proper grain line, which help in checking the grain and fit of the garment.

☐ Natural waistline for the standard figure in each pattern size is marked by a short straight line, and the words "natural waistline." Check waist length measurement from this point and shorten or lengthen according to your needs.

GLOSSARY OF SEWING TERMS

Following directions of any kind requires a pretty thorough knowledge of the terminology. By using this glossary you can check your own sewing vocabulary and add new terms. Keep it handy for quick reference and browse through it when you have time. The larger your knowledge of terms, the easier sewing becomes.

A

Allowance Extra fabric outside the seam line, or within the garment, to accommodate gathers, tucks, shirrings or bloused effects.

Appliqué Small piece(s) of fabric applied as decorative trimming by hand or machine.

Armhole The opening in a garment for the arm. It is faced or bound, or a sleeve is set into the opening.

Arrowhead Tack A small, hand-embroidered, triangular trim detail used on tailored garments as a reinforcement stay at the ends of pleats, vents, pockets.

B

Back-Stitch A small hand-stitch that looks like machine-stitching on the right side but with stitches overlapping on the wrong side.

Bands Strips of fabric, ribbon or bias applied to edges or set into garments to finish or decorate. They may be cut on the bias or straight of grain.

Bar Faggoting Decorative trim used between seams and created by wrapping your needle with thread and making parallel bars from edge to edge.

Bar Tack Hand-worked decorative trim used across ends of pockets, buttonholes, etc., to reinforce the ends.

Basic Pattern A pattern printed on non-woven fabric, fabric, or paper assembled and altered for correct garment fit. Used then as a guide to compare with other patterns to make correct pattern alterations.

Basting A loose, long, temporary stitch made by hand or machine. Usually made with a contrasting coloured thread.

Beading A narrow open-work insertion through which ribbon can be run. It is usually placed between fabric edges but can also be used with lace edges.

Belt Carrier A thread or fabric loop used to hold belt in place.

Belting A stiff ribbon-like banding used inside a waistline as a stay, or covered with fabric and used outside as a belt.

Bevelling *See* Grading.

Bias The 45-degree diagonal of a fabric. It is used when you need "give" in your material.

Bias Band A strip of bias used to finish edges or decorate a garment.

Bias Facing A strip of bias-cut fabric used to finish curved edges.

Bias Seam Binding A bias rayon, silk or nylon binding used to finish curved raw edges.

Bias Tape A bias cotton binding used to bind, face or pipe curved edges. Comes in double or single fold.

Bishop Sleeve A long sleeve, wide at the bottom and gathered into a band.

Blanket Stitch A decorative edge finish formed by looped, interlocking stitches.

Blend A mixture of different fibres in one yarn, or different yarns in one fabric, each lending its own characteristics to the fabric.

Blind-Stitch A form of hemming made by catching only one thread of the outer fabric.

Bodkin A blunt needle with an eye or a pin on the end used for threading tape, elastic or ribbon through beading or casing.

Body Measurements Actual measurements of the body—bust, waistline, hip, back waist length—used to purchase the correct pattern. Also, measurements given on the back of the pattern envelope that are correct for the size and figure type of a specific pattern.

Boning Stiff piece of bone, plastic or metal used within a seam or along a dart to give added support or fit in a bodice or hip area.

Box Pleat Two side pleats which turn away from each other.

Braid A woven novelty trim finished on both edges. Comes in cotton, wool, rayon and nylon in a variety of widths and weights and can be applied by hand or machine.

Breakline The roll line of a lapel when it turns back from the garment.

Bridle A strip of pre-shrunk tape that is applied behind the breakline of a lapel to prevent stretching.

C

Canvas Firmly woven fabric used for coat interfacing. Can be of linen, cotton, wool or hair fabric.

Cartridge Pleats Unpressed, rounded pleats used decoratively.

Casing A hem with an opening so that ribbon or elastic can be drawn through.

Catch-Stitch A cross-stitch used to hold raw edge in place securely.

Chain-Stitch A decorative stitch formed by interlocking loops.

Chalk Tailor's chalk is a firm grade of chalk used for marking pattern lines and fitting marks. French chalk is a powder that can be dusted on your hands to keep them fresh and your garment unstained.

Clean Finish An edge finish for facings, hems or seams in non-bulky fabrics that ravel. Turn under raw edges $1/_4$ inch and machine-stitch close to turned edge.

Clip A short cut into the seam allowance of a garment which allows a corner or a curved area to turn and lie flat.

Cord Piping A cord which is encased in bias fabric and used to finish and decorate edges, waistlines, buttonholes, and for soft furnishings.

Couching An embroidery stitch in which a long, heavy double thread or cord is laid along a design and caught in place by another thread at equal intervals.

Crease A folded line pressed into the material.

Crosswise Grain The grain of the fabric that runs

from selvage to selvage at right angles to the lengthwise grain.

Crow's Foot A triangular-shaped thread design used as an end stay for pleats and pockets.

D

Dart A stitched fold of fabric tapering to a point at one or both ends, used to shape a garment to fit the curves of the body.

Design Allowance Extra ease in a garment to permit blousing, tucking or shirring.

Diagonal Basting A temporary stitch used to hold two layers of fabric together without slipping.

Directional Cutting, Stay-Stitching, Stitching, and Pressing Working with the grain of the fabric to retain the original shape. The pattern is marked with small arrows on each seam indicating the direction in which to work.

Drape Soft folds of fabric controlled by pleats or gathers.

Dress Form A duplicate of the human figure made of padded fabric, wire, paper or plastic. Helpful for fitting or draping a garment.

Dressmaker's Carbon Carbon of many colours used with a tracing wheel to mark construction lines.

E

Ease When one section of a seam is slightly fuller than the section to which it is joined, the fullness is distributed evenly without gathers or puckers and pressed so that the threads within the fabric are crowded closer together. This ease allows shaping for curved areas such as the bust in princess line, set-in sleeves, etc.

Ease Allowance An allowance in measurement over and above the given body measurements of a pattern. This ease allowance gives needed room in a garment for it to be comfortable and allow for movement.

Edge Finish Any finish applied to the raw or cut edge of fabric, such as hemming, binding, stitching, fringing, overcasting, zigzagging or pinking.

Edging Any lace, tatting or novelty trim with one straight edge and one decorative edge.

Edge-Stitch A line of stitching placed close to a finished edge of a garment.

Elastic Thread Thread made with a rubber core that gathers fabric as you stitch. Can be applied by machine as well as by hand.

Embroidery Machine- or hand-stitching worked for decorative effect.

Emery Bag A small bag filled with an abrasive powder used to sharpen and remove rust from pins and needles.

Entre-Deux Another term for beading or veining; it is an open-work strip that can be inserted between fabric edges and run through with ribbon.

Even Basting Large stitches equally sized and spaced, used for temporary joining.

Extension Any additional fabric jutting out beyond a seam or a centre marking.

Eyelet A small hole in a garment, finished by hand-stitches or a metal ring to hold the prong of a buckle. Also used to give lacing effect with ribbon, yarn or cording.

F

Facing A piece of fabric, fitted or bias, applied to finish the edges of neckline, armhole and openings in a garment.

Faggoting A trim placed between seams. It is either handmade or commercially purchased as tape.

Fashion Stitches Decorative stitches used for trimming. Made by hand or with sewing machine.

Fastenings Hooks, eyes, snaps, buttons, etc., used to close garments.

Featherboning Light-weight, fabric-covered boning that is used for support of seams in strapless bodices, wide belts, etc.

Feather Stitch Blanket stitches that are slanted to create a decorative pattern.

Felling A slanted hemming stitch used in tailoring to attach undercollar to coat.

Fibres Natural or man-made substances used to form the yarns of fabrics.

Figure Type The classification for various figures according to height and body proportions. Within each figure type are various size ranges.

Filling The yarns interlaced at right angles to the warp yarns to produce fabrics. These run across the fabric from selvage to selvage.

Findings *See* Notions.

Fish Dart A dart that tapers at both ends, generally used at waistline.

Fitting Adjusting pattern or garment to fit your individual figure.

Flap A piece of fabric that hangs loose and is attached at one edge only. Found on pockets.

Flat-Fell Seam used on shirts, slacks and other tailored garments in which one seam is trimmed and the other stitched over it. Gives a flat, finished seam on both sides of the garment.

Flounce Circular, gathered or pleated length of fabric that is applied to the bottom of skirts, curtains or furniture.

Fly Front Closing that conceals buttons or zipper, usually associated with men's trousers, topcoats and Chesterfield-type coats.

French Chalk *See* Chalk.

French Knot Decorative hand-stitch in which the thread is twisted around the needle and brought down through the fabric at almost the same spot to form a small dot.

French Seam A double-stitched seam that looks like a plain seam on the right side and a small neat tuck on the wrong side. Used on straight seams and as a finish for sheer fabrics or infants' clothes.

French Tack A thread bar fastening used to hold two pieces of a garment together loosely. Used to attach lining to coat at hemline.

Fringe Decorative edge finish purchased by the yard or formed by ravelling the edge of fabric.

Frog Decorative closing formed by looping braid, bias binding, or cording. Usually associated with Oriental style garments.

G

Gathering One or two rows of stitching, either hand or machine, that are drawn up to form even fullness.

Gauging Fullness drawn up in uniform-sized deep folds of fabric where a long length of fabric is to be gathered into a small space. This produces a decorative effect.

Gimp A heavy thread that is often used on worked buttonholes.

Glove Stitch Decorative top-stitching made by taking the same size stitch on both sides of the work.

Godet Triangular or shaped piece that is set into skirts, curtains, etc., for added width at the bottom.

Gore Tapered or flared section of fabric that is narrow at the top and wide at the bottom. Usually refers to a skirt section.

Gorge Line Part of the seam line that joins the collar and the facing. It extends from the crease or roll line to the notch.

Grading Trimming all the seam allowances within a seam to different widths to eliminate bulk. The interfacing seam allowance is always trimmed close to the seam.

Grain The direction of fabric threads. The yarns running parallel to the selvages form the lengthwise

grain; the yarns running from selvage to selvage form the crosswise grain.

Grain-Line Arrow The arrow line printed on a pattern indicating the exact grain-line for each garment piece. Place this printed line along one yarn of the fabric, lengthwise or crosswise, as indicated on the pattern.

Guide Sheet Printed instruction sheet included with each pattern giving specific detailed instructions for the complete construction of each pattern view in that particular pattern.

Gusset A small triangular or shaped piece of matching fabric set into a slash or seam to give added ease and shaping. Usually placed at underarm.

H

Ham A ham-shaped cushion that is used for pressing or moulding shaped areas and curves.

Hand-Pricking A variation of the back-stitch used for applying zippers by hand or as an edge finish on a tailored garment.

Hand-Rolled Hem A fine edge finish for sheer fabrics or for a scarf, sash or ruffle formed by rolling raw edge between fingers and hemming by hand.

Heading Area above the pleating or gathering line of a casing, flounce or ruffle.

Heavy-Duty Thread Heavy-weight thread used for sewing on buttons or sewing on heavy fabric such as sailcloth, drapery or upholstery fabric.

Hem An edge finish formed by folding back the raw edge and stitching it by hand or machine. The depth of the hem and the method of stitching depend on the garment and type of fabric.

Hemline The marked line at the bottom of a garment where the hem is turned.

Hemstitch A decorative open-work stitch made by drawing lengthwise threads of the fabric and fastening the crosswise threads in clusters.

Honeycomb Stitch A basic smocking stitch worked alternately on two rows at a time. Fits smoothly over curved areas since it tends to spread and close like an accordion.

I

Insertion A piece of lace or decorative banding (straight on both edges) set into a garment for trimming.

Inset A piece of fabric inserted in a garment for fitting or decorative purposes.

Interfacing A suitable fabric sewn between the

garment and facing to give added body, shaping and support to the garment. Usually used along edges, in collars, cuffs, pockets, waistbands.

Interlining A suitable fabric sewn and shaped the same as the garment, placed between the garment and lining to give added warmth.

Inverted Pleat Two side pleats which turn toward each other.

Invisible Stitch Used for hems and attaching facings and interfacings in tailoring.

K

Key To match pattern markings or seam edges on the sections to be joined.

Kick Pleat A short pleat at the lower edge of a skirt. It is formed by an extension cut on the centre or side seam and is top-stitched across the upper edge to hold it in place.

Kimono Sleeve Bodice and sleeve cut in one piece with or without a shoulder seam.

Knife Pleats Series of pleats that turn in the same direction, are usually equal in width and are pressed straight to the hem.

Knot-Stitch See Lock-Stitch.

L

Lap To place one piece of fabric over another.

Lapel Upper edge of a coat front that turns back.

Lapped Seam A seam used for yokes and applied pieces such as gussets. One seam allowance is lapped over the other seam allowance and top-stitched.

Layering Another term for grading, staggering or bevelling; trimming one seam allowance narrower than the other to eliminate bulk.

Layout The way the pattern pieces are placed on the fabric for cutting. The pattern guide sheet has diagrams showing the easiest and most economical way to place the pattern pieces on the fabric for each width of fabric, pattern size, and pattern view.

Lazy Daisy Stitch Embroidery stitch that is a long chain stitch arranged to form a flower.

Lengthwise Grain The yarns in the fabric that run parallel to the selvage. It usually has a greater number of yarns to the inch, is stronger and will stretch less than the crosswise grain.

Lingerie Hem A rolled hem that is caught with two overcast stitches at intervals of $1/8$ to $3/8$ inch gathering it in puffs.

Lingerie Seam Supposedly "rip-proof"; made by pressing both edges of a seam to one side and top-stitching with a zigzag stitch along the edge.

Lining A suitable fabric constructed in the shape of a garment to cover and finish the inside of the entire garment or a section of it. It can also give shaping and prevent stretching.

Link Buttons Two flat buttons held together with several threads covered with blanket stitches. Used as cuff links.

Lock-Stitch Stitch used to secure thread at beginning and end of stitching, made by releasing presser foot and stitching in one place several times.

Loop A fastening, which extends beyond the finished edge, used on closings with no lap. Can be made of thread, cording or fabric.

M

Machine-Basting A long machine-stitch used in place of hand-basting. Can be pulled out easily.

Machine-Gather One or two rows of long machine-stitches pulled up to hold fullness evenly.

Machine Hem A hem stitched in by machine. Usually found in sportswear, curtains or slip covers.

Marking Transferring all necessary pattern symbols to the wrong side of the fabric by one of the various methods best suited to the fabric.

Matching Joining construction markings.

Military Braid A flat rayon or metallic braid used as a trim.

Mitre Diagonal joining of two pieces of fabric or lace that meet at a corner.

N

Nap The short fibres on the surface of the fabric that have been drawn out from the yarns of the fabric and brushed in one direction.

Needle Board A board covered with fine steel wires set vertically for use in pressing velvet and other nap or pile fabrics.

Notch A small diamond-shaped printed marking or group of markings on the cutting edge of the pattern that indicate where fabric edges match corresponding edges.

Notions All dressmaking supplies that are used in the construction of a garment: thread, zippers, tape, buttons, etc.

Nylon Closure Tape Nylon tape with a fleece side and burr side which adhere firmly to each other, used for fastening openings, belts, etc.

O

Open-Work Decorative insertions of open designs and patterns; can be made by hand or machine.

Outline Stitch An embroidery stitch made with a short back-stitch worked from left to right.

Overcasting A small, slanting stitch placed over the raw edge of fabric to finish the edge and keep it from ravelling.

Overhanding A straight stitch used to hold finished edges together when a strong, flat, invisible seam is needed, as in table linen, undergarments, sewing on lace or patching.

Overlap Part of a garment that extends or laps over another part.

P

Padding Stitch Tiny, diagonal hand-stitches used to hold interfacing to the fabric securely on tailored garments. The stitches do not show on the right side of the garment.

Permanent Basting Any type of basting with matching thread that remains in the finished garment.

Pick-up Line The centre fold line of a dart or tuck.

Picot An edge finish made by cutting through a line of machine hemstitching.

Piecing Sewing two pieces of fabric together when more width is needed as in a circular skirt; should always be done on grain.

Pile Fabric woven with a third set of yarns forming tufts or loops on the surface of the fabric. Loops may be cut or uncut. Velvet, velveteen, corduroy, terry cloth are examples.

Pin-Basting A method of joining seams before stitching them. Place pins at right angles to edge and an even distance from the edge.

Pin-Fit To pin and adjust the garment to your figure before permanent stitching.

Pin Tucks Tucks pressed on a thread of the goods and stitched close to the edge.

Pinch Pleats Cluster of pleats used in drapery headings. Made by dividing one pleat into several smaller ones.

Pinking A notched seam finish cut with pinking shears. Can only be used on fabrics that do not ravel badly.

Pins Dressmaker or silk pins—rustproof and sharp—used to hold pattern and fabrics together and to hold pieces of fabric together.

Piping A fold of bias fabric, ribbon or braid inserted in a seam. Used in dressmaking, with or without cording.

Pivot Refers to way of stitching a sharp corner. Leave the needle in the fabric, lift the presser foot, turn the fabric to the desired angle, lower the presser foot and continue stitching.

Placket Opening in a garment that allows for ease in dressing. Plackets are closed by means of snaps, hooks and eyes or zippers.

Plain Seam The stitching together of two pieces of fabric placed right sides together. Most common seam used in sewing.

Pleats Folds of fabric used to control fullness.

Pocket Stay A strip of interfacing sewn to the wrong side of a pocket opening for reinforcement.

Pre-Shrink Treatment of fabrics so that size will not be appreciably altered by washing or dry-cleaning.

Prick Stitch *See* Hand-Pricking.

Q

Quilting Stitching several layers of fabric together in an all-over design.

R

Ravel To draw yarns out from along the edge of the fabric to form fringe.

Regulation Stitch The permanent stitching placed in a garment, usually 12 stitches per inch. May be varied in length to suit the fabric.

Reinforce To add strength to corners and areas of great stress by adding rows of stitching or a patch of fabric.

Revers Wide shaped lapels on a garment.

Reversible Fabric that has been finished so that either side may be used or a garment finished so that it may be turned and worn on either side.

Ric Rac A saw-tooth-edge braid made in cotton or metallic thread. Can be applied as a flat braid or set into a seam.

Rip To open a seam by pulling out or cutting the stitching

Rolled Hem *See* Hand-Rolled Hem.

Ruffle A band of fabric that is gathered or pleated and applied to an edge as trimming.

Running Stitch The simplest form of hand-stitching; small stitches that appear the same on both sides of the fabric, used for gathering.

S

Saddle Stitch A decorative top-stitch made by taking longer stitches on top and shorter ones underneath.

Sag The stretch that occurs in the bias grain of

garments after hanging, or the effect of strain on any part of a garment.

Satin Stitch An embroidery stitch made by rows of flat stitches placed close together.

Scallop An edge finish made up of a series of semi-circles.

Seam The line or fold formed by stitching two pieces of fabric together.

Seam Allowance The fabric edge that extends beyond the stitching line. The normal seam allowance in all patterns is $5/8$ inch unless it is marked and printed otherwise on the pattern.

Seam Finish Finish applied to a raw edge to control fraying and ravelling.

Seam Roll A long, firmly padded cylinder that is used for pressing seams.

Selvage The narrow woven border on the lengthwise edges of the fabric.

Shank The stem between the button and the fabric to which it is sewn; may be part of the button or can be made with thread when the button is sewn on.

Shaping Materials Appropriate fabric used as interfacing, underlining, interlining or lining in a garment.

Shell Edge A narrow hem that is stitched by hand and stitched over the edge at measured intervals to form scallops. Used on lingerie.

Shell Tuck A tuck that is sewn by hand with a stitch taken over the edge at measured intervals to form scallops.

Shirring Two or more rows of gathers.

Shrinking Contracting of fabric usually resulting from washing or dry-cleaning. Most fabrics are now treated by manufacturers to control shrinkage.

Side Pleats Also called Knife Pleats.

Size The measurement classification within a figure type which allows for variations in body measurements such as bust, waist, and hip. Each figure type has a range of sizes.

Sizing A chemical finish applied to a fabric to give it added body or stiffness.

Slash An even cut in the fabric along a straight line. This is a longer cut than a clip. Slashes are usually finished with a seam or facing.

Sleeve board A small, narrow, well-padded board for pressing sleeves.

Slip-Basting Invisible hand-basting, put in from the right side.

Slip-Stitch Tiny hand-stitches taken through and under a fold of fabric where the stitching must be invisible.

Slot Seam A seam which has an underlay of fabric and resembles an inverted pleat.

Smocking A decorative way of gathering a piece of fabric into regular folds; done before the garment is made up.

Soutache A narrow rayon braid with rounded edges used for decorative effect. Can be curved or shaped easily.

Spanking Pounding or flattening fabric with heat and steam to shape it. Used primarily on woollen fabrics.

Stab-Stitch A stitch in which the needle is brought in and out of the fabric at right angles. Used for sewing on buttons or as an edge stitch.

Stay Tape or fabric sewn into a section of the garment to reinforce the section and hold it securely in position. Used at waistlines, under gathers or shirring.

Stay-Stitching Line of regular-length machine-stitches made in the seam allowance $1/8$ inch inside the seam line, to prevent bias and curved edges from stretching.

Steam Press To press a garment using steam produced by moisture and a hot iron to remove creases, raise nap in pile fabrics and shrink out fullness in woollens.

Stiffening Fabric such as crinoline, horsehair or non-woven interfacing used to stiffen parts of a garment.

Straightening Manipulating fabric to correct grain-line; pulling out a crosswise thread of the fabric and then cutting along that line.

Straight of Goods This refers to the lengthwise grain or crosswise grain of the fabric.

Sunburst Pleats Pleats that are wider at the bottom than at the top.

Surplice Front closing that is cut on the diagonal.

T

Tack To hold two pieces of fabric together at a point with tiny hand-stitches.

Tailor's Tack Method of marking pattern symbols with temporary loose basting stitches sewn through double layer of fabric and cut apart when pattern is removed.

Tailoring The technique of shaping and moulding the garment throughout the construction processes in making a suit or coat.

Taping Sewing tape on the back of fabric for reinforcement at points of stress.

Tension The degree of looseness or tightness of bobbin thread and needle thread in machine-stitching.

The bobbin thread and needle thread should lock evenly together in the fabric.

Termination Point Marking placed at the end of a tuck or dart to guide in matching the layers of fabric exactly.

Top-Stitching A line of stitching on the outside of the garment, usually placed close to a finished seam or a finished edge.

Trapunto Quilting in which only the design part is padded.

Trim To cut away excess fabric in the seam allowances after the seam has been stitched.

True Bias Exact 45-degree diagonal of the fabric. When cut on this line, material will have the most "give."

Tubing A hollow cylinder of fabric used for button loops and decorative trim.

Tucks Straight folds of fullness evenly stitched.

Twill Tape A woven cotton tape used as a stay, drawstring or ties.

U

Underlap A part of a garment that extends or laps under another part.

Underlay An additional piece of fabric placed under a section for the purpose of joining as in a pleat or slot seam.

Underlining A suitable fabric used to back a section or an entire garment. It is used to give body and shaping and to prevent sagging and stretching of the outer fabric.

Understitching A row of machine-stitching through the facing and seam allowance close to a seamline. This holds the facing to the seam allowances and prevents the facing from rolling to the outside.

Unit Construction Organisation of sewing procedure so that an entire garment section is completed before it is joined to another.

V

Velvet Board Another name for a needle board.

Vent A lapped, finished opening on the hem edge of a sleeve, jacket or skirt.

W

Warp The yarns that run lengthwise in a woven fabric. The filling yarns are interlaced with them at right angles.

Weights Metal discs which are covered with fabric and sewn in cowl necklines or in the hemlines of coats and jackets.

Welt An applied strip of fabric used to finish the lower edge of slashed pocket. It is stitched on three sides and left open at the top.

Whip Stitching two finished edges together securely with tiny slanting stitches.

With Nap Designation for fabric that must be cut with all the pattern pieces laid in one direction. This includes napped fabrics, pile fabrics and those with a one-way design produced by light reflection (sateen, satin), printed or woven with an up-and-down direction.

Woven Seam Binding A straight-edged rayon, silk or nylon binding used to finish raw edges of hems or as a stay. It cannot be shaped or used on curved edges.

Y

Yardage The amount of fabric needed to make a particular garment. The back of the pattern envelope has a yardage chart. This gives the exact amount of fabric necessary for each view and size for the various widths of fabric.

Z

Zigzag Stitch A machine-stitch made by the movement of the needle from side to side rather than in a straight line. The stitch is made with a zigzag attachment or an automatic machine. Used to stitch two edges of fabric together, finish the raw edges of seams, stitch plain seams for greater elasticity, apply appliqués, mend tears or make decorative stitching.

Zipper A closure made of metal or nylon chains attached to tape so that it can be stitched into a placket.

Zipper Foot Machine foot with one prong for stitching in zippers or piping. Right, left or adjustable attachments are available.

CHAPTER 3

THE RAW MATERIALS — FABRIC, SHAPING MATERIALS, NOTIONS

The basis of any fashion is, of course, the materials of which it is made. Fabric, thread, buttons, trimmings and the like are the seamstress' raw materials—her paint and canvas. Top designers use fabrics as fine artists do paint—subtly, skilfully, dramatically creating fashions that are exciting and beautiful. Many home dressmakers haven't achieved this perfection, but everyone should understand how different materials handle and the effects they create. Then putting a costume together will not be thought of as a flat jigsaw puzzle, but instead, as the moulding and draping of fabric to create the desired result.

THE ART OF FABRIC SELECTION

Fabrics are a lot like people. They have very distinct personalities and behaviour patterns. They can be stiff and unyielding; crisp and businesslike; soft, fluttery and feminine; even whimsical and fun. Studying the personality of fabrics is almost as interesting and profitable as studying people. The more you know about them, the more you enjoy them, and the more success you have in dealing with them.

If a garment is to be completely successful, the personality of the fabric must be used to full advantage. It should be flattering to you, expressive of your personality, and completely suitable to the design and the occasion. In short, the fabric in a garment as well as the design must be in good taste. Developing perfect taste in fabric selection is not an easy task, but neither is it an impossible one. It takes study, experimentation and probably a few mistakes before one unerringly selects the right fabric for every design.

Suggested Fabrics

When choosing fabric for a particular design, check the pattern envelope for "Suggested Fabrics." Here are listed the designer's choices of fabrics having the proper weight and drapability for the design. Your choice needn't be confined to these selections, but you should look for fabrics similar in weight and drapability. In Chapter 4 you will find a complete "Glosary of Familiar Fabrics" with their descriptions and suggestions for their use.

Before you decide on a fabric, study the sketch of the design and determine the general silhouette of the garment. Hold the fabric in these same general lines. Does it poke out when it should fall in graceful folds? Will it gather softly into shirring at the waist? Will it hold crisp pleats? Will it pouf if a bouffant effect is needed? If the design is a moulded one, will the material be firm enough to retain the shape?

Learning to understand fabric and how it will shape in a garment takes two things—practice and observation. Practice feeling fabrics, all sorts of fabrics. Observe their behaviour carefully. Look at the fabrics used in ready-to-wear garments. Check pattern publications to see which fabrics the experts select for various styles. Soon you will be able to look at a fabric and visualise it in a specific design, or look at a pattern and see it in a particular fabric.

There are two artistic factors that play a part in fabric selection—texture and colour. Four basic elements are involved in texture: the light reflection which determines a fabric's sheen or dullness; the touch, its roughness or smoothness; the look, its richness or plainness; and the handle, which means the weight, body and drape. As to colour, in addition to the optical illusions you can create with the right choice of colour, as outlined in Chapter 1, there are other considerations in selecting colour for your wardrobe. Which colours go well with each other and how much of each to use is an important decision you will have to make.

TEXTURE

Each of the elements of texture will have an influence on the total appearance of the garment and the figure wearing it. Whether a fabric is shiny or dull, whether it has a look of elegance or an everyday air, will make it more or less suitable for you and for the occasion. Surface roughness or a smooth silky look will determine to a large degree the type of garment for which a fabric can be used, as will its body and its ability to be draped softly, pleated crisply or moulded sleekly.

Texture and Individuality

Just as certain styles seem more suitable for certain personalities, so do textures. For instance, three career women with comparable figures may select the same suit pattern. The first wants to look cool, crisp and efficient. She selects a smooth worsted wool in a conservative colour. The second likes casual clothes with a bit of country about them. Her choice is sturdy, casual wide-wale corduroy. The third prefers the feminine look, and chooses a soft, airy bouclé woollen. Each suit is in good taste. The fabric is appropriate

for the style and expresses the personality the individual wishes to convey. Always select the texture that makes you feel your best at all times.

Texture and the Design

Texture and a pattern design should be thought of together, so that they will not be in conflict. If a design calls for a bouffant effect, select a fabric that creates poufs naturally. However, if the design shows soft folds, be sure not to use a crisp or stiff fabric. Just like people, fabrics are more successful if they are doing what they like to do.

In defining texture, the word "handle" is often used. The handle, or weight and draping quality of the fabric, will determine to a great extent the designs for which it may be used. The way to determine and understand the handle of a fabric is to become a "fabric feeler." Touch it, drape it in folds, hold it up to see how it falls.

Textures for the Occasion

Usually one thinks of selecting the right clothes for an occasion, without consciously considering the appropriateness of the fabric. Obviously, there are certain elaborate fabrics which are never worn in the daytime. Satins, brocades, sequined fabrics are strictly for evening wear. On the other hand, there are fabrics and textures which seem more suited to city, country or resort wear.

Generally, clothes for the city and for business are best fashioned in fine-textured fabrics that are conservative in feeling. Recently, the range of "city" fabrics has been considerably extended. Tweedy materials, homespun fabrics, nubby woollens are being used to create more casual-looking city clothes. Textures which wear well, resist soil and keep their shape are not only more practical for city wear, but more appropriate.

For the country, the rougher, sturdy fabrics look marvellous, and are in the right setting. The style of clothes for the country is more casual because living is more leisurely there. The textures should carry out the same theme of casual comfort.

Resort wear is the most fun of all. Here all the whimsical, funny, even bizarre fabrics and textures look right at home. The wild prints that are wrong for the suburbs are very right in the carefree atmosphere of the resort. For those who don't visit resorts, the same sort of textures can be used for at-home enter-

taining. Again, when the whole atmosphere is one of fun and relaxation, let the fabrics help set the mood.

Although certain fabrics are strictly evening fabrics, many popular daytime fabrics are now appearing in very effective evening fashions. The plaid woollens, formerly worn by schoolgirls in skirts and dresses, appear in sleek, informal evening sheaths. Soft, drapable wool jersey is cut into a "little nothing" dress that is perfectly right for today's casual entertaining. However, many of these fabrics can be called "novelty" fabrics as far as evening wear is concerned, and usually look right only on younger girls or women with youthful figures and appearances. Soft flannel sheaths can be very striking for informal evening wear with the right sparkly jewelry; in summer many of the new "dressy" cottons and silky synthetics are perfect choices for evening ensembles. But when you want to feel really dressed up and ready for a big night, try the real evening fabrics. You'll feel more gala. There is something special about the luxurious feel of a silk crêpe or satin, the rustle of taffeta or brocade, that makes you feel your elegant best.

Combining Textures

Being well dressed would be a simpler task if someone could just devise a hard-and-fast rule about combining textures, colours and lines. There just isn't any. Some women seem to have a sixth sense when it comes to co-ordinating a costume; most of us have to work at it.

The basic concept in combining the elements of any artful creation, be it a painting or a Paris costume, is unity of idea, with some variety. When working with textures, it generally means using sheers with sheers, heavyweights with heavyweights. Quite obviously, you do not add a wool tweed cummerbund to a nylon chiffon gown, nor a draped chiffon blouse to a cotton corduroy suit. However, some of the subtleties of selecting just the right textures in a costume are less obvious.

The only way to become adept at combining textures is to study the effect of one texture on another, and to observe various textural combinations used in fashion. Experiment with different combinations when planning a costume. When you sew your own, this is easier to do than when purchasing garments. You can take swatches of your garment along with you as you shop for blouses, accessories or other fabrics which will be combined with the garment you make.

COLOUR

The second factor you have to consider in choosing a fabric is colour. While the colour is often more obvious than the texture, it creates just as many problems because of the profusion of colours that exist. It is so easy to employ too much colour or the wrong kind, unless you learn to follow a few basic guides based on the principles of design.

Chart a Colour Scheme

In planning your wardrobe, it is most important that you have a definite colour scheme in mind. Unless you do, the various garments and accessories you make or buy will not seem to belong together. This lack of co-ordination will cause colours to clash or, what may be even worse, leave you with gaps in your wardrobe. A lovely suit without the right blouse can hang in the closet for months.

In order to avoid this unhappy situation, there are certain things you can do. First, decide on the colours which are most becoming to you. If you like one especially well and it can be used as a basic colour, then make this your background colour. Naturally, a basic colour should be one which will combine nicely with a variety of other colours.

Usually, you will use the basic colour for garments you plan to wear for several years, such as a coat or a suit. This is the most satisfactory plan for "carry-over" clothing, for it allows you to introduce unusual or livelier colours as accents in your wardrobe and change them from time to time without discarding the major garment.

Dark colours and those that create a neutral effect are the ones most frequently used for basic colours. Black, navy blue, brown and gray fall into this category. Although brighter colours can be used as basics, it is usually best to avoid them unless you can afford to change your entire wardrobe frequently. A person seems to tire of colours of high intensity more quickly than of those in more subdued hues. There is no reason for a basic colour to give your wardrobe a monotonous look if you learn to employ colour wisely and with imagination.

As soon as your basic colour is chosen, you should look at all other colours with it in mind. Each new piece of apparel you select should be chosen to blend with your basic colour. Gradually, you will evolve a colour scheme which will make your entire new wardrobe more attractive and satisfying to wear.

Colour in the Balance

Proper balance of colour is important, especially when forceful and weak hues are used together. A good rule to follow at such time is that the larger the area to be covered, the less intense the colour should be; the smaller the area, the brighter the colour can be.

The amount of a colour to use is also a matter of proportion. Subtle variations in the tone and the amounts of colour used will create an interesting effect, while too much repetition of one colour can become monotonous. For instance, the identical hue used for a hat, bag, gloves and shoes will create a less pleasing effect than if you were to choose one dark, one light and one bright tone of the same colour.

Remember, too, that a light colour has power to attract the eye and hold attention. This makes it possible for you to camouflage figure irregularities by drawing the eye to your most attractive feature. If several light areas are used, the eye will dart from one to the other. Unless they are placed advantageously, they can cause the figure to appear shorter and stouter. But a rhythmic feeling can be developed in a design if the colours are placed properly and used in correct amounts. The eye will seem to glide from one hue to the repeated one.

Colour Harmony

Naturally, it is important for any colour combination to give a feeling of harmony. To produce such an arrangement, colours should seem to belong together. This may be done by combining related colours in a monochromatic or an analogous harmony. It may also be achieved by using contrasting colours in a complementary harmony. Whichever you choose, one colour should be emphasised with the others playing subordinate roles.

PATTERNED FABRICS

Prints, plaids, checks and stripes can add a delightful excitement to an otherwise drab wardrobe. However, it is important to select a patterned fabric that is flattering to the wearer.

Analyse the Design

The size of the fabric design should be in proportion to the size of the wearer. Small prints, miniature checks, narrow stripes seem best for the petite figure, larger designs for the taller. Large, bold prints, dramatic plaids and stripes should be worn only by someone with a model girl's figure. Usually the medium-sized print with an indefinite outline will be most flattering to the average figure.

Because of their versatility, prints have become a part of everyone's wardrobe. However, to select one which embodies the elements of good design is not always easy. The oft used principle of "unity with variety" is a good rule to follow. Motifs should be related. They should be placed so that the eye glides rhythmically from one motif to the next. Try an artist's trick. Hold the fabric at arm's length and study it through half-closed eyes. Do the designs and colours seem to blend in a pleasing harmony? If they do, you have probably chosen a good design.

Then the mood of the print should be considered. Some create a formal or conservative feeling; others a frivolous, gay spirit. Some seem demure; others exotic. Never allow the design to seem more important than you. Remember, you are simply selecting a background for your personality.

THE PRACTICALITIES OF FABRIC SELECTION

Once you have chosen a fabric that you like, one that is suitable for your pattern and appropriate for you, there is another point you will have to check at the store, and this is whether or not the fabric has a straight grain.

THE IMPORTANCE OF GRAIN LINES

Since the entire appearance of the garment may depend on whether the various sections are cut properly on the straight grain of the fabric, you should check fabric before purchasing it to see if the grain is straight. If it is not, then you will have to decide whether you can successfully straighten it yourself. Although fabrics are always originally woven on grain, finishing or printing processes will often pull them off-grain. In some cases a permanent finish may lock the threads in the off-grain position and the fabric can never be straightened. Drip-dry fabrics, in particular, should be carefully checked.

Testing for Position of Grain Lines

To test the grain of a fabric before you buy it, fold the fabric back on itself, matching the selvages. If the end of the fabric has been torn, see if the torn end is exactly at right angles to the selvage. If the fabric has been cut straight across the end, then try to follow a single crosswise thread to see if it is exactly parallel to the end of the fabric. Be sure to check carefully any prints with a regular design. It may be that the fabric was printed in an off-grain position and when straightened the print pattern will be distorted.

On plaids or prints having a regular design at right angles to the selvage, make the following test. Unroll about a yard of the fabric from the bolt. Fold back about one-half yard. Match the selvages carefully, making the fold at right angles to the selvage. Now, see if the design is parallel to the folded line (12). If it

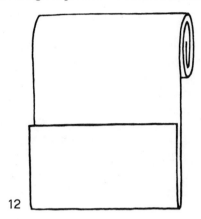

12

is a wash-and-wear or permanently finished fabric and is more than one-half inch off grain, don't buy it. You will never be able to straighten it and have a satisfactory garment.

It is rather difficult to determine grain straightness in knits, since most of them are produced in circular or tubular form with no lengthwise finished edges. The only way to check grain, before you buy the fabric, is to fold back about one-half yard and match the lengthwise folded edges carefully. This makes a fold at right angles to the edges. See if a single rib is at right angles to the folded line.

SHAPING MATERIALS

Shaping materials have been in existence for centuries. Look at the costumes in a museum. Elaborate metal and bone hoops, bustles and other contraptions gave fantastic shapes to garments of the past. Shaping materials are no less important today than they were in the days of Marie Antoinette, but fortunately for us, light-weight, shape-retaining fabrics do the job. They are much more comfortable to wear and work with.

Not only do shaping materials help shape the garment, but they also add to its durability. Below is a list of the jobs that shaping materials can be expected to do.

☐ Prevent sagging and stretching of knitted or loosely woven fabrics at points of strain, such as skirt backs.

☐ Give greater crease-resistance to all fashions.

☐ Add firmness and body to fashion details such as necklines, pockets or to the entire silhouette.

☐ Create fashion effects such as yokes, stand-up collars, peplums and stand-away flares.

☐ Strengthen edges where buttons, buttonholes, hooks and eyes are used.

☐ Tailor a fashion and help ensure perfect fit.

☐ Increase the life of the garment.

☐ Add warmth to a garment.

Selecting Correct Shaping Fabric

Choosing the proper shaping materials for a garment is almost as important as selecting the right fashion fabric. Picking just the right one will take almost as much thought and consideration. You will have to choose a shaping material with two major points in mind. First, is it right for the fashion fabric—the proper weight and colour—and second, what effect will it create in the garment? Will it stiffen it, make it soft and drapable, or just firm enough? The basic criteria for selecting shaping materials are:

☐ Correct weight—no heavier than the fashion fabric, unless you want a very crisp, standing effect.

☐ Proper finish and texture—should be somewhat similar to the fashion fabric.

☐ Right degree of stiffness and flexibility—it should suit the silhouette of the garment, or be able to take the shape of a specific detail.

☐ Shrinkage control—be sure to read the hang tags to see that the cleaning is the same for fabric and shaping material.

☐ Colour—try to match the fabric colour as nearly as possible; shaping materials may show through some fabrics.

The best way to determine which shaping material to use is to test the effect by draping the fabric and shaping material over your hand. Decide how they combine. Feel the two together to get an idea of the weight and texture; hold them up to see how they drape. Carefully consider how the two will shape into the silhouette of the garment.

How to Use

Shaping materials are used in a garment in four different ways, each having a slightly different purpose. They can be used as underlining, lining, interfacing or interlining.

UNDERLINING. A piece of shaping material usually cut in the shape of the design section of the garment, and used to back that section. The main purpose of underlining is to give shape to the garment and add to its crease-resistance and wear. The two pieces, garment section and underlining, are treated as one during construction.

LINING. Similar to underlining, except that it is constructed separately from the garment pattern pieces and joined to a major seam. Lining will not only shape the garment and add to its wear, it will provide a nice finished look to the inside of the garment.

INTERFACING. A piece of shaping material cut in the shape of a facing section and placed between the facing and the garment. Its purpose is to add firmness to the section, usually an edge, and help it retain its shape.

INTERLINING. Cut in the shape of a lining section and used between a lining and the design section. It is often used in coats or jackets when shape and added warmth are needed. Interlining is constructed separately and catch-stitched to the garment facing before the lining is sewn in.

Usually patterns indicate when shaping materials should be used. Study the chart shown here before choosing your shaping material.

WHAT MAKES THE SHAPE

USES	SHAPING MATERIALS
1 To tailor heavy coats and heavy suiting fabrics	Heavy Weight: Vilene Solena Oswilena hair canvas
2 To tailor medium-weight woollens and synthetics; to give crisp effect to firm cottons and linens	Vilene—medium-weight Vilene—Iron-on Solena—medium-weight Oswilena—medium-weight Staflex Iron-on Muslin Cambric Taffeta
3 To give soft shaping to medium-weight fabrics; to give crisp shaping to light-weight fabrics	Vilene—light-weight Solena—light-weight Staflex Iron-on Also: organdie, permanently finished cotton, crêpe, batiste, light-weight muslin, fine net, light-weight hair canvas
4 To give soft shaping to light-weight fabrics; to give crisp shaping to sheers and laces	Staflex Iron-on Also: net, organdie, organza, marquisette, lawn.

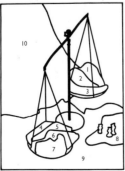

4 The luxury of silk makes it a firm fashion favourite. It is used for evening wear, lingerie, nightwear, dresses, coats and suits.
1 Silk taffeta. **2** Screen printed silk douppion. **3** Screen printed silk serge. **4** Jacquard woven tie silk. **5** Screen printed antung. **6** Silk poplin. **7** Screen printed silk milanese. **8** Silk bridal brocade. **9** Silk chiffon. **10** Panel print on silk georgette.

Photograph by courtesy of The Silk Centre

5 Cotton — the most widely used of all the world's fibres — is available in an incredible variety of weights and textures for all types of garments, furnishings and domestic textiles. It can be dyed in any colour, from the delicately subtle to the excitingly vivid. **1** Plissé. **2** Embroidered voile. **3** Cotton knit. **4** Marcella piqué. **5** Colour woven batiste. **6** Lurex striped ombré voile. **7** Heavy textured cotton. **8** Printed voile. **9** Broderie anglaise. **10** Seerloop gingham. **11** Printed lawn. **12** Corduroy. **13** Cotton lace. **14** Cotton satin. **15** Printed furnishing repp. **16** Satin striped cotton. **17** Corded gingham. **18** Basket weave cotton. **19** Heavy textured cotton. **20** Fancy woven voile.

Photograph by courtesy of The Cotton Board

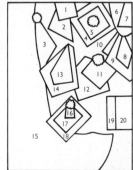

NOTIONS AND TRIMS

Patterns and fabrics do not cover the entire list of items you'll need for your sewing. There is a whole group of interesting items called notions and trims which are essential to the completion of a garment.

The essential notions which you must have for a garment are listed on the back of the pattern envelope. Thread, zippers and seam binding will almost invariably be mentioned. Buy these, plus any others listed, at the same time you purchase your fabric.

Zippers

Zippers are typed according to their purpose: neck zippers, dress placket zippers, skirt placket zippers, trouser fly zippers, and light-weight and heavy-weight separating zippers for jackets. Some are adjustable.

You'll have no problem selecting the type and length zipper you need. Your McCall's pattern tells exactly which to choose in the section marked "Notions" on the back of the envelope. Select one in the colour closest to your fabric colour. If you can't find an exact match, then select a shade darker.

Recently there have been developments in the zipper industry resulting in two new zippers which add a great deal to the fashion look of garments. The "invisible" zipper is as thin as a seam line and the zipper teeth are completely invisible behind tapes. The conventional lap covering usually required to conceal a zipper is not even necessary. It is used for skirts, slacks and shorts. The application of this zipper is somewhat different from standard, so be sure to check the instructions accompanying the zipper.

There is also the nylon zipper with nylon coils that mesh. It is a lighter, more flexible zipper than the metal chain and is easily repaired in a few seconds. It takes colour beautifully and keeps the coils permanently coloured.

Nylon Tape Closure

This type of closure is especially useful for fastening openings on belts, waistbands, jackets, slip-covers and for attaching removable collars and cuffs. It is a bit too bulky to use in most dresses or skirts. The tape is an inch wide and comes in yard or more lengths which can be cut to the size you need. There is a wide colour range; select the one closest to your fabric colour.

Snap Fasteners

These are available in silver and black and should be rustproof. They should be used where there is little strain, never to replace a button. Sizes vary from size 000, the finest, to 10, the largest. There is a complete range of sizes for every weight of fabric. Some need no sewing, just tapping in place.

Hooks and Eyes

These also come in silver and black and some are covered. Again, select ones that are rustproof. They are useful where there is tension on a garment or an inconspicuous closing is needed. The eye can be either a straight bar type for use on overlapping edges, or the round type for edges that just meet. There is a complete range of sizes.

Gripper Snap Fasteners

These may be bought in separate units, or they can be purchased already applied to tape. A kit is available for applying the fasteners. A wide colour range is available and some have decorative designs on them. Although they can replace buttons, they are mainly used in women's sports jackets, children's playclothes, baby clothes, men's shorts, and soft furnishings.

Buttons

The size and number of buttons needed for a garment are listed on the pattern envelope. There are two basic types of buttons: the shank, which is sewn to the garment under the button face, and the sew-through type. Buttons are available in wood, bone, plastic, metal, glass, leather, jet, pearl, fabric or crocheted, and there are kits for covering your own buttons easily and quickly.

Choose buttons that are best suited to your fabric and your size, considering the colour, texture, design and style of the garment. Be sure to select washable buttons if they are to be placed on a washable garment.

Bias Seam Tape or Binding

This is used as a trim edge finish or as a finish for raw edges on the inside of garments. It comes in assorted colours and is available in cotton percale, nainsook, rayon or silk. The fabric closest to your garment fabric should be selected, so it will react to washing or cleaning the same as the rest of the garment. It is purchased as single-fold, double-fold or wide bias tape. Rayon and silk bindings are single fold and are used to finish curved seam edges and hems. Double-fold cotton bias tape is most useful as a trim since it is already folded and easily applied. For use as a facing, it is best to use the single fold. The cotton percale tape used for trimming is also available in stripes, checks, plaids and small prints and can add a gay finish to summer sportswear or children's clothing. The wide bias tape is used for quilt binding or edge trimming. See page 230 for complete directions on how to apply bias seam bindings.

Woven Seam Binding

A straight woven tape with finished edges. Used to finish hem edges, and as a stay to eliminate stretching of a seam. It is available in rayon, silk or nylon, and in assorted colours. Various widths are usually available.

Bias Skirt or Hem Facing

This is a bias strip $2^1/_2$ inches wide with folded edges. It is used for facing hems when the skirt is not long enough for a self hem or when a very bulky fabric is used and a hem would produce an unsightly bulge. It comes in assorted colours and is of percale, nainsook or rayon taffeta.

Twill Tape

A cotton tape used in tailoring to tape edges and roll lines as well as seams to prevent stretching, especially in heavyweight fabrics or very stretchable materials. It has a sturdy twill construction that has no stretch or give. It is available only in black or white and in widths of $1/_4$ to 1 inch. The $1/_4$ inch is used for tailoring, the $3/_8$ to $5/_8$ inch for making ties on garments or for taping seams. The 1-inch is not readily available since it is used mainly in upholstery work.

Cording

Cording is used to pipe edges and seams, tucks, buttonholes, in loops and frogs, and in shirring. It is available in various sizes. The fine cable cord is excellent to use for piping buttonholes and for fine piped edges. The heavyweights can be used for drawstrings or heavy cord belts. When using cord for seams at the waistline or for edge trims, select the size cord needed for your fabric and for the effect you desire. Cording comes in white only because it is covered by the fabric.

Cord Piping

This is a fine cording covered in bias cotton for use as a decorative edge trimming. It is available in assorted colours and provides a neat decorative finish for faced edges and seams.

Braid Trims

There is a wide assortment of novelty braid trimming available, including fold-over braid, middy braid, soutache (very fine braid), shell and novelty trims. The pattern may indicate the type of trim needed, or you can use your own judgment.

Elastic

Available as thread or in various widths up to several inches. Ordinarily it is made of nylon or rayon and is limited to white, pink and black. The elastic thread is sometimes found in light blue, brown, navy and gray in addition to the regular white, pink and black.

Belting

The width and yardage needed for making belts is listed on the back of the pattern envelope. You may cut your own belt interfacing or backing from heavy interfacing fabrics, buckram, heavy canvas or grosgrain ribbon. However, the commercial beltings are quite fine and easier to use. They come plain, rubber-backed or leather-backed and are made of heavy cotton or rayon. Belting can be purchased by the yard or in standard belt length packages. Also very popular are belt and buckle kits that come by waist size and in widths from $1/_2$ to 3 inches.

Buckles

The size buckle needed will depend upon the width of the belt. The inside measurement of the buckle should be slightly wider than the width of the belting used. Buckles are available in bone, wood, plastic, metal, leather, pearl or fabric-covered, and with or without a prong. The kits for covering buckles are very easy to use, and provide a nice self-belt finish to a garment. Select the type and shape buckle which is best suited to the garment style and any buttons or trims used.

Shoulder Pads

The style in shoulder padding changes with the look of fashion. The size, shape and thickness will vary according to the fashion of the shoulder line and to the shape of your shoulders. Today, pads are used mainly to correct figure faults, for example, to build up narrow or rounded shoulders in garments which normally do not require their use. Commercially, several shapes of shoulder pads are available in styles for blouses, dresses, suits, coats. Dress and blouse pads are usually covered in fabric, or you can cover them in the dress fabric. Suit and coat pads are usually purchased uncovered; they are placed between the garment and the lining.

Featherboning

Featherboning is used wherever stays and stiffening are needed—in strapless bodices, hoop skirts, high collars, wide belts and cummerbunds. The boning is covered in cotton or synthetic fabric (white or black) and it can be stitched to the garment or encased in a lining. The width and yardage needed is listed on the pattern envelope of the garment requiring it.

Stays

These are metal, plastic or bone strips in various pre-cut widths and lengths and are used for strapless bodices, points in collars, cummerbunds. The length, width and number needed are listed on the pattern envelope.

Zigzag Wire Stays

These are spring wires which are flexible and adjustable in length. Because of their flexibility, they are almost invisible when used in necklines or collars or for formal gowns. They are inserted inside the seam and attached to the seam allowance. They come in either black or white and in several lengths.

Horsehair Braid

Horsehair braid is a stiff woven braid used for hemming the edge of light-weight full skirts and lace garments to give the hem support. It is available in widths from $1/_2$ inch to $3^1/_2$ inches in black or white.

Weights

Round lead weights available in various sizes are used to weight the hem edges of jackets and coats, or for weighting necklines and collars for a particular fashion effect.

Petersham Ribbon

Petersham ribbon or tape for making or stiffening skirt bands can be purchased with or without boning. It is available in white, black, and sometimes in other colours from the larger stores.

CHAPTER 4

FABRIC FACTS

"Little lamb, who made thee?" might be a logical question to ask today when viewing a mound of fuzzy lamb's wool in a fabric department. Years ago the question would have been silly because everyone knew a sheep on a hillside provided the origin. Today it may come from a laboratory and be composed entirely of man-made fibres.

Although the vast, wonderful array of new fabrics which appear each year are a delight to see, they can at the same time be bewildering. Years ago, women took pride in being able to identify a fabric by looking at it and feeling it. Now, this is almost a lost art. Because of new methods of manufacture, identities have become confused so that man-made fabrics may resemble wool; cotton, silk; silk, linen. In fact, fabrics can look, behave and feel just about any way man wants them to. It all depends on what is done to the fibre when converting it to cloth.

Because sewing and pressing techniques vary according to the material, it is important that you understand the three factors—fibre construction and finish—which influence the manner in which a fabric is handled. Try to be as knowledgeable as possible about these matters. It will make your sewing easier, and make you a better-dressed woman.

THE FIBRES

Less than fifty years ago, all fabrics were made of natural fibres. There was wool from the sheep; cotton from the cotton plant; silk from the silkworm cocoon and linen from the flax plant. Today we have the same natural fibres and a tremendous variety of new synthetics which originate in a test tube. Terms such as "polyamides" "cellulose triacetates," "polyesters" and "acrylics" appear everywhere. You may never see a polyamide or care to see one, just as you may never see a cotton plant or care to see one, but you really should know what these fibres will do for you.

To guide you through the maze of modern fabrics, a list of them is given here. Important characteristics and general tips on sewing and care are also noted. New fibres and fabrics will be appearing regularly. Try to keep up-to-date by reading magazines, such as *McCall's Pattern Fashions*.

THE BLENDS

Technicians in the textile industry are constantly experimenting with blends to improve the appearance and serviceability of fabrics. Wool is blended with man-made fibres to make it washable, more crease-resistant, lighter in weight. Cotton is blended with nylon to make it stronger, quick-drying and silkier in appearance. Some of the blendings are quite successful, but others may fail to give the performance expected.

The secret of perfect blending is in the balance of fibres. A 100 per cent synthetic of Dacron, Orlon, Terylene, nylon and others less well known will do exactly what is claimed. These synthetics are usually

FIBRE AND SOURCE	EXAMPLE OF FIBRE	CHARACTERIS-TICS OF FIBRE	SEWING TIPS AND GENERAL CARE
NATURAL			
SILK (cocoon of silkworm) (See Colour Plate 4)		Lustrous, luxurious, drapes well. Is naturally resilient and strong. Takes brilliant dyes. Comfortable. Absorbent. Can be mixed with wool, cotton and man-made fibres.	Dry clean or hand wash only in lukewarm water with well dissolved soap flakes. Squeeze gently, do not rub or wring. Rinse thoroughly. Turn garment inside out during rinsing. Roll in a towel to remove surplus moisture — do not machine dry. Hang to dry in a cool airy place, in required shape (avoid direct heat or sunlight) on a plastic hanger. Press most fabrics when damp on wrong side. Use a moderate iron (silk setting). Iron wild silk fabrics, i.e. Shantung, Douppion, Crepon, Antung and Honan silk, when bone dry. Other silks should be evenly damp when ironed. *Sewing:* Press material before laying on pattern. Pin selvages together before cutting out, using fine steel pins. Tack pinned edges together. This avoids tendency to slip. Tack to tissue paper for support when machining sheer silk fabrics, e.g. chiffon. Use a fine machine needle and sew with silk thread. Press with a cool iron on wrong side.
ANIMAL (protein) WOOL (hair fibres of various animals, most commonly sheep). Others include mohair, cashmere, vicuna, camel's hair and alpaca. (See Colour Plates 2 and 3)		Wool is naturally absorbent, flame resistant and has exceptional qualities of insulation. It is warm to wear in winter and the light-weight cloths are cool in summer. Light and medium-weight cloths mould to the body and drape well. When treated, wool can be made moth-proof, shrink-proof, shower-proofed, stain-resistant, permanently creased or pleated and also given lasting flat-set finishes. It will not hold a static electrical charge and therefore does not attract dust or dirt. Wool dyes well and is very comfortable to wear. Different grades of wool from the 450 breeds of sheep are blended together to provide garments for all purposes as well as upholstery and curtaining material, carpets and wool felts.	Dry-clean unless labelled washable, then follow manufacturer's instructions. (Hand-wash gently in lukewarm water with mild detergent or soap flakes. Avoid bleach. Do not boil.) Do not rub, or stretch by squeezing or wringing. Rinse very well in clean lukewarm water. Knitted articles can be spin-dried or rolled in a towel. Lay flat to dry, or on plastic hanger, in correct shape. Dry away from heat. Use a press cloth and a moderate iron when pressing. Air well after pressing. *Sewing:* Sponge before sewing, unless fabric has been treated with shrink resistant process. Can be eased in or shrunk during construction to give perfect fit.
VEGETABLE COTTON (seed pod of cotton plant)		Versatile, strong, durable, highly absorbent; blends well with other fibres, can be dyed any colour,	Very easy to wash by hand or machine. Whites can be bleached, boiled and spin-dried. Cotton can

FIBRE AND SOURCE	EXAMPLE OF FIBRE	CHARACTERISTICS OF FIBRE	SEWING TIPS AND GENERAL CARE
(See Colour Plate 5)		available in wide range of weights and constructions. Great affinity for chemicals — can be given shrink-resistant, crease-resistant, flame-resistant, water-repellent properties. Will take stretch, glaze, emboss and raised finishes. Used for all types of clothing, furnishings, domestic textiles, etc.	be finished to prevent shrinkage. Easy-care cottons need little or no ironing. Many untreated cottons improved by the use of starch. Press with a hot iron while damp. *Sewing:* Most cottons are very easy to sew, do not fray easily and are little subject to seam slippage.
LINEN (flax fibres) (See Colour Plate 6)		Cool, comfortable, absorbent. Has a crisp fresh appearance. Can be blended with natural and man-made fibres. Frequently a crease-resistant finish is applied.	Washable as for cotton. Press with a very damp cloth on wrong side. Slight shrinkage during washing is restored when fabric is pressed under light tension. *Sewing:* Cut, don't tear, to straighten ends. Ravelling edges need special finishing; zigzag stitches are satisfactory.

MAN-MADE FIBRES

FIBRE AND SOURCE	EXAMPLE OF FIBRE	CHARACTERISTICS OF FIBRE	SEWING TIPS AND GENERAL CARE
VISCOSE RAYON (See Colour Plate 7)	*Standard rayon* Courtaulds rayon. Filament and staple. Filament rayon is also available with textured and slubbed effects. *Modified rayon* Sarille. Crimped rayon staple. Durafil. High-tenacity and abrasion resistant staple. Vincel. Polynosic fibre giving fabrics with good stability in washing. *Duracol* is a registered trade-mark of Courtaulds Ltd., and is used to denote their spun-dyed yarns and fibres. All above fibres are produced by Courtaulds Ltd.	The fibre is exceedingly versatile and is used in many types of fabrics either alone or mixed with natural or other man-made fibres. Fabric is pleasant to handle, and drapes well. Characteristics, particularly of Vincel, are similar to cotton. Good moisture absorption. Can be textured, crêped, moiréed, and a wide range of finishes applied to give different textures. Dyes well. "Spun-dyed" yarns are available to give a high degree of colour fastness particularly for checks, stripes and jacquard designs. Hard-wearing, moth-proof and mildew resistant. Non-static properties make it particularly suitable for linings.	Avoid oversoiling. Dry clean or wash often. Rayon fabrics may often be washable at 60° C - 140° F. in a machine, but knitted fabrics are preferably washed in hand-hot water (48° C — 118° F.) by hand. BUT always look for a label giving precise instructions, and ALWAYS in the absence of a label check that the colour is fast. Handle light-weight fabrics carefully when wet, since some rayon loses strength in wet state. To damp down for ironing, roll in a damp towel rather than by sprinkling. Iron with a medium hot iron (rayon setting) while still damp.
ACETATE (Cellulose acetate) (See Colour Plate 7)	Dicel (British Celanese Ltd.). Acetate filament yarn and staple fibre. Dicel Duracol (British Celanese Ltd.). Spun-dyed filament acetate yarn. Dicel KN (British Celanese Ltd.). Acetate filament yarn with latent crimp.	Fabrics have a rich, attractive appearance. Soft, luxurious and smooth. Drapes beautifully. Used extensively in dresswear, hand knitting yarns and furnishings. It can be spun-dyed to give a high degree of colour fastness, taking sharp and brilliant colours. Prints well. Moth and mildew resistant. Does not deteriorate with age,	Avoid oversoiling. Evening wear should be dry cleaned frequently. Most other fabrics can be hand washed, but use only *warm* water (40° C — 104° F.) Hot water can be damaging to acetate. Squeeze gently, do not wring. Avoid spin drying for longer period than the minimum required to remove excess water. Iron with a warm

FIBRE AND SOURCE	EXAMPLE OF FIBRE	CHARACTERISTICS OF FIBRE	SEWING TIPS AND GENERAL CARE
		and will give lasting wear if properly cared for.	iron (rayon setting) on the wrong side while still damp. Beware of spilling acetone (nail vanish remover) as it damages acetate fabric. *Sewing:* Use sharp cutting-out scissors, fine steel pins and needles. Use a synthetic fibre sewing thread to avoid seam pucker after washing. Seams on the bias should be taped. Make sure that all trimmings are washable if you intend the garment to be washable. Use a soft padded surface for pressing to avoid seam impressions.
CELLULOSE TRIACETATE (See Colour Plate 10)	Tricel (British Celanese Ltd.). Filament yarn and staple. Tricel Duracol (British Celanese Ltd.). Spun-dyed filament yarn and staple. Arnel (American Celanese Co.).	Similar in appearance to acetate. Soft, comfortable fabric, which drapes beautifully. Tricel staple blends well with natural and man-made fibres. Excellent resistance to shrinkage and stretching. Resists soiling and is easy to wash. Quick drying and suitably constructed fabrics require little or no ironing. Crease-resistant. Takes permanent pleats well as long as fabric contains more than 55% Tricel.	Except for permanently pleated Tricel, washable both by hand and machine. Do not wring and avoid spin-drying. (Tumble drying is satisfactory.) Avoid bleach. Minimum iron garments should be preferably hand washed in warm water (40° C — 104° F.) avoiding squeezing. An extra rinse in hand-hot water removes creases in drip-dry garments. Hang up to drip-dry — in proper shape of garment on a hanger. Durably pleated garments must be drip-dried. When ironing is necessary, iron while still damp or use a steam iron, set at "wool." Dry-cleaning — by perchlorethylene only — not trichlorethylene. *Sewing:* Use tissue under seams to prevent marking right side while pressing. Use sharp cutting-out scissors, sharp pins and fine needles.
ACRYLIC (more than 85% acrylonitrile) (See Colour Plate 11)	Acrilan (Chemstrand Ltd.). Courtelle (Courtaulds Ltd.). Orlon (Du Pont Ltd.).	Fabric has warm, exceptionally kind soft luxurious handle. Light in weight, yet strong and hard-wearing. Resilient. Non-irritant. Crease-resistant, resilient. Correctly made garments will not shrink or stretch. Can be durably pleated. Mothproof and mildew resistant. Blend well with natural or man-made fibres. Not affected by sunlight.	Wash before garment looks dirty. Exceptionally easy to machine or hand wash. Use warm water (40° C. — 104° F.). Do *not* boil. Avoid wringing. Squeeze out moisture and allow to drip-dry in proper shape of garment on a plastic hanger. Rinse thoroughly to avoid graying. A small amount of soapless liquid detergent in the final rinse will help to keep a good colour. Avoid bleach. Spin dry for a short time only when garment

FIBRE AND SOURCE	EXAMPLE OF FIBRE	CHARACTERISTICS OF FIBRE	SEWING TIPS AND GENERAL CARE
			is quite cold, or permanent creases will result. Knitted articles do not felt after repeated washing, and these are ready-to-wear as soon as dry. Dry flat on a towel with no ironing: some woven and knitted garments made from blended yarns with natural fibres may require a light pressing with a cool iron on the wrong side when fabric is practically dry. Always use a damp cloth and avoid excessive mechanical pressure, particularly at seams, pockets and other areas of multiple thicknesses. *Sewing:* Choose washable notions. Perfect seam tension is absolutely essential to avoid puckers in seams. Avoid ripping out or pressing until fit is assured. Use sharp cutting-out scissors. Sew with good quality cotton, nylon or Terylene thread. Do not stretch the material as you guide it through the machine.
MODACRYLIC (35—85% acrylonitrite staple fibres)	Dynel (Carbide & Carbon Chemicals Co.). (American imported fabric.) Verel (Tenesee Eastman) (American imported fabric.)	Warm, strong fabric. Moth and sunlight resistant. Crease resistant. Bulk without weight. Coatings (fur-like fabrics of 100% Dynel blended with acrylics). Has soft luxurious feel, drapes well, crease-resistant. Dyes beautifully. Flame-resistant.	Wash easily, dry quickly. In fur-like form should be treated as fur. Follow Acrylic washing instructions. Use very cool iron or shrivelling will result. Iron on wrong side. *Sewing* (see Acrylics)
Modacrylic filament yarn	Teklan (British Celanese Ltd.). Continuous filament yarn. Zephran (Dow Chemical Co. Ltd.). (American imported fabric.)	Flame-proof, even after repeated washing and dry cleaning, strong, hard wearing, soft, warm and light fabric which washes easily, dries quickly and is dimensionally stable. Highly resistant to damage by sunlight, bacteria and insects. Crease-resistant. Used to make a wide variety of dress fabrics, night wear, and household textiles.	Hand or machine wash in hand-warm suds, rinse well and drip-dry. If ironing is necessary, use a cool iron when fully dry.
POLYESTER (See Colour Plate 9)	Terylene (I. C. I. Ltd.). Filament yarn and staple fibre. Crimplene (I. C. I. Ltd.). Modified high bulk Terylene filament yarn. Dacron (Du Pont Company Ltd.). Filament yarn and staple fibre (American imported fabric.)	Even light-weight fabrics are very strong and abrasion resistant. Durable. Resilient. Crease-resistant. Shrink-resistant. Resists stretching. Fabric drapes well, mothproof and mildew-resistant. Retains durable pleating. Absorbent. Easily washed and dried. Now leading fibre for curtain material and dress fabrics which	Spot cleans and washes easily due to low moisture absorption. Use hand-hot water (48° C. — 118° F.). Wash by hand or machine, but do not spin dry or wring as permanent creases may result. Handle sheer weight fabrics carefully. Rinse well. Shake off excess moisture or roll in a towel if desired. Hang up in shape. Ironing depends on

FIBRE AND SOURCE	EXAMPLE OF FIBRE	CHARACTERISTICS OF FIBRE	SEWING TIPS AND GENERAL CARE
		have excellent resistance to light degradation. Staple fibre blends well with other natural or man-made fibres.	fabric — often not necessary, or only brief touch of a *cool* iron. According to other fibres used. Crimplene — turn garment inside out before washing as above, accessories removed. If pleated wash by hand. Press with a cool iron under a damp cloth. Use bleach only when essential. *Sewing* (see Acrylics). Material cannot be "eased in" or shrunk during construction, so correct cutting is important. Use Terylene thread and non-shrink linings and interlinings.
NYLON (polyamide) (See Colour Plate 8)	Nylon 6 6 (pronounced "six, six") (British Nylon Spinners Ltd.). Bri-Nylon continuous filament and staple fibre. Nylon 6 (six) (British Enkalon Ltd.). Enkalon.	Extremely strong and durable — exceptionally abrasion resistant. Even lightweight fabrics have high tensile strength even when wet. Naturally elastic, and therefore particularly suitable for jersey and stretch fabrics. Nylon fabrics drape well and are soft to touch. Can be set to a permanent size and shape during manufacture — will not stretch or shrink. Can be durably pleated. Fast-dyes well in a wide range of good clear colours. Flame resistant. Mothproof and mildew resistant. Easily washed and dried. Nylon staple improves strength and durability of fabrics with which it is blended.	Wash frequently using hand-hot water (48° C. — 118° F.). — rather hotter for white fabrics, but do not boil or permanent creases may result. In hard water areas use a soapless detergent. Use plenty of water and rinse thoroughly. Do not use bleach. Dries quickly at room temperature. Drip-dry (use plastic hangers). Do not wring. Squeeze gently. Spin dry for a short period only or roll in a towel. Do not expose to direct heat or strong sunshine. Little or no ironing required (particularly knitteds) but fabrics look better if pressed with a *cool* iron. Best ironed nearly dry on the wrong side. *Sewing* (see Acrylics).
STRETCH YARNS	Bri-Nylon (British Nylon Spinners Ltd.). Many different kinds of nylon, some having their own brand names, e.g.: Agilon (British Nylon Spinners Ltd.). Courtolon (Courtaulds Ltd.) and other crimped nylons. Helanca (John Heathcoat Ltd.) nylon and Terylene yarns. Ban-Lon (Joseph Bancroft Ltd.) bulked nylon. Bri-Nylon is also used in combination with a variety of natural and synthetic fibres, e.g. linen, viscose, wool, etc.	Warp stretch pulls parallel to selvage edge. Weft pulls across to fabric width. Two way stretch pulls in both directions. Fine soft handling material produced in a variety of weaves including knitted and jersey materials. Used for ski-pants, trousers, slacks and sports wear.	Washable, and dry cleanable. Hand or machine wash in luke-warm water, rinsing thoroughly. Avoid bleach. Dry away from direct heat. Use a *cool* iron only, on the wrong side, if required. *Sewing:* Check manufacturer's directions for care (see Chapter 7). A zigzag stitch is very satisfactory to stitch or re-stitch seams and as a hem finish. Use nylon thread and a fine needle and stitch at a slow even speed using a small stitch (14 to the inch).

FIBRE AND SOURCE	EXAMPLE OF FIBRE	CHARACTERISTICS OF FIBRE	SEWING TIPS AND GENERAL CARE
RUBBER	Lastex (Lastex yarn and Lactron Thread Company Ltd.). Rubber cored covered yarn.	High stretch recovery used in corsetry and swimwear.	
ELASTOMERIC YARNS	Vyrene (Lastex yarn and Lactron Thread Co.). Blue "C" Spandex (Chemstrand Ltd.). Spanzelle (Courtaulds Ltd.) Continuous filament yarn. Lycra (Du Pont Ltd.). Multifilament.	Naturally supple, resilient fabric with high stretch recovery, used in corsetry and swimwear and any garment where stretch is required. Extremely durable, light, porous and comfortable. Resistant to seawater, sunlight and suntan oils and perspiration. Can be sewn with no note of needle-tacking, and danger of laddering is reduced. Some fabrics are fully dyeable in a wide variety of colours.	
METALLIC	Rexor (Metallic yarns). (Porth Textiles Ltd.). Lurex & Lurex 50 C (Metallic yarns). (Dow Chemical Co. Ltd.).	Non-tarnishing metallic yarn which can be used with any basic fibre in both woven and knitted applications, used for both fashion and furnishing materials. Non allergenic and non irritant — due to fine film covering the metal.	Can be safely dry cleaned or washed depending on basic fibre. Dry cleaning is advisable for rayon brocades. Use a *cool* iron (rayon temperature) with a damp cloth, on the wrong side. Do *not* use a hot iron or film covering will be destroyed. *Sewing:* Check that material has no one-way sheen. Stitch as for basic material, ignoring the metallic altogether.
SYNTHETIC FOAM	Foam backers: (Lintafoam Ltd.). (Perrofoam Ltd.). (Caprofoam Ltd.).	Flexible spongelike, porous material used for interlining and interfacing. Light weight, non allergenic, non toxic, odourless, gives warmth without weight. When bonded with another fabric, gives resilience and shape retention to the fabric. Crease resistance. Used for coats and jackets.	Follow manufacturer's instructions for care. Most British foam-backs are dry cleanable. *Sewing:* See complete instructions for handling in Chapter 7. Place pattern on *fabric* side. Pin within the seam allowance. Use large stitch (8-9 per inch). Tape all seams with linen tape. Reverse each pattern piece after cutting. No neatening required. Press on wrong side using a dry pressing cloth.
GLASS	Fibreglass (Fibreglass Ltd.) (Deeglas Fibres Ltd.) (Turner Bros. Asbestos Co. Ltd.)	Glass yarn for home furnishings; curtaining and industrial uses. Resists moth, mildew, sunlight; fireproof and non-absorbent. Does not deteriorate with age. Crease-resistant, does not shrink, stretch or sag. Reflects and filters light.	Avoid machine washing and dry cleaning. Hand wash by swishing lightly in warm soapsuds or detergent. Do not rub. Rinse well. Drip-dry over clothes line or rod. Do not use clothes pegs. Do not iron. *Sewing:* Test fabric for correct stitch; tension. Use mercerised thread, long stitch, loose tension, light pressure, sharp needle. Line with fibreglass only.

washable and highly crease-resistant. They won't shrink, stretch or lose shape. When they are combined with other fibres, usually the natural fibres, these same characteristics are partially added to the fabric, but only in proportion to the percentage of synthetic fibre in the fabric. If the fabric is to give the performance of the synthetic, the synthetic fibre must compose at least 50 per cent of the blend. In many cotton and rayon blends, the synthetic fibre must constitute 65 per cent of the fabric for the blend to react as the synthetic.

When confronted with a fabric that is composed of two or more fibres, it is often a problem to know just how to handle the combination of fibres to get the best results in your garment. The various percentages of fibres in the fabric will be listed, and reliable manufacturers will state how the fabric should be cleaned. Don't think that just because a woollen has some man-made fibre in it, the fabric is washable. Be sure that the man-made fibre is at least 50 per cent of the fabric and the tag clearly states that the fabric may be washed. Don't assume that just because a cotton contains a little nylon, it won't shrink. The nylon may be there just to add sheen or to make the fabric stronger. Be sure that the tag or label states that the fabric will not shrink more than one per cent. Even then, it's often best to test the fabric for shrinkage. (See the shrinkage test on page 97.)

FIBRES INTO FABRIC

Man has been making cloth to cover himself since his very earliest history. He probably started with the skins of animals and then learned how to pound fibres from bark, bonding them into cloth. Weaving and knitting followed. Despite all our wonderful scientific advances, we still haven't found any new methods of making cloth. Man still must weave, knit or bond fibres into fabric.

From these three basic methods of making a cloth, a huge technology has evolved. Man can weave fabrics in an endless variety of textures; he knits them in all sorts of interesting stitches, and bonds them with heat, moisture and chemicals.

Woven Fabrics

Most of our fabrics are woven. In weaving, two systems of yarns are interlaced at right angles to each other. The type of yarn used, the way the yarns are interlaced, even the colours of the yarn produce an infinite variety of interesting fabrics in look, feel and reaction.

It isn't so important for you to know how these weaves are made, but it is important to know what they will do, how they will look when you make them up in a garment. When you purchase fabric you should know if the weave is a sturdy one or if the very nature of the weave allows the fabric to stretch, and what will happen when the garment is worn. Although less important, it's nice to know what the different weaves are and what they are called, so when you read and hear about various fabrics you can at least have a mental picture of what the fabric looks like (13) p. 52.

Surprising as it may seem, there are basically only three methods of weaving: the plain weave, the twill weave and the satin weave. They vary in the way the lengthwise threads or warp yarns are crossed by the crosswise threads or filling (weft) yarns. But there are many, many ways to vary each of these basic weaves.

PLAIN WEAVE. This is the most common of all weaves. Each filling yarn goes over one warp yarn and under the next alternately. Every second warp yarn is raised in the loom, the filling shot across, then the alternate warp yarns are raised, and the filling shot across again.

When warp and filling yarns of the same size are closely woven and equally spaced, the plain weave is the strongest of all weaves.

Familiar fabrics made with a plain weave are: batiste, broadcloth, challis, gingham, muslin, madras. And there are many, many more.

One major variation of the plain weave is the *Basket Weave*. Double yarns are used in a plain-weave pattern, instead of the usual single yarn. This produces a very loosely woven fabric, which stretches easily and drapes well. The looseness of the fabric makes it less durable and not very satisfactory for clothing; it is very likely to stretch out of shape quickly in a garment.

The *Rib Weave* which has ribbed or corded effects in either the warp or filling direction is another variation of the plain weave. The rib may be produced by alternating fine yarns with coarse yarns, or single yarns with double yarns. In general, ribbed fabrics are not as long-wearing as plain-woven ones, especially when the ribs are rather thick, because the coarser yarns tend to pull away from the finer ones, resulting in splits and tears in the fabric. The entire yarn is also exposed to abrasive wear and is less durable.

WEAVES

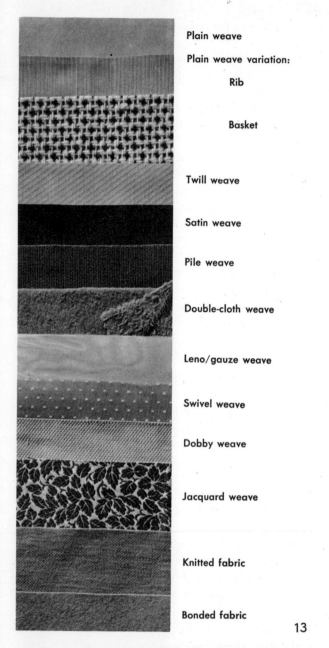

Plain weave

Plain weave variation:

Rib

Basket

Twill weave

Satin weave

Pile weave

Double-cloth weave

Leno/gauze weave

Swivel weave

Dobby weave

Jacquard weave

Knitted fabric

Bonded fabric

13

Changes in the direction of the twill weave's diagonal lines produce variations such as the herringbone, corkscrew, entwining and fancy twills.

SATIN WEAVE. This is the weakest type of weave. Similar to the twill in construction, the yarns are more widely spaced, producing long floats which lie on the surface and receive most of the wear. Satin weaves produce smooth, lustrous fabrics. Satin and sateen are made with a satin weave.

There are many variations of each of these weaves. To help you recognise the most popular of these special weaves a brief description of each is given here:

PILE WEAVE. This fancy weave uses both the plain and the twill weaves in construction. An extra warp or filling yarn is woven into the basic construction. This additional yarn is drawn up from the surface of the fabric forming loops. The loops may be cut or closely sheared as in velvet, or left uncut as in terry cloth.

DOUBLE-CLOTH WEAVE. In double-cloth, two fabrics are woven on the loom at the same time, one on top of the other and interlaced in construction. Two different weaves can be used; for example, a twill on one side, a plain on the other. These fabrics are frequently bulky. If made of warm, woolly fibres, they can give great warmth. Fabrics representative of double-cloth weaves are blanket cloth and upholstery fabrics of all types.

LENO WEAVE; GAUZE WEAVE. Very light-weight meshy fabrics are woven with the leno loom. Basically the plain weave is used with the second warp yarn twisting around the first warp as it passes alternately over and under the filling yarn, locking the filling in position. Some major fabrics woven on leno looms are marquisette, netting, mesh shirtings.

TWILL WEAVE. This weave is formed by the filling crossing at least two warp yarns before going under one or more yarns, with a shift to the right or left in succeeding rows forming diagonal ridges on the face of the fabric. Basically, twills are not as tight a weave as the plain weave, since the yarns are not as tightly interlocked. However, most twills are woven of sturdy yarns and give good service. They are often preferred for suits, coats and work clothes because of their rough and interesting texture. A few fabrics representative of the twill weave are: gabardine, drill, serge, whipcord, foulard, surah.

LAPPET and SWIVEL WEAVES. In both these weaves, decorative dots, circles or other small figures are woven on the surface of the fabric while it is being constructed in the loom. In the swivel weave, yarns are cut when the fabric is completed. Since the yarns cannot be securely fastened, the designs may pull out when the fabric is handled in washing. The lappet weave has the designs stitched in the fabric while it is being woven. The ends of the threads are fastened so they will not pull out easily. Dotted swiss is produced by both these methods. The lappet weave dotted swiss is preferable to the swivel weave.

DOBBY WEAVE. Special looms are needed for dobby weaves, which produce small geometric designs in the fabric. Although this weave does make use of floats, they are usually small enough not to affect the wear of the fabric. The most familiar of the dobby weaves is the popular bird's-eye, which is a small diamond pattern with an eye in the centre.

JACQUARD WEAVE. The marvellous damasks, brocades and tapestries are made on the Jacquard loom. The easiest explanation of the loom is that it is controlled by perforated paper patterns similar to player piano rolls, and is capable of producing intricate patterned designs. Floats are inevitable in the Jacquard weave because of the elaborate designs and may affect durability unless the fabric is compactly constructed and of good quality. Damask, brocade, tapestry and matelassé are all Jacquard weaves.

Knitted Fabrics

Knitted fabrics are in fashion. They seem to answer a demand for clothes that are practical, comfortable and still good-looking. More and more fibres are being turned into attractive knit patterns and made into all types of garments from underwear to evening clothes.

When buying a knit, remember that it is a resilient fabric. The fact that it is formed of loops makes it springy, stretchy and more elastic than woven cloth. These qualities can be both an advantage and a disadvantage. Knits stretch and contract with the body, making them wonderful for active wear. They usually spring back into shape. After long wear, however, they may become stretched and start to "bag."

Knits come in marvellous patterns, in all sorts of weights and in a myriad of textures. They drape well and do not wrinkle easily. However, because of their elasticity they may cling to the body and they do require special handling. Before sewing a knitted fabric be sure to read the special directions on page 99.

Bonded Fabrics

The oldest method of making cloth is by bonding fibres. Early man pounded the bark of trees and through pressure created a cloth. A French monk placed wool in his sandals to relieve foot pain. He discovered that the moisture, pressure and heat matted the wool fibres, interlocking them to form a sort of wool cloth. Thus, felt was born.

For dressmaking there are only two types of bonded fabrics you are likely to work with: felt and the non-woven shaping materials. There is no elasticity or resilience to these fabrics, and they will tear under stress. The edges will not ravel or fray. They will not drape, but many are thermoplastic, which means they shrink and shape with the application of heat and moisture. This quality is fine if you are making a shaped garment, but it can present problems in pressing.

FABRIC FINISHES

If you've mastered the fibres, and know about weaves, you have one more step to go. There is another process involved in the manufacturing of fabrics which will have a decided effect on a fabric's action and behaviour—the finishing. This includes all those wonderful treatments which make fabrics shrink-resistant, crease-resistant, colour-fast, drip-dry, mothproof.

You will discover a host of trade names, like Mitin, Sanforized, Calpreta. Most of these finishes are patented processes and the only way to discover what the name means and the purpose of the finish is to consult a list, such as the one here. Many of these finishes accomplish several purposes. New finishes appear almost daily, so keep up to date by reading about them in current magazines.

Shrinkage Control Finishes

Sanforized (*Cluett, Peabody & Co. Ltd.*) A trade mark appearing on woven cottons and cotton blends indicating that the fabric has been treated to prevent more than 1 % shrinkage or stretch in any direction, when washed.

Tebilized (*Tootal, Broadhurst Lee Co. Ltd.*) This is a name applied to fabrics which have satisfied certain standards of crease and shrink resistance. Dylan (*Stevensons Dyers Ltd.*) Is a registered trade mark denoting that goods carrying the mark are made from wool, or mixtures containing wool, have been shrink-resist treated by processes approved by "Dylan" laboratories and passed their standards of washability. Woven fabrics, made-up garments, hose, knitted garments, knitting wools and blankets are treated in this way.

Quintafix (*The Bradford Dyers' Association Ltd.*) A process giving crease and shrink resistance to cotton dress fabrics.

Quintesse (*The Bradford Dyers' Association*) A process giving crease and shrink resistance to rayon crêpe fabrics.

Calpreta Fixt (*Calico Printers' Association Ltd.*) Finish renders furnishing fabrics dimensionally stable so that they will neither shrink nor stretch.

Rigmel (*The Bradford Dyers' Association Ltd.*) Finish for cotton shirtings and overall fabrics.

Rigmel Prystene (*The Bradford Dyers' Association*) Shrink-resist non-iron finish for cotton shirtings and blouse fabrics sheds creases in the wash.

Rigmel C-CL (*The Bradford Dyers' Association*) Shrink-resist, non-iron chlorine resisting finish for cotton shirtings.

Fortesse Finish (*The Bradford Dyers' Association*) Shrink-resist finish for furnishing fabrics.

Permo Finish (*The Bradford Dyers' Association*) Non resin finish for wool and worsted cloths, sheds wearing creases, retains intentional creases.

Crease-Resistant Finishes

Calpreta Crease Resist 44 (*Calico Printers' Association Ltd.*) A crease and shrink resistant finish used for rayon materials.

Tebilized (*Tootal Broadhurst Lee Co. Ltd.*) A name applied to fabrics which have reached a certain high standard of shrink and crease resistance.

Everglaze and Minicare (*Joseph Bancroft and Sons (England) Ltd.*) A trade mark that identifies fabrics treated for crease, stretch and shrink resistance.

Quintafix, Triple Three, Sereno, Rigmel C-CL, Prystene (*Bradford Dyers' Association Ltd.*) are all crease shedding and shrink resistant finishes.

Stretch Finishes

Calpreta Stretch Finish (*Calico Printers' Association Ltd.*) New finish which gives pure cotton fabrics a stretch of about 20% — the finish is permanent. If drip-dried, fabrics need little or no ironing.

"Lastique" (*British Silk Dyeing Co.*) A finishing process for imparting stretch to fabrics in wool, rayon and all blends of natural and man-made fibres.

No-Iron Finishes

Calpreta Carefree-Wringable, Calpreta Carefree Sheen (*Calico Printers' Association Ltd.*) are non-resin crease and shrink resistant finishes for cottons which can be spin dried, wrung out or tumble dried and still require little or no ironing.

Calpreta Carefree Cotton Finish (*Calico Printers' Association Ltd.*) for drip-dry no-iron cottons.

Quintafix, Rigmel C-CL, Prystene (*The Bradford Dyers' Association*) are drip-dry and crease resistant finishes. Tebilized Double Tested (*Tootal Broadhurst Lee Co. Ltd.*) Finish gives crease resistance and smooth drying qualities to cotton, linen and rayon.

Everglaze Minicare (*Joseph Bancroft and Sons Ltd.*) Such fabrics need little or no ironing.

Moth-Proofing Finishes

Mitin (*The Geigy Co. Ltd.*) Non-toxic compound used for the durable proofing of wool mixtures and fabrics composed of other animal fibres against moth and beetle damage, applied during dyeing or finishing.

Fortesse (*Bradford Dyers' Association*) A rot and pest proof shrink and stretch resistant finish for cotton and rayon fabrics. Especially suitable for tropical weight fabrics.

Shell Dielmoth (*Shell Chemical Co. Ltd.*) Finish for woollen fabrics, which does not affect colour, odour, or handle of material. Lasting process applied during manufacture, which is not affected by washing.

Water-Repellent Finishes

Scotchgard (*Minnesota Mining and Manufacturing Co. Ltd.*) This is a fluorochemical oil and water-repellent finish. Stain-repeller is a fluorochemical which imparts oil and water-repellency to fabrics. Oil borne or water borne stains bend up on the surface of the fabric and can be quickly and neatly blotted away.

Can be bought by the yard in furnishing fabrics (loose covers) but not as yet for dressmaking. Garments treated in this way carry a swing ticket and sewn-in label.

Velan, Dipsanil (*Imperial Chemical Industries, Ltd.*) Non-silicone durable water-repellent finishes. I. C. I. also produce several silicone finishes which give water-repellency on all natural and synthetic fabrics.

Calpreta (*Calico Printers' Association Ltd.*) Stain-resistant and water-repellent finishes which are used on cotton, nylon, Terylene and rayon fabrics.

Cravenette (*The Bradford Dyers' Association*) is a shower-proofing finish for cotton, union and woollen rainwear. Also Cravenette Wash and Wear Finish for cotton rainwear.

Dri-sil (*Midland Silicones Ltd.*) Process imparts soft handle with water and stain resistant characteristics.

Flame-Resistant Processes

PROBAN *(Proban Ltd.)* A permanent anti-flame finish applicable to all cellulosic materials and blends.

Insulating Processes

MILIUM *(Deering Milliken, U.S.A.)* A lining fabric with a metal insulating treatment that gives warmth in winter, coolness in summer.

Colour-Fast Processes

Vat dyeing is one of the processes widely used on cotton, washable rayon, and linen fabrics to keep their colour fast to laundering, sun fading and rubbing. In recent years a class of dyes known as reactive dyes has been introduced which also give fast dyeings on cotton and other cellulosic fabrics.

Some of the larger textile concerns are endeavouring to institute a label system, to indicate those fabrics which reach a certain standard of colour-fastness.

GLOSSARY OF FAMILIAR FABRICS

We've talked about fibres, we've talked about finishes, we've talked about weaves, now let's talk about specific fabrics. When you read the list of suggested fabrics on a pattern envelope you should know what is meant by dimity, voile, madras, corduroy. This glossary has been compiled to help you identify the fabrics which you are most likely to use (14).

Barathea Made of silk or rayon warp with a woollen or worsted filling. Various weaves are used to produce this fine-textured cloth, which is usually of high quality. It comes most often in black.

GLOSSARY OF FAMILIAR FABRICS

14

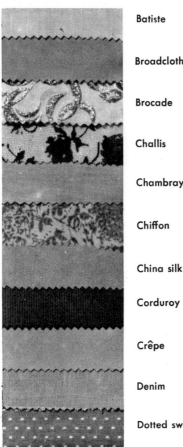

- Batiste
- Broadcloth
- Brocade
- Challis
- Chambray
- Chiffon
- China silk
- Corduroy
- Crêpe
- Denim
- Dotted swiss

- Faille
- Flannel
- Gingham
- Jersey
- Lace
- Lawn
- Linen
- Moiré
- Organdie
- Organza
- Peau de soie

- Piqué
- Satin
- Seersucker
- Shantung
- Surah
- Taffeta
- Terry cloth
- Tricot
- Velvet
- Voile

Bark Crêpe A woollen or rayon fabric that has rough, barklike surface interest. Used for coats and in upholstery.

Batik This is a method of printing cloth, rather than a special weave, fibre or finish. Design areas are covered in wax and colour applied. When the wax is removed, the design appears in white on a coloured background.

Batiste Soft, sheer cotton fabric woven in a plain weave. It comes in white, solid colours and prints, and is very suitable for soft dresses.

Bedford Cord A cloth made by using a variation of the plain weave in which cords run the length of the fabric. It can be woven of any of the major fibres, but is generally of wool or cotton. It is used for coats, suits, uniforms.

Bengaline Cross-rib material with filling yarn coarser than the warp to produce the corded effect. Usually made of silk, rayon, wool or cotton in various widths and is used for dresses, coatings and ribbons.

Bouclé Usually found in woollens, this cloth is woven with a novelty yarn which has tightly curled loops. It does appear in some cottons and other fibres, and is very popular in knitted fabrics.

Broadcloth Usually a plain, closely woven cloth made of wool, cotton or silk, broadcloth may be made in a number of weaves. Cotton broadcloth has a fine crosswise rib and a lustrous finish.

Brocade A decorative fabric which has a raised pattern woven in relief against a background. It is made of a variety of fibres and often has metallic threads forming the raised or embossed pattern. Depending on its weight, it may be used for clothing or upholstery.

Burlap A plain-weave coarse fabric made from jute or allied yarns. Comes natural or may be dyed in a variety of colours or prints.

Butcher Rayon Rayon fabric with a linen weave.

Calico A plain-woven cotton which is printed with small designs. It comes in various qualities depending on the texture and fineness of the yarn used.

Camel Hair A coating fabric made from the natural-coloured hair of the camel, frequently mixed with wool. It is a soft napped fabric, noted for its warmth and light weight.

Cashmere A soft finish fabric made entirely from the hair of goats from Kashmir or from fine wool mixed with the hair, widely used in coats, suits, sweaters.

Challis A light-weight soft wool, cotton, rayon or combination of fibres made with a plain weave and usually printed with a small design. Usually used for dresses and blouses.

Chambray Smooth, lustrous fabric made of coloured or dyed warp threads, and white or contrasting colour threads in the filling, producing an iridescent effect. Usually, it is a cotton fabric, but may be made in a combination of fibres. It is sturdy, launders well, and is easy to work with.

Cheviot A heavy-weight twill-weave woollen or worsted with a rough, hairy surface, similar to tweed. Ideal for sportswear.

Chiffon Very sheer, light-weight, transparent cotton, silk, nylon, rayon or blend of fibres made in a plain weave with fine, highly twisted yarns. It is a dressy fabric, and is often used for soft draping over other heavier firmer fabrics.

Chino A sturdy cotton fabric, made in plain or twill weave and fairly lustrous. It is used extensively for summer uniforms and sportswear.

Chintz A glazed, crisp cotton of a closely woven plain weave, usually printed with bright and gay colours. It is used a great deal for drapery and loose covers. In lighter weights, it is very adaptable to gay summer dresses and sportswear.

Corduroy A very strong, durable cotton pile fabric with rounded ridges or wales of pile running lengthwise. The wales come in various widths. Suitable for casual clothes and sportswear.

Covert A twill weave usually made of woollen or worsted yarn but can be cotton, rayon or spun acetate. Fabric woven with yarns of two shades of the same colour so that fabric has a speckled effect. Used for coats, suits, sportswear.

Crêpe Light-weight fabric of silk, rayon, cotton, wool, synthetic or a combination of fibres. It is characterised by a crinkling of the surface, obtained by using either hard-twisted yarns, chemical treatment, special weaves or embossing.

Damask Woven designs similar to those of brocade are found in damask, but the cloth is a finer, thinner construction. It is made of silk, cotton, linen, rayon and some blends of synthetics. Widely used for table linens, damask is available in various qualities at all price ranges.

Denim Twill-weave cotton woven with coloured warp and white filling yarns. Gives a strong fabric that launders well. Popular for work and play clothes.

Dimity Thin sheer cotton fabric with corded stripe or check effects made by weaving heavier threads in a pattern using a plain weave. Popular for dainty dresses, lounge wear.

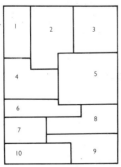

6 The materials shown in this picture are all 100% linen, all of which are specially treated for crease-resistance, and some are pre-shrunk. Note the delicate, yet intense, colouring and the range of textures available using the same fibre. Being cool, linen is used for tropical suiting, dresses, coats, suits, trousers, skirts and blouses, slacks, shorts and other sportswear.

1 Toning ombré cotton embroidered linen. **2** Irish linen, dress or suit weight. **3** Exactly toning all over cotton embroidery. **4** Spaced motif embroidered in ombré cottons on natural background. **5** Bold design embroidered in ombré cottons on white or natural linen. **6** Dress weight Irish linen. **7** Fine smooth 'handkerchief' linen. **8** Classic design embroidered in white cotton on many ground colours of Irish linen. **9** Heavy weight slubbed linen. **10** Simple, spaced eyelet design embroidered in cotton on Irish linen.

Photograph by courtesy of "Moygashel" Stevensons & Sons Ltd.

7 Fabrics in rayon and acetate are available in a variety of textures and are used for blouses, dresses, evening wear, sportswear and lingerie, as well as household furnishings. **1** Viscose ribbon lace. **2** Acetate and viscose slubbed fabric. **3** Textured acetate and nylon organza. **4** Slubbed acetate. **5** 100% rayon linen. **6** Printed acetate surah. **7** Escorto gold seal 100% rayon. **8** Acetate satin. **9** Rayon velvet.

Photograph by courtesy of Courtaulds Ltd.

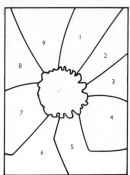

Dobby Any fabric woven on special dobby looms. Can be of cotton, rayon or silk. Fabrics have small woven designs such as dots, geometric figures, floral motifs. Widely used for shirts, blouses, dresses.

Doeskin A fine quality, smooth finish, satin weave wool fabric with a slight nap. Used for coating, suiting or sportswear. Also made in twill-weave rayon napped on one side.

Dotted Swiss Sheer cotton fabric made of a lappet or swivel weave, with woven dots in it. Used for blouses, dresses, children's clothes, curtains.

Douppion A silk yarn which is uneven, irregular and of a large diameter. Used in cloth of the same name, as well as pongee, shantung and other slubbed silks.

Drill A durable closely woven cotton fabric of medium weight; when dyed, drill is the basic cloth of khaki and ticking.

Duck A closely woven, durable, heavy cotton fabric. Use depends on its weight.

Duvetyn A very softly napped wool fabric, or a silk which has a suède-like downy nap. It looks like a compact velvet, drapes well and wears well.

Facecloth A fine velour-like woollen cloth with a a high-gloss finish.

Faille Silk or rayon fabric with a flat crosswise rib effect, similar to grosgrain, but finer. Used for dresses, suits and coats.

Fake Fur Woven or knitted fabrics made of cotton or synthetic fibres to simulate the fur of animals. Used wherever real fur might be used.

Felt Bonded fabric created by interlocking threads through moisture, heat and pressure. Widely used in millinery, most felt has wool fibre as the base, but it can be made of almost any fibre.

Flannel A soft, loosely woven cloth of either plain or twill weave which the dull finish may conceal. Flannel comes in many weights and textures, is usually slightly napped, and can be made of cotton, wool or rayon. Used for suits, dresses, coats and, in cotton, for nightwear and sport shirts.

Fleece A heavy-weight woollen with very long nap used for coats. It is inclined to be bulky, and may be difficult to sew.

Foulard A soft, twilled silk or rayon, usually printed in small figures. It is very popular for neckwear, and is also used for soft dresses, blouses, robes.

Gabardine A sturdy cotton, rayon or wool fabric with a simple twill construction, giving steep diagonal lines on the face of the cloth. It is widely used in suits, coats, sportswear of all kinds.

Georgette A light-weight silk crêpe with a pebbled effect. Has exceptional stiffness and body for its weight due to the yarn twist in weaving. Can be white, dyed or printed.

Gingham Plain-weave cotton of medium weight, which comes in checked, plaid or striped designs. It comes in various grades; better ginghams are soft, evenly woven.

Grosgrain A strong corded silk or rayon fabric used for ladies' suits and millinery.

Homespun Usually a plain-weave wool or cotton fabric which looks as if it were hand-loomed. The yarns used are rather thick, producing a fairly heavy-weight fabric.

Hopsacking A coarse plain-weave cloth of wool or cotton which is not very closely woven. Some hopsacking may be of a basket weave. It is used primarily for coats and suits.

Jacquard Any fabric woven on the looms named after the inventor, Jacquard, which make it possible to weave intricate and fancy designs into cloth. Brocades, damasks and tapestries are all the result of Jacquard weaving.

Jap Silk A very soft light-weight plain-woven silk, used primarily for linings. It is simulated in some rayon lining fabrics.

Jersey A smooth, plain-knit fabric of wool, cotton, rayon, silk or synthetic blends. Usually jersey has a dull surface and excellent draping qualities. Widely used in dresses, shirts, sportswear, underwear.

Lace Open-work fabric made with bobbins, needles or hooks. The threads form a design. Can be hand- or machine-made. Used for trimming or for entire garments.

Lamé Any fabric in which metallic threads are used in the weaving for decorative purposes. Used mainly for evening wear.

Laminate A layer of fabric which has been fused with a layer of foam; currently the term is widely used for fabrics fused with foam rubber. Used to give warmth without weight.

Lawn Fine, sheer, crisp-finished cotton or linen of plain weave. It is crisper than voile, less crisp than organdie. In white, solid colours and prints. Popular for children's clothes, summer dresses, nightwear.

Linen Strong, lustrous fabric of plain-weave flax fibse. It comes in three major weights: handkerchief linen, which is very sheer; medium-weight, dress-weight linen; and heavier-suiting-weight for tailored garments.

Madras A plain cotton weave, usually in strongly coloured plaids, stripes and checks which will "bleed" slightly when washed. Named after the region in India where it was originated. Used for shirts, dresses, blouses.

Marquisette A gauze-weave mesh fabric, very light in weight. It is made of cotton, rayon, silk or nylon and is used for curtains or dressy evening fashions.

Matelassé Fancy fabric made on dobby or Jacquard looms. The patterns are raised, giving a quilted effect. It is made of silk, rayon, cotton or wool.

Melton A dull, non-lustrous wool fabric used for coatings and outer garments. Fabric gives excellent wear since the finishing process covers up all interlacings of the yarns giving a "solid" fabric.

Mohair Generally a soft, woollen fabric, made in plain and twill weaves, which is napped with goat hair. Fabric is glossy and lustrous, sometimes formed in loops on the surface.

Moiré Any fabric which has a wavy, water-marked finish. Most moiré is taffeta, treated to have a wavy, watery effect.

Monk's Cloth A rough basket weave, made of coarse cotton or linen fibres. Used mostly for loose covers, curtains.

Mousseline de Soie Muslin made of silk or rayon with a crisp, firm finish; resembles chiffon. Used primarily for evening wear.

Muslin A substantial plain-weave cotton, fairly strong and heavy. It comes in various grades and qualities. Cheap muslin is sized or filled with a starchy substance which washes out; better grades are made of stronger, finer fibres.

Nainsook Soft, fine cotton fabric similar to batiste, but of coarser yarn. Light in weight, of plain weave, it resembles a soft-finished dimity. It is durable and launders well.

Net or Netting Open-weave fabric with knots coming at each corner of the square. Can be cotton, rayon, silk, or nylon and ranges from very light-weight to heavy fabric.

Non-woven Fabric Fabric made by bonding fibres together with an adhesive agent or by fusing rather than weaving, spinning or knitting.

Organdie Sheer, stiff, transparent plain-weave cotton cloth, which usually is treated for permanent stiffness.

Organza Thin, transparent, stiff fabric of rayon or silk used for evening wear.

Ottoman A crosswise-ribbed fabric similar to faille or bengaline, but with much heavier ribs, often spaced with finer ribs between. Can be made of wool, cotton, silk or rayon covering cotton cords.

Oxford Cloth Plain-, basket- or twill-weave cotton, often used for shirting. It is fairly heavy cloth in which two yarns travel as one in the warp, and one filling yarn is equal in size to the two-warp yarns.

Paisley Any cotton, wool, or rayon which is printed with the traditional scroll design which originated in Paisley, Scotland.

Peau de Soie The name means "skin of silk" and denotes a soft, good-quality silk satin cloth which has a rather dull, grainy appearance.

Percale Closely woven plain-weave cotton fabric of smooth yarn. Widely used in white and pastels for fine sheets, it may also be printed for dress fabric.

Pile Fabrics Any material that to some degree resembles fur in that it has a fairly heavy nap or loops, cut or left uncut, on the face of the fabric, hiding the basic weave underneath. Fur fabrics, terry, velvet, corduroy are all classed as pile fabrics.

Pima A very fine quality cotton fibre strong and lustrous, named after Pima County, Arizona, where it was originally grown.

Piqué A medium- or heavy-weight cotton fabric with raised cords running lengthwise. The cords can be of various widths, and several novelty weaves are available, such as waffle and bird's-eye piqués.

Plissé Cottons with a puckered effect put in by a special finish. They may be plain or printed in cottons ranging from lawn to organdie weights. Most plissés have permanent puckered effects; in cheaper plissés, puckers may wash out.

Polished Cottons Generally, a plain-weave cotton which has a glazed finish, mechanically applied. Many weights and grades of cotton fabric are polished through these methods.

Pongee Usually raw silk in a natural tan colour which has a rather uneven, crude texture. It also refers to cotton or rayon cloth of similar weight and texture, which comes in solid colours or prints.

Poplin A standard dress goods material in which the filling is heavier than the warp, producing a somewhat uneven ribbed effect. It can be of wool, silk or rayon, but is most commonly a medium - or heavy-weight cotton fabric.

Puckered Nylon A fabric originally made by weaving pre-shrunk and non-shrunk nylon yarns together. Other methods are also used to create permanent puckering, usually in stripes.

Pure Dye Silk Silk goods which are not weighted with metallic finishes to give them a heavier handle and stiffness. Too much weighting reduces the strength of the fabric, making the fibres break.

Raw Silk Silk from the cultivated silk worm, before any processing has been done to remove gum.

Rep A fabric with a ribbed effect.

Sailcloth A very strong, durable canvas. Can be made of linen, cotton, or nylon. Used largely for play clothes and in upholstery.

Sateen A cotton cloth woven with the standard satin weave used for silk and rayon satin. It is highly lustrous, used widely for linings in washable garments.

Satin Silk or rayon in satin weaves, producing a highly lustrous, slippery fabric used for evening wear, linings and lingerie.

Seersucker A dull-surfaced medium-weight cotton with crinkly stripes on a plain surface, produced by a plain-weave crêpe variation. Widely used for summer clothes.

Serge Diagonal worsted, wool, rayon or silk in a fine twill weave. A standard fabric for tailored suits; it is rugged, of high texture and smooth appearance.

Shantung A rough silk in a plain weave which has large irregular filling yarns which give it a slubbed effect. Cotton and rayon are often used to simulate this.

Sharkskin A medium- to heavy-weight sleek fabric with a slightly lustred and textured weave. It is made in wool, rayon, silk and synthetics. It is very popular for tailored suits, slacks and sportswear.

Suède Cloth Plain-weave cotton napped on one side to look like leather suède.

Suiting General term used for any fabrics which are suitable for coats, suits. Includes many weaves, textures and various fibres.

Surah Twill-weave silk, rayon or synthetic which is suitable for soft, tailored garments. Available in solid colours, prints, and plaids, often used for neckwear.

Taffeta A closely woven, smooth fabric of plain weave with a crisp finish, and usually with a sheen to its surface. Formerly all taffeta was silk; now, rayon or synthetic fibres compose much of the cloth.

Terry Cloth A cotton fabric with uncut loops on one or both sides used extensively for towels since it is absorbent and requires no ironing. It is popular for beach and sportswear as well.

Ticking A drill cloth of twill construction which has alternate stripes of white and coloured yarn. Used mainly for pillow and mattress covers, in recent years it has become a novelty sportswear fabric.

Tricot A fine-waled knit fabric, used a great deal for underwear and nightwear, also for gloves. It is commonly made of rayon, nylon or cotton.

Tulle Silk, nylon or rayon sheer cloth with a hexagonal mesh construction. It is a stiff fabric, used for bouffant gowns, bridal veils and for dance costumes.

Tussore A sturdy, rough silk fibre sometimes called wild silk. The cloth is very coarse, rough and usually quite loosely woven.

Tweed A rough-surfaced fabric, usually woven in two or more colours to obtain some sort of pattern, check or plaid. Originally tweed was a rough homespun of heavy woollen, but today the term covers almost any fabric which is nubbly, of variegated colours and has a roughened look. Tweeds are usually woollens; however, cotton tweeds, silk tweeds and synthetic tweeds have become popular in the past decade.

Velour Thick-bodied, soft, close-napped fabric, used mainly as a suit or coat fabric. Wool velour is constructed like a broadcloth with an erect nap that is thick and full. Nylon velour is also very popular for dressy at-home fashions.

Velvet Pile fabrics with plain or twill back and warp yarns forming the pile. They may be of all silk, rayon, nylon or cotton, but are usually made of a silk or synthetic fibre with a cotton back.

Velveteen Cotton velvet with short, thick pile and a dull surface. Widely used for evening fashions.

Vicuña A soft woollen material made in textures ranging from dress weight to mens' overcoatings.

Voile Light, sheer, thin, transparent cloth, which is similar to organdie and lawn. It is less stiff than these, drapes well and tends to cling to the body.

Waffle Cloth A textured cotton similar to piqué that is woven on a dobby loom in a fine honeycomb weave.

Wash-and-Wear Any fabric which can be washed, dried and then worn again with little or no ironing.

Whipcord A worsted similar to gabardine but with a steeper or more pronounced twill. Dry and harsh to touch, it is a strong, springy fabric preferred for riding clothes and sharply tailored garments.

Wincey A strong material of wool or wool and cotton used for shirts, etc.

Woollens Woven wool fabrics of short, fuzzy fibres which have not been highly twisted.

Worsteds Popular class of wool cloth made of choice wool fibres which are smooth, strong and more highly twisted than the woollen fibres.

Zibeline A wool coating fabric with a long, rather wiry, lustrous nap of straight fibres laid over in one direction.

CHAPTER 5

THE TOOLS OF THE TRADE

*A pleasant place to work and the correct tools are a "must" for sewing enjoyment.
Try to establish a sewing centre in your home. It will make it possible for you
to sew efficiently and to utilise moments snatched from a busy schedule.*

A PLACE TO SEW

Years ago a special room was set aside for sewing. Equipment was always ready to be used and sewing could be left in place for future work. Today few women are lucky enough to have this ideal arrangement. Usually, sewing and equipment must be packed away between sewing sessions. However, if you give this matter careful thought, perhaps you can find a tiny space in a closet, a hall, a corner of the kitchen or a guest room which can be fitted for sewing. Use your ingenuity and design a sewing nook for yourself.

14

Organisation and planning are the keys to good results in a limited space. Utilise as many portable aids as possible. A sewing screen placed in a corner of a room can be decorative on one side but very functional on the other. Put pegboard on the back with hooks to hold yardsticks, tapes and small shelves for boxes and tools. Hide your sewing table, machine and pressing equipment behind the screen. Although the equipment is out of sight, it will always be handy for using.

Be sure the area where you sew is well lighted. Don't depend on machine lighting alone. Select a straight-back chair without arms. It should fit your back adequately, so you will be comfortable for long sewing sessions. A full-length mirror convenient to your sewing area is a must.

If you can arrange a three-way mirror it will be even better. The mirror panel needs to be only wide enough to take in your figure, but it must be long enough so you can stand quite close and see yourself from the top of your head to your toes. Then you will be able to judge the entire effect of your garment and make the necessary adjustments in length or placement of details easily and accurately.

ESSENTIAL TOOLS

The equipment you need depends on the amount and type of sewing you do. Each year new devices appear on the market. Watch for these on notions counters of your local stores. Often you will find an inexpensive item that can save hours of sewing time and help create a more professional look.

Not every seamstress needs every piece of equipment. However, these items are essential to successful and easy sewing:

- Sewing machine.
- Attachments—adjustable zipper foot and seam guide.
- Dressmaker's shears—bent handles, $6^{1}/_{2}$ to 8 inches long.
- Scissors—sharp points, 3 to 6 inches long.
- Tape measure—folded, 60 inches long, reversible.
- Yardstick.
- Ruler—transparent with $^{1}/_{8}$ inch markings, 6 inches long. Also one 12 inches long.
- Tracing wheel.
- Dressmaker's carbon paper (tracing paper).
- Tailor's chalk or chalk pencil.
- Dressmaker or silk pins.
- Thimble.
- Pin cushion.

- Needles—assorted sizes.
- Thread—various types and colours.
- Pressing equipment—iron, ironing board, pad, cover, sleeve board, press cloth, tailor's ham, sponge.
- Full-length mirror.

In addition to the necessary equipment, there are many other sewing aids which are useful. The items below do not comprise a complete list of available equipment but are among those you may find most helpful.

- Sewing machine attachments other than those listed above.
- Pinking or scalloping shears.
- Buttonhole scissors.
- Seam ripper.
- Thread clips.
- Cutting board.
- Hem marker.
- Hem gauge.
- Emery bag.
- Needle threader.
- Loop turner.
- Bodkin.
- Stiletto.
- Tweezers.
- Seam roll.
- Clapper.

- Point presser.
- Needle board.

Keep your small equipment neatly arranged in a handy sewing box or basket. If you do not have a specially designed one, divide the area with smaller boxes to ensure tidiness. Be sure thread ends are caught in the notch on each spool.

Whenever you purchase equipment, check the quality. Buy good tools and give them excellent care. They are a form of investment which should pay dividends in length of service and performance. To help you shop wisely, here are some helpful suggestions for selecting various types of equipment.

Cutting Tools

Look for shears and scissors made of steel by the hot-drop forge method, which ensures a sharp cutting edge that can be reconditioned (15). The manufacturer's literature accompanying the cutting tool will give this information. Take along a few scraps of fabric when purchasing shears or scissors. Cut with the entire length of the blades and release the fabric. If a thread of the fabric is caught, the cutting edges of the blades are imperfect. Check the points. Select cutting tools joined with a bolt or screw rather than rivets, which may loosen and cannot be tightened.

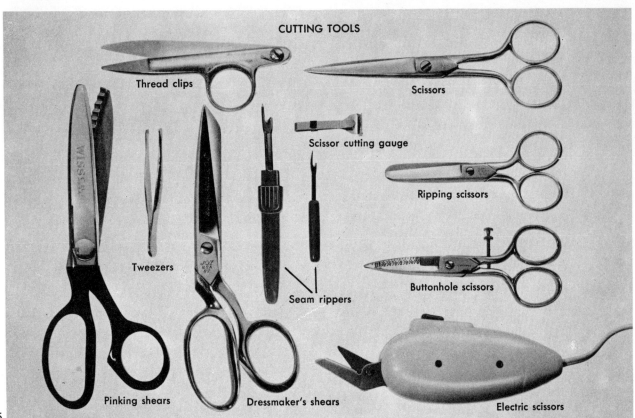

CUTTING TOOLS

Thread clips

Scissors

Scissor cutting gauge

Tweezers

Seam rippers

Ripping scissors

Buttonhole scissors

Pinking shears

Dressmaker's shears

Electric scissors

15

Shears and scissors do require some care. Handle them as you would surgical instruments. Lay them down; don't drop them. Keep them dry and occasionally oil them at the screw. Reserve them only for your sewing; don't use them for cutting paper or other general household tasks. When they become dull, your cutlery repair shop will sharpen them.

DRESSMAKER'S SHEARS. Select bent-handled shears that have a small ring handle for the thumb, a large ring handle for the second and third fingers. Do not buy straight-handled shears; the blades won't rest flat on the table when cutting, and you will not get as accurate a cutting line. Choose a length of $6^1/_2$ to 7 or 8 inches; these will be better than the shorter 6-inch length. Left-handed sewers should take advantage of the left-handed shears which are available in the $7^1/_2$-inch length.

SCISSORS. In contrast to shears, scissors are straight and have identical rings for handles. Select scissors 3 to 6 inches long with double sharp points. Keep your scissors handy at the machine for trimming, clipping threads and light cutting.

PINKING OR SCALLOPING SHEARS. Pinking shears have zigzag edges, and scalloping shears scalloped cutting edges. They are excellent in finishing seams to prevent ravelling of fabric edges. Pinking shears are available in lengths from $5^1/_2$ to 10 inches. The 9- and 10-inch lengths will give a deeper zigzag than the standard $7^1/_2$-inch size. Scalloping shears come only in $7^1/_2$- or 9-inch lengths.

BUTTONHOLE SCISSORS. A handy item if you make a lot of garments with machine-made buttonholes, these are designed to cut open buttonholes accurately, and can be adjusted for different buttonhole lengths.

RIPPING SCISSORS. With care you won't be subjected to much ripping, but if you must, these will be helpful. The blunt point cuts open stitched seams without cutting the fabric. They hold and pull the threads as you cut the seam stitches.

SEAM RIPPER. This inexpensive item is used for ripping seams and can sometimes be used as buttonhole cutters. Although it is efficient, it should be used with great care. Otherwise you may find yourself cutting the fabric.

THREAD CLIPS. A real time-saving little clipper that can be used effectively for snipping threads and making the small clips needed for marking or for curved seams. It has one ring which fits over the little finger, and is operated by squeezing with the palm of the hand.

ELECTRIC SCISSORS. This is a relatively new and expensive item. It is valuable to sewers who may have arthritis or find some difficulty in manipulating shears for long periods of time. For general sewing, electric scissors really are not a necessity, but may be a useful luxury. They operate on AC current; cut thin or heavy fabric.

SCISSOR CUTTING GAUGE. When long strips of fabric need to be cut, this gauge is a tremendous help. It fits on the point of the scissors and may be adjusted to various widths. It ensures even widths of cloth and facilitates cutting a large quantity of material in a short time.

CUTTING BOARD. A real boon to the person with no cutting space. The board folds easily for storage, and is marked with inches in each direction to allow for accurate placement of fabric. Material can be pinned right to the board. It measures 40 by 72 inches and folds to a mere $12^1/_2$ by 40 inches for storage.

Measuring Tools

A perfect fit requires perfect measurements of body, pattern and fabric. Accurate measuring tools are essential for accurate sewing so be sure you have the ones you need (16).

MEASURING TOOLS

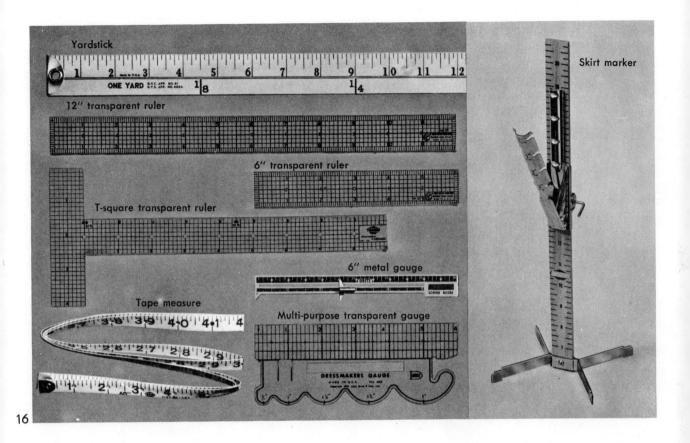

TAPE MEASURE. Select an oilcloth or plastic tape measure; paper ones may tear and linen ones may stretch. The fold-up type is the easiest to use and store. You'll need one which measures 60 inches and has the numbers clearly printed on both sides of the tape. Metal tips on either end will help the tape to lie flat and keep ends from fraying.

YARDSTICK. The best yardsticks are made of maple or hickory and finished to a satiny smoothness which will not catch on even the most delicate fabrics. Since they are inexpensive, take time to find a good one. You'll need your yardstick for checking grain lines and for other general marking purposes.

RULERS. Transparent, flexible rulers are best. You can see to mark details such as buttonholes, and the flexibility makes it possible to measure slight curves. Buy those with $1/8$-inch markings, since sewing directions are given in $1/8$-inch measurements; you need a 12- or 18-inch ruler and a short 6-inch one. A little metal gauge with a sliding marker is also handy. It may be adjusted to fractions of an inch and is useful for measuring tucks, spacing buttonholes and other small construction details.

SKIRT MARKER. If you do a lot of sewing for others, or have to do your own hem marking, you'll find this instrument more than worth its weight in gold. It provides a much quicker and more accurate method of marking hems than when a yardstick is used. Skirt markers come in various types—pin markers, chalk markers, and combination pin-chalk markers. The pin marker gives a more accurate marking. Chalk marks tend to be too thick, and the chalk does not come out of some fabrics.

Marking Tools

Because of the many types of fabric you use, you may need several different devices for marking pattern

DRESSMAKER'S CARBON. Dressmaker's carbon comes in packages of one colour or assorted colours. It is wisest to buy the assorted packs and use

MARKING TOOLS

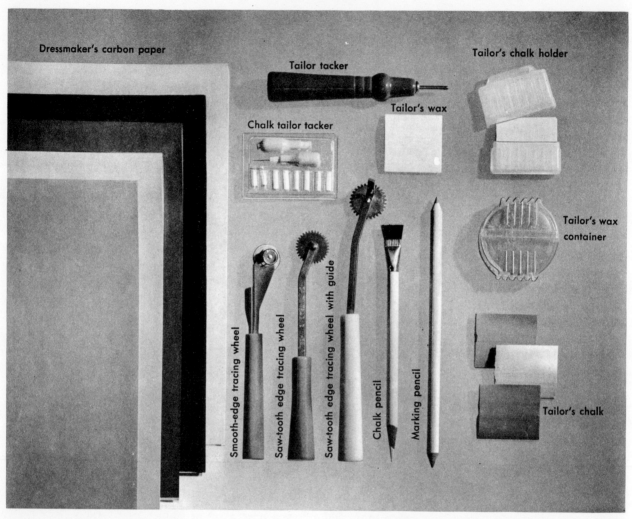

Dressmaker's carbon paper

Tailor tacker

Tailor's chalk holder

Chalk tailor tacker

Tailor's wax

Tailor's wax container

Smooth-edge tracing wheel

Saw-tooth edge tracing wheel

Saw-tooth edge tracing wheel with guide

Chalk pencil

Marking pencil

Tailor's chalk

17

symbols (17). Not all fabrics can be marked in the same way, just as they can't be cut and stitched in the same way.

TRACING WHEEL. The tracing wheel is available in needle-point and saw-tooth edges as well as with a smooth edge. The needle-point style is used for marking heavy fabrics; the saw-tooth style for most light- and medium-weight fabrics.

The newest tracing wheel has a smooth edge, allowing the pattern tissue to remain intact. The wheel rolls along pattern markings and transfers them through the dressmaker's carbon to the wrong side of the garment fabric. (Complete instructions for marking appear in Chapter 7.)

the colour closest to your fabric colour when tracing. Carbon markings may show through very sheer fabrics, so always test a scrap of fabric before tracing on the garment pieces.

Chalk is used on fabrics which cannot take the carbon, or for marking which will later be removed (trims, grainlines, etc.). It rubs off very easily when the marking is no longer needed. Tailor's chalk is made in flat 2-inch squares in white, black, red and blue. White and blue are least likely to stain fabric. You should have both of these colours. The chalk pencil gives a thinner, more accurate mark. It is easier and less messy to handle.

TAILOR'S WAX. Use this with caution; it does not wash out and may not disappear with dry-cleaning. The wax is clear or white in colour and should be used only on woollens which will not take the softer chalk. Be sure you mark only on the wrong side of the fabric.

TAILOR TACKER. This metal tool marks both sides of the fabric through dressmaker's carbon. Dots are marked by placing the point sharply down on the fabric; straight lines by drawing the tool along. The tracing wheel is actually easier to use.

packages of 100, but if you're going to do a large amount of sewing, buy them in the large economy one-pound box. For very heavy fabrics, there are coarser pins, size 14, and lower numbers for upholstery work.

NEEDLES. Buy the big assorted packages of needles that have all of the 10 sizes you'll need. Generally "sharps" of medium length are used for sewing; 9 or 10 for sheers; 6 or 8 for medium-weight fabrics; 1 to 5 for heavy materials. For very fine hand sewing use "betweens", which are short needles. For basting and millinery, select "milliners," which are no longer than sharps. "Calyx-eyed sharps" have large eyes

SEWING EQUIPMENT

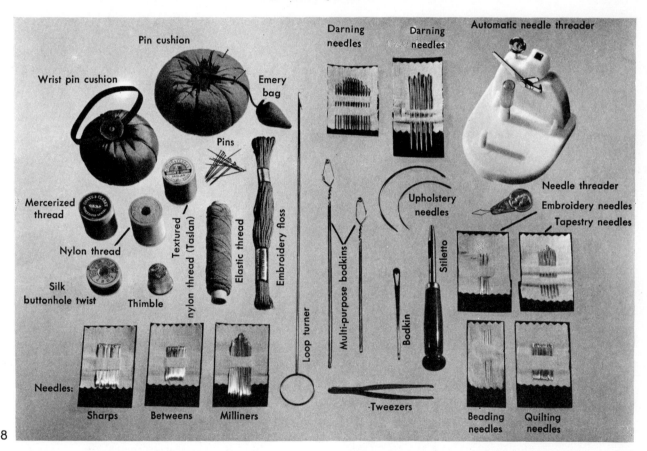

18

Sewing Equipment

Sewing is a meticulous craft, so select your tools with care (18). Many a fine dress has been marred by such a small item as a wrong pin or needle.

PINS. Select only the sharpest and the finest rust-proof dressmaker or silk pins. Numbers 15, 16 and 17 are suitable for most fabrics. You may buy small

making them easier to thread. When sewing on delicate silks, you may wish to purchase enough very fine needles to use in place of pins.

SPECIAL NEEDLES. Special tasks require special needles:

☐ Embroidery — long, sharp, large-eyed crewel needles. Similar to "sharps," these have a large eye

for easy threading of embroidery yarn or thread.
☐ Upholstery—large, curved needles which are designed to slip in and out of heavy fabric easily.
☐ Darning—long, coarse needles with large eyes.
☐ Leather and Fur—three-cornered pointed needles called "glover's needles."
☐ Beading—needles which are very fine and long, especially designed for beading.
☐ Quilting—short, between-type needles.
☐ Millinery—long, thin needles used for millinery tacking.

NEEDLE THREADER. If you have an eyesight problem, or just find threading needles a chore, use a needle threader.

THIMBLE. You should always use a thimble for hand sewing. Your sewing will be more comfortable, and the results more perfect. The metal ones are more durable than the plastic type. Find one which fits the middle finger of the hand holding the needle. Look for a firm, snug fit. If the thimble seems to slip off easily, wet the end of your finger. The moisture creates suction and holds the thimble in place.

PIN CUSHION. If you want a purely decorative pin cushion, then select at random the one which you find the most attractive. If you want real service, then use the wrist type. A plastic or elastic wrist band keeps it in place. It never slips away or gets hidden among patterns and fabric just at the time you need it. The cushion is usually sponge rubber or sawdust.

EMERY BAG. You may find one on your pin cushion. This is a small bag with an abrasive inside which removes rust from pins and needles. You can also purchase them separately. Use it to keep pins and needles clean and free from rust.

THREAD. Thread, like fabric, is made of various fibres and in various weights suitable for certain types of sewing. Always select the one best for your fabric.

Thread is made in almost as many colours as fabrics are. Select a colour slightly darker than the cloth with which it is to be used. The thread sews in lighter than it appears on the spool. Use a contrasting colour for basting—one which is easily seen when it is time to remove the stitches.

Mercerised Cotton Thread. Most often used for general sewing.

Silk Thread. May be used on fine woollens and silk fabrics, since it produces a finer stitching line. When working on fine fabrics, silk thread is an excellent choice for basting because it slips in and out of fabric easily and can be pulled out without marring the fabric. It's also good for basting pleats because it does not mark fabric when pressed.

Nylon Thread. Should be used on synthetics and their blends. The textured nylon thread such as Taslan is highly recommended for stitching all wash-and-wear fabrics to prevent puckering of seams or may be used for hemming and hand-stitching when garment is sewn with mercerised thread. Never use a synthetic thread on cotton or linen which will have to withstand high temperatures in pressing. Synthetic threads usually require a looser upper and lower tension on the machine, and a fine needle.

Elastic Thread. Used for gathering or for shirred effects which are either machine- or hand-stitched. It is used only as bobbin thread.

Buttonhole Twist. Silk thread comes on 10-yard spools. Use it for decorative stitches, handworked buttonholes, sewing on buttons and as the bobbin thread when gathering large sections of fabric. It is stronger than cotton thread and slips easily through the fabric, making gathering a much easier task.

Embroidery Silks. Used for decorative stitches and most embroidery. It comes in 6-strand twists; your pattern will indicate the number of strands to use in embroidered designs.

Needles and Thread

Thread and needle should be considered together. The weight of the fabric determines the size of needle and thread. To help you find just the right size, a special chart is shown here. In using the chart, remember that fabrics of the same general description may vary. You should always test the thread on a scrap of the fabric you are using. You will notice that on the chart there is a column showing the approximate number of machine stitches to the inch. Use this guide for fine sewing.

WEIGHT OF FABRIC	TYPES OF FABRIC	THREAD	HAND	NEEDLES MACHINE	MACHINE
Very Sheer	Batiste, chiffon, fine lace, marquisette, organdie, net	Silk Fine mercerised 50 Synthetic 50	9	Fine 9	15-20 stitches to inch
Sheer	Dimity, dotted swiss, handkerchief linen, lawn, sheer crêpe, voile, synthetics	Silk Fine mercerised Synthetic 50	9	Fine 11	12-15 stitches to inch
Light Weight	Chambray, gingham, percale, taffeta, satin, sheer woollens, silk, challis, synthetics and blends	Mercerised cotton 40-50 Synthetic 75 Silk	8	Medium 14	12 stitches to inch
	Plastics	Synthetic thread or Mercerised cotton	9	Fine 9—11	10 stitches to inch
Medium	Muslin, chintz, dress linen, piqué, flannel, jersey, broadcloth, corduroy, crêpe synthetics and blends	Mercerised cotton 40-50 Silk Cotton Synthetic	8	Medium 14	12 stitches to inch
Medium Heavy	Denim, velveteen, terry cloth, tweeds, drapery fabrics, twill, gabardine, coatings, fleece, synthetics and blends	Mercerised cotton 40 Silk Synthetic	6	Medium Coarse 14—16	10 stitches to inch
Heavy	Upholstery fabric, sailcloth, ticking, heavy denim	Heavy-duty mercerised cotton 24 Cotton 24 or 36	4,5	Coarse 16—18	8-10 stitches to inch

Miscellaneous Equipment

The more you sew, the more uses you will discover for various other pieces of equipment. A few which are most helpful are:

☐ Loop turner to help in turning tubing to the right side.

☐ Stiletto for punching eyelets and holes in fabric and leather.

☐ Bodkin for threading elastic, fabric and tape through casing.

☐ Tweezers for removing threads from ripped seams.

Sewing Machine

With the many brands and models available, it may be difficult for you to select a new machine and be confident you have purchased the best machine for your money and one which will meet your needs for years to come. Visit the dealers in your area and request demonstrations of their machines. Consult consumer reports. After you have narrowed your selection down to one or two machines, you may find it advisable to rent a model so you can test its performance.

In making your decision, you will have to decide between a straight-stitch and a swing-needle (automatic) machine and between the cabinet and portable models. The type and amount of sewing you do, the space you have for a machine and your budget will influence your choice.

If you use the machine only for plain sewing, patching and mending, you may find the straight-stitch sewing machine satisfactory. This type sews forward and backward and usually can be released for some free-motion darning. The needle moves up and down in a straight line. Usually some attachments are available for the various machines.

The more versatile swing-needle or zigzag machines have a needle that moves from side to side as well as up and down, making it possible to do many of the finishing details and decorative stitches without the use of attachments. The swing-needle or automatic machines vary greatly in the amount of decorative stitching they will do. Some machines are built to use templates, which produce distinctive patterns; others require just a twist of a knob. If you plan to purchase an automatic machine consider the difficulty of operating the decorative controls in case you expect to do special stitching. If you are not mechanically inclined, choose a machine that is easy to set.

Some machines are constructed with slanting needles, allowing for better visibility. Both straight-needle and swing-needle machines can be obtained with this type of needle.

Your next decision will be whether to select a cabinet or portable model. The cabinet model costs more, but it does provide extra work space, a convenient storage space for your equipment, and is easier for quick use. Cabinets are available in all periods of furniture style, and can be a decorative piece of furniture. Usually the cabinet model machine is a heavier machine, capable of handling heavy and bulky fabrics.

When space is limited, budgets limited, or the machine must be moved frequently, the portable is a more practical purchase. Take care to select a portable that is capable of handling fairly heavy and bulky fabrics. Inexpensive, light-weight portables may be too light to handle any but light- or medium-weight fabrics and will "slip" around the table when in operation. Beware of second-hand portables that are merely the regular heavy sewing head set into a cheap, unwieldy carrying case. These may be inadequately wired, and have a cheap motor attached that cannot be efficiently controlled.

Before you purchase your machine, test and check the construction and performance. A diagram of a standard model machine with the major parts identified is shown here. Become familiar with all the parts, then use the following questions as a checklist for judging the quality of a machine.

Long-Life Design

☐ Is the wiring located where it will not be pinched, and is it protected against wear and oil drip?

☐ Are service parts carried in stock and is repair service readily available?

☐ Is the cabinet well constructed; hinges sturdy; legs well braced; leaf well supported and level when opened?

☐ Is a guarantee offered on the machine?

Easy-to-Use Features

☐ Are the upper tension setting and stitch-length controls easy to see and read?

☐ Is the lamp well placed to throw light where needed?

☐ Are there adjustable lock positions for the forward and reverse stitching controls?

☐ Does the machine stitch forward and backward, plus have a quick release mechanism for darning and embroidery?

☐ Is the foot or knee speed control comfortably placed?

Good Operation

☐ Is the machine quiet and free from objectionable noise and vibration?

☐ Is the machine easy to start and stop, and does it run smoothly at all speeds?

☐ Are the needle and bobbin easy to thread?

☐ Do two pieces of fabric stitched together travel between the foot and feed dog evenly at the same rate?

☐ Is the bobbin winder easy to use and does it fill the bobbin evenly?

Easy-to-Care-for

☐ Are the coverplates easily removable and all parts readily accessible for cleaning, oiling and greasing?

☐ Is the light bulb easy to replace?

☐ Is the machine easy to dust and wipe clean?

After you purchase your machine, it is important that you learn to operate and care for it efficiently. All new machines have accompanying instruction manuals which illustrate the parts of the machine and give full instructions for all phases of operation and care. If you buy a second-hand machine and receive no manual, contact a dealer in your area who handles the brand machine you purchased. He will either be able to provide a manual or demonstrate the operation of the machine. Remember that each machine may vary in the placement and type of parts, so no matter how many machines you have operated in the past, study the manual before attempting to operate one that is unfamiliar.

Winding the Bobbin

Wind the bobbin using thread which is identical to upper thread. It must be wound evenly and should never be so fully wound that it is tight in the bobbin case. If the bobbin has thread on it, remove it before winding new thread, or the new thread will not wind evenly or feed easily when stitching. Bobbins wind differently on the various machines, but generally there is a spool pin for the thread located below the balance wheel. The thread is placed on the spool pin, run through a bobbin tension disc, and then to the bobbin which is placed on a spindle. Always release the stop-motion screw on the balance wheel by turning it toward you. Raise bobbin winder and press it against the handwheel. Hold thread end to start winding, and wind until the bobbin is full.

Threading the Machine

Always check your instruction manual for proper threading. Your machine simply won't work if it isn't threaded exactly according to plan. Although upper threading of machines may vary according to the placement of the parts, it does follow a general pattern. The thread is placed on the spool pin on top of the machine head, then through a thread guide to the tension mechanism, through another thread guide to the take-up lever, through another thread guide, and inserted into the needle. Be sure that the thread is placed through the needle in the correct direction. After the machine is threaded, draw about 5 inches of thread through the needle.

The bobbin should be placed in the bobbin case carefully, so that the bobbin will move in the correct direction. Follow the directions in the manual for the machine you are using. It is important that the bobbin thread be placed behind the presser foot before stitching begins. To draw bobbin thread up through the needle hole, insert the bobbin in the bobbin case, leaving about 3 inches of bobbin thread outside the bobbin, as shown in your manual. Close the bed plate. Raise take-up lever to its highest point. Turn the wheel by hand until the needle goes down and up so take-up lever is again at its highest point. Pull the end of the needle thread and a bobbin thread loop will appear through the needle hole. Pull end of bobbin thread through needle hole with scissors, and place both bobbin and needle threads diagonally behind and under the presser foot.

Inserting the Needle

You will have to change needles in your machine when one breaks or when you need a different size for various weights of fabric.

Generally size 14 needles are used for normal sewing, but various fabrics may require a heavier (size 16) or a finer (size 11) needle. If you are in doubt about what needle size to use for your fabric, check the chart on page 67. In case a different numbering system is used for the needles on your machine, the manual will give you the necessary information.

Every sewing machine needle has a short groove at the eye on one side and a long groove on the other. When inserting a needle in a machine, the long groove must always face the side from which the machine is to be threaded. On most machines, the last thread guide will indicate the direction in which the thread must enter the needle. Be sure the flat side of the needle is facing in the direction opposite to the thread. Raise the take-up lever to its highest point, and insert the needle upward into the needle clamp as far as it will go and tighten needle clamp screw.

Stitching

Test the stitching on a scrap of fabric. Never operate

a threaded machine without fabric. The threads will become tangled and the feed will be damaged.

To stitch, raise the take-up lever to its highest point, place the needle and bobbin threads diagonally behind and under the presser foot. Place the larger amount of fabric to the left of the head and the part to be stitched to the right. Lower the needle into the fabric by turning the balance wheel toward you. Lower the presser foot and start stitching with a slow, even speed. Place your hand so your fingers are guiding the fabric lightly. Be sure the weight of the left arm is not resting on the fabric causing uneven feeding. Guide the fabric, but do not force or pull it through the machine.

When you have completed the stitching, raise the take-up lever to its highest point by turning the balance wheel toward you so the tension is released. Raise the presser foot; remove the fabric by drawing it to the back and left of the needle; cut threads.

There are various types of seam guides to help you stitch in a straight line. Lines on bed plate, a special attachment, or tape placed on bed plate can be used.

Correct Tension

After you have stitched your scrap of fabric, check it for correct tension. If the tension is correct, the stitch will be perfectly locked in the fabric and the needle and bobbin threads perfectly balanced so that the stitch appears the same on both sides of the fabric. When tension is incorrect, with either the needle or bobbin thread too tight or too loose, stitching will not appear the same.

Inspecting the line of stitching is the only way to check tension. It is important that the tension be checked on each type of fabric used, since tension requirements vary for some fabrics. If your stitching on the test scrap does not appear exactly alike on both sides of the fabric, then determine if the needle or bobbin thread needs adjusting. To do this, stitch diagonally across a square of your fabric, folded on true bias. Hold the stitching tightly at each end between thumb and forefinger and pull with an even gradual force until the thread breaks. The broken thread is always the one with tight tension. When the tensions are balanced, both threads break together and require more force to break.

If tension does need adjustment, it is better to try to adjust the upper tension. Most machines have a numbered tension dial with numbers ranging from 0 to 9. To increase turn upper tension toward the higher numbers; to decrease toward the lower. Never move more than two numbers at a time, then re-check the tension by stitching a scrap of the fabric.

Adjusting bobbin tension is more difficult, and should only be attempted if tension cannot be corrected with an upper tension adjustment. The bobbin case has a small tension screw which, when turned in the correct direction, will increase or decrease tension. Be sure to check your manual or ask your dealer to find the proper bobbin tension screw and direction for increase or decrease.

Correct Pressure

The amount of pressure influences the ease with which fabric will flow through the machine when stitching. Pressure should be heavy enough to keep two thicknesses of fabric travelling at the same rate; light enough to keep fabric from being marred by the feed dog. The surface finish, weight and texture of the fabric will determine the amount of pressure needed. To test for correct pressure, feed a double thickness of fabric through the machine and adjust the thumb screw until the fabric moves under the presser foot easily and shows no feed marks.

The pressure thumb screw is located on the top of the machine head and controls a spring which connects with the presser foot mechanism. It can be raised and lowered either by turning or a press-release mechanism. Check your manual or with your dealer on the correct operation of pressure control.

Stitch Length

There is no test for checking the correct stitch length for various fabrics. However, the chart on page 67 prescribes the proper stitch length for most fabrics. Generally, a shorter stitch (16 to an inch) is needed for sheer, fine fabrics; a medium stitch (12 stitches per inch) for medium weights; a long stitch (8 to 10 to the inch) for heavy, coarse fabrics. There are also certain special stitches used for basting, gathering, reinforcing, which require different lengths of stitches.

The stitch regulator is usually placed on the right side of the machine. It lists numbers from about 7 to 20. A bar is placed in the centre of the numbered plate and stitch length is regulated by moving the bar to the number indicating the number of stitches desired. The stitch regulator also controls the forward or backward motion of the feed dog. Usually by raising the stitch regulator to the highest point, you are able to stitch backwards.

Care of the Machine

A sewing machine, like any piece of equipment, needs some care and cleaning. When not in use, keep your machine covered to prevent dust from settling on it. Also, fabric will leave deposits of lint around the feed dog and bobbin case which must be removed fairly often.

You should have a lint brush especially designed for cleaning sewing machines, and a piece of cheesecloth or lintless cotton. If a brush was not provided with your machine, you can purchase it at most sewing notions counters. To remove lint deposits, remove the throat plate of the machine and brush the lint and dust from the bobbin case and feed mechanism. Following the instructions given in your manual, remove the entire bobbin case if possible, and remove all lint, fluff and loose threads or foreign matter which has collected. Dust the entire machine, using the cloth, and brush out hard-to-get-at crevices.

Periodically, it is necessary to oil and lubricate the machine. If you use it every day, do this about every six weeks. If you use it infrequently, then every three to four months should be sufficient. Use only regulation sewing machine oil. Apply it sparingly, using only one drop of oil for every oiling point. Although machines vary greatly the places which require oil on most standard models are illustrated in diagrams 19, a, b, c.

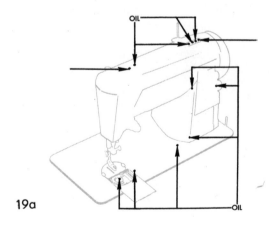

19a

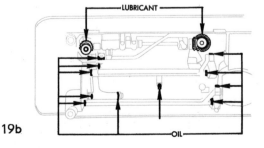

19b

When the machine has been thoroughly oiled, run it slowly for several minutes to allow the oil to work into the moving parts. If you do not plan to use the machine immediately, place a scrap of fabric under the presser foot and lower the needle. The fabric absorbs the excess oil that might drain down through the machine. The machine will be ready to use when you take it out again and there will be no danger of getting oil spots on your garment.

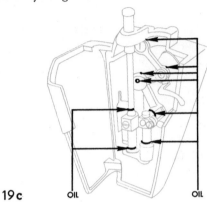

19c

Repairing Tips

There is nothing more frustrating than to be in the middle of constructing a garment and have the machine go wrong. Although major repairs should only be made by qualified repair men, there are certain minor adjustments you can make yourself when a machine operates incorrectly. If your machine develops one of these common ailments, check the possible causes suggested. If these remedies do not correct the trouble, then call your service-repair man.

Breaking of Needles - Causes

- Incorrect size of needle for thread and material (see chart, page 67).
- Needle bent.
- Pulling of material when stitching.
- Needle striking improperly fastened presser foot or attachments.
- Crossing too thick a seam using too small a needle.

Breaking of Needle Thread - Causes

- Knot in needle thread.
- Incorrect threading.
- Upper tension too tight.
- Needle not inserted in needle clamp as far as it will go.

- Needle blunt or bent.
- Needle in backwards.
- Thread too coarse for needle.
- Roughened hole in throat plate.
- Incorrect arrangement of thread when starting to sew.

Breaking of Bobbin Thread - Causes

- Incorrect threading of bobbin case.
- Bobbin thread tension too tight.
- Knot in bobbin thread.

Skipping of Stitches - Causes

- Needle not inserted in needle clamp as far as it will go.
- Needle in backwards.
- Needle threaded incorrectly.

- Needle blunt or bent.
- Needle too small for thread.
- Needle too short.

Puckered Seams - Causes

- Tension too tight.
- Stitch too long for material being sewn.
- Wrong presser foot. Use only the presser foot provided for each particular machine; they are not interchangeable.

Sewing Machine Attachments

When you purchase your new machine, check the attachments included in the price of purchase, and those which are available at additional cost. Attachments make sewing easier and provide opportunities for decorative sewing. Don't neglect them; learn to use them effectively. They not only save time, but make sewing a more creative and interesting experience.

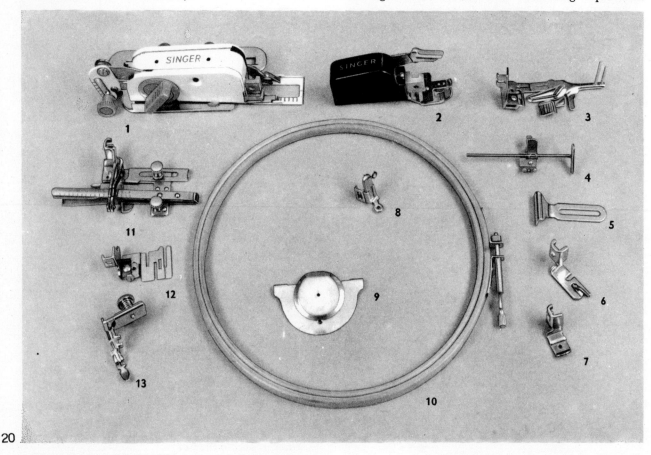

1 Buttonhole Attachment	**6** Foot Hemmer	**10** Machine Embroidery and Darning Frame
2 Blind Stitcher	**7** Gathering Foot	**11** Tucker
3 Multiple-slotted Binder	**8** Darning Foot	**12** Edge Stitcher
4 Quilter and Guide	**9** Feed Cover Plate for Machine Embroidery and Darning	**13** Zipper or Piping Foot
5 Cloth or Seam Guide		

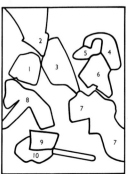

8 Fresh, charming and feather light, these examples of some of the newest Bri-Nylon fabrics are chosen from ranges designed for summer and evening dresses, and are also available in many other colours.
1 Printed sparkle chiffon. **2** Flare-free net. **3** Printed chiffon. **4.** Chiffon. **5** Printed chiffon. **6** Sprigged voile. **7** Printed crinkle voile. **8** Printed sparkle chiffon. **9** Chiffon. **10** Chiffon.

Photograph by courtesy of British Nylon Spinners Ltd.

9 Terylene can be used by itself or in blends with cotton, rayon, flax or silk for fabrics used for men's, women's children's and household textiles. Crimplene, bulked Terylene yarn, is made into knitted jersey fabrics and knitwear.
1 Terylene-cotton corduroy. **2** Terylene-wool worsted. **3** Terylene-wool worsted with a filament warp. **4** Terylene-linen. **5** Terylene-cotton. **6** 100% Terylene spun voile. **7** 100% Terylene lawn. **8** 100% Terylene crêpon. **9** 100% Crimplene. **10** 100% Crimplene piqué.

Photograph by courtesy of Imperial Chemical Industries Ltd.

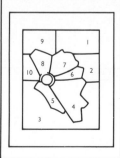

Before purchasing any additional attachments, talk to your dealer about the work each will do and have him demonstrate the operation of each. Decide which of the attachments will be practical for your needs. If you make only simple garments with few decorative details, then you will probably use only a few of the attachments. However, if you enjoy making garments with your own original ideas for trimming, you will use many of them. In selecting attachments, be sure that they will fit your make and model machine.

The zigzag machines require fewer attachments than the straight-stitch type, while the automatics vary widely in the amount of work they do without attachments, so that no accurate list can be made to apply to all automatics. However, listed below are the ones most frequently used on the straight-needle machines, what they do, how to use them and whether they are necessary or optional—see also (20) p. 72.

ZIPPER PIPING FOOT. The zipper piping foot is designed for stitching close to a raised edge and can be adjusted to either the right or left side of the needle. The hinged feature of the foot ensures even feeding over pins or heavy layers of fabric formed by crossed seams. It is used for covering cord, applying cording into seams, and most frequently for zipper application. It is essential to have one, since no zipper can be successfully applied by machine without it.

CLOTH OR SEAM GUIDE. Seam guides help ensure more accurate seam widths on both straight and curved seams, as well as provide a guide to accurate top-stitching. Most new machines have the seam markings on the plate of the machine, but if yours does not, you can purchase an inexpensive type which attaches to the machine bed, or you can make your own simply by placing cloth adhesive tape across the bed of the machine, with accurate markings on it, $5/8$ inch and $1/2$ inch from the needle. In stitching, keep your eyes at the edge of the seam guide or marking on the tape to direct the fabric correctly.

BUTTONHOLER. Standard models have templates which are inserted in the buttonholer and guide the machine in making various sizes of buttonholes from $5/16$ to $1\,1/16$ inches. There is also a special template for eyelets. Each buttonhole attachment has a dial which makes it possible to adjust the bight (width) of the stitch used. Both straight and keyhole buttonholes can be made. The buttonholer is easy to operate and works well on most fabrics. If you wish to make even, attractive buttonholes, you'll definitely need this

attachment. The buttonholes are not only quicker to 'make than the hand-worked type, but they're stronger. For best results, use two rows of stitches.

DARNING FOOT. This is a spring foot which facilitates darning and machine embroidery by holding the fabric down safely.

FEED COVER PLATE FOR MACHINE EMBROIDERY AND DARNING. This plate is only necessary on those machines which do not have any other way of dispensing with the feed, which is not used in darning or machine embroidery.

MACHINE EMBROIDERY AND DARNING FOOT. This attachment is essential for machine embroidery or darning as it holds the material taut and firmly in position.

BLIND STITCHER. This attachment performs a type of slip hemming stitch which is invisible on the right side of the material. It is sometimes called a blind stitch hemmer.

NARROW OR FOOT HEMMER. The attachment forms and stitches a perfectly turned hem, without previous basting or pressing. The hem formed is about $1/8$ inch in width, and is very useful when finishing the edges of ruffles, and for applying lace, ric rac braids or any finished trim to an edge in one operation. Hemmers which make wider hems are available for some machines.

RUFFLER. This attachment is capable of making uniform gathered or pleated frills, and will make and apply frills to another section at the same time. Some models are also equipped to apply piping to a frill or to make a frill and attach it with a facing in one operation. It is a relatively simple attachment to operate, and is most valuable in making household items such as curtains, loose covers and bedspreads which require long lengths of frilling. It is also useful in making children's clothes which have gathered skirts and petticoats.

MULTIPLE-SLOTTED BINDER. Excellent for applying various widths of commercial or self-fabric bias binding to a straight or curved edge, the binder ensures uniform application and eliminates tedious pinning and basting of binding. It is most often used to add decorative bound edge-trims and to bind seams on fabrics which ravel a great deal. It is particularly useful for making household items such as café curtains with bound edge-trim, aprons, and for adding neat, bound finishes to all types of garments.

GATHERING FOOT. Do not confuse this attachment with the ruffler. The gathering foot does what its name implies—gathers fabric as it is stitched. It will produce uniform rows of shirring with the fullness locked in every stitch.

EDGE-STITCHER. This has five slots that serve as guides when stitching must be uniform and accurate on the edge of the material. It is most helpful when sewing together bands of lace, making lace insertions, making French seams, piping edges, or for making pin tucks up to $1/4$ inch deep.

TUCKER. Used for making uniform tucks from $1/8$ to 1 inch in width; the tucker is equipped with two scales: one regulates the width of the tucks, the other ensures equal spacing between tucks. It can be used

effectively for creating cross tuck effects, pin tucks or regular tucks.

QUILTER. The quilter has a short open foot and an adjustable or removable space guide that may be used to the right or left of the needle to guide the quilting stitches in even rows. It is especially useful for quilting padded fabrics, and some models are adaptable as an embroidery foot which permits following curved lines with ease and accuracy.

PRESSING EQUIPMENT

Expert pressing is as essential to the good looks of a garment as expert sewing. Keep pressing equipment (21) as handy as the sewing machine; it should be used almost as often as the machine. For tips on how and when to press, check Chapter 8.

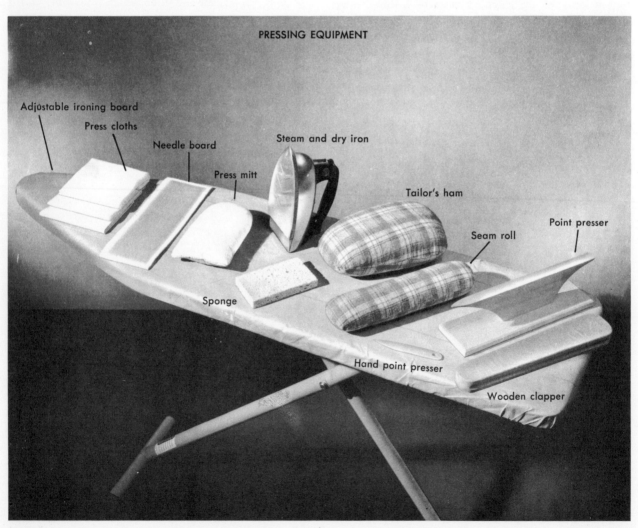

PRESSING EQUIPMENT

Adjustable ironing board
Press cloths
Needle board
Press mitt
Steam and dry iron
Tailor's ham
Point presser
Seam roll
Sponge
Hand point presser
Wooden clapper

21

Iron

A combination steam-dry iron is best; one with a temperature control essential.

Ironing Board

Obtain an adjustable one. They are most comfortable because you can adjust them to your height. Metal boards are more durable than wooden ones and do not warp.

Ironing Board Pad and Cover

Select a pad that will last. The foam rubber or plastic foams are quite durable. Heavy cotton padding is inclined to wear more quickly and scorch easily. The best covers are the silicone-coated ones or the asbestos type, since they do not become scorched as easily as the cotton drill or duck ones. Be sure that the cover and pad you select fasten securely to the board and fit it well.

Press Cloths

The commercially treated cloths are very inexpensive. Closely woven cheese-cloth also makes an excellent press cloth. The open texture allows the steam to go through but the weave keeps fabric surface from shining. A dry wool press cloth under a damp cheese-cloth is helpful for problem materials that shine.

Sponge

Used to dampen fabric as you press. It gives an even amount of moisture to an area.

Press Mitt

If all garments were composed of straight or angled pieces, these wouldn't be essential. Since garments curve as often as they lie straight, you need a curved cushion to press and shape the curved detail. The mitt is a small padded mitt that slips over the hand.

Tailor's Ham

This is a ham-shaped cushion also used for pressing curved and shaped details. It is essential if you plan to do any sort of tailoring. Inexpensive hams are available commercially, or you can make your own. Cut two oval pieces of firmly woven cotton or light-weight wool about 8 by 12 inches. Sew the ovals together and leave an opening. Turn right side out and stuff firmly with wool scraps, kapok or sawdust. The secret of a successful ham is packing it firmly. For best results soak the scraps and stuff them into the ham while still wet. Shape it as you pack and pack until it is solid. Then sew the opening closed with an overhand stitch.

Seam Roll

This is a padded rolled cushion to place beneath the seam when pressing. It will keep ridges from forming along the seam line. Commercial ones are available.

Wooden Clapper

When tailoring garments, purchase the clapper. It is a shaped wooden block which is pounded against steam-dampened fabric for the purpose of flattening edges and pressing seams flat.

Point Presser

Again, this item is mainly used for tailoring, but is useful for almost any garment making. It is a thin, shaped wooden board used to press open the seams in corners, points and other difficult areas.

Needle Board

To prevent the pile of velveteen, velvet and other pile fabrics from matting, use the needle board. The fabric is placed face down on the needles so that the pile fits between the needles and can be pressed without marking.

CHAPTER 6

THE EASY RULES OF PATTERN ALTERATION

If you have purchased your pattern in the correct figure type and size for your type of figure, most of your pattern worries should be over. However, the pattern is made for the average person, and since everyone differs in contour, you may find that your figure deviates slightly from the average. This makes it necessary to make a few adjustments to the pattern to achieve a professional look. Having a garment that is accurately fitted to your individual figure is half the joy of sewing.

Knowing exactly what alterations to make in your pattern to achieve this perfect fit comes with experience . . . sometimes sad experience. Often a beginner will blithely cut a pattern in expensive fabric, only to find, when it is completed, that the garment just doesn't fit properly. It may be too late, then, to do anything about it. This will never happen if you become familiar with your own individual contour and learn the simple adjustments to make in your tissue pattern so that you can cut correctly for a perfect fit.

A BASIC PATTERN

If you truly want to make clothes with a perfect fit, you should first make a basic pattern. Although this takes time in the beginning, it will save a great deal of time and even money as you continue to sew. No longer will your sewing be experimental. It will have a professional look.

The basic pattern can be made in two ways: by using inexpensive fabric for a slim skirt and a standard bodice with set-in sleeves; or by using the McCall's Try-on pattern made of non-woven material. Naturally the Try-on will be easier to use because it is designed especially for this purpose. All the pattern markings are printed on the pattern. The pattern can be cut, adjusted to the figure, stitched and used again and again as a guide for altering other patterns of a

similar silhouette. Try-on patterns are available in Junior Petites, Number 50; Misses' and Junior sizes, Number 100; Half sizes, Number 200. They can be ordered through any McCall's pattern dealer.

One big advantage in purchasing the Try-on is the instruction booklet which accompanies it, giving directions for altering the pattern for various figure irregularities. Also, the Try-on provides not only a dress pattern but additional pieces for various facings, collars, cuffs, and waistband. These can be used to make a dress, blouse, and skirt in a variety of styles. In fact it allows you to be your own designer and to create variations of the basic dress (22).

However, if you decide you would rather make your basic from cotton fabric, buy a tissue pattern of a simple, basic dress in your figure type and size. Use firmly woven fabric such as percale or muslin. Lay out the pattern and cut. Transfer all pattern markings to the fabric.

22

Using the Basic Pattern

EASE. In order to use a basic pattern successfully you must understand the meaning of "ease." Ease is the amount of fullness built into every pattern to allow room for a person to move. It is the amount added to body measurements so that a garment isn't skin-tight. Even a very fitted sheath has ease.

Although body measurements are standardised, the amount of ease isn't. Each pattern company decides how much ease is needed in its patterns. This is the reason why the fit of a garment in one brand of pattern is not identical with another although the size is the same.

The standard amount of ease in a McCall's pattern is:

Bust—$3^1/_2$ inches in a basic bodice. Evening bodices which are designed to fit snugly may have less.
Waist—$^1/_2$ inch.
Hip—Approximately $2^1/_2$ inches in slim skirts.
Back Waist Length—$^1/_4$ to $^3/_8$ inch.

You may want a little more or less, depending on how tight you wear your clothes; however, these are average amounts of ease for today's fashions.

The style and the design of the pattern also influ-

ence the ease allowance. A garment with the sleeve and bodice cut in one piece will have more ease through the bodice than a fitted garment with a set-in sleeve. A blouson style will have more length than a fitted bodice. This is known as design ease and changes with fashion.

ADJUSTMENTS. Trying to measure pattern pieces and decide whether the ease allowance is correct for you is a difficult and uncertain task. The use of a basic pattern avoids this confusion because it can be adjusted until it fits perfectly. After the basic has been fitted, identical alterations can be made on each pattern you use. If you add $^1/_2$ inch to the waist length of the basic, then you will add $^1/_2$ inch to the length of other bodice designs, such as blouson, a dropped waistline, an Empire line, in order to retain the same proportions the designer intended. The same thing applies to horizontal or around-the-figure measurements.

FITTING. Assemble the basic garment by machine-basting the seams together. Then the stitches may be pulled out easily to make adjustments. It is impossible to fit a garment accurately if it has been pinned or hand-basted together. Try the garment on and check

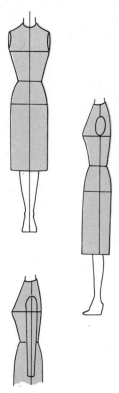

23   POSITIONS OF GRAINLINES

these points to determine if the basic pattern fits:

☐ Grain lines at chest, bust, waist, hip and upper arm are straight and parallel to the floor (23).

☐ Grain lines at centre front and back are perpendicular to the floor (23).

☐ Garment hangs gracefully and smoothly when you are standing straight.

☐ Garment has sufficient fullness throughout for movement in sitting, bending and walking.

☐ Bodice length is correct both above and below the grain line at front and back bustline.

☐ Skirt is correct length.

☐ Sleeves are correct length above and below the elbow.

☐ Neckline fits smoothly, without gaping or pulling.

☐ Centre front and back seams are in the centre of the figure.

☐ Side seams lie halfway between front and back, perpendicular to the floor.

☐ Shoulder seams lie straight across the shoulder.

☐ Sleeve seams lie across the tip of the shoulder for normal unpadded shoulder. As amount of padding increases the sleeve seam moves out on the shoulder.

☐ Bodice darts point directly to the fullest part of the bust.

☐ Hip darts end just above fullest part of the hip.

☐ Elbow darts are even, with centre dart pointing directly to point of elbow when arm is bent.

ADJUSTING YOUR PATTERN

Whether you are using a tissue paper pattern or altering your basic pattern, the adjustments will be made in the same way. To help you solve your adjustment problems, below are described the most common fitting ailments that women have, and the pattern adjustments which will remedy each situation.

Since many of these adjustments suggest the use of the McCall's Easy-Rule Guide, you should understand how it is used to shorten and lengthen pattern pieces.

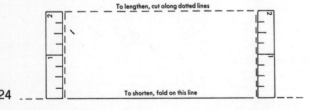

This simple device (24), printed right on the pattern,

simplifies the process greatly and ensures accuracy. *To lengthen:* cut along the dotted line marked on the pattern. Spread the pattern to your requirements using the printed ruler. Place tissue paper underneath the pattern and pin or tape into position to fill the gap.

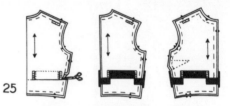

Re-draw seams and pattern markings to retain the original shaping of the pattern (25). *To shorten:* crease along the straight line marked on the pattern and fold a straight pleat to remove the necessary amount, using the printed ruler marking. Re-draw seams and pattern markings where necessary, again to retain the original shaping of the section (26).

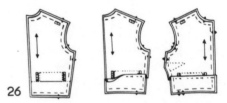

Bodice Alterations

When making any bodice adjustments remember that you need an ease allowance at the bustline of about $3\frac{1}{2}$ inches more than your body measurement for movement and comfort.

Problem

High Bust Bodice fullness for bust falls below bust so that bodice is too tight at actual bustline and too full below bustline; bust darts too low (27).

Low Bust Bodice fullness for bust is above bust; bust darts too high (28).

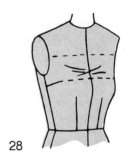

28

Problem

Smaller Than Average Bust Folds falling across bust; dart fitting too full for curve of bust; grain lines of fabric droop at bustline (30).

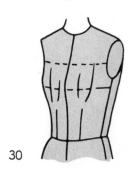

30

Solution

Alteration to Lower or Raise Bust Darts Mark the position of the point of the bust on the pattern. Lower or raise the point of waistline dart an amount equal to

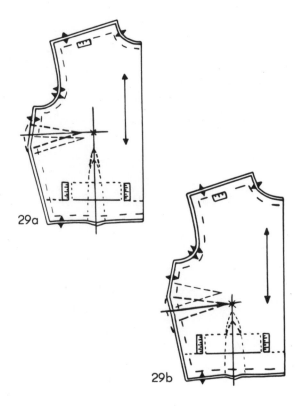

29a

29b

Solution

Alteration for Smaller Than Average Bust Draw a line through the centre of underarm dart and waistline dart until the two lines meet (31a,b). This point marks the point of the bust. Draw a line from point of bust to shoulder, halfway between shoulder and neck edge. Slash pattern from the lower waistline edge along the vertical line to within $1/8$ inch of shoulder seam. Slash pattern on horizontal line to $1/8$ inch of point of bust. Overlap the cut edges of vertical slash at point of bust, decreasing the bust the desired amount, tapering slash from shoulder line to waistline. This will overlap the underarm slash edges, also automatically decreasing both darts. This is necessary since the smaller bust needs less shaping. Pin or tape pattern in position.

the distance from the original point to the new bust point (29a, b). Re-draw the waistline dart from the new point to the waistline marking, keeping the darts in the same curve as original darts. Raise or lower underarm dart from new point keeping dart seamlines parallel to original dart lines. Re-draw the underarm seamline. If bust is very low it is often more flattering to eliminate the waistline dart and take up fullness at waistline seam with gathers rather than darts. This will give a softer shaping for the bust.

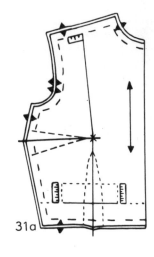

31a

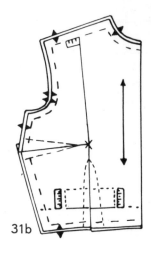

31b

Problem

Large Bust Wrinkles pulling across bust; dart fitting not sufficient for curve of bust; grain line of fabric pulls up at bust (32).

32

34

Solution

Alteration for Large Bust Cut the pattern as directed for the small bust. Spread the pattern on vertical slash at bust point increasing the bust as required, tapering from shoulderline to waistline (33). This will automatically spread the underarm slash. Place tissue underneath and pin or tape in position. The underarm and waistline darts have been increased, which is

Solution

Alteration for Narrow Shoulders Draw a vertical line through the inch rule marking to a point even with the armhole notch (35a). Draw a line from this point straight across to the seamline at armhole. Slash on marking and overlap edges at shoulder seam to remove desired amount. This overlaps the edges at the horizontal slash. Pin or tape the edges in position. Re-draw the shoulder line straight from neck edge to shoulder edge. Make the same alteration on bodice front (35c) and back (35b). If pattern has no Easy-Rule, draw a vertical line halfway between neck edge and shoulder seam, slash, and overlap as suggested above.

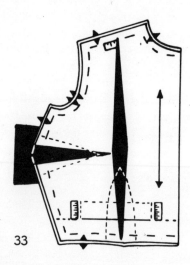

33

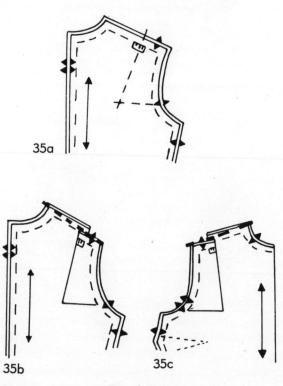

35a

35b   35c

desirable as a large bust needs additional dart shaping. Re-draw the darts from the centre point of slash at end point of original dart to the waistline and underarm markings (33).

Shoulder Alterations

Problem

Narrow Shoulders Shoulder seamline extends beyond top of shoulder and sleeve seam falls over edge of shoulder (34).

Problem

Broad Shoulders Bodice pulls from armhole to shoulder seam; shoulder seamline does not reach tip of shoulder and sleeve cap rides up (36).

36

Solution

Alteration for Broad Shoulders Cut pattern in same manner as described for altering narrow shoulders. Spread the slash at shoulder seamline to increase the desired amount (37). This automatically spreads the slash to the armhole. Place tissue paper underneath and pin or tape in position. Re-draw the shoulder line straight from neck edge to shoulder edge. Make the same alteration on bodice front and back.

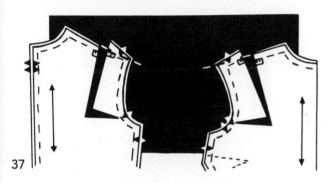

37

Problem

Sloping Shoulders Wrinkles slope from neckline to armhole and fall in folds; fabric grain line drops at armhole in both bodice front and back (38).

38

Solution

Alteration for Sloping Shoulders Mark amount that must be removed from the shoulder seam at armhole. Draw a new shoulder seam from the neck edge to armhole edge. Remove equal amount from shoulder seam on bodice front and back. To retain the shape of

armhole, lower the underarm seam the same amount as was removed from the shoulder seam, bringing armhole back to its original shape (39).

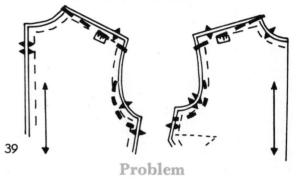

39

Problem

Square Shoulders Bodice has wrinkles pulling from the shoulder to bust and shoulder blades; fabric grain line pulls up at armhole in front and back (40).

40

Solution

Alteration for Square Shoulders Let out the shoulder seam at armhole edge. Insert a piece of tissue paper under shoulder seam and underarm and pin or tape it in position. At armhole edge mark the amount that must be added to the shoulder seam. Draw a new shoulderline from the marking to the neck edge. Add equal amounts to the shoulder seams on bodice front and back. To retain the shape of the armhole, raise the underarm the same amount as was added to the shoulder seam, bringing the armhole back to its original shape (41).

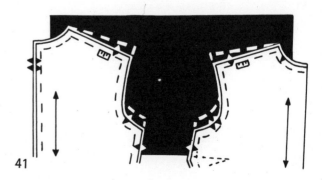

41

Problem

Erect Posture   Fold falling from neckline to shoulder blades in bodice back; fabric grainline drops at shoulder blades in centre back (42).

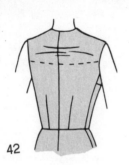

42

Solution

Alteration for Erect Posture   Shorten centre back at shoulder blades. Slash pattern back straight across from centre back to armhole seamline about 4 inches below neckline. Overlap edges of slash at centre back to remove the necessary amount, tapering the slash to the armhole seamline. Pin or tape in position. Re-draw the centre back line straight to restore the original grain line. This will decrease the neckline. You will have to use the pattern as a guide to restore the neckline and shoulder seams to the original size and shape (43).

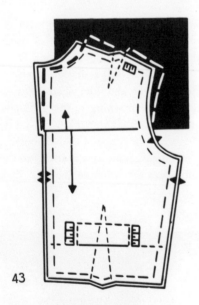

43

Problem

Round Shoulders   Bodice wrinkles pull from neckline in back toward shoulders; grain line pulls up at the shoulder blades in centre back (44).

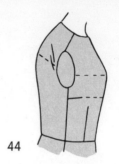

44

Solution

Alteration for Round Shoulders   Lengthen the centre back at the shoulder blades. Slash pattern back, about 4 inches below neckline, straight across from centre back to armhole seamline. Spread the slash apart to add the necessary amount at centre back, tapering slash to armhole seamline. Insert a piece of tissue underneath and pin or tape in position. Re-draw centre back straight to restore the original grain line. The neckline will be increased, so use the pattern as a guide to restore the neckline and shoulder seam to its original size and shape (45).

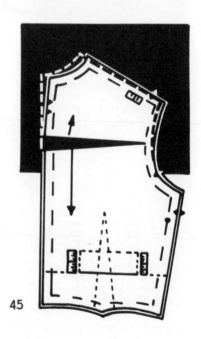

45

Problem

Uneven Shoulders   One shoulder higher than the other (46, 47).

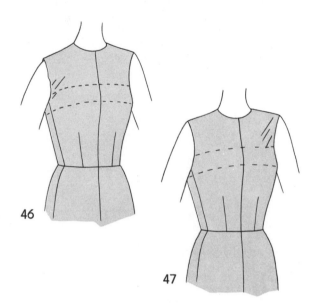

46

47

decrease the neckline. Using the pattern as a guide, restore neckline seam to its original size and shape.

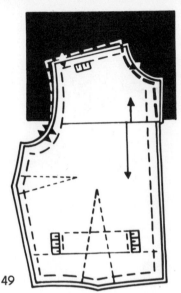

49

Neckline Alterations

Necklines should fit smoothly and hug the body closely, neither gaping nor pulling. If alterations are made on the neckline, the same alterations should be made on its facing and the original width of the facing retained. If a collar is to be applied to a neckline that has been changed, the collar must also be altered an equal amount for it to fit and lie smoothly.

Solution

Alteration for Uneven Shoulders Try inserting a small shoulder pad on the side of the low shoulder to conform to the higher side. If this does not work, the pattern will have to be altered. If the bodice fits correctly on the lower side, make the alteration for square shoulders only on the high side; if bodice fits higher shoulder, make sloping shoulder alteration on side of the lower shoulder.

Problem

Hollow Chest Folds falling across bodice front from neckline to chest; grain line drops across chest at centre front (48).

Problem

Thin Neck Neckline falls away from neck and falls in folds (50).

48

50

Solution

Alteration for Hollow Chest Shorten centre front at chest. Slash bodice front, about 4 inches below the neckline, straight across from centre front to armhole seamline (49). Overlap edges of slash at centre front the necessary amount, tapering to the armhole seamline. Pin or tape in position. Re-draw the centre front line straight to restore the original grain line. This will

Solution

Alteration for Thin Neck Build up the neckline. Pin or tape a piece of tissue paper underneath the neckline edge. Build up the neckline the desired amount. Add the same amount to bodice front and back. Alter the facing in the same manner and restore the original width of the facing (51, page 84).

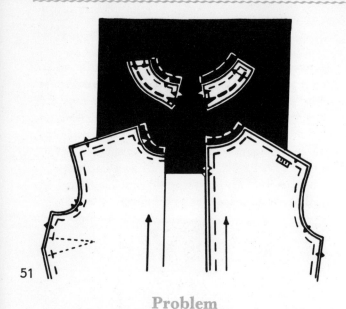

51

Problem

Full Neck Neckline pulls and wrinkles around neck and is too tight (52).

52

Solution

Alteration for Full Neck Lower the neckline. Cut out neckline of bodice front and back the necessary amount to fit neck smoothly. Alter the facing in the same manner and restore the original width of the facing (53).

53

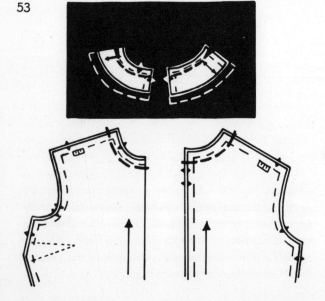

Problem

Open Neckline That Gapes Neckline is too big and hangs away from the neck (54).

54

Solution

Alterations for Open Neckline That Gapes Take in the neckline. Pin tiny darts in the pattern tissue evenly around the neck edge of bodice to remove necessary amount. Do not make darts more than $1/8$ inch in width at the seam line on neck edge. Make the same alteration on the neckline facing (55).

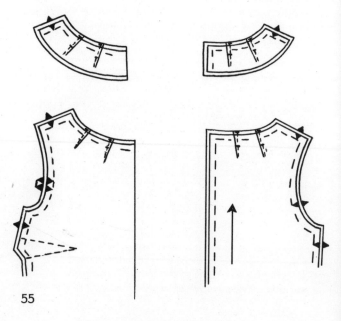

55

Waistline Alterations

Problem

Small Waistline Skirt falls below natural waistline; bodice too full at waistline (56).

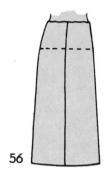

56

Solution

Alteration to Decrease Waistline To take in the waistline 2 inches or less, divide the total amount to be decreased by four and remove this amount from each side seam allowance. This will decrease the waistline evenly on each side both front and back. Taper from waistline to underarm seam in the bodice and from waistline to hipline in skirt (57). If you need to take in the waist more than 2 inches, take in each dart slightly (not more than $1/4$ inch) at waistline tapering to the point.

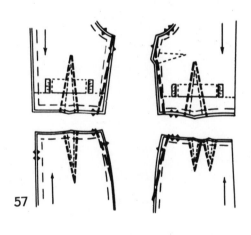

57

Problem

Large Waistline Waistline of skirt rides up above natural waistline and wrinkles pull around waist (58).

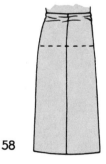

58

Solution

Alteration to Increase Waistline To let out the waistline 2 inches or less, divide the total amount to be added by four and increase each side seam edge this amount (59). This will increase the waistline evenly on each side both front and back. Taper from waistline to underarm seam in bodice and from waistline to hipline in skirt. If you need to increase the waist more than 2 inches, let out each dart slightly (not more than $1/4$ inch) at waistline tapering to the point.

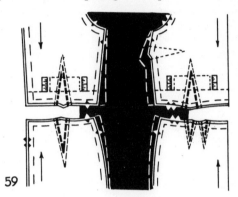

59

Problem

Large Abdomen Waist pulls across front in bodice and skirt, and waistline rides up at centre front; side seams of skirt swing toward front; fabric grain line goes up at centre front (60).

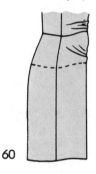

60

Solution

Alteration for Large Abdomen Increase bodice and skirt in width and length across abdomen. Draw a line through the waistline dart and a line straight across from centre front to side seamline about 3 inches above and below waistline in both bodice and skirt. Slash on markings. Spread the slash at dart the necessary amount and then spread slash to side seamline sufficient to bring centre grain lines back to normal straight grain. Place tissue behind slashes and pin or tape in position. Re-draw waistline darts in centre of slash bringing them back to normal position and size (61 a, b) p. 86.

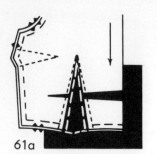
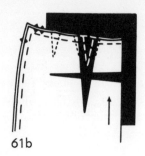

61a   61b

Skirt Alterations

When making any skirt adjustments, remember that you need an ease allowance at the hipline of $2^1/_2$ inches more than your body measurement for movement and comfort.

Problem

Small Hips   Skirt too full over the hipline, falls in folds over hip; fabric grain drops at side seams (62).

62

Solution

Alteration for Small Hipline   To decrease hipline 2 inches or less, divide the total amount to be decreased by four and take an equal amount off each side seam edge front and back. Taper from waistline to hem (63).

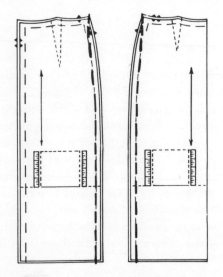

63

Problem

Large Hips   Skirt pulls across hipline and tends to ride up; fabric grain line goes up at side seams (64).

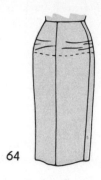

64

Solution

Alteration for Large Hipline   To increase hipline 2 inches or less, divide the total amount to be added by four and add an equal amount to each side seam allowance front and back. Taper from waistline to hem (65).

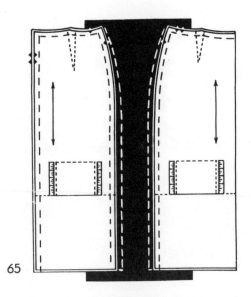

65

Problem

Small Hip Curve   Skirt stands away from body hip curve from waist to thigh (66).

66

Solution

Alteration to Decrease Hip Curve   Determine the amount needed to be taken off curve. Draw a new hip curve on the pattern front and back from waistline to fullest part of hipline. Taper the line (67).

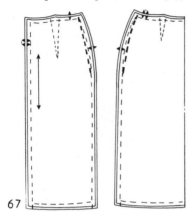

67

Problem

Sway-Back   Folds or wrinkles form across the centre back between waist and hip (68).

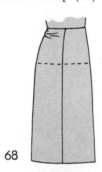

68

Solution

Alteration for Sway-Back   Shorten at centre back. Slash pattern about $3^1/_2$ inches below waistline, straight across from centre back to side seamline. Overlap edges of slash to remove the necessary amount and pin or tape in position. Re-draw the centre back line straight to restore the original grain line. This decreases the back waistline measurement which is usually desirable with a sway back. To make the bodice back waistline fit the skirt, take in the bodice darts at waistline (69a) the amount removed from the centre back of skirt, taper to the point of darts. However, if you need the original waistline measurement, increase the side seam of the skirt the same amount as was removed from the centre back, tapering from the waist to hip. Re-draw the skirt dart to straighten it (69b).

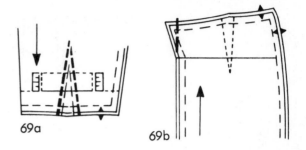

69a   69b

Problem

Large Derrière   Skirt wrinkles across the derrière, tends to ride up in the back; fabric grain goes up in the back; side seams swing toward the back (70).

70

Solution

Alteration for Large Derrière   Increase width and length of skirt back at fullest part of derrière. Slash the pattern through the centre of waistline dart and spread the pattern the necessary amount. Cut straight across the pattern about 7 inches below the waistline from centre back to side seam. Spread pattern sufficiently to return the centre back grain line to normal straight grain. Insert a piece of tissue underneath and pin or tape in position. This has increased the size of the dart allowing for the larger curve. To maintain the size of waistline, divide the amount added and increase darts an equal amount (71).

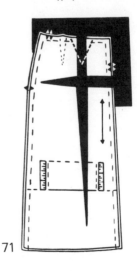

71

Small Derrière Skirt falls in folds across the derrière and tends to sag at back; grain line drops in centre back of skirt (72).

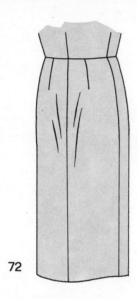

72

Alteration for Small Derrière Decrease length and width of skirt in centre back. Slash pattern back section through the centre of the waistline dart and overlap the edge of the slash to remove the necessary amount. Slash straight across the pattern about 7 inches below the waistline from the centre back to side seam. Overlap the edges of the slash sufficiently to bring the centre back grain line to its normal straight grain position. The size of the waistline dart has been decreased, which is desirable since less dart fitting is necessary for a flat derrière. Re-draw the dart from the waistline marking to the point (73).

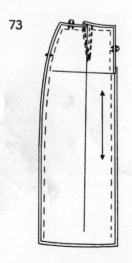

73

Sleeve Alterations

Binding Sleeve Cap Sleeve pulls and wrinkles across top of sleeve (74).

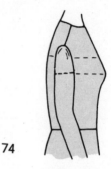

74

Alteration for Binding Sleeve Cap Let out the underarm area. Raise the underarm edges of the sleeve by about $3/8$ inch and add $3/8$ inch to the side seams of the sleeve. Re-draw the line, tapering to nothing. Adjust bodice front and back the same. Add $3/8$ inch to underarm seam and $3/8$ inch width at the underarm side seam, tapering to nothing at waistline (75).

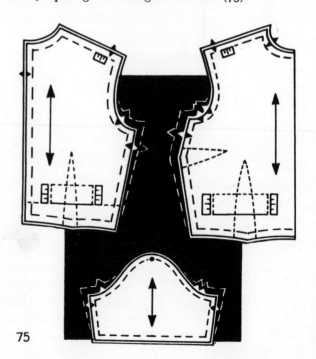

75

Large Upper Arm Sleeve pulls and wrinkles across fullest part of sleeve; fabric grain pulls up at the centre of sleeve (76) p. 89.

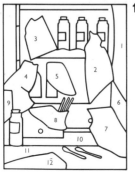

10 Tricel is available in a wide range of fabrics and garments. It is used for woven and knitted fabrics, suitable for dresses, blouses and lingerie. Blended with other fibres it is also available as lightweight suiting, rainwear, pleated skirts, washable trousers and children's wear.

1 Tricel grosgrain. **2** Tricel lawn. **3** Tricel printed surah. **4** Tricel voile. **5** Tricel printed jersey. **6** Tricel printed surah. **7** Tricel jersey. **8** Tricel shantung. **9** Tricel printed sparkle surah. **10** and **11** Tricel rayon rough spun. **12** Tricel rayon tartan.

Photograph by courtesy of Courtaulds Ltd.

11 Courtelle, a popular and versatile fabric, is available in textures suitable for dresses, suits, skirts, coats, and evening wear. The fleece is excellent for pram or cot covers, blankets and housecoats.

1 Courtelle jersey. **2** Courtelle viscose linen spun. **3** Courtelle viscose linen. **4** Printed Courtelle jersey. **5** Courtelle crêpe. **6** Woven Courtelle and wool tweed. **7** Courtelle fleece. **8** Courtelle pile fabric (not washable). **9** Woven Courtelle and wool tweed. **10** Courtelle printed cotton.

Photograph by courtesy of Courtaulds Ltd.

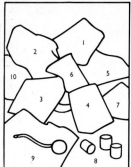

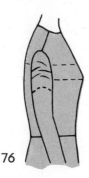

76

Solution

Alteration for Large Upper Arm Increase width of sleeve cap (77). Slash the sleeve pattern straight through the centre from the lower edge to the circle on seamline at cap of sleeve. Slash straight across pattern at fullest part of sleeve cap from seamline to seamline. Spread the pattern through centre slash increasing sleeve at fullest part the necessary amount and tapering to seamline at cap and lower edge. This will automatically overlap the edges of the slash across the sleeve cap. Insert tissue under slash and over cap of sleeve and pin or tape in position. Measure the amount decreased by the overlapped edges at centre of sleeve and add this amount to cap of sleeve, restoring the original length. Re-shape the sleeve cap to normal curve. Alter the bodice front and back at side seams so that the sleeve will fit with the normal ease allowance. Add half the amount of the increased width at fullest part of sleeve to the front and half the amount to back side seams tapering to nothing at the waistline.

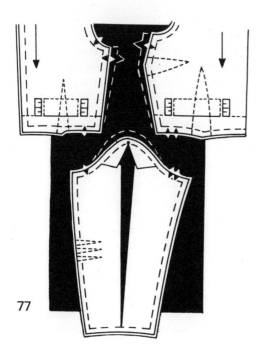

77

Problem

Sleeve Width Too Full Sleeve is too full and too wide at lower edge (78).

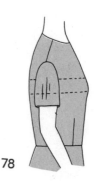

78

Solution

Alteration for Full Sleeve Slash the pattern through the centre of the sleeve to the circle at sleeve cap seamline (79). Overlap the slash edges decreasing the necessary amount at hem and tapering to seamline at cap. Pin or tape in position. Re-draw grain line straight and parallel to centre of sleeve and straighten the lower edge of the sleeve.

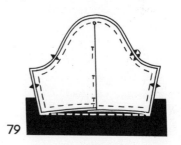

79

Problem

Sleeve Width Too Narrow Sleeve is too narrow; pulls and wrinkles at lower edge (80).

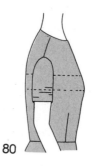

80

Solution

Alteration for Narrow Sleeve Slash the pattern through the centre of sleeve to the circle at seamline of cap. Spread the slash, increasing the sleeve the necessary amount at hem and tapering to sleeve cap. Insert tissue under the slash and pin or tape in position. Re-draw grain line parallel to centre of sleeve and straighten the lower edge of the sleeve (81).

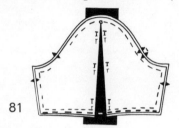

81

Alterations for Slacks and Trews

The trews fashions of today create special fitting problems. A snug fit is demanded, but the garment must not be too tight at any point. It is important that major alterations be made on the tissue, since little can be done once the garment has been cut. If you have a number of fitting problems, it would be wise to test the pattern in an inexpensive fabric. Once you achieve the perfect fit for your figure, use this as a basic pattern for all kinds of trews in your wardrobe.

Trouser patterns should be bought by hip measurement. However, there are other measurements which are needed to alter your pattern properly, so have someone take the following measurements for you.

Waist—The waistline can be taken in or let out

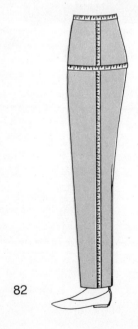

82

very easily, so do not use this measurement as a guide for buying your pattern (82).

☐ Hip—This is the important measurement to keep in mind when buying your pattern. Take the measurement 7 inches down from the waist (82).

☐ Instep—This measurement is taken over the instep and around the heel. It determines how narrow the pants can be at the ankle and still be able to get over the foot without an opening (83).

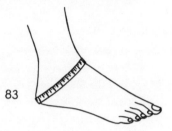

83

☐ Length of Crotch—Take this measurement in sitting position. Take the measurement from the side waistline down to the seat of the chair (84).

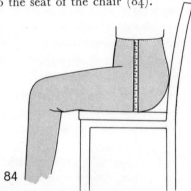

84

☐ Waist to Ankle—Take this measurement from the side waistline to the ankle to get the total length (82).

Before cutting your fabric, check your pattern according to the procedure listed below. Make the alterations necessary for your figure. Some further adjustments may be necessary in the first fitting, but at least you can cut with the assurance that the pattern has been proportioned to your individual measurements.

Start by making all lengthwise adjustments on your pattern. Once the length of the crotch and the length of the trews have been established, you will be able to mark the location of the hipline on your tissue.

ADJUSTING LENGTH OF CROTCH

Draw a line across the pattern at right angles to the grain line from the widest part of the crotch to the side seam. The length of the tissue from the waistline to this pencil line should be the same as your crotch length taken in the sitting position plus $3/4$-inch ease.

If the pattern is too long, crease along the Easy-Rule

Guide line and fold a tuck to take up the desired amount (85).

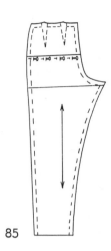

85

If the pattern is too short, cut apart along the dotted lines indicated by the Easy-Rule Guide. Spread the pattern apart the desired amount and insert a piece of tissue (86)

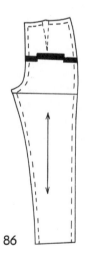

86

ADJUSTING THE LENGTH OF THE TREWS Measure the length of the pattern from waistline to lower edge. This should be the same as your measurement from waist to ankle.

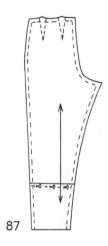

87

☐ If the pattern is too long, take a tuck along the Easy-Rule Guide line in the leg (87).
☐ If the pattern is too short, cut and spread the tissue using the Easy-Rule Guide (88).

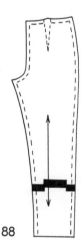

88

LOCATION OF THE HIPLINE. Measure down 7 inches from the waistline and draw a horizontal line on the pattern. A coloured pencil will make this line more visible. The hip measurement of your pattern will be taken at this point.

Now you are ready to make the crosswise adjustments on your pattern. Your pattern was purchased by hip measurement so we will start from the hipline and make all other adjustments accordingly.

ADJUSTING THE HIP. Take the hip measurement of your pattern at the hipline marking you made on the tissue 7 inches down from the waist. There should be a 2-inch ease. If the tissue does not measure 2 inches more than your body measurement then the pattern will have to be adjusted.

If the pattern is too big, take a vertical tuck parallel to the grain line and avoiding any dart markings. Carry the same width tuck down the entire length of the pattern (89).

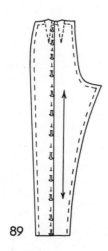

89

If the pattern is too small, slash the tissue in a vertical line parallel to the grain line and avoiding any dart markings. Spread the tissue the necessary amount and insert a piece of tissue down the entire length of the pattern (90).

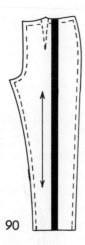

90

ADJUSTING THE WAISTLINE. You will have a better fit if the waistline is eased to the waistband. Make the waistline of the pants $1/2$ to $3/4$ inch

larger than the waistband measurement. The waistline can be increased or decreased by adjusting the darts. Each dart can be taken in or let out as much as $1/4$ inch but no more (91, 92). If this adjustment is not sufficient, the side seams can be altered also. Divide the additional amount needed by four and increase or decrease each side seam edge this amount. Taper to hipline, being careful not to change the hip measurement (91, 92).

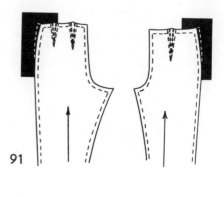

91

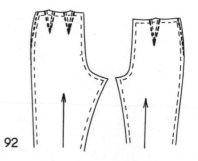

92

ADJUSTING THE WIDTH OF THE LOWER EDGE. Measure the lower edge of your pattern at the hemline. There should be a minimum of 1-inch ease at the lower edge in order to slip over the foot without an opening. However, the person with heavier legs will find that a little extra width will be more becoming to her. If the pattern does not measure at least an inch more than your instep measurement, you will have to alter the tissue.

If the pattern is too small, determine the amount to be added and divide by four. Add this amount to each of the four seam edges at the hemline. Taper from hemline to hipline on the outside seams and from hemline to crotch on the inside seams (93).

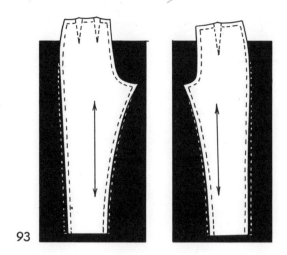

93

If the pattern is too large, the extra amount can be taken out of the pattern now or pin-fitted out later. The person with very slim legs can safely take the extra fullness out of the tissue at this time. Divide the total amount to be taken out by four. Take this amount off each of the four seam allowances at the hemline and taper to hipline on the outside seams and crotch seam on the inside seams (94). The person with legs on the heavy side would be wise to leave the extra fullness until the first fitting. When you try on the garment, it is very easy to pin-fit and taper the legs to a becoming width.

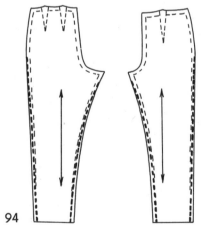

94

ADJUSTING THE WIDTH OF THE LEG.

There is no standard amount of ease required for the width of the leg. This is a matter of personal preference and depends so much on the size and shape of the leg muscles. A person with heavy legs will not be able to fit her trews as tightly as the person with slim legs.

If you have heavy thighs, add to the inside leg seams, front and back, at the crotch, tapering to the lower edge. Do not add to the side seams. This will do nothing for tightness through the thigh area. Tightness in the thigh means that you need more width in the crotch as well as the leg, and adding at this point will give you both. Width of crotch refers to the thickness of the body from front to back. This cannot be measured but it is important to the fit of pants. It cannot be adjusted by adding to the side seams of a pattern.

Thigh muscles that bulge in the front even on a slim leg can cause a fitting problem. Add to the inside leg seam of the front only and taper to hemline (95). Do not add to the inside leg seam of the back. This will only succeed in giving a baggy seat.

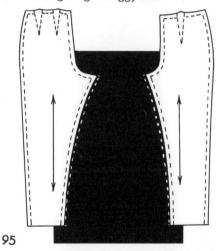

95

If you have very slim thighs, you will need to decrease the inside leg seams front and back at the crotch and taper to lower edge (96). You need less width in the crotch and the leg, and this can never be accomplished by fitting it out at the side seams.

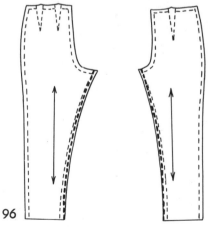

96

In additon to these general rules for adjusting trews patterns to your figure, there are a few special alterations that you may need in order to take care of specific figure problems. If you have one of the problems listed on pages 94-95, adjust your pattern accordingly.

ALTERATION FOR SWAY-BACK. This problem is handled in the same way as for a skirt. The wrinkles across the back (97) are removed by taking out the extra length at centre back. Slash straight across the back to the side seam about $3\frac{1}{2}$ inches below the waistline (98). Overlap slash lines to remove the necessary amount. Re-draw the centre back seam and the darts if they have been affected. This has decreased the back waistline which is normally desirable with a sway-back. However, if you need the normal waistline width, add the amount trimmed from the centre back to the side seam tapering to the hipline (98).

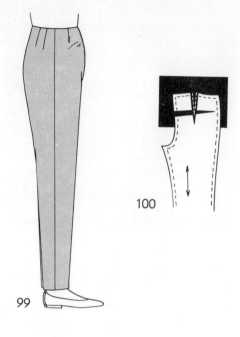

99

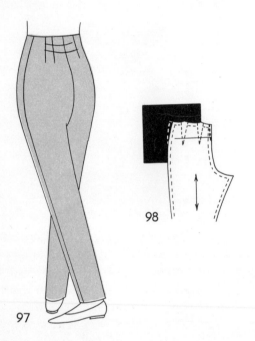

98

97

ALTERATION FOR PROTRUDING HIP

Extra dart fullness released at the point of the hip bones will take care of this problem (101). Reposition the dart so that it comes in line with the hip bone. Increase the width of the dart and for some figures the dart may need to be shortened. The larger dart releases more fullness over the hip bone. This makes the waistline smaller, so now you will have to add the difference at the side seam and taper to the hipline (102).

ALTERATION FOR LARGE ABDOMEN. This adjustment may also apply in a lesser degree to the average figure wishing to wear fitted trews without a girdle as well as to the person who wants to wear a lighter-weight one than she is in the habit of wearing. You may never need to consider such an alteration for a skirt but fitted trews emphasise the slightest figure fault (99). Slash through the centre of the waistline dart and spread the tissue the necessary amount. Slash straight across the front about 3 inches below the waistline seam (100). Spread the amount necessary to bring centre grain lines back for normal straight grain. Insert tissue under slashes. Adjust waistline darts in the middle of the slash bringing them back to their original position and size.

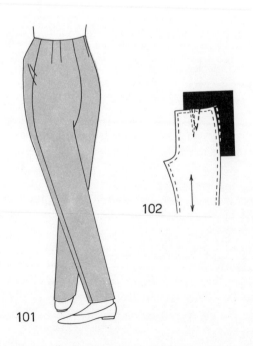

102

101

ALTERATION FOR LARGE DERRI-ÈRE.

There are several adjustments for this, depending on the degree of your problem (103). First try making the back darts deeper and longer (104). The deeper darts will give more fullness and the longer darts will drop that fullness lower where it is needed. Add to the side seam to compensate for the amount lost in the waistline measurement by taking the darts deeper. Taper from waistline to hipline. If more fullness is needed, then add at the inside leg seam on the back. This will add length and width to the back crotch measurement without getting a baggy seat.

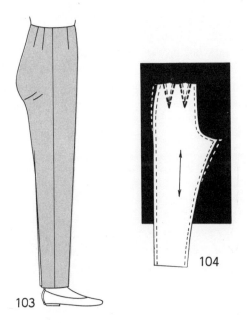

103

104

ALTERATION FOR FLAT DERRIÈRE.

For this type of figure (105), the pattern is going to have too much length and width across the back. Lift the pattern across the back to take out the extra length. Do this by slashing straight across the back to the side seam about $3^{1}/_{2}$ inches below the waistline (106). Overlap slash lines to remove the necessary amount and re-draw the centre back seam. Shallower darts will give less fullness across the back. Decrease the darts and take out the extra waistline width at the side seam. Taper from waistline to hipline. For this figure problem, make the dart nearest the centre about $1^{1}/_{2}$ inches longer than the other dart. This distributes the dart fullness and gives a smoother fit. Remove the extra fullness below the hipline by decreasing the inside leg seam of the back at the crotch and tapering to the lower edge.

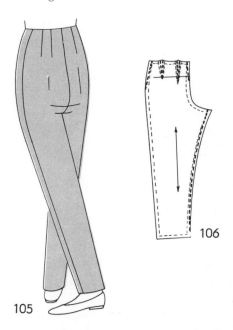

105

106

Fitting Basic Pattern for Trews

Machine-baste the trews together for the first fitting. Hand-basting will not give an accurate fit for such a snug garment. The way you assemble the trews is very important to the fit. Stitch the side seams first and then stitch the inside leg seams. Stitch the front and back crotch in a continuous seam. All men's trousers are made this way and it makes them hang better. Baste the waistband in place for the first fitting.

During the first fitting make any necessary adjustments. The legs can be tapered to the most becoming width for you. When tapering the legs, pin-fit the same amount on the inside and outside leg seams. Do not do all the tapering from the side seam.

Make all necessary adjustments and try the garment on again to check the fit. When you achieve perfect fit, take the time to transfer all the adjustments made on the fabric to your tissue pattern. Now you have a pattern perfect for you. You can use this basic pattern for all trews that you make and save a lot of time in experimenting with alterations on new patterns.

CHAPTER 7

GROUNDWORK FOR ACTION

You have your pattern altered to fit you; you've bought your fabric, and now you're more than ready to start cutting and sewing . . . and that is exactly what you will be able to do after one more preliminary step. Before you can put your shears to work, you will have to be sure the fabric is ready to cut. Each of the three types of fabric—woven, knitted and bonded—requires slightly different handling when you prepare it for cutting, as well as when you cut, mark, and finally sew.

PREPARING WOVEN FABRICS

Most of the fabrics you use will be woven, composed of lengthwise and crosswise threads interlaced at right angles to each other. These lengthwise and crosswise threads are referred to as the grain of the fabric. The lengthwise grain runs parallel to the selvages, the crosswise grain from selvage to selvage (107).

Fabrics are always woven with the crosswise grain at exact right angles to the lengthwise grain; the lengthwise threads are held taut in the loom and generally there are more of them than crosswise threads. These additional threads make the lengthwise grain stronger than the crosswise grain and less likely to stretch. Because of this, it is best to have the lengthwise grain follow the length of the body, since greater strength is needed lengthwise when stretching, bending and sitting. You will want the additional stretch of the crosswise grain across the body for movement.

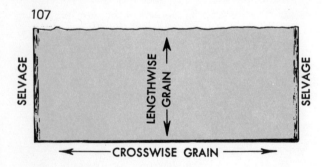

107

Checking Position of Grain Line

After you have purchased the fabric, be sure to check the grain again by either tearing or cutting it along one crosswise thread. To tear it, clip the selvage; then place the left thumb on top of the material and the right thumb underneath and tear quickly, straight across the fabric. Sheer, pile, ribbed and loosely woven fabrics should not be torn, but should be checked by pulling one crosswise thread. Clip the selvage and gently pull one crosswise thread. Ease the fabric along the thread as you pull it out to help prevent breaking the thread. Cut across the fabric on the pulled thread from selvage to selvage (108).

108

After each end has been torn or cut along one crosswise thread, lay the fabric flat on a large surface. Fold it in half lengthwise matching the selvages accurately. If the crosswise ends match evenly and are at right angles to the selvage edge and the fold, the grain of the

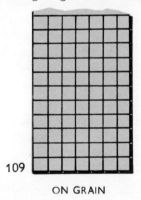

109

ON GRAIN

fabric is straight (109). If the crosswise ends do not match evenly or are not at right angles to the selvage edge and the fold, the fabric is off-grain (110, 111).

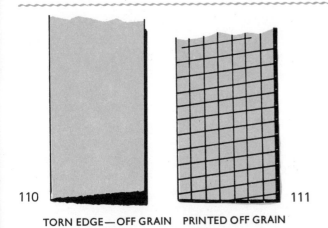

110   111

TORN EDGE—OFF GRAIN   PRINTED OFF GRAIN

113

Straightening Fabrics

There are several ways to straighten off-grain fabrics, depending on the type of the material. For cottons, silks, linens, wools and some synthetics which have no permanent finishes, first try straightening the grain by stretching the fabric. Place the fabric on a flat surface and pull the fabric on the true bias in the direction opposite to the higher off-grain edges (112). Continue stretching until the crosswise threads are at right angles to the lengthwise threads. If this method does not work, you will have to use one of the other methods suggested here.

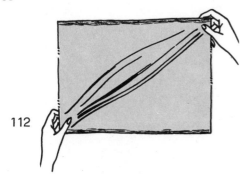

112

If the fabric is washable, fold the piece in half lengthwise matching the selvage and ends of the fabric evenly. Baste the selvage edges together, and the ends together evenly. Fold the fabric loosely and immerse in water (113), until it is completely wet throughout. Place it on a flat surface and pull gently on the bias in the direction opposite to the higher off-grain edges until the crosswise threads are at right angles to the lengthwise threads. Drape straightened fabric over clothes line, clothes rack or shower rod until it is dry. Do not try to dry it in an electric dryer; the motion may distort the material again. When dry, press smooth and flat with a steam iron or a dry iron and damp press cloth. After the fabric has been completely pressed, remove the bastings along the edges.

For woollens and other fabrics that are not washable, you should follow a slightly different procedure. Fold the fabric in half lengthwise, matching selvages and ends evenly, and baste together along the selvage edge and ends. Place a sheet in warm water and wring it as dry as possible. If the sheet is too wet, it will give the wool fabric a puckered, washed look. Lay sheet on a flat surface and place folded fabric flat on sheet (114). Fold sheet in half over fabric. Fold loosely and allow it to remain folded for eight to ten hours. Remove the fabric carefully and place it on a flat surface to dry, first pulling gently on the bias to straighten the grain. When completely dry, press flat and smooth with steam iron or dry iron and damp press cloth.

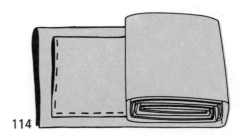

114

Shrinking Fabrics

Another important point to check before you purchase any type of fabric, woven or knitted, is whether the fabric has been pre-shrunk. Most fabrics today have been processed for shrinkage, but you will still find some inexpensive cottons, linens, washable rayons and blends of less than 65 per cent synthetic fibre which may not have this noted on the bolt. They may very well have been processed, but unless it is specifically stated that shrinkage is less than one per cent, be careful. You may still buy the fabric, but be sure you test it for shrinkage before you cut it for a garment.

To test for shrinkage, cut a 6-by-6-inch square of

the fabric and trace its exact outline on a piece of paper. Wash the square of fabric in warm water, let it dry and press it. Compare it with the tracing to see how much, if any, shrinkage has occurred. If you do find the fabric shrinks, then shrink the entire piece by one of the methods described on page 97 for straightening the grain. Use the immersion method for washable fabrics; the damp-sheet method for non-washable.

Woollens will often require some shrinkage, unless they are tagged "ready for the needle" or have some sort of label or tag stating that they have been shrunk. Even when you plan to have the garment dry-cleaned, you will need to shrink woollen if it has not been pre-shrunk. The steam-pressing used in shaping the garment during construction will cause the fabric to shrink if it hasn't been treated. It is safest and easiest to have a dry-cleaner shrink wool fabrics. However, you can shrink it yourself using the damp-sheet method outlined on page 97.

Silks which are to be dry-cleaned, synthetics or blends containing 65 per cent synthetic fibres require no shrinking. Felt is created by a bonding and shrinking process, so any further shrinkage should be avoided.

Be sure to shrink and straighten any inner shaping materials you use, if they are not pre-shrunk. Do the same for any notions such as zippers, grosgrain ribbon or tape which will be placed in a washable garment. Most of these items, except the ribbon, have the notice "washable" on the package, and will not need shrinking, but be sure to check.

PREPARING KNITTED FABRICS

These, too, should be checked for straightness of grain and shrinkage. Remember in the knitting process, the fabric is produced by a series of interlocking loops formed by one or more yarns. As the loops are interlocked they form chains in both directions of the fabric. The chains running the length of the fabric are called "wales," and correspond to the lengthwise grain of woven fabric. The chains running across the fabric are called "courses" and correspond to the crosswise grain of woven fabrics. The bias of the knitted fabric is the diagonal grain formed by placing the wales on top of and parallel to the courses, the same as in woven fabric.

If the fabric is a man-made one such as nylon jersey, the fabric occasionally becomes distorted and locked in an off-grain position. It is impossible to straighten, so you should avoid buying such fabrics if they are much off-grain. If you do buy one, you will have to cut each pattern piece individually following a lengthwise rib to preserve the grain lines. The same is true for wool or cotton knits termed "washable." They have been permanently finished and cannot be straightened.

Wool and cotton knitted fabrics which have no permanent finish can be straightened by folding the fabric along a single lengthwise wale, basting it in position and steam pressing the folded edge. Using this as a selvage, straighten the fabric as you would a woven fabric by stretching it into position.

PREPARING BONDED FABRICS

Felt and non-woven fabrics are formed by several methods, but none of them have a grain since the fibres are meshed and locked together. Pattern pieces may be laid and cut in any direction. The commercial products usually have been treated to prevent shrinkage, but check the hang tags or bolt to make sure. With wool felt, avoid steam pressing as much as possible, since this tends to shrink the fabric a great deal.

SPECIAL HANDLING FOR PROBLEM FABRICS

Although most fabrics you will be using are easy to handle, there are a few types that require special attention. Beginners would do well to avoid these fabrics until they have had a little practice on easy-to-work-with, firmly woven cottons and woollens. Then these problem fabrics will offer little or no difficulty if you follow a few simple suggestions in preparing, cutting and sewing them.

Chiffon

Chiffon tends to be slippery and will slide when being cut, unless a non-slippery surface is used. An old sheet or tablecloth on the cutting surface should suffice. Be sure to use fine dressmaker pins and cut with very sharp shears. Use a fine machine-stitch (15 to 18 to the inch) and a fine machine needle. The feed dog may catch the fabric surface, so it's best to stitch over tissue paper, which may be torn away after stitching. Preferred seam finishes for sheer fabrics are the French seam and hand-rolled edges, since these are the least conspicuous. Wider seams show through. When facings are needed, it is best to make the entire garment section double, rather than have the edges show through to the right side of the garment.

Crêpe

The spongy quality of crêpe, which makes it drape so beautifully, also tends to make it stretch when being machine-stitched. To prevent stretching, stitch over tissue paper. Fit crêpe garments fairly snugly; they usually stretch after wearing. However, don't fit too tightly, or your garment will pull and stretch in all the wrong places. Allow crêpe garments to hang at least overnight before marking the hem, since the fabric tends to stretch when hanging. Press it lightly, always using a press cloth to prevent shine.

Felt

Felt does not present many difficulties in construction. It may be cut in any direction since it has no grain. It does not ravel, needs no edge finish, and usually felt garments have no hems. Choose very simple patterns for felt, without a great many construction details. It is hard to ease seams in felt. Use lining fabric or iron-on tape for facings when required to avoid bulky seams. Use a fairly long machine-stitch and medium tension. Press felt with a warm, dry iron; steam-pressing tends to shrink it.

Fur Fabric

When working with the fabulous fakes, follow the layouts and directions for cutting napped fabrics. Baste seams together by hand before stitching, since the pieces tend to slip when machine-stitched. Use a light tension on the machine, and a long stitch (8 to 10 to the inch). Use a needle to smooth pile out of the seams on the right side of the fabric. Slash darts and press open with tip of iron and a dry press cloth. Never use a steam iron; it will mat the fabric. Use lining fabric for facings, and hooks and eyes, snaps or loops for closings. Buttonholes should be avoided, since they are very difficult to manipulate in heavily napped fabric.

Jersey

For jersey or any knit fabric that comes in a tubular form, you may have to cut the tube open following a lengthwise rib if the pattern layout shows the pieces cut singly. Open flat, square off ends, and steam-press to remove fold creases. Pin pattern securely to wrong side of the fabric to keep edges from rolling. Stay-stitch each piece immediately after cutting to prevent its stretching out of shape. For permanent stitching, use a long machine-stitch (10 to 12 to the inch) with loose tension. Stretch the material slightly without pulling. For extra reinforcement, double-stitch or tape seams at points of stress such as waistline, underarm, elbows of long sleeves. Hang garment for at least twenty-four hours before marking hemline. Line jersey garments to prevent them stretching out of shape.

Double-Knitted Fabrics

Double-knits are wonderful fabrics for the home dressmaker, and present few problems in handling. Choose patterns suitable for jersey or light-weight wools, avoiding bias-cut skirts because of the excess stretching. If your double-knit is very light-weight, you may want to line it with Jap silk, but in general these knits are not lined because you want to retain the suppleness of the fabric. You may line suit jackets with soft silk crêpe or Jap silk. Pre-shrunk muslin makes a good interfacing, but you may choose any woven interfacing that is not too firm or bulky. A firm, straight taffeta petticoat or fitted slip is recommended for wear under the knits.

Follow a lengthwise rib for correct layout; straighten knit by pulling on the true bias. Stay-stitch all curved or bias edges. Use mercerised thread and a medium stitch of 12 to 15 to the inch, testing tension and pressure on a scrap of fabric before you begin. Keep seams stretched lightly as you stitch to prevent stitches from popping later. Use your zigzag machine for permanent stitching and for seam and hem finishes. You may also finish the hem edge by overcasting, or by pinking and edge-stitching with 2 rows of machine-stitching, then complete with a tailor's hem.

Stay shoulder seams and waistlines with woven seam binding to prevent stretching. For waistbands, use pre-shrunk grosgrain belting as interfacing in a band cut double on the lengthwise grain of the knit. Buttonholes may be bound or machine-made, and you will want to reinforce the area with organdie or muslin.

Lace

A lace garment is transparent and delicate and should be completely lined. If you intend to make a special slip for the garment, then you may like to line with nylon net. If you want to build the slip into the garment then taffeta the same colour as the lace is a good choice. If the fabric is not lined, use matching net or marquisette for facings.

Select a simple pattern design without centre seams or elaborate seamings, to avoid breaking up the lace designs. Use machine or hand appliqué to join lace sections; stitch lace over tissue.

A fold of net or transparent horsehair makes a good hem finish, depending on the stiffness required. When using lace with a scalloped edge or border, let that be at the hem. The scalloped edge of a flouncing may be cut away as a band and applied to any part of the garment, e.g. hem. Stitching should then follow the inner cut edge of the scalloping.

Many dress laces are made from a combination of different fibres, and dry cleaning is therefore strongly recommended. All-cotton or all-nylon laces, e.g. those intended for lingerie, can be laundered at home, by floating in mild lather, squeezing in a towel, and drying flat. Washing machines or spin driers are not recommended. Use a medium, not hot, iron in all cases. Press, textured side down, on a well padded board.

Laminates

There are a variety of laminates available to the home dressmaker; woven cottons, jersey and knitted laminates will be found most frequently. Your choice of a pattern will be determined by the fabric. The jersey or knitted laminates present no particular problem in pattern selection; however, if you choose a firmly woven cotton laminate, do not select any design calling for eased seams, such as princess lines or normal set-in sleeves, because with these laminates you cannot ease a long seam to a shorter one without forming gathers.

Smooth pattern flat and trim to the marked cutting line before using to prevent tearing of the tissue. Use sharp shears to cut these fabrics. Tailor's tacks, chalk or pins can be used to transfer pattern markings, but the tracing wheel and dressmaker's carbon do not mark successfully.

To stitch laminates, loosen pressure on presser foot; use a looser tension and longer stitch (10 to the inch). Because its foam underside prevents the fabric from feeding evenly, you must use tissue on each side of the fabric if you stitch on the wrong side. Tear tissue away after stitching.

Stay-stitch all bias and curved seams. To control stretching of bias seams, place tissue under fabric and seam binding on top of the seamline, and stitch the binding in with the seam. Grade all seam allowances to prevent bulk; trim wide darts to $5/8$ inch and press open, forming a triangular pleat at the point. Faced edges should be top-stitched to keep them flat. Press laminates on the right side only with a steam iron and press cloth. Be careful not to touch the foam side with the iron.

Net

Net presents very little trouble. Seams on net garments may be trimmed without ravelling. The number of stitches to use per inch on the machine depends on the size of the mesh, so test a scrap before doing any permanent stitching. Transparent horsehair provides a nice finish for the hem, but is not essential.

Nylon

The biggest problem in working with nylon and some of the other pure synthetics is seam puckering. Stitching tends to draw seamlines and ripple the fabric on either side. Bias or off-grain seams pucker less than straight lengthwise ones, so it's best to select a style with flared gores cut with bias seams. When stitching nylon, always use a fine machine needle, and either nylon or mercerised thread. Use a fairly small stitch (12 to 15 to the inch) and loosen both bottom and top tensions as much as you can to produce a good stitch. Avoid stitching over pins. As you stitch, use the same technique suggested for jersey, stretching the seam slightly but allowing the fabric to feed normally under the presser foot.

Pile Fabrics

Velvets, velveteens, corduroys and velours require special handling because of their napped surface. Follow layouts given for napped fabrics, being certain that all pattern pieces are laid in one direction. For a very rich colour, let the nap run upward toward your face; for longer wear, run the nap toward the hem. Use fine pins and silk thread to prevent marring the surface. On velveteen, avoid the bulk of double thickness by using chiffon or taffeta for facings. Use a long machine-stitch (10 to 12 to the inch) and avoid top-stitching the garment. Then press according to the instructions given in Chapter 8 (pages 117—121).

Sheer Fabrics

Treat all sheers as you would chiffon. Use full-skirted, classic shirtdresses or dressy evening designs. Sheers will have skirts of double layers of fabric, and often matching separate or built-in slips. Slips may be taffeta or cotton satin; interfacings are organdie, organza, or net. Add required yardage for double skirt and for deep hem; sheers must have a hem of at least 6-10 in on the outer skirt. Circle sheer skirts have a narrow, hand-rolled hem.

Stretch Fabrics

There are three types of stretch fabrics available to the home dressmaker: warp or lengthwise stretch, generally used for ski pants or slacks; filling or crosswise stretch, generally used in jackets, skirts or dresses; two-way stretch used in ready-to-wear for bathing suits. Most of the stretch fabrics on the retail market for home-sewing are the warp type. The home dressmaker should be careful to choose the type of stretch the pattern calls for.

Care should be taken to prevent stretching the fabric when cutting or marking. Use sharp shears to cut, and stay-stitch all curved and bias edges before beginning construction. Stitch with a small zigzag stitch to allow seams to stretch without thread breakage; avoid pulling the fabric in stitching. You may use synthetic or mercerised thread.

If stretch fabric ravels, you must use a secure seam finish: overcast edges, use your attachment or machine to zigzag near the seam edge, or turn under and edge-stitch.

If buttonholes are part of your design, place a small patch of interfacing under the buttonhole to prevent stretching. You may steam-press stretch fabrics, but don't use pressure.

Be sure to check the bolt of fabric for cleaning instructions. Fabrics made of rubber must be washed, since dry-cleaning will tend to stiffen and swell the rubber fibre. Nylon or Helanca stretch fabrics are both dry-cleanable and washable.

Sequin and Beaded Fabrics

The glamorous sequin and beaded fabrics are "cycle" fabrics which return to popularity at frequent intervals. Usually it is best for the home dressmaker to sew these fabrics by hand, using a fine back-stitch, as these will break machine needles, or often the machine needle will break the sequins or beads in the stitching. If you don't want to sew by hand, try a scrap of your fabric on the machine, always stitching on the wrong side of the fabric, using a regulation stitch (12 to 15 to the inch). These fabrics vary according to the number of sequins or beads sewn to the fabric so they may sometimes be successfully stitched on the machine.

Metallic Fibres

Metal thread woven into other fibres adds a touch of glitter but presents a few problems. Metallic fabrics must be pressed with a moderately hot iron, or they may melt under high heat. Pin marks can mar the surface when the fabric has a high percentage of metal, so it's best to place all pins in the seam allowances. Most metallic fabrics tend to ravel badly so seams should be overcast and bound buttonholes should be avoided.

PRESSING

The final step in preparing your fabric is the pressing. Press the fabric on the wrong side, always pressing with the grain lines. Remove all wrinkles and creases, especially the folded crease lines. On crease-resistant fabrics the fold line may be difficult to remove, and a damp press cloth will be needed. If the crease cannot be pressed out, refold your fabric and avoid this line as you cut, otherwise the crease will show on the finished garment. For tips on what method to use in pressing various fabrics, see Chapter 8.

LAYING OUT THE PATTERN

Laying pattern pieces on fabric is anything but a haphazard affair. Easy sewing is possible only if you know exactly how to place patterns on fabric and cut them out accurately. If it is not done with care and skill, the garment simply will not go together easily and correctly, and it will never hang properly.

Prepare a Cutting Surface

The first thing to do is to find a large cutting area, large enough for the entire length of fabric if possible. A large table is best; just be sure to protect the surface if necessary. You may also wish to pad a very slippery surface such as Formica. The cutting boards mentioned in Chapter 5 provide just the right padding. If you haven't a suitable table, then use the floor, protecting

2. CUTTING LAYOUTS FOR ALL SIZES

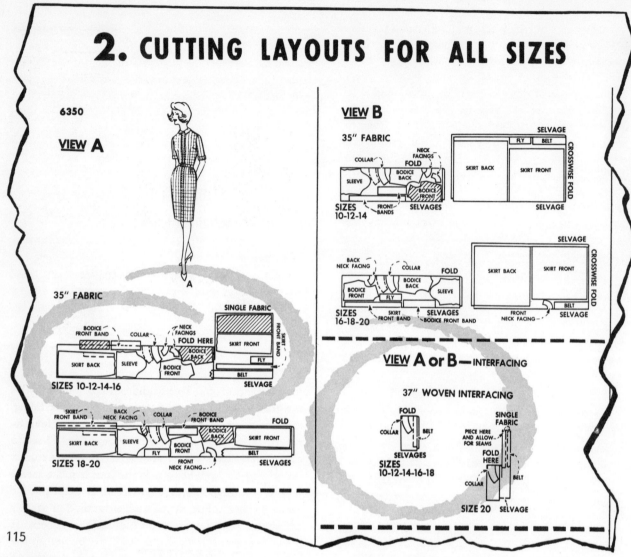

115

your fabric from dirt by placing an old sheet or clean paper beneath it. Never use the bed for laying out and cutting fabric. You will find it does not give firm enough support for accurate cutting because the fabric and pattern pieces do not lie flat.

Circle the Correct Layout

If you have not circled the layout to be used, do it now (115). Find the correct layout diagram on the instruction sheet for the size pattern and the width of fabric you are using. Be sure to circle the layouts for lining, interfacing or contrasting fabrics if they are necessary for your design.

Sort Your Pattern

Open the envelope and sort through the pattern pieces, selecting only those you need for the version you are making. Check each piece with the layout diagram and the diagram of pattern pieces on the back of the pat-

tern envelope. Be sure to select all the pieces you need, and check to see that all pieces are marked with the same size and pattern number. Put the other pieces back in the envelope; they only add confusion and are likely to get lost if left loose.

Press the Pattern

Press each pattern piece flat, using a very low temperature on a dry iron. Moisture or steam will shrink and pucker the tissue pattern, and it will no longer be the true size.

Fold Your Fabric

Fold the straightened and pressed fabric as illustrated on the layout diagram. Always fold on the straight grain of the fabric: lengthwise fold on a single lengthwise thread parallel to the selvage; a crosswise fold on a single crosswise thread with the selvages folded back on themselves. Fold the fabric with right sides together, unless it is necessary to match design motifs in the fabric which are only visible on the right side.

Pin Pattern to Fabric

Start laying the pattern on the fabric as shown in the diagram. You may be one who loves to devise her own layouts, but by and large it is wisest to use the ones shown in the instructions. Rest assured, pattern experts have worked to give you the most economical layout possible for your fabric width. The diagrams are drawn to scale and show the exact placement of each piece.

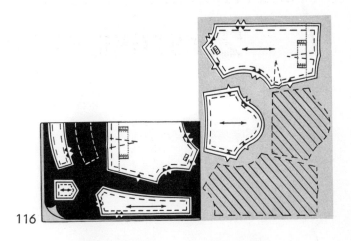

116

Always lay out the entire pattern on the fabric before you cut one snip of it. If your cutting area is not quite large enough, place a few pieces of the pattern on the fabric, secured with just a few pins, carefully roll this section up, and continue laying the pattern until it is completely laid out. You want to be sure there is ample yardage before you cut, not afterwards when it is too late.

Usually all the pattern pieces are placed on the wrong side of the fabric when the fabric is folded. When single thicknesses are cut, the pattern pieces are normally placed on the right side of the fabric. This ensures that the right and left sides of the garment, if they are not identical, will be placed correctly on the right side of the fabric. McCall's patterns have an extra margin of tissue outside the double cutting lines. This is designed to make the printed pattern accurate and to help you cut more accurately. Remember you can overlap these margins to the cutting line when laying out the pieces. The margins fall away as you cut your fabric.

McCall's patterns are laid out with the printed side up unless the layout shows a shaded piece. The shading indicates that the piece should be placed with the printed side down on the fabric. This usually occurs when the same piece is used for a right and left section and the piece is placed printed side up one time; printed side down the other. If a piece is drawn with a dotted line, it means the piece is to be cut identically a second time (116). If a pattern piece has a single printed line, marked "place on fold," lay it face up with the printed line exactly along the straight grain fold of the fabric (117).

Check Grain Lines

Each pattern piece has a printed grain-line arrow-marking indicating the correct grain for that section of

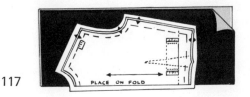

117

the garment (117). To lay the pattern piece on the correct grain easily, place the pattern on the fabric with the grain line parallel to the selvage for lengthwise grain or parallel to the crosswise fold. Measure with a yardstick or ruler from each end of the arrow to the selvage or fold, being sure that each point measured is an equal distance from the edge. Place pins at each end and centre of the printed grain-line arrows before you attempt to pin the edges of the pattern. It is essential that the grain placement be secured so the piece does not slip out of position while the rest of it is pinned (118).

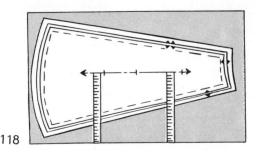

118

After the grain-line arrows are pinned, smooth the tissue out from the grain-line arrow until it lies flat and smooth on the fabric. Pin the corners and the long outside edges of the piece, placing pins parallel to the cutting edge within the seam allowance. Use just enough pins to keep the pattern in position while cutting; too many will distort the edges (119) p. 104.

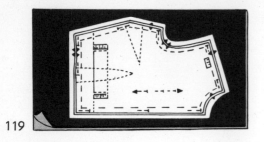

119

Cut all notches outward when you cut (120) so they will be easily seen when you have to match them in construction. Remember to cut double or triple notches in one continuous strip across the top of the notches as indicated by the printed line.

Cut out all the pieces before going on to the next step of transferring the markings to the fabric. This will speed up both cutting and marking time.

If you own pinking shears, save them for finishing raw edges after seams are stitched. Do not use pinking shears to cut out your pattern and fabric. They tend to pull the fabric, easily distorting the pieces, and you will not have a clean cutting edge from which to measure the seam allowance.

CUTTING THE FABRIC

Get out your well-sharpened, bent-handled dressmaking shears and start to cut. Keep the fabric flat on the cutting surface by placing one hand flat on the tissue and fabric as you cut. Cut with long, even strokes in the direction of the fabric grain. The fabric grain direction is indicated on each edge of the pattern by small directional arrows printed on the seam line. Cutting with the grain will produce a cleaner raw edge, one that is less likely to ravel.

When cutting a McCall's pattern, cut directly between the double line printed on the pattern. If you are accurate in your cutting, you will have the exact $5/8$-inch seam allowance intended for the piece. If you use a pattern from another company, measure from their cutting line to the seamline to determine whether you should cut inside the cutting line or outside to maintain the correct $5/8$-inch seam allowance.

USING McCALL'S SPECIAL FEATURE PATTERNS

The patterns with special features such as McCall's Instant and proportioned-to-height patterns require slightly different handling when laying them out and cutting them. This does not mean that they are more complicated to use; on the contrary, they are usually easier.

Instant Patterns

Instant Patterns are printed with all of the pattern pieces on one large piece of tissue paper so that the layout is already done for you. Each piece of pattern is positioned so it will be on the correct grain line of the fabric, which eliminates checking each piece for grain perfection. Again, the layout is designed for the most economical use of fabric.

When using an Instant Pattern, you have to buy the exact amount of fabric indicated on the yardage section of the pattern envelope. Check the width and length of the fabric needed for your size and purchase only that amount.

Straighten and press the fabric as you would any other material. Fold it as illustrated in the pattern guide sheet. Pin the pattern in place on the correct grain, fastening each piece securely to make cutting accurate, then cut it out. That is all there is to it.

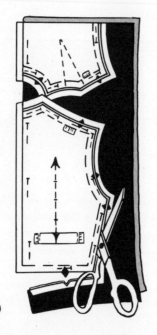

120

12   There is a no more enchanting fabric than lace. Deceptively fragile, lace is available in a multitude of fashion colours suitable for both evening and day wear. Choose a simple pattern which will accentuate the innate beauty of the material.

Lace fabrics by courtesy of British Leavers Lace Association. Italian lace negligée set by courtesy of Harrods, London

13 The gleam, glint and sheen of these varied fabrics is extremely eye catching, particularly for evening wear.

1 Single knit rayon Duracol jersey and Lurex 50 C. **2** Double knit jersey wool with Lurex 50 C. **3** Diolen and Lurex 50 C. **4** Rayon and Lurex 50 C. **5** Wool double jersey Jacquard with Lurex 50 C. **6** Gold Lurex lamé. **7** Featherweight lamé nylon, rayon and Lurex 50 C. **8** Hand woven Ceemo tweed with Lurex. **9** Crystal nylon and Lurex 50 C.

Photograph by courtesy of the Dow Chemical Co. (U.K.) Ltd.

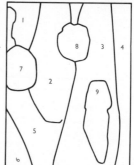

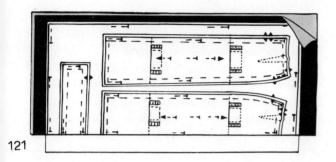

121

One word of caution for those who find it necessary to alter their patterns before cutting. If alterations must be made, you will have to cut out the separate pieces of the pattern and alter them. Then lay them out again just as you would a regular pattern (121).

Proportioned Patterns

McCall's Proportioned Patterns are designed for the tall (5′ 8″), medium (5′ 6″) and short (5′ 3″) figures. All the darts, lengths and proportioning details of the design are clearly marked on the pattern for these three heights.

Some of the Proportioned Patterns have separate bodices and skirts for each individual height all packaged in one envelope. Each of these pieces is clearly marked "tall," "medium" or "short" (122). Double-check to be sure you have selected the correct pieces for your height. Once a piece is cut the wrong height, there is little you can do to correct it.

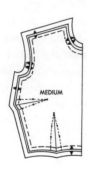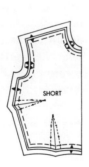

TALL   MEDIUM   SHORT

122

Other Proportioned Patterns will have only one pattern piece for bodice and skirt with darts, pleats and other details specified for each height. These pattern pieces are actually proportioned for the tall figure, with instructions printed on the piece for shortening it to fit the medium or short figure. Remember to do any alterations necessary and cut the hemline along the appropriate printed marking before you lay the pattern on the fabric. Cut the adjusted pattern just as you would any other pattern (123).

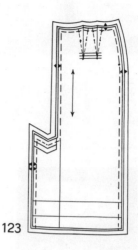

123

FABRICS REQUIRING SPECIAL LAYOUTS

Some fabrics require special handling in pattern layouts. Remember, you should always use a pattern which is specifically designed for fabrics needing special handling such as napped, pile, one-way textures or designs, plaids, stripes, checks, prints, border prints and lace. If a pattern is suitable for one of these, the illustration on the front of the envelope will show this and the "Suggested Fabrics" section will list it. The time may come, however, when you want to use one of these fabrics and can't find a style you like specifically designed for the fabric. Another style can be selected as long as you know exactly how to work with the fabric you have selected. Check the following suggestions and instructions before you begin to cut.

"With Nap" Layout

When yardage requirements on the back of the pattern envelope list fabrics "With Nap," it means that a layout is given in which all the pieces are placed on the fabric in one lengthwise direction (124) p. 106. This is necessary since napped or pile fabrics reflect light differently, depending on their direction or, in the case of some fabrics, the design may have a definite up-and-down direction.

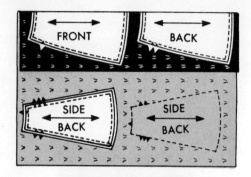

124

If you use a pattern which does not give yardage for "With Nap" fabrics, and plan to use one, then read the instructions on page 22 for computing the exact yardage you will need when using napped fabrics. Fabrics which must be cut according to napped layout are:

Napped Fabrics

Short fibres are brushed and raised to the surface of the fabric; the fibres are usually brushed smoothly in one direction. Some napped fabrics have woven raised loops, as well. Commonly used napped fabrics are wool broadcloth, camel's hair, fleece, some flannels, doeskin, melton, cashmere and suède cloth. To test the direction of the nap, rub your finger over the lengthwise surface of the fabric. If the surface feels smooth, the direction is referred to as down; if it is rough, the direction is up. Most napped fabrics are cut with the nap running down toward the hem.

Pile Fabrics

These are woven with a third set of threads that form a looped or tufted surface on the fabric. Common pile fabrics are velvets, velveteens, corduroy, velour, fur fabrics and terry cloth. Test the direction of the pile as you do for napped fabrics. For a richer colour and greater light reflection, cut velvets, velveteen and corduroy with the pile surface running toward the face. Fur fabrics and terry cloth should be cut with the pile surface running down.

One-Way Textures

Fabrics which reflect light differently when held up or down. These include satin, sateen, some brocades, damask, chino and some gabardine and flannels.

One-Way Designs

Any fabric which has a woven or printed design that has a definite up-and-down direction.

When using any of these fabrics, first determine the direction you wish the fabric to take in the garment. To place all the pattern pieces in one direction lengthwise, you may have to work with the fabric unfolded, if your pattern design has a definite right and left. Most of the time, however, you can work with a centre lengthwise fold. If the pattern requires two full-width layers, cut it along the crosswise fold and reverse the under layer so that right sides of both layers are still face to face but with the nap going in the same direction.

Plaids, Stripes and Checks

If you select a pattern which is not specifically designed for these fabrics, problems will arise. These fabrics must be matched at seam and design lines if the garment is to be at all attractive. Try to find a pattern that has straight seams and little detailing. Eased seams, bias seams, or a large number of pattern pieces will add to your matching problem.

EVEN PLAIDS. On these the designs are balanced in both lengthwise and crosswise direction and are the easiest plaids to work with. Determine how you want the design lines placed on your figure. The vertical lines should be evenly arranged from the centre front and back so that the right and left sides of the garment will be the same. Check, too, to see if you want a particular construction line placed on the horizontal design of the plaid. Straighten the fabric, if needed. Fold the fabric through the centre of a plaid design, according to the diagram given for "Without Nap" fabric in the pattern layout. Be sure to match the lines of the plaid accurately when folding so that all corresponding lines are directly over one another.

Place the pattern pieces on the fabric so that the

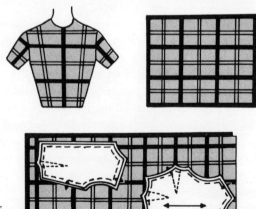

125

lines of the plaid will be correctly placed as previously determined on the figure. Put the centre front and centre back fold, seam lines or markings in the middle of the desired plaid design (125). To match the design at all seams, place corresponding notches on the same line and colour of the plaid. McCall's numbered notches will easily help you determine which notches match. When pockets or other detailing will be applied to the garment, be sure to match these with the lines of the plaid at the place on your garment they will be sewn.

Pin, cut and mark the sections carefully so that the garment will be identical on both sides. Slip-baste seams before machine-stitching for accurate matching.

UNEVEN PLAIDS. These plaids have an unbalanced design in both lengthwise and crosswise directions and are the most difficult plaids to work with. They should be avoided by the beginner, but for the experienced sewer with time and patience they present a challenge and are well worth the time and effort. The unbalanced design lends itself to more variety and interest in the plaid and makes up into a most attractive garment if the pattern is appropriate for the fabric. Remember to select a pattern with as few construction lines as possible. Plaid is most effective if it is not cut up by a lot of seams. For instance, never select a large plaid for a princess-line garment.

Uneven plaids should be cut on the bias forming a chevron at centre front and centre back seams (126). If you do not want the fabric cut bias, then the plaid is matched all in one direction going around the body with no centre seams. Although there are directions available for cutting an uneven plaid half on the wrong side and half on the right side of the fabric in order to

make the plaid match at a centre front seam, it is best not to do this. There are very few fabrics that do not show a difference if the dress is cut half on the wrong side of the fabric.

EVEN STRIPES. These are stripes in which the colour and width of stripes are repeated consecutively either lengthwise or crosswise of the fabric. They are the easiest to work with. Fold the fabric so that the stripes are identical on each side of the fold. Lay the pattern on the fabric, following the "Without Nap" layout and placing the pieces so that the stripes will be properly positioned on the figure (127, 128). Put corresponding notches on the same stripe design for correct matching.

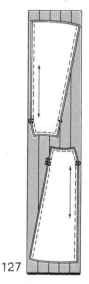 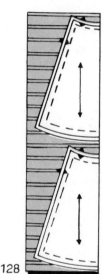

127   128

UNEVEN STRIPES. Stripes of this type are more difficult to work with since there is not an even repeat. Any stripe with variety in colour or width of the stripes

 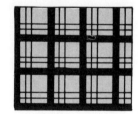

126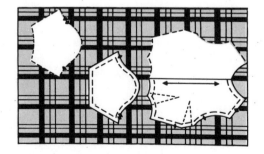

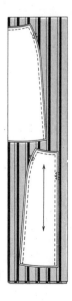

129

is considered an uneven design and requires extra thought and care in matching. Place the predominant stripe in the centre of the figure and cut the pattern according to a "With Nap" layout (129).

Like uneven plaids, uneven stripes are matched all in one direction rather than trying to make the right and left sides of the garment symmetrical (129). Uneven stripes are also very effective if cut on the bias so that they form a chevron at centre front and centre back.

CHECKS. These are treated in the same way as an even plaid. The checks should be matched at all seamlines and centred on the figure.

Prints

First check to see if the print has a regular directional pattern. If so, then treat it as a napped fabric. If not, then you will merely want to space the print attractively on the figure (130).

Large prints and some medium-size prints should be spaced to give the most pleasing effect. Hold the fabric up to your figure and test the placement of the design. Usually the dominant motif is placed in the centre front and back of the bodice and skirt and in the centre of the sleeve. Match large designs at seam lines whenever possible. Place the pattern seam lines, not the cutting line, on the design lines you want to match. It is best to work with large prints folded right side out when you lay out the pattern so that you can more easily determine the proper spacing of the print.

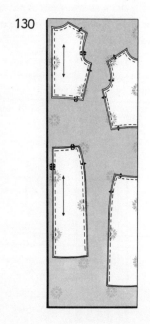

130

Border Prints

A border print usually appears along one lengthwise edge of the fabric. Select a pattern with straight or nearly straight side seams in the skirt, if you really want to use the border effectively (131). Place the pieces on the crosswise grain, if you want the border at the hemline of the garment. Other details which can use borders effectively are straight sleeve edges, squared necklines or styles with fairly wide ruffled borders.

When placing pattern pieces on the fabric, arrange them so the border design will match at seam lines. If you make a bordered skirt, be sure to shorten or lengthen the pattern piece before cutting out the fabric, so that you do not have to cut away the border when you mark the hem.

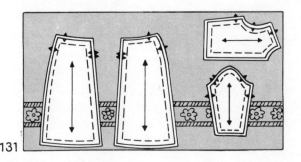

131

Lace

If lace has a scalloped or finished edge, then treat it as a border print. When working with any lace, try to keep the motifs centred and intact as much as possible. Place the motifs properly on the figure, just as you would a large print. Always underline lace so that the pattern of the lace is not lost by the conflict of darts, seams and slip straps showing through.

MARKING THE FABRIC

Once all your pattern pieces are accurately cut, you will want to transfer all the pattern markings to the fabric. If you don't, you will have a very difficult time deciding where the different pieces go. No matter how experienced a seamstress you are, always mark each piece. It is the only way to avoid needless errors.

There are several methods of marking the fabric. It is wise to select the one most suitable for the fabric being used. One method cannot be employed for all types of material.

Tracing Wheel and Carbon

This method works on most fabrics. However, it cannot be used on sheers, which will show the markings on the right side, or on heavy or napped woollens on which the markings won't show. Buy the non-wax type of dressmaker's carbon in the colour closest to your fabric colour. Test a scrap of the fabric before marking the whole garment to see that the markings show clearly on the wrong side of the fabric but do not show through on the right side. Be particularly careful in using white and pastel fabrics to be certain that the marks disappear when washed or dry-cleaned. Also be sure that the tracing wheel does not mar the fabric.

To use the carbon, place the marking side of the paper next to the wrong side of the fabric. If the fabric was cut double, place a piece of carbon paper in each layer next to the wrong side of both pieces of fabric. In this way they will both be marked at the same time. You may have to remove a few pins in order to place the paper smoothly between the two thicknesses. Place the fabric piece on a smooth, hard surface. If you use a table top which is likely to be marred, place a fairly firm board beneath the fabric. Use a ruler as a guide and run the wheel along the side of the ruler. (132) Do not use heavy pressure, just enough to make the markings visible. Transfer all markings. At the termination point of darts, tucks, pleats, ets., mark a short straight line across the point. Use two short crossed lines to indicate circle markings. The same method is used with the tailor tacker, which is used like a stylus.

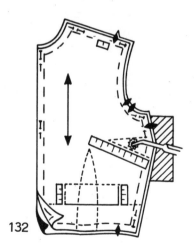

132

Tailor's Tacks

This method can be used on any type of fabric, and is especially good for heavy or knobbly woollens, fine silks and sheers. Once the garment is made, the thread markings are easily pulled out and will not mark the fabric in any way. Use darning cotton or embroidery thread for the tailor's tacks. They do not slip out as easily as other threads. Always use a contrasting thread so that the marks can be easily seen (133).

Using double thread, take a small stitch at the point

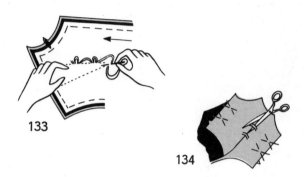

133

134

to be marked through the pattern and fabric. Leave an inch or more thread end. Take a second stitch in the same position leaving a small loop. Then take a stitch at the next marking, leaving the thread loose between the two markings. Continue in this manner until all markings have been made on the section. Cut the thread between markings. Unpin the pattern from the fabric and remove it carefully by pulling threads through the tissue. Spread the two layers of fabric apart; cut the threads between the layers, leaving thread tufts in each piece of fabric (134).

Tailor's Chalk

This marks easily and can be removed usually by brushing or rubbing the surface of the fabric. A white chalk pencil is even better to use than the old-fashioned tailor's chalk. It can be sharpened to give a much more accurate, thin line. Chalk in either form is a quicker method of marking than the tailor's tacks, and is a good method to use if the fabric will not take carbon well. On knobbly or heavy woollens, the chalk will not mark well. Always mark on the wrong side of fabric.

Place pins through the pattern and fabric at the positions to be marked (135), with the pins pointing toward the centre of the garment. Remove the tissue pattern by slipping it off the marking pins, and mark the position of the pins with tailor's chalk (136). Both layers of the fabric can be marked without re-pinning, if the right sides of the fabric are together and the wrong sides out. Mark the top side and then turn the fabric over and mark position of pins on the underside.

Tailor's chalk markings are also used in fitting.

When the garment is being fitted right side out, pin in any necessary alterations. Remove the garment, turn inside out and chalk mark the position of the pins on the wrong side of the fabric. Further instructions for fitting garments can be found in Chapter 8.

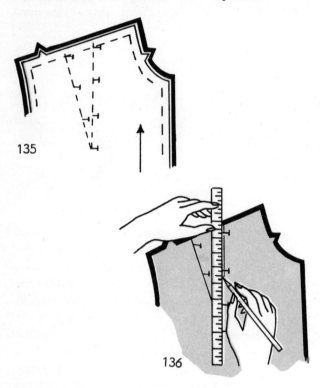

135

136

Clip Marking

This method is not recommended for beginners, since they are very likely to clip too far into the seam allowance. However, an experienced sewer may find the clip marks easy, since they can be done in the same operation with cutting the garment. Using sharp shears, take a small clip no longer than $1/8$ inch in the seam allowance with the point of the shears (137). This marking is used to identify centre front and back, top and bottom of pleats, tops of darts, tucks and fold lines.

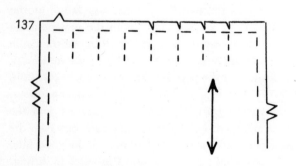

137

Basting

This is used for marking the centre front and centre back lines (138) and the straight lengthwise and crosswise grains at the cap of a set-in sleeve to help in fitting the garment and seeing that proper grain lines are maintained.

BASTING STITCH ALONG FOLD

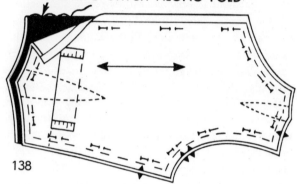

138

When it is necessary to transfer pattern markings from one side of the fabric to the other, use a machine- or hand-basting stitch. Buttonholes, placement of trimmings and pleats are often marked in this way. Test fabric first before machine-basting to be sure the stitching does not mark the fabric when basting is removed.

REMOVING THE PATTERN

After the fabric is completely marked, you are ready to put the parts of your garment together. Remember this is similar to doing a jig-saw puzzle. Unless the parts are joined correctly, the finished design will never appear as the artist or designer intended.

The thought and efficiency with which you work will influence the perfection of your garment and the satisfaction you receive from making it. Try to handle your materials as little as possible. Study the sewing guide and directions on pattern pieces carefully before the pattern is removed so that you know exactly what you are to do.

Some people prefer to leave the pattern pinned to each section until they are ready to work on it. Others like to remove all the pattern pieces before starting to sew, identifying each section of the garment by initialing it on the wrong side in tailor's chalk (SF for skirt front, BB for bodice back). If this method is used, be sure to identify the small facing pieces carefully since these tend to look alike. Mark the wrong side of your fabric if difficult to distinguish the right side.

The pattern should be removed carefully, folded neatly and returned to the pattern envelope. A pattern can be used several times if it is handled with care. Keep the envelope handy for ready reference in case a direction is not clear or a marking has become indistinct.

It will also be helpful if you keep all parts of a section together. Place them so that they may be joined without unfolding. This keeps the fabric in good condition. As soon as possible, hang up the various sections. Unnecessary wrinkles do not appear if this is done.

139   140

STAY-STITCHING

Many people find it helpful to stay-stitch edges which may stretch before the garment pieces are sewn together. It is especially useful if you can sew only for short periods of time, making it necessary to give your material more handling than is usually needed. On some stretchy fabrics, stay-stitching is absolutely essential.

Stay-stitching is simply a row of machine-stitching placed on a single thickness of fabric close to the seam line (139, 140). It holds those all-important grain lines of the fabric in position, and helps prevent curved and bias edges from stretching. It is not necessary to stay-stitch straight seams.

Using matching thread and a regulation machine stitch (12 to 15 stitches to the inch), stitch $1/_8$ inch from the seamline ($1/_2$ inch from edge for $5/_8$-inch seam allowance) in the same direction as the grain of the fabric. On McCall's patterns, the grain direction for cutting and stitching is indicated on the tissue pattern by small arrowheads printed on the seam line. Normally, stay-stitching is done from the wide to the narrow edge of a pattern piece. If you are in doubt about the direction of the grain of a particular area, rub your finger lightly along the cut edge. If the threads separate, you are rubbing against the grain; if the threads stay flat, you are rubbing with the grain. When the direction of the grain changes, as on deep necklines, collars, waistlines on circular skirts, stitch from one edge to the centre, lift the needle and cut the thread. Then stitch from the other edge to the centre, lift the needle and cut the thread.

Some fabrics will tend to slip and shift when stitched. In this case it is best to stitch each fabric piece to tissue paper. Place the tissue paper next to the wrong side of the fabric. Stitch through the fabric and tissue paper. Leave the fabric stitched to the tissue until the construction sewing has been completed. Gently rip the tissue paper away when finished.

CHAPTER 8

BLUEPRINT
FOR THE PROFESSIONAL

Throughout this book, you will find constant reference to the "professional-looking" garment . . . the kind you want to have. Defining the term, it means a garment that looks as if it came from the finest couturier house, even if it is a housecoat.

There are many factors which contribute to the professional look. The way you work is one important aspect; the originality you add to the design; the way you fit the garment to your figure for a made-to-measure appearance; and the careful pressing of each detail so that by the time the last stitch is made, the garment needs just a quick press to make it ready to wear.

This chapter is concerned with developing your professional aptitude and skills. Beginners take note. Start immediately to work like a pro. Veterans, check the suggestions. Many of them will simplify your work and help you turn out garments that completely satisfy your own desire for truly fine work.

To test your own professional skill you may want to make a dress, following the chart in this chapter. This outlines each step that gives a garment the look of having been made by an expert craftsman. Once you've followed this method, you can apply the principles you learn to every other garment you make. Soon you will be working with the skill and speed of the finest dressmakers.

THE PROFESSIONAL APPROACH

Sewing habits vary with each personality. Some seamstresses practically refuse to make a garment unless they can finish it at one sitting. Others have temperaments which allow them to sew only an hour or two at a time. The latter group is more likely to have a better looking garment; the former will have more garments in a shorter time. You have to establish your own philosophy, whether you want fewer garments of good quality in your closet or many garments of lesser quality.

Sewing, like any skill or art, takes planning and organisation if the results are to be satisfactory. Plan your sewing time, if possible. Always have all your equipment handy—pattern, fabric, notions, and, above all, have the ironing board, iron and all pressing equipment set up right at hand. It's too much of a temptation to think you can forget pressing a detail simply because it means going into another room or filling the steam iron. Pressing is absolutely essential to a good-looking garment.

If you are inclined to become bored or nervous at the machine, then plan to spend no more than two hours at a time. Organise your work into planned sessions. Fit the pattern at the first session, cut and mark at the next, stay-stitch and stitch the darts and press at the next, construct each section at a time throughout the next few sessions, working only until that first feeling of impatience, frustration or case of "nerves" sets in.

It is best to plan sewing time after other essential household work is done, so you can devote your mind to your sewing and not sit there feeling guilty because the dinner isn't started or the dessert made. You're likely to start making mistakes and just waste your time. Dress comfortably, and stay as neat as possible.

ASSEMBLING YOUR GARMENT

For beginners, the easiest and least time-consuming method for assembling a garment is to complete each type of construction process wherever possible before proceeding to the next. This may not be the procedure outlined in the Easy Sewing Guide for your pattern, but for the beginner, this system has certain advantages:

☐ Each construction process is a learning process and should be mastered before proceeding to the next.

☐ There is less chance of error when following only one process at a time.

☐ It is time-saving, since each process can be done with the same machine-stitch at the same spot. There is no running from the machine to the ironing board and back to the machine.

☐ Short amounts of time can be used to advantage when each construction process is done at one time.

Place a flat surface, such as a table, next to the sewing machine so you can lay all the garment pieces flat when you are not working with them. Working carefully and neatly is one of the secrets of a well-finished garment. Treat the fabric as you would the finished garment. Don't overwork it. Ripping needless stitching caused by not stitching correctly the first time, unnecessary handling and trying on, can make a garment look worn out before it is even finished.

Complete each construction process wherever possible during the assembling of your garment by using the following outline as a guide.

☐ Make all necessary pattern alterations.

☐ Straighten the fabric.

☐ Press the fabric.

☐ Fold the fabric for correct layout following the diagram on the Easy Sewing Guide.

☐ Lay all the pattern pieces on the fabric.

☐ Pin all pattern pieces securely on the correct grain of the fabric.

☐ Cut out all the garment pieces.

☐ Transfer all markings.

☐ Remove all tissue pattern pieces.

☐ Stay-stitch all curved and bias edges of each piece.

☐ Baste the construction details—darts, tucks, etc.— and the sections of the garment together and fit correctly before stitching permanently; chalk-mark corrections on wrong side of fabric.

☐ Stitch all darts, dart tucks, and pleats, fastening thread ends securely wherever necessary and cutting thread ends close to the fabric.

☐ Press lightly.

☐ Stitch all plain seams that can be stitched before a collar, pockets, etc., are applied.

☐ Finish seam allowances in appropriate manner.

☐ Press seams.

☐ Apply collars, sleeves, pockets and other garment details, studying the Easy Sewing Guide. There are some of these steps which must be completed before other seams are joined.

☐ After completion of the garment, give it a final pressing, or for tailored garments, send them to be professionally pressed.

The Easy Sewing Guide will not follow this procedure, because these guides are designed for seamstresses with some skill and experience. Most of the pattern guide sheets are based on a unit method of construction in which the bodice is completed, the skirt completed, the two joined and small finishing details such as zipper application and hems done as the last process. After you know basic sewing constructions, you may find that working with your garment in units is a quicker way of assembling it. You should try both methods and find the one which works best for you and gives you the most satisfactory looking garment.

To illustrate the method of assembling a garment

by completing each construction process before proceeding to the next, in the professional way, this Guide to Easy Sewing chart has been designed. This has been "use-tested" in a large number of schools

1 STEP I DARTS

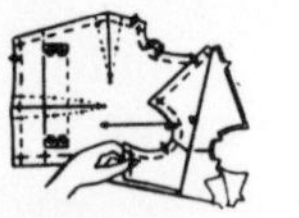

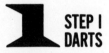

1. Remove pattern pieces from fabric.

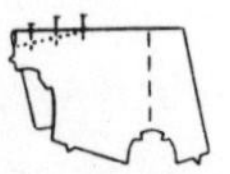

2. To make darts in bodice front, bodice back and sleeves, fold fabric, right sides together, on centre marking of dart. Match stitch-line markings accurately. Place pins at right angles to stitching line at each end of dart and then at centre.

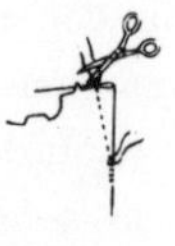

3. Stitch darts from wide end tapering to point. Remove pins as you stitch. Take three stitches along fold line at point. Reverse the stitching direction and stitch back three stitches on the original stitching line to fasten ends of thread. Clip threads at both ends of darts.

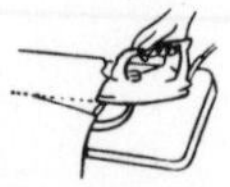

4. Press each dart. Use a tailor's ham and an iron regulated for your fabric. Press on each side of stitching, then press front darts toward centre front; back darts toward centre back; underarm darts toward waist; and sleeve darts toward wrist.

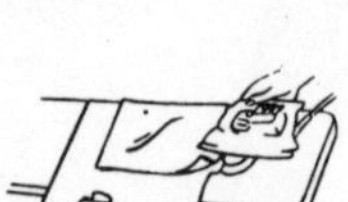

5. Finish by pressing on right side of fabric, using a press cloth. Always press with grain of fabric.

2 STEP 2 SEAMS

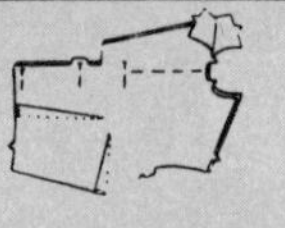

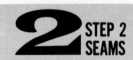

1. Place two front bodice sections together at centre front seam, right sides of fabric together, matching edges evenly. Place pin at lower edge at right angles to and directly on the seamline. Match and pin markings for end of centre front opening. Pin notches together.

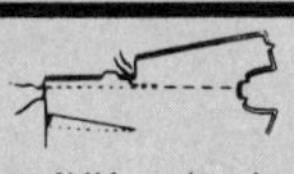

2. Stitch seam 5/8" from edge using 12 stitches to the inch and a seam guide. Stitch evenly and at a moderate speed from lower edge to marking for centre front opening. Remove pins as you stitch. Stitch back three stitches to fasten ends of thread. Clip threads at both ends of seam.

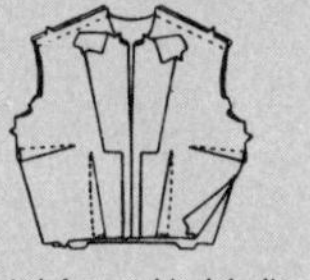

3. Pin and stitch front and back bodice sections together at shoulders, right sides together, stitching from neck edge to armhole. Clip threads at both ends of seams.

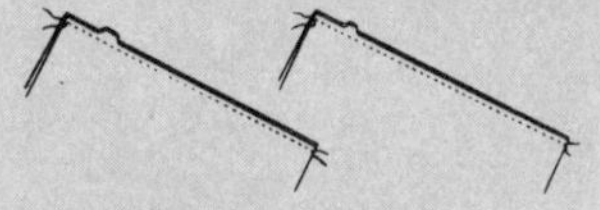

4. Pin and stitch front sections of skirt together along centre front seamline, right sides together, beginning at lower edge. Remove pins as you stitch. Clip threads at both ends of seam. Pin and stitch back sections of skirt together at centre back seamline in same manner.

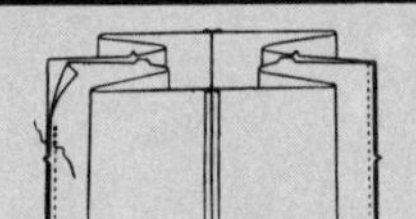

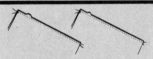

5. Pin front and back sections of skirt together at side seams, right sides together. Stitch left side seam from lower edge to marking for placket opening. Stitch back three stitches to fasten ends of thread. Stitch entire right side seam starting at lower edge. Remove pins as you stitch. Clip threads at ends of seams.

6. Edge Finishes:
Fabrics that do not ravel:
Trim edges with pinking shears, 1/8" from edge.
Fabrics that ravel slightly:
Stitch 1/4" from edge and pink close to raw edge.
Fabrics that ravel:
(a) Finish with machine zigzagging.
(b) Stitch close to edge and hand overcast.

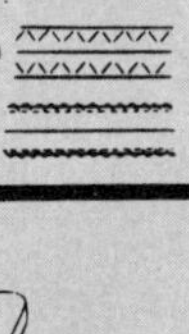

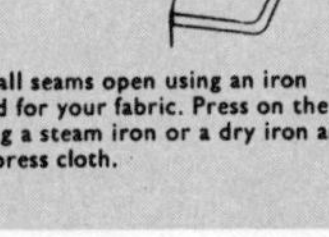

7. Press all seams open using an iron regulated for your fabric. Press on the wrong side using a steam iron or a dry iron and a damp press cloth.

3 STEP 3 COLLAR

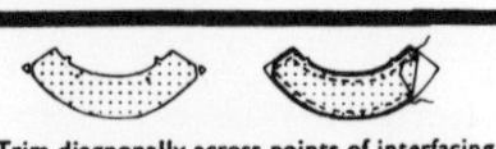

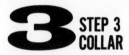

1. Trim diagonally across points of interfacing 3/4" from edge to remove bulk from corners. Baste interfacing to wrong side of undercollar.

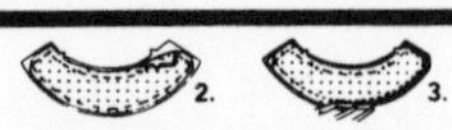

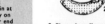

2. Pin undercollar to upper collar, right sides together. Match edges evenly. Stitch on seamline around outer edges, leaving neck edge open. Take a diagonal stitch across points.
3. To grade seam allowances: trim interfacing close to stitching; undercollar to 1/8"; and upper collar to 1/4". Clip curve at 1/2" intervals to seamline and trim diagonally across points, 1/8" from stitching line.

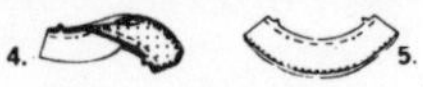

4. Turn collar to right side. Press seam allowance toward undercollar.
5. Understitch edge, stitching undercollar to seam allowance close to seamline between points. Stitch into points as far as possible. Draw threads to inside and tie ends. Clip threads.

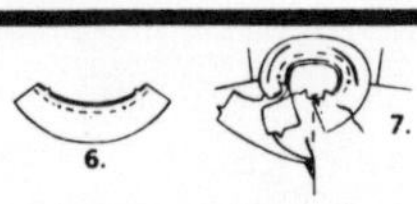

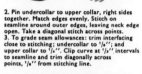

6. Press collar flat and baste neck edges together.
7. Pin collar to bodice at neck edge, right sides up, matching notches, centers and markings. Place pins at right angles to edge. Hand-baste in place.

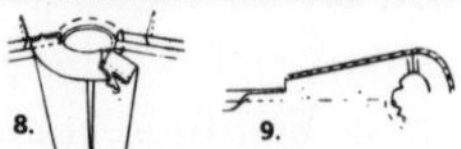

8. Stitch back facing to front facing sections right sides together, at shoulders. Clip threads. Trim seam allowances to 1/4". Press seams open.
9. Turn under 1/4" on unnotched edge of facing and hand-baste. Machine-stitch close to edge. Remove basting and press.

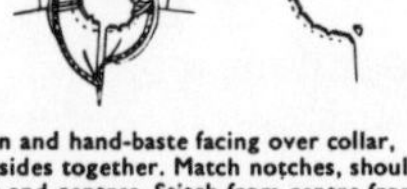

10. Pin and hand-baste facing over collar, right sides together. Match notches, shoulder seams and centres. Stitch from centre front opening around the neck edge. Tie ends of thread securely at front edges. Clip threads. To grade seam allowances: trim bodice to 3/8"; collar to 1/4"; facing to 1/8". Clip curve at 1/2" intervals to line of stitching. Trim diagonally across corners at front neck edge.

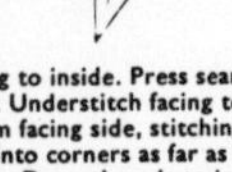

11. Turn facing to inside. Press seam allowance toward facing. Understitch facing to seam allowance from facing side, stitching close to seamline and into corners as far as possible at centre front. Draw threads to inside and tie ends. Clip threads.

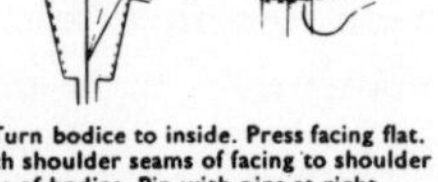

12. Turn bodice to inside. Press facing flat. Match shoulder seams of facing to shoulder seams of bodice. Pin with pins at right angles to edge of facing. Catch-stitch edges of facing to bodice seam allowances.

4 STEP 4 BOW

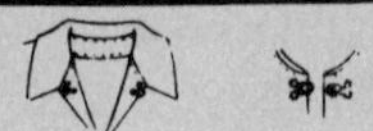

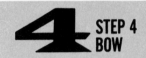

1. Close neck edge with hook and eye. Sew hook to inside right front edge with overhand stitches around the holes and three stitches across end of hook and through facing. Sew round eye to inside left front with eye extending beyond the edge. Use overhand stitches around holes and take three stitches across each side of eye and through facing.

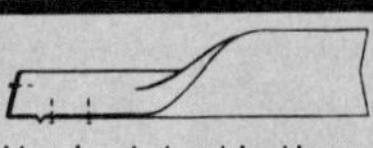

2. Fold bow lengthwise, right sides together, matching notches and cut edges. Pin edges together with pins at right angles to and directly on the seamline.

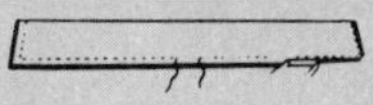

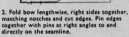

3. Stitch around cut edges, leaving a 2" opening at centre of bow for turning. Grade seam allowances and trim diagonally across points, 1/8" from stitching line.

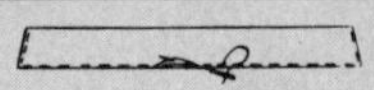

4. Turn bow to right side through opening. Pull out the corners with a pin. Baste along seam edges. Turn in the edges of opening and slip-stitch together. Press.

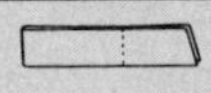

5. Fold bow in half and bring ends together. Match dotted lines and pin at right angles to line. Stitch together along dotted lines.

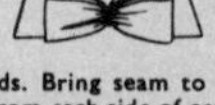

6. Spread ends. Bring seam to centre of bow. Gather 1/4" from each side of centre marking with a hand running stitch. Draw up gathers to 1 1/4" and fasten ends of threads.

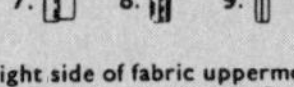

7. With right side of fabric uppermost, make pleat in knot on lines indicated. Baste in place along folded edge. Press.
8. Fold knot, right sides together, and match notches. Stitch a 3/8" seam along notched edge. Press seam open.
9. Turn knot to right side. Place seam at centre of knot and press flat.

10. With pleat on the outside, place knot over centre of bow.

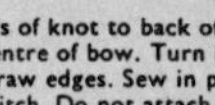

11. Bring ends of knot to back of bow. Sew one end to centre of bow. Turn in other end 3/8" and lap over raw edges. Sew in place with a hemming stitch. Do not attach bow until dress is finished.

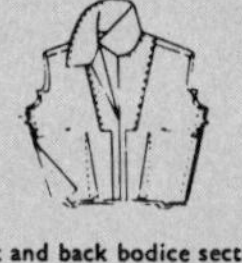

12. Pin front and back bodice sections together at underarm, right sides together. Stitch entire right underarm seam starting at armhole. Remove pins as you stitch. Stitch left underarm seam from armhole to marking for placket opening. Stitch back three stitches to fasten ends of threads. Clip ends of threads on both seams. Press seams open.

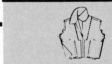

and has been proven to be of great help to students of sewing. Following the chart, you can hardly help turning out a garment that you'll be proud to wear anywhere (141).

5 STEP 5 SLEEVE

1. Stitch around top of sleeve on the seamline. Use 12 stitches to the inch from underarm to first notch; change to 6-8 stitches to the inch between notches; back to 12 stitches from notch to underarm seam.

2. Pin and stitch sleeve seam. Clip seam allowance to seamline at hemline marking. Press seam open using a sleeve board.
3. Turn up lower edge of sleeve on hemline and baste in place.

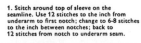

4. Pin sleeve into armhole, right sides together, matching underarm seams, notches, small dots and centre point of sleeve to shoulder seam.
5. Starting at centre point of sleeve, pull up bobbin thread until sleeve cap fits armhole. Pin and baste sleeve firmly in place.

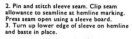

6. Shrink out any fullness in sleeve cap by pressing sleeve and armhole seams together from the sleeve side.

7. Try on bodice and check the following places for fit. Make any necessary adjustments.

. Waistline seam at natural waist and parallel to floor.
. Centre front seam and centre back basting line in middle of figure and perpendicular to floor.
. Side seams halfway between front and back and perpendicular to floor.
. Shoulder seams straight on top of shoulder.
. Bodice darts pointing directly to fullest part of bust.
. Sleeve seamline falls across tip of shoulder.
. Sleeve length is becoming.
. Neckline fits smoothly.
. Sufficient ease throughout for movement.

8. Stitch sleeve into armhole with sleeve uppermost on machine. Seam allowance at top of sleeve is turned toward sleeve and left turned up at underarm. Finish sleeve and armhole seam allowances separately.

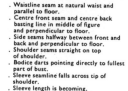

9. Turn under lower edge of sleeve ¹/₄''. Stitch close to folded edge.
10. Baste upper edge of hem to sleeve. Sew hem to sleeve with a tiny slip-stitch. Remove bastings. Press on a sleeve board.

6 STEP 6 WAISTLINE

1. In preparation for gathering the upper edge of the skirt, thread the top of the machine with regular sewing thread; bobbin with heavy duty thread. Adjust machine for 6-8 stitches per inch.

2. Stitch each of the four skirt sections separately. With right side of fabric uppermost, start at placket seamline and stitch along the seamline of upper edge of skirt to centre back seam. Leave ends of thread 2'' long. Place a second row of stitching ¹/₄'' above in the seam allowance. Leave ends of thread 2'' long. Stitch each of the other three skirt sections in this manner.

3. Cut waistline stay from woven edge seam binding using the waistline stay pattern. Transfer all pattern markings to the seam binding with carbon and tracing wheel.

4. Pin centre of waistline stay to seamline at upper inside edge of skirt. Place ends of stay even with placket edges. Match centre fronts and centre backs and place large circle at right side seam. The small circles are placed in line with notches on upper edge of skirt.

5. Pull up bobbin threads until gathers fit waistline stay. Adjust gathers evenly. At left front section of skirt, adjust gathers so that fullness starts ¹/₂'' from placket seamline. Baste stay to skirt.

6. Pin skirt to bodice, right sides together. Match placket edges, centre, notches and right side seams. Baste in place, being careful to keep gathers flat in seamline.

7. Try on complete dress. Pin placket opening on seamline. Check fit of waistline. Seam should be at natural waistline and parallel to floor.

8. Thread bobbin with regular sewing thread. Adjust machine for 12 stitches to the inch. Stitch waistline seam with the waistline stay uppermost. Clip threads. Remove bastings. Press seam allowance toward bodice.

7 STEP 7 ZIPPER

1. Pin left side opening closed, right sides together, matching waistline seams.

2. Machine-baste placket opening using 6-8 stitches to the inch.
3. Press seam open.

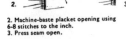

4. Attach zipper foot to machine and adjust to right-hand side of needle. Change machine stitch to 12 stitches to the inch. Open the zipper. Place face down on back seam allowance. Match bottom of zipper chain to beginning of machine-basting with teeth on seamline. Stitch zipper to seam allowance close to teeth from bottom to top. Sew through zipper tape and back seam allowance only. Clip threads.

5. Adjust zipper foot to left-hand side of needle. Close zipper and turn face up. Press fabric away from zipper forming a fold in back seam allowance along zipper. Stitch from bottom up through seam allowance and tape close to zipper teeth.

6. Spread garment flat and turn zipper face down over front seam allowance. There will be a small pleat at top and bottom of placket. Starting at seamline, hand-baste across top of zipper, down the front side and across the bottom.

7. Turn dress to right side. Adjust zipper foot to right-hand side of needle. Using the basting as a guide, stitch across the bottom of the zipper. Raise presser foot, pivot fabric, lower presser foot and stitch an even distance from the seamline to top of zipper. Raise presser foot, pivot fabric, lower presser foot and stitch across top of zipper. The top-stitching on the front of the zipper application should be an even distance from the seamline, and will be stitched through front of dress, front seam allowance and zipper tape. Pull threads to wrong side and fasten securely at each end of zipper. Clip threads.

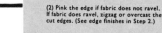

8. Press zipper application. Remove hand-basting and machine-basting from the seamline.

8 STEP 8 HEM

1. Put on the dress and the shoes to be worn with it. Stand in normal posture position with feet together. Have someone mark skirt at correct hem length for you, measuring an even distance from floor.

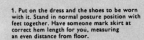

2. Take off the dress. Turn up hem on marked line. Baste close to folded edge. Press.
3. Mark width of hem using a ruler or hem gauge and trim hem allowance evenly.

4. The hem edge is finished according to the fabric.

  a. The turned and stitched hem is used on fabrics to be machine-washed.

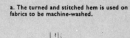

(1) Turn under the edge ¹/₄''. Stitch along folded edge, leaving just enough room to slip a needle through the fold when hemming the skirt.

(2) Baste upper edge of hem to skirt. Slip-stitch hem in place.

  b. The dressmaker hem may be used on all other fabrics.

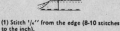

(1) Stitch ¹/₄'' from the edge (8-10 stitches to the inch).

(2) Pink the edge if fabric does not ravel. If fabric does ravel, zigzag or overcast the cut edges. (See edge finishes in Step 2.)

(3) Baste hem in place ¹/₂'' from the upper edge.

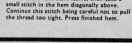

(4) Turn hem back so that folded edge of skirt falls along line of stitching on hem.

(5) Sew hem to skirt with a French hemming stitch. Working from right to left, pick up one thread of the skirt fabric, then take a small stitch in the hem diagonally above. Continue this stitch being careful not to pull the thread too tight. Press finished hem.

5. Sew bow to right front neck edge of dress with overhand stitches.

FITTING

The real reward of sewing your own is having a perfect fit in every garment you own. You can spend hours and hours doing meticulously careful construction, but unless it is properly fitted, the garment will not look professional.

Most of the fitting should be done in the pattern before the garment is cut out. Actual fitting of the garment should include only minor changes such as repositioning darts, slight taking in or letting out of seams. Until you become really expert at altering your pattern, you may find that you will have to do some fitting of the garment after it is cut and basted together.

To prepare a garment for fitting, be sure that all curved and bias edges are stay-stitched. Machine-baste the garment together before you do any permanent stitching. Use a non-matching colour thread so that you can see the basting when it is to be removed. This will eliminate the possibility of forgetting to stitch permanently a construction detail that is only basted. Never hand-baste a garment for fitting. The basting pulls and stretches and does not give an accurate fit. The garment always ends up tighter after it is stitched.

Stitch all darts, tucks and construction details and press them lightly. Don't press hard, since the markings may be difficult to remove if refitting is necessary. Machine-baste shoulder seams, underarm seam, and front and back seams of the garment. Pin up the hem of the skirt, and join the skirt and bodice together at the waist by overlapping the seam allowances and pinning along the seam line.

Put the garment on, right side out, over the undergarments you will be wearing with the finished garment. Always fit a garment right side out. Because the left and right sides of the body are never identical, one side may need to be fitted while the other may not. If there are noticeable differences between the right and left sides of the body, be sure not to fit the garment too snugly or the differences will be more apparent. Try to make the figure appear as symmetrical as possible. Wear the correct shoes, and have the correct width of belt if one is part of the design. Pin in shoulder pads if they are to be used. Fit suits over blouses or sweaters, jumpers over blouses or sweaters, jackets over blouses and skirts, and coats over dresses or suits.

Determine the fit of your garment by checking the following points:

☐ Sufficient fullness at all points for movement, standing, bending and sitting. A garment is not worn by a

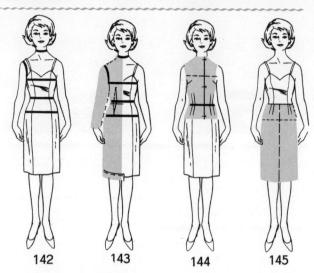

142   143   144   145

mannequin but by a moving figure and, therefore, must have ease allowance for this.

☐ Grain lines at bust, waist, hip and upper arm are parallel to the floor (142, 143).

☐ Grain lines at side seams, centre front and back are perpendicular to the floor (144, 145).

☐ Centre front and back seams are in the middle of the figure (145).

☐ Side seams are straight and placed halfway between the front and back.

☐ Shoulder seams lie straight across top of shoulder.

☐ Bodice length is correct above and below the waist and waistline seam fits snugly at natural waist. To find your natural waist, bend to the side and place your hand on bend. This is your natural waistline.

☐ Skirt is the most flattering length for your figure within the fashion range (143).

☐ Sleeve length is correct above and below the elbow, with centre elbow dart pointing to the tip of the elbow when the arm is bent.

☐ Bodice darts point directly to the fullest part of the bust (143).

☐ Hip darts point to the fullest part of the hip and end just above this point (145).

☐ Sleeve seam line lies across the outer edge of shoulder (142, 143).

☐ Neckline fits smoothly without pulling or gaping (144).

If any of these fitting points is not correct, the correction should be pinned in, removing the basting wherever necessary.

Fitting Shoulders

The area of fitting which is most important to the entire "hang" of a garment is the shoulder and neck area. Not only is it most important, it can cause the greatest difficulty in fitting. To help you fit the shoulders properly, here are suggested corrections for the most common fitting problems.

SLOPING SHOULDERS. Remove the basting at shoulder seam. Smooth up any wrinkles formed around the armhole and pin in a new shoulder seam, tapering from neck edge to sleeve edge. This makes the seam at sleeve edge wider than at neck edge to take care of the slope. When the garment is removed, the underarm will have to be lowered the same amount as was removed from the shoulder seam. Re-baste the shoulder seam and check the alteration.

SQUARE SHOULDERS. Open the basted seam, smooth out the wrinkles and pin in a new shoulder seam, tapering out from neck edge to sleeve edge. The sleeve edge will be the narrower end of the tapered seam. If a sleeve is to be inserted, the sleeve seam will have to be tapered also to fit smoothly in the enlarged armhole.

NARROW SHOULDERS. Move the sleeve about $1/2$ inch higher on the shoulder—taking a deeper seam allowance on the shoulder than in the sleeve. If this still doesn't take care of the extra width, then take small darts at mid-shoulder in both front and back bodice. For best results this alteration should be done in the pattern before the garment section is cut.

Fitting Necklines

Necklines are another area which cause some problems in fitting. Again, adjustments should be made in the pattern. If you failed to make adjustments, or the adjustments were not correct, you can do some fitting in the garment.

TIGHT NECKLINE. If the neckline is too tight, lightly chalk the correct depth on the garment and recut. Remember to recut the facing in the same way.

LOW NECKLINE. If the depth of the neckline is too low and the neckline is the jewel type, you might try adding a bias edging of the fabric to fill in around the neckline, or a shaped band or facing turned to the outside.

SCOOP NECKLINE. Scooped necklines the gap of which cannot be fitted very successfully once you have cut the garment: this alteration definitely should be made in the pattern. The shoulder seams can be about $1/4$ inch on each side of the neckline. If this doesn't correct the gaping, place a row of machine-basting around the neckline. Ease the fabric and shrink out the excess fullness until the neckline lies smoothly.

All scooped necklines fit better if the facing is cut slightly smaller than the neck edge, and the neck edge eased to the facing.

DEPTH OF NECKLINE. If in doubt about the depth of a neckline there is an easy way to test it before cutting your fabric. Cut the facing pieces from muslin or a scrap of fabric and stitch up the shoulder seams. Cut away the seam allowance on the facing neck edge. Put the facing on over your head and place the seams on the shoulder seams of the dress you are wearing. You will be able to see just where the neckline of the dress will come on you.

Final Alterations

After the correct fit has been achieved, remove the garment. Mark any corrections on the wrong side of the fabric by turning the garment inside out and marking the position of pins with tailor's chalk or white pencil. Remove the pins from the outside of the garment and re-pin along the markings on the inside. Baste the garment again, and check the fit. Keep checking until you are satisfied that you have a perfectly fitted garment.

Remove the basting wherever the construction seams meet or cross each other, or where it is necessary in order to stitch construction details. For example, the neckline may have to be finished before side seams are joined, so the side seam bastings will have to be removed.

For fitting slacks and shorts, check the section under Trews Alterations in Chapter 6. Complete instructions for pattern alteration and fitting procedure are outlined there.

PRESSING

Pressing is as important to the professional look as any sewing technique you will master. It is absolutely essential to the good looks of a garment. Keep your ironing board and iron as handy as your sewing machine, and as close to it as possible. Unless you are using drip dry fabrics, you should press each construction detail completely after it has been stitched before proceeding to the next step. Unless you do this, you will not be able to stitch the next step smoothly and evenly, and your garment will have a home-made look. Don't expect to correct everything with a final pressing. It just isn't the same. Once you recognise and accept the fact that time spent in pressing as you work is the best investment for a home dressmaker you are well on your way to becoming a professional.

However, if you are using wash-and-wear fabrics, finger-press a seam until you are sure the stitching line is in the correct place. Press marks are difficult to remove in this type of fabric.

Before you begin to press, read any pressing instructions given on the hang tag or on the bolt of fabric. Check the chart in Chapter 3 which gives special instructions for man-made fibres. Be sure you know the fibre content of the fabric. If you aren't sure what temperature will be best, or have neglected to find out the fibre content, then test a scrap of your fabric. Beginning with the lowest setting on iron, increase temperature until you can iron the fabric smoothly and easily. Always use a press cloth to prevent shine when necessary to press on the right side of the garment.

To press successfully, raise and lower the iron as you move across the fabric, using a gentle up and down motion. This will keep the fabric grain in its original position. Pushing the iron across the fabric will tend to stretch it and distort the grain. When pressing any bias sections which are easily stretched, move the iron in the direction of the straight grain. For example, in pressing a bias skirt, pressing diagonally with the grain will keep the hem edge even. If you press straight up from hem to waistline, the most bias sections of the skirt will hang longer at the hem than the portions cut on straight of grain.

Steam-pressing is necessary on almost all fabrics to achieve a professional-looking garment. Test a scrap of your fabric first to be sure that it does not water-spot. If it does, use an extra dry press cloth next to the fabric to prevent spotting. Press with a steam iron or a dry iron and a damp press cloth. The steam iron may be satisfactory for some fabrics, but many materials require more steam than you get from the home steam iron. A damp press cloth in addition to the steam iron may be needed, particularly in tailoring.

There are many commercial press cloths on the market but a piece of closely woven cheesecloth makes an excellent one. The texture allows the steam to pass through but the weave protects the surface of the fabric from shine. Wet half of the cloth and squeeze out the excess moisture. Fold the dry and wet sections together and wring the cloth to dampen both sides evenly. Use one, two or three layers of the cheesecloth depending on the amount of moisture you need for the area being pressed, but never place a really wet press cloth on your garment.

The bottom of the iron must be kept clean at all times. Starch and sizing collect on the surface of the iron and will mark fabric. When the iron is cool it may be cleaned off with soap and water. If the iron is warm, sprinkle scouring powder on wax paper and slide the iron over it.

Press the fabric and the tissue pattern pieces before pinning the pattern to the fabric since it is impossible to cut accurately when fabric or pattern are wrinkled. Press the pattern pieces with a dry iron; steam will shrink the tissue.

Cotton and Linen

Use a high temperature and press on the wrong side wherever possible. On light-coloured fabrics, you may be able to press directly on the right side. On dark colours, use a press cloth when pressing on the right side to prevent shine. To obtain flat smooth edges you will always need moisture and steam-pressing. Press all seams completely dry to avoid puckering.

Wool

Use a moderate temperature plus moisture—either a steam iron or a damp press cloth and a dry iron. Press on the wrong side as much as possible. Sometimes top pressing or pressing on the right side is necessary. To protect the right side of the fabric, use a dry wool press cloth under the damp press cloth. Press fabrics that shine easily over a needle board or cover the end of your ironing board with a piece of wool fabric. Moisture is very necessary in shrinking out fullness and shaping wool, but do not press a wool garment while it is wet. The garment will shrink and the elasticity of the fabric will be destroyed.

Silk

Use a medium temperature and press on the wrong side. Silk requires less moisture than other fabrics, and it water-spots easily. Always press with a dry press cloth or a piece of tissue paper next to the fabric to prevent water-spotting.

Man-Made Fabrics

Use a low temperature setting since most man-made fabrics melt or fuse at a high temperature. Repeated pressing of some white synthetics with too hot an iron will cause yellowing. Press on the wrong side as much as possible. If right-side pressing is necessary, protect the fabric with a press cloth. Test a scrap of your fabric for the correct temperature and for water-spotting before ironing your garment. If fabric water-spots, use a dry press cloth next to the fabric.

Blends

Press according to the directions for the most delicate fibre in the blend. Be sure to test a scrap of your fabric for the correct temperature setting and water-spotting before applying moisture or a steam iron to your garment.

Wash-and-Wear Fabrics

Use a steam iron or a dry iron and a damp press cloth. Be sure to try to press out the centre fold crease before cutting out your garment. If the crease will not press out, as is the case with some fabrics, re-fold your fabric and cut garment sections to avoid this crease mark. Press darts and seams lightly for the first fitting. Pressed creases are difficult to remove from these fabrics if changes have to be made.

Pile Fabrics

Velvet, velveteen and corduroy should be steam-pressed on a needle board to keep from matting and flattening the pile. Place the fabric face down on the needle board with a damp press cloth on wrong side to steam-press. If you do not have a needle board, stand the iron on end and place a wet press cloth over it. Holding the fabric lightly, draw the wrong side of the velvet across the iron. Be careful not to hold the fabric tightly as it will finger-mark.

A pile fabric garment can have the wrinkles removed most easily by hanging it in a steaming room. Turn on the hot water, and when the room is filled with steam hang the garment on the shower rod. After the wrinkles have disappeared, let the garment dry thoroughly before touching it. This steam-pressing in the shower is an excellent thing to remember when travelling. It takes the packing wrinkles out of most fabrics and saves having to carry a travelling iron.

Laminated Fabrics

Press on the wrong side of the fabric with a press cloth. Never touch the foam side with the iron. Use steam-pressing during construction. To press on the right side, use a damp press cloth and a dry cloth under it if the fabric shines.

Lace and Embroidered Fabrics

Press on the wrong side. To keep from flattening the design, place the fabric face down over several layers of Turkish towelling. Do not press on the right side or you will flatten the design.

During the construction of a garment, the pressing of each detail after stitching is essential to the final appearance. It is so much easier and more accurate to press and shape small areas of the garment as you work. Press on the wrong side as much as possible and use a press cloth. There are different methods of pressing and it is important that you use the correct one for the construction detail being pressed.

Seams

Press along the stitching line before pressing the seam open. Place flat sections on the ironing board and curved sections over a tailor's ham. Always put the wrong side of the fabric uppermost. Hold the seam allowances open with the fingers and press with the point of the iron along the stitching line. Avoid seam imprints by pressing over a seam roll or by placing strips of brown paper between the seam allowance and the garment. Press two or three inches at a time on a curved seam to avoid stretching the seam out of shape. If the seam allowances are to be pressed to one side, press the seam open first and then to the side to give a smooth, clean line.

Before joining seams where one section has to be eased to the other, shrink out the fullness in the eased section. After placing a line of stitching along the area to be eased, draw up and distribute the fullness evenly. Place the section over a curved surface such as a tailor's ham with the wrong side of fabric up. Steam-press along the seam allowance to the line of stitching shrinking out the fullness. Using the tip of the iron, press into the seam line over the ham to retain the curved shaping beyond the seam line. Press again after the seam has been stitched placing the curved area over the ham.

Darts

Press on both sides of the dart using the point of the iron along the line of stitching, then press the dart to one side over a tailor's ham. Press from the wide part of the dart to the point, shrinking out fullness at the point. If a ridge is formed by the fold of the dart on the right side of the fabric, slip a piece of heavy brown paper between the dart and the fabric. In bulky fabric, trim the dart $1/2$ inch from the stitching. Place over a tailor's ham and press the dart open along the seam, using the tip of the iron. Fold a triangle at the point of the dart.

Vertical darts, such as at waistline and shoulder, are usually pressed toward the centre front or centre back. Horizontal darts such as bust and elbow darts are pressed down.

Tucks

Place flat on the ironing board, right side up. Press along line of stitching on both sides of tuck with the tip of the iron, using a press cloth. Then press the tuck to one side, again using the press cloth. Turn to the wrong side and press along the line of stitching.

Press released tucks in the same way as regular tucks but do not press flat beyond the line of stitching.

Dart Tucks

Place over a tailor's ham with wrong side of fabric up, and press along the line of stitching. Then press to one side as for a regular dart. Turn to the right side. Press along line of stitching, using a press cloth. Do not press flat beyond the line of stitching.

Pleats

Place the basted pleats flat on the ironing board, right side up. Using a press cloth and steam, press lengthwise along the pleat folds. Turn to the wrong side and press the pleats in the same way. If the pleated section has a hem, press the pleats only to the hemline until the hem has been turned up. After the garment is completed, remove the bastings and press the pleats again on both the right and wrong sides. Use steam and a press cloth to remove basting thread marks.

Gathers

Place the gathered section on the ironing board, wrong side up. Smooth the fabric flat below the gathered section and press into the gathers with the point of the iron. Lift the gathered edge as you press into the gathers to keep from forming creases. Never place the iron flat along the line of gathering or you will form creases and destroy the full effect of the gathers. When one edge is gathered, press the seam allowance away from the gathered edge. When two gathered edges are stitched together, use a seam roll to press seam allowance open for less bulk.

Faced Edges

After the facing has been stitched to the garment, press the seam open with the tip of the iron wherever possible. Use the point presser to open seams in corners. Curved areas will have to be clipped and seams graded before seam can be pressed open. Understitch when necessary and turn facing to inside. Press flat along the edge with a damp press cloth for best results. Pressing the seam open first, and then pressing both edges in one direction, gives a flatter finish. On collars and faced edges, where the seam line should not show along the edge, roll the seam lines slightly to the underside and press in this position. Edges of wool garments can be flattened further by pounding the edges with a wooden clapper while there is still steam in the fabric. See Chapter 14 for full tailoring instructions.

Plackets

A zipper application should be pressed over a tailor's ham to retain the curve of the hip seam. Close the zipper. Press from the right side with a press cloth. Slip a piece of brown paper between the chain and the fabric to keep the imprint of the zipper from pressing through to the right side. Press to within an inch of the top of the closed zipper. Do not try to press over the bulk of the pull tab; open the zipper to press the top of the application.

Sleeves

Press the armhole seam line from the sleeve side with the sleeve and armhole seam allowances together. Place the seam line on the edge of the sleeve board and press several inches at a time. Continue around the armhole, pressing from the cut edge to the stitching line. Press in the same way with the garment side uppermost. Then press the seam allowance at the top of the sleeve into the sleeve, leaving the underarm portion turned up.

Press the lower edge of sleeves on the right side with a press cloth to retain the circular shape. If pressed on the wrong side, the inner facing or hem may become stretched, causing the lower edge to ripple.

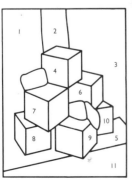

14 On the back of your pattern you will find reference to "materials with nap". These are fabrics with a pronounced pile, sheen or one-way design which will require special care in estimating the amount of material required and in placing the pattern on the material when cutting out.

1 and **2** Metallised fabrics. **3** Velvet. **4** Suedette. **5** Nylon fur fabric. **6** One-way patterned brocade. **7** Woollen velour. **8** Woollen facecloth. **9** Corduroy. **10** Mohair. **11** Ocelot fur fabric.

Fabrics by courtesy of John Lewis of Oxford Street Ltd.

15 Flame-resistant materials.
The number of young lives lost each year from fire is terrifying. Parental peace of mind may be bought for a negligible extra cost per yard. Choice is limited but will increase to meet public demand.
1 Dressing gown with Proban flame-resistant finish. **2** Printed cotton winceyette with Proban finish. **3** Teklan (available in made-up goods only). **4** Printed Clydella with Proban finish. **5** and **7** 100% woollen nun's veiling. **6** Printed cotton winceyette with Proban finish. **8** Fibreglass curtain material. **9** Shelley rug, made of flame-proof Dynel fibre.

Hems

After marking the hemline, place the garment wrong side up on the ironing board. Turn the hem along the markings and press the fold lifting the iron with each stroke. Do not push the iron along the folded edge. This will stretch and ripple the edge. After the hem has been trimmed evenly, press again in position. If the skirt is straight, press the hem flat working from fold edge to hem edge. If the skirt hem has fullness, place a gathering thread $^1/_4$ inch from the edge. Match the seams, then draw up the thread and distribute the ease evenly from seam line to seam line, until the hem fits smoothly. Use a damp press cloth to shrink out the fullness in the hem allowance. A heavy piece of brown paper placed between the hem allowance and the garment will prevent a ridge on the right side. Press again after hem has been finished

Final Pressing

If you have done a thorough job of pressing as you worked, the final pressing will be greatly simplified. This should be just a matter of pressing out wrinkles caused by working on the garment and touching up the edges to remove basting marks and any shiny spots.

Some people prefer to send their wool garments to the tailor for a final pressing, particularly with fabrics that are very difficult to press, since he has special steam and heavy pressing equipment. A tailor can flatten the seams and edges of your garment. However, he can never build in the shaping that you have lost by failing to press and shape as you work. He can improve an unpressed garment, but he can never give the garment a professional finished appearance unless you have done your work well.

CHAPTER 9

CONSTRUCTION DATA — STITCHES AND SEAMS

This chapter and the next few following contain complete instructions for all basic techniques of sewing. Beginners will find them helpful for describing in detail stitches of finishes which may be mentioned in a pattern guide sheet without specific directions. And even an experienced seamstress may discover that a brief "refresher course" will remind her of details she may have forgotten, or bring her up to date on techniques and methods that have been developed since she learned to sew. Remember that your success as a home dressmaker depends on how well you master the very elementary techniques.

MACHINE STITCHES

Machine stitches are divided into two types—straight (146) and zigzag (150). The straight-needle machine makes only straight stitches, unless a special attachment is used; whereas the zigzag machine can create both.

Regulation Stitch

This is the stitch (146) used for permanent stitching such as seams, darts and tucks. The length and tension of the stitch may vary according to the fabric used. (See page 67.) On most medium-weight fabrics, the regulation stitch is about 12 stitches to the inch; sheers require a finer stitch (16 to the inch); heavy or coarse fabrics generally take 8 to 10 stitches to the inch.

146

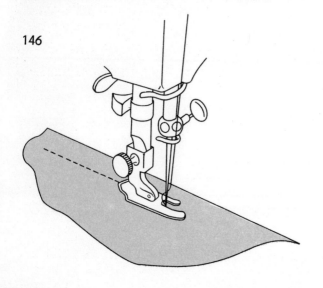

Basting Stitch

Basting stitches are used for temporary joining of sections or details which may require reworking when the garment is fitted or for marking. Use the longest stitch on the machine (6 to 8 per inch) and a contrasting thread (147) so that the markings and bastings are easily seen and easily removed. Use the same tension on the machine as you do for permanent stitching on your fabric. To remove basting, clip the needle thread every few inches and pull out the bobbin thread using small, sharp-pointed scissors.

147

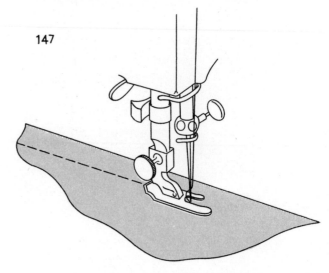

Stitching for Gathering

Sections which require easing or gathering should be stitched with a long stitch (6 to 10 to the inch) in matching colour thread. Leave long threads at the ends of the stitching (148). Anchor threads at one end around a pin, then pick up the bobbin thread at the other end and gently draw it up to form the amount of easing or gathering needed. The shorter stitch (10 to the inch) will form finer easing or gathering; the longer (6 to the inch) will create fuller easing or gathering. Sometimes a heavier thread is used on the bobbin.

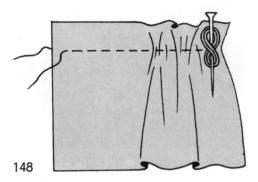

148

Stitching for Reinforcement

Areas where there is strain or a need for reinforcement, such as points of collars, cuffs, gussets, pointed faced openings of necklines, underarm seam of kimono sleeves, will need a finer, tighter stitch, usually 16 to 20 stitches to the inch (149).

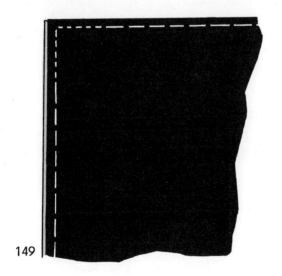

149

Zigzag Stitch

Automatic machines are capable of making the zigzag stitch but a straight-needle machine will require special zigzag attachment (150).

The zigzag may be used to stitch seams in jersey and loosely woven fabric with bias seams, giving greater elasticity which helps prevent seam splitting. It can also be used as a seam finish for edges that ravel by

stitching close to the raw edge or by overcasting the edge.

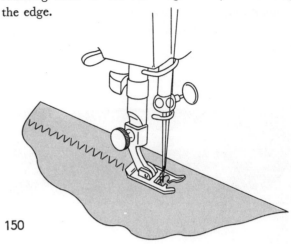

150

HAND STITCHES

Permanent hand stitches are usually worked from right to left unless the directions state otherwise (151, 152). If you are left-handed you may have to reverse the direction of the stitching. All the diagrams shown here are designed for a right-handed person. Begin and end any permanent hand stitches with tiny back-stitches on the wrong side of the garment to hold threads securely.

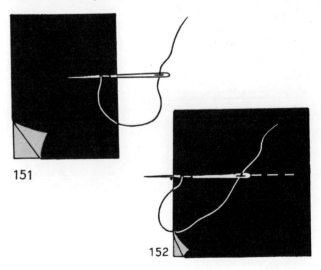

151

152

Running Stitch

This is the simplest form of hand stitch (153) p. 124. It is used for gathering, quilting, mending, tucking and seams that do not require much strain. For easing and gathering, take stitches $1/16$ to $1/4$ inch in length, pass the needle through the fabric several times and then pull the needle through. Continue across gently easing the fullness. For a permanently stitched seam use tiny stitches $\frac{1}{16}$ to $\frac{1}{8}$ inch in length. Do not draw the thread up; keep it flat and smooth in the work. On sheer fabrics use the tiny $\frac{1}{16}$-inch stitch; on heavier woollens a $\frac{1}{8}$-inch stitch may be the smallest you can make.

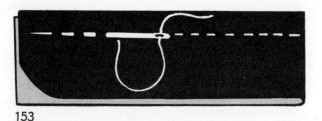

153

Basting Stitch

A basting stitch is used to hold two or more pieces of fabric together temporarily, to transfer construction symbols from wrong to right side of fabric and to indicate guide lines. Use a contrasting thread so the basting stitch can be easily identified when permanent stitching is made and the basting is removed. The stitch is a larger version of the running stitch, about $\frac{1}{4}$ to $\frac{1}{2}$ inch in length, depending on the weight of the fabric and how securely the pieces of fabric should be held together (154, 155).

EVEN BASTING. Used when there will be some strain on the seam. Make stitches about $\frac{1}{4}$ inch long, even on both sides of fabric (154).

154

UNEVEN BASTING. Used in seams where there is little or no strain or as a guide line for stitching. Take long stitches on one side of fabric and short stitches on other side (155).

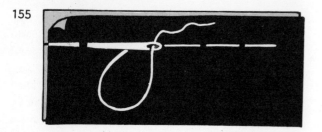

155

DIAGONAL BASTING. Used to hold several layers of fabric securely together. Stitch through the fabric at right angles to the fabric edge (156). This gives a diagonal stitch on the upper side and a short horizontal stitch on the underside. It is used to hold interfacings, linings and facings in place during fittings.

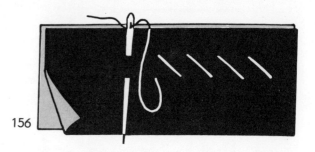

156

SLIP-BASTING. Most often used when matching seams in plaids or stripes or to baste alterations made on the right side. Fold under the seam allowance on one side of the seam and press flat. Then place this over the other section of the seam, right sides up, matching accurately at the seam line and pin. Place the needle through the seam line on the underside and back through seam line (157). Take stitches about $\frac{1}{4}$ inch in length. Place the needle through the seam line fold and out on the fold line. Continue in the same manner. No stitches will show on the right side, while on the wrong side there is a regular basting stitch.

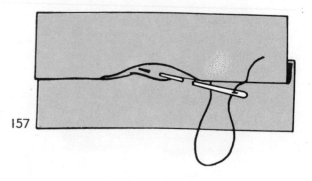

157

Back Stitch

Back-stitching is used to stitch a seam securely or permanently. It looks like machine-stitching on the right side (158), but stitches overlap on the wrong side. Take a small running stitch ($\frac{1}{8}$ inch long) through the fabric on the underside. Take a stitch back, placing the needle in the fabric at the beginning of the first stitch and bringing it out a stitch ahead. Continue in this manner working across the fabric.

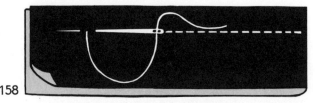

158

Half Back-Stitch

Used as a decorative stitch. The needle is carried back only half the length of the first stitch (159). This looks like a running stitch on the right side, but stitches overlap on the wrong side.

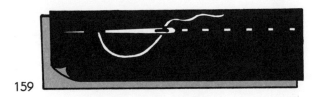

159

Prick Stitch

A variation of back-stitch and half back-stitch, the prick stitch is used for applying zippers by hand. The needle is carried back only one or two threads of fabric (160).

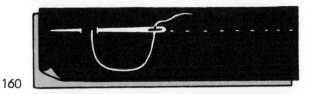

160

Slip-Stitch

The slip-stitch is used when stitching should not show, but it isn't very strong. It differs from the slip-basting stitch in the length of the stitches. Place a stitch through the fold of fabric (161) about $1/8$ to $1/4$ inch in length. Pick up only one or two threads of the under fabric. Continue in this manner taking a stitch through the fold and then in the under fabric.

161

Hemming Stitch

A slanting stitch which shows on the wrong side and is stronger than the slip-stitch. Used for all types of hemming. Take up one thread of the garment fabric and then bring the needle through the fold of the hem edge (162). Stitches should not show on the right side.

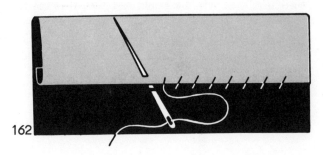

162

Catch-Stitch (Herringbone)

This is a fairly loose but secure stitch used to hold raw edges of facings and interfacings. Working from left to right, take a small stitch through the upper fabric from right to left, then pick up one or two threads in the under fabric from right to left. Do not pull the stitches tight. The threads will cross each other between stitches (163).

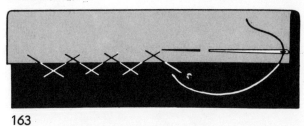

163

Invisible Stitch

Sometimes called the French hemming stitch. This stitch is used for hems and for attaching facings and interfacings in tailoring. Fold hem or facing back on garment. Working from right to left, pick up a thread of the garment, then pick up a thread of the hem or facing diagonally above. Do not pull stitches tightly (164).

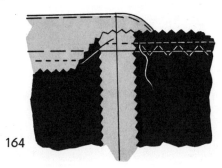

164

Overhand Stitch

This is used when a strong, secure and invisible seam is needed. It is often used on table linens, to sew on lace, to patch and for hems. Fold and press back the two seam allowances and place the fabrics right sides together with seam lines matching (165). Place the needle through the back fold and then through the front fold, picking up only one or two threads each time. Bring the needle out diagonally to the left. This produces a straight stitch. The stitches are kept close together.

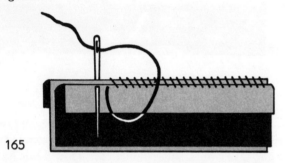

165

Whipping Stitch

This may be used in place of the overhand stitch, since it serves the same purpose, or in tailoring. The only difference between the two stitches is that the whipping stitch produces slanting stitches, taking stitches over the edge (166) with needle in a straight position. Again, take only one or two threads of fabric.

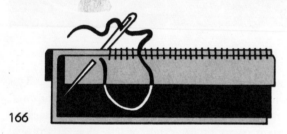

166

Overcasting

This stitch may be used on raw edges, either single or double, to prevent them ravelling. Take stitches over the edge with the needle held in a slanting position.

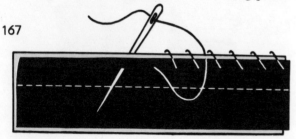

167

Stitches should be close together and an even distance apart. Keep the depth of the stitches uniform (167).

Pad Stitch

This stitch is very similar to diagonal basting stitch (156). It is a shorter stitch, and the underside of the stitch is much shorter, catching only one or two threads (168). It should be almost invisible on the outside. It is used to tack interfacing to collars and lapels of tailored garments. (See page 253 for instructions on using this stitch in a tailored garment.)

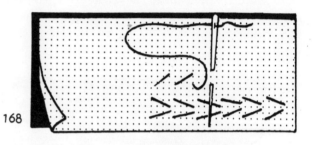

168

SEAMS

Pinning

Although it is possible to stitch seams without pinning them, this requires a great deal of skill and control. Normally, seams are joined first with pins, then basted or permanently stitched. To pin plain seams correctly, place the two pieces to be joined together evenly on a flat surface. Insert pins at right angles to the seam line with the pin holding the two fabrics securely together along the seam line (169). This prevents the two fabrics from shifting on the seam line while you are basting or stitching. Place a pin at each end, matching edges, and then at the notches before pinning the remaining area.

169

If you are working with an eased seam, pinning will be slightly different (170). Place the fabrics together with the section to be eased on top toward you. Place pins at right angles to the seam along the seam line. Put them very close together leaving slight fullness between pins in the eased section (170). This can be done easily and evenly if you roll the fabric over your finger as you join the two sections with the pins.

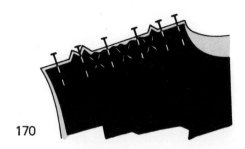

170

When you pin a crossed seam (where two or more seams cross each other), first be sure the stitched seams match. Place a pin through the middle of the stitched seams at the seam line and place pins on either side of seams on the seam line (171).

171

To pin a lapped seam, turn under the seam allowance on the section to be lapped and place it in position. Place pins at right angles to the fold edge close to the fold through all thicknesses (172).

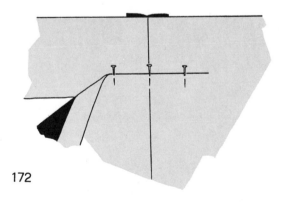

172

Stitching

Usually a pinned seam is taken directly to the sewing machine and either machine-basted or permanently stitched. If it is a seam which will not require addi-

tional fitting such as a centre front seam, or the joining of a facing to a neckline, it is permanently stitched. Seams which may need refitting should be machine-basted. In either case, you'll want to remove the pins as you stitch. Most machines are equipped with a travelling foot which rocks backwards and forwards over the pins, so an entire seam can be stitched and the pins removed after stitching. However, this is not the best method, since many fabrics may require slight easing of the top layer because the two thicknesses do not travel through the machine at exactly the same rate. When a seam is pinned such fabric is likely to bunch at the pins, unless it is carefully eased. It is better to stitch slowly, removing each pin with your right hand just before it reaches the edge of the machine foot (173). Keep a pin cushion handy on your wrist or at the right side of the sewing machine, and place the pin in it as soon as you remove it from the fabric.

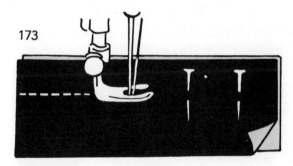

173

DIRECTION OF STITCHING. Seams should always be stitched so that both ends and edges match accurately. Stitch on the exact seam line indicated by the pattern piece. Usually this is $^5/_8$ inch unless otherwise noted. Stitch seams in the direction of fabric grain just as you cut and stay-stitch with the grain (174, 175).

174

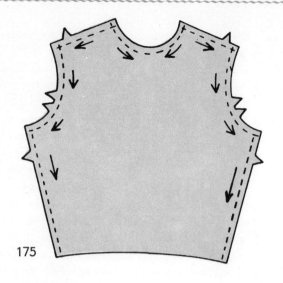

175

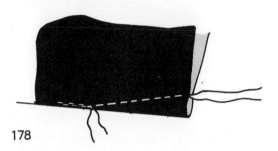

178

Take several stitches back over the stitches in the seam by adjusting the machine for back-stitching. Since you must stitch directly back over the seam, it is easier to turn the machine wheel by hand to do these back-stitches (178).

SECURING ENDS. When stitching seams or darts permanently, the machine-stitches should be secured at each end. There are several ways to do this. At the end of a seam, the needle and bobbin threads can be clipped, leaving enough thread to tie the two together several times in a knot (176).

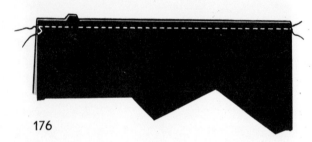

176

When stitching does not reach an edge, the two threads can be pulled to one side of the fabric and tied securely in a firm knot. To do this, gently pull the bobbin thread until the loop of needle thread is visible. Catch this with the end of a pin and pull it through, so both threads are on the same side of the fabric (177).

Very skilled seamstresses may wish to try the lock-stitch. However, if this is not done accurately, the needle thread may jam in the bobbin case of the machine. Practice several times on a scrap of fabric before trying it on a garment. To do the lockstitch, leave the needle in the fabric at the end of stitching. Raise the presser bar very slightly (this is the tricky part—the presser bar must be raised just the slightest bit), hold the fabric securely, and take several stitches right over the last stitch.

After threads have been fastened securely, clip the ends close to the fabric, using very sharp scissors. Be careful not to clip the fabric. You may find the little thread clippers suggested in Chapter 5 very helpful for this operation. Do not neglect clipping these threads. The garment will look much neater, and further sewing will be easier, since there will be no loose threads to catch in other stitching or on the presser foot.

Trimming

In working with a pattern, you'll find that you will have to trim many seams. This means that you cut away both allowances to an even width. Seams are trimmed to reduce bulk, particularly at faced edges (179).

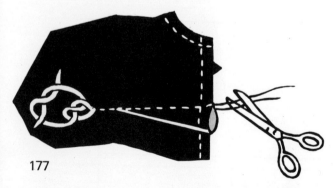

177

Back-stitching is an excellent way to secure threads, but it does require a little practice at the machine.

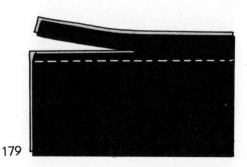

179

Grading

Grading a seam allowance means that the layers of fabric are cut to different widths, with the wider seam allowance next to the outside fabric. When there is an interfacing joined in a seam, trim this close to the line of stitching. Grading eliminates a ridge being formed by the bulk of several layers of fabric in a seam allowance (180).

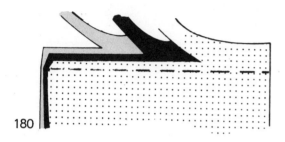

180

Clipping

Most curved seams, such as necklines, princess seam lines, collars, kimono sleeves at the underarm, require clipping in order to make the seam lie flat. On an inward curve, grade seam allowances and clip to the stitching line about $1/4$ inch apart (181). On outward curves, grade seams and make notches to line of stitching about $1/4$ inch apart (182).

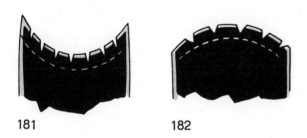

181   182

Types of Seams

In garment construction there are several types of seams. The type to use in a garment is determined by the fabric and the design of the garment. For example, if you are working with a sheer fabric, you'll use a French seam which won't show through the sheer fabric. When making a man's sports shirt, the flat-fell seam is used since it is stronger and will hold up under the stress given this sort of garment. You should know the various types of seams and how to construct them, as well as where they are commonly used in a garment.

PLAIN SEAM. The seam most frequently used to join two sections of fabric. Pin two pieces of fabric, right sides together, and stitch (183). Sometimes backstitches are used for this joining. Press seam open and finish seam edges.

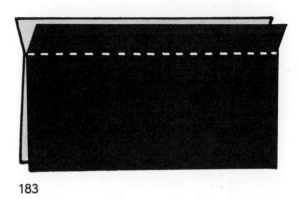

183

PLAIN EASED SEAM. When two pieces to be seamed together are slightly unequal in length, the longer piece must be eased to the shorter. Although this easing provides shaping for a curved area of the body, the seam should appear smooth. It is often found at the bust, elbow and shoulder seam of a garment. To construct the seam, place a row of long stitches (6 to 10 to the inch) on the seam line of the longer piece of fabric between the markings for easing. Pull up the bobbin thread of this row of stitches until the seam edge of the longer piece is the same length as the shorter one. Distribute the ease evenly and steam-press to shrink out any fullness at the seam line. Pin the two pieces together and stitch the seam, keeping the eased seam on top as you stitch (184).

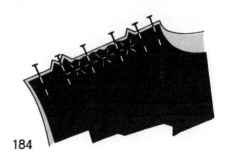

184

PLAIN SEAM JOINING BIAS PIECE AND STRAIGHT PIECE. If one section of fabric to be joined at a seam is bias and the other on the straight grain, place the bias section on top; ease if necessary and stitch with the bias section up toward you (185). To control stretching of bias seams, place woven seam binding along the seam line and stitch the tape to the seam as you are stitching the seam (202).

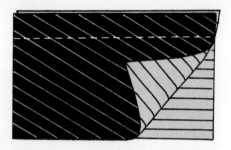

185

PLAIN SEAM JOINING NAPPED FABRIC AND SMOOTH FABRIC. When one section to be joined in a seam is napped and one is smooth fabric, place the smooth section on top. Stitch with smooth fabric up toward you (186).

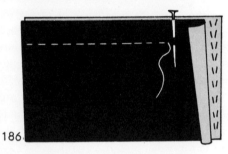

186

PLAIN SEAM, TOP-STITCHED. A top-stitched seam not only adds a decorative effect to a garment, it also provides a strong seam construction. It is similar in appearance to the lapped seam. Stitch a plain seam (183) and press the seam open first, then press both seam allowances toward the section to be topstitched. Place a row of stitching close to the seam line, stitching on the right side of the garment through both seam allowances (187).

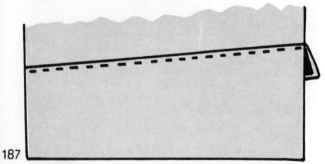

187

PLAIN SEAM, DOUBLE TOPSTITCHED. This seam is mainly used for a decorative trim, although it does provide a strong seam. Stitch a plain

seam and press the seam open. Top-stitch on the right side an equal distance on both sides of the seam line (188).

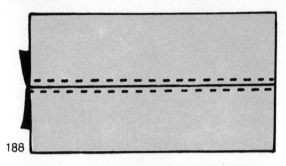

188

LAPPED SEAM. This seam is most often used for yokes and applied pieces such as gussets. One section is lapped over the other and top-stitched (189). Fold under the seam allowance on the section to be lapped and press flat. Place the sections together, right sides up, matching the fold to the seam line accurately and baste in position. Stitch close to the folded edge through all thicknesses.

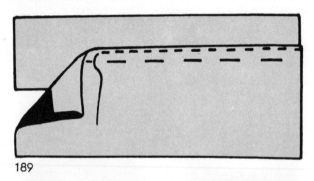

189

SINGLE LAPPED SEAM. This seam is used for joining seams in interfacings and interlinings because it gives the least possible bulk. Seam allowances are lapped one over the other, matching seam lines. Stitch on the seam line and trim both seam allowances close to stitching (190).

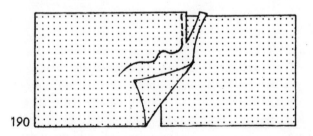

190

TUCKED SEAM. This is a decorative seam finish. The lapped seam is stitched back from the edge to form a tuck (191).

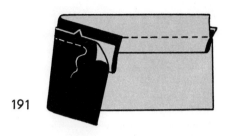

191

WELT SEAM. This seam is similar in appearance to the flat-fell seam on the right side. It is also good for heavy fabrics since it gives a smooth, flat finish without the bulk of a flat-fell seam. First stitch a plain seam, press it open, then press the seam allowances toward one side. Trim the underneath seam allowance to $1/4$ inch and press the other seam allowance over trimmed edge. Stitch close to the raw edge (194).

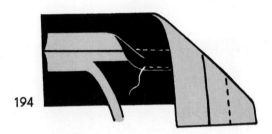

194

FLAT-FELL SEAM. This strong, sturdy seam construction is used for sportswear, men's sports shirts, children's clothes and pyjamas. Garments which will receive a great deal of stress or must withstand repeated washing will be sturdier if constructed with flat-fell seams. However, avoid using the construction on bulky fabrics; the seam is thick and difficult to construct in a heavy, bulky fabric. Place the pieces to be joined wrong sides together, and stitch a plain seam (183). Press the seam to one side and trim the lower seam allowance to $1/8$ inch (192). Turn under the raw edge of the other seam allowance and place over the trimmed edge. Stitch close to the folded edge through all thicknesses.

DOUBLE WELT SEAM. This seam construction for the double welt seam is the same as for the welt seam. It does give a sturdier seam construction, and gives the same appearance as the flat-fell seam. The only difference between this and the welt seam is an additional row of stitching placed close to the seam line through all thicknesses (195).

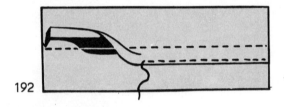

192

195

HEMMED-FELL SEAM. This seam is similar to the flat-fell seam and begins with a plain seam (183) on the wrong side. The under layer is trimmed to $1/8$ inch and the upper edge is turned under, pinned and slip-stitched by hand (193), catching only a single thread of fabric. This eliminates machine-stitching on the right side and gives an inconspicuous finished seam on the wrong side.

FRENCH SEAM. This is a particularly good seam for sheer fabrics and is used for infants' clothes because it leaves no unfinished seam edges. Place the fabrics, wrong sides together, and stitch a plain seam $3/8$ inch from the edge. Trim the seam allowances to $1/8$ inch or less. Turn the garment with right sides together and press flat at the seam line. Pin and stitch on the regular $5/8$-inch seam line marking (196). In infants' clothing, this seam construction is often done by hand.

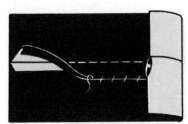

193

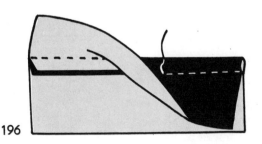

196

MOCK FRENCH SEAM. This seam is similar in appearance to the French seam and is often used in similar fabrics. It is easier to construct, especially in curved seams, such as those of set-in sleeves. First stitch a plain seam (183), with right sides of the fabric together. Turn in the raw edges of the seam allowance $^1/_4$ inch toward the centre seam line. With the folded edges meeting, stitch them together close to the folded edge (197).

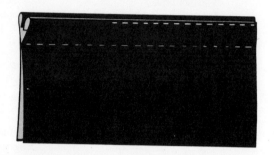

197

FRENCH SEAM WITH ONE EDGE HEMMED. This seam is used on bodices and areas of a dress made of sheer fabric that requires fitting. Make a plain seam (183). Trim one edge to $^1/_4$ inch. Turn under raw edge of other seam allowance and hem by hand along stitching line (198).

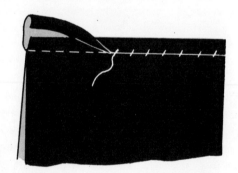

198

SLOT SEAM. This is primarily used as a decorative seam because of the tucked effect which results (199). The pattern may have slot seams as part of the design detail, or you may wish to devise your own, using the seam on yokes, side skirt seams, sleeves, pockets. A strip of fabric is placed under the seam. It may be the same fabric or a contrasting colour or fabric, and may be cut on the straight of the goods or on the bias. To construct the seam, turn under the seam allowances on the seam line and press flat. Cut a strip of fabric on the desired grain, the length of the entire seam, and approximately $1^1/_2$ inches wide. Place a row of basting stitches down the centre of the

strip. With right sides up toward you, place the seam line folds so they meet exactly at the centre basting line. Baste in position close to the folded edges. Top-stitch through all thicknesses an even distance from each side of the centre marking to produce the desired width tuck.

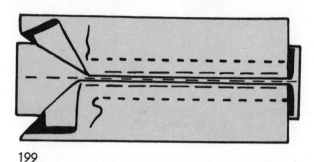

199

PIPED SEAM WITHOUT CORD. This is a decorative seam often used in neckline seams with a facing and at the waistline. Use a folded bias strip of fabric, ribbon, bias tape or braid. Place it on the right side of one section of the fabric with the fold extending the desired amount beyond the seam line toward the main part of the garment (200). Baste. Place the other section in position, right sides together, and stitch seam. Press seam allowances to one side.

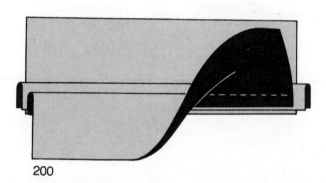

200

PIPED SEAM WITH CORD. This is also used as a decorative finish, and is similar to the piped seam without cord (201). Encase the cording inside a bias strip, using the zipper piping foot. (See page 233.) Place the piping on right side of one section of the fabric to be joined, with the stitching on the piping matching the seam line. The piping should face toward the main part of the garment. Baste. Then place the other section in position, right sides together, and stitch, again using the zipper foot on the sewing machine. Press seam allowances to one side. If the seam is bulky, grade the seam allowances (180).

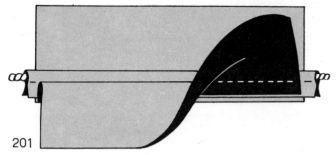

201

Special Problems

TAPING A SEAM. When a seam must be very sturdy, or when it must be prevented from stretching, the seam is usually taped (202). This is often necessary with waistline seams and shoulder seams, or when stitching bias seams in loosely woven fabrics. Place a strip of woven seam binding with the centre of the binding on the seam line. Stitch in position at the same time you are stitching the seam.

202

SEAMS IN INTERFACING. Seams in interfacing are lapped, stitched and trimmed to eliminate bulk. See instructions for the Single Lapped Seam on page 130.

STITCHING SEAMS OVER TISSUE. In fabrics such as jersey, sheers, or smooth, slippery fabrics which tend to slip, stretch or pucker, or if the feed dog of the machine mars your fabric, you should stitch through tissue paper. Place a piece of tissue under the fabric, and another on top. After the stitching has been completed, tear the tissue away (203).

203

SEAMS WITH INWARD CORNERS. When applying a facing to a square neckline, or at any point where there will be an inward corner in the seam,

stitch to within $1/_2$ inch of the point, change the length of the stitch to a short stitch (14 to 16 to the inch) and stitch to the point (204). Raise the presser bar, pivot, lower presser bar and stitch for $1/_2$ inch. Change back to the normal stitch length and continue the seam. Grade the seam allowances and clip diagonally through seam allowance to point.

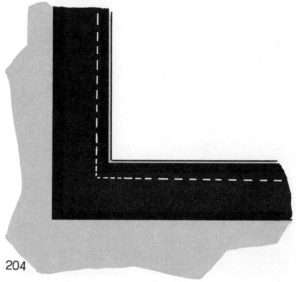

204

SEAMS WITH OUTWARD CORNERS. In collars which have outward points, or any part of the garment where two pieces are seamed to form an outward corner, stitch to within $1/_2$ inch of point, shorten stitch to 14 to 16 to the inch and stitch to point (205). Raise presser bar, pivot, lower presser bar, take two stitches across point, raise presser bar, pivot, stitch for $1/_2$ inch, then adjust to normal stitch length. Grade seam allowances; clip diagonally across point close to stitching; clip diagonally on each side of point.

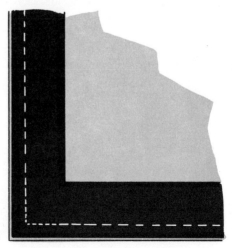

205

Seam Finishes

No garment is complete unless the raw edges of seams are finished. This prevents ravelling, and gives the garment a neat appearance on the inside. The type of finish to use will vary according to the fabric and the design of the garment. For example, fabrics which hardly ravel at all can be finished merely by pinking the edges. Those which are very "ravelly" and bulky, loosely woven fabrics need a more secure finish. Unlined jackets need a very neat finish since the inside of the jacket is often on display.

PINKED OR SCALLOPED EDGES. For fabrics that are firmly woven and do not ravel, a pinked or scalloped edge is sufficient. Using pinking or scalloping shears, cut along the raw edge. Hold shears firmly and cut with long even strokes (206, 207).

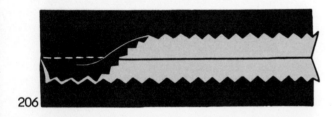
206

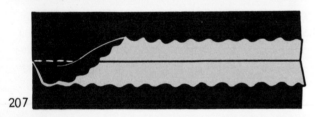
207

EDGE-STITCHED EDGES. To finish a seam for fabrics that ravel slightly, machine-stitch $1/8$ inch from the raw edge (208). To give a more secure finish, machine-stitch $1/4$ inch from the edge, and then trim $1/8$ inch from the edge with pinking or scalloping shears (209).

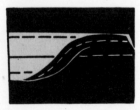
208

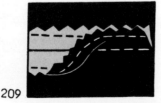
209

ZIGZAGGED EDGES. For fabrics that ravel and need a secure finish, zigzag stitch close to the raw edge, using an automatic machine or a zigzag attachment (210). The depth and width of the zigzag stitch is determined by the weight and closeness of the weave of the fabric. Use a smaller stitch on firmly woven fabrics and a wider stitch on loosely woven fabrics.

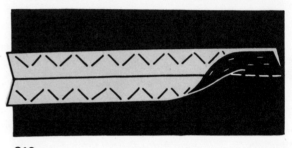
210

OVERCAST EDGES. A hand finish similar to the zigzag is made by the overcast stitch (211). Take small, even stitches over the raw edge and be careful not to pull the stitches tight. If the seam has been stitched with both seam allowances to one side, overcast both edges together (212). A row of machine-stitching close to the raw edge serves as a guide for keeping overcasting stitches even.

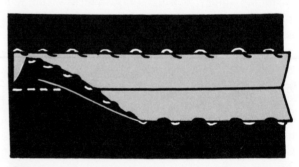
211

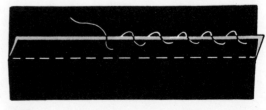
212

TURNED AND STITCHED EDGES. The turned and stitched edge finish is used for non-bulky fabrics. Fold under the raw edges $1/4$ inch and then machine-stitch $1/8$ inch from the edge (213).

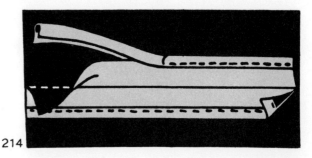

214

213

BOUND EDGES. For heavy or bulky fabrics, the edges are bound with woven or bias seam binding depending on whether seam is straight or curved (214). Fold and press the tape so that the under section is $1/16$ inch wider than the upper section. Having the under edge just slightly wider will help ensure stitching through both edges of the binding. Place the binding over the edge and machine-stitch close to the edge.

ROLLED EDGES. On sheer fabrics, a trim finish is the rolled edge. Stitch a plain seam, press both seam allowances to one side and trim to $3/8$ inch. Roll both seam allowances together, using your thumb and forefinger, to the line of stitching. Sew over the edge close to the line of stitching with a whipping stitch (215) Keep stitches evenly spaced and do not pull tight

215

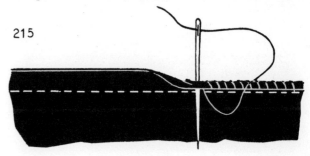

CHAPTER 10

CONSTRUCTION DATA

In garment construction you work in three dimensions. You not only join sections, but you shape them to fit the curves of the body. There are various ways that garments are shaped, depending on the amount of curve needed in the garment and the design of the garment. Shaping is formed by curved seams, darts, tucks, pleats and gathers. Then, to help your garments hold their shape, you apply facings, interfacings and linings.

DARTS

Darts are the most frequently used shaping construction. In fact, you'll seldom make a garment that doesn't have some sort of dart shaping in it. Darts are placed on the garment so that the rounded fullness they produce is at the fullest part of a body curve. For example, bust darts should point to the fullest part of the bust; waistline darts in a bodice should also point toward the fullest part of the bust and end about 1 ½ inches below; hip darts should end just above the fullest part of the hip; elbow darts should point toward tip of the elbow when the arm is bent; shoulder darts should point toward the shoulder blades.

It is best to machine-baste darts in your garment before you stitch them permanently. Since the placement of the darts may vary according to the contours of your individual figure, adjustments may be necessary when fitting the garment.

Darts should always be pressed over a curved press mitt or ham to give the proper curve to the garment. Waistline darts and shoulder darts are pressed toward the centre front or centre back. Bust and elbow darts are pressed down. When pressing any dart, place the dart over the curved cushion, wrong side up. Press along each side of the stitching, in the direction of the stitching, then press the dart to one side (216). Reverse the garment and press it on the right side. Be sure your garment will take the direct heat of an iron — if not, use a pressing cloth (217). Additional tips on pressing can be found in Chapter 8.

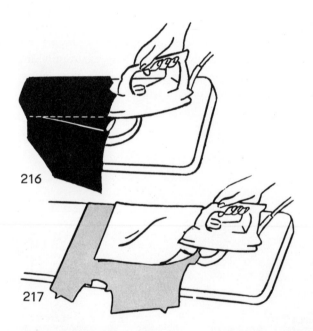

Dart constructions, like seam constructions, vary according to the area they are to shape and the design of the garment. The most frequently used dart constructions are:

Standard Dart

Fold the dart on the fold-line marking, right sides of fabric together, matching stitching line markings accurately. Pin in position, placing pins on the stitching line at right angles to it (218). Baste, if you wish. Stitch, beginning at the wider edge, to the point taking the last two or three stitches directly on the fold (219). This is extremely important in order to eliminate a tuck at

HOW A PATTERN IS CREATED

From McCall's film

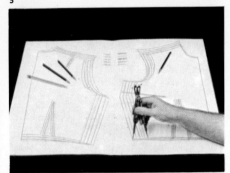

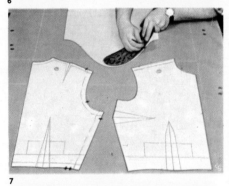

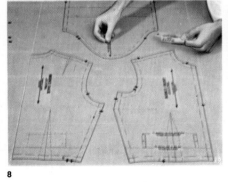

1 The pattern is designed, and sketched with several variations.

2 The finished sketch.

3 In the design department, the pattern maker cuts out and pins up the pattern in muslin, using a dressmaker's model.

4 After approval, the muslin dress is sewn up, as shown on sketch, with variations.

5 From the muslins, a manilla pattern is cut and stamped with the necessary markings.

6 The pattern is graded to all sizes within the size range.

7 The manilla pattern is placed under tracing paper and reproduced.

8 Printed markings are added to the tracing. The finished tracing is printed.

9 The fabric editor chooses suitable fabrics and widths for the suggestions on back of the pattern envelope and the coloured artwork is completed for the front cover.

10 The instruction sheet for making up the garment is worked out and printed.

11 The pattern, envelope and instruction sheet is printed.

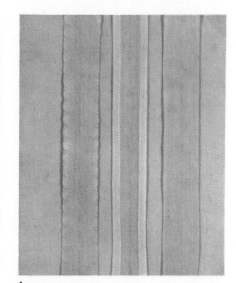

AUTOMATIC MACHINE PROCESSES 1

1 Buttons and buttonholes.
2 Invisible hemming for all garments.
3 Tucks for dresses, blouses, children's clothes.
4 Seam neatenings for all garments.
5 Narrow hem, run and fell seam, attachment of lace edging, machine rolled hem.
6 Decorative lace insertions for lingerie.
7 Decorative lace insertions with machine embroidery, for dainty blouses and dresses.

Photograph by courtesy of Singer Sewing Machine Company Ltd.

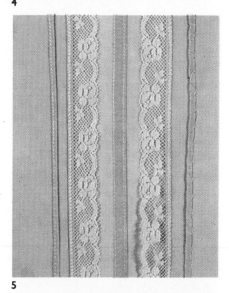

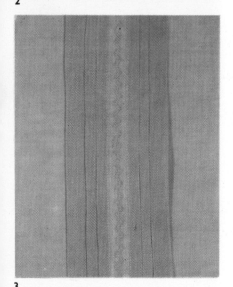

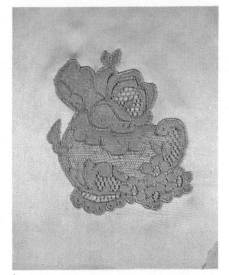

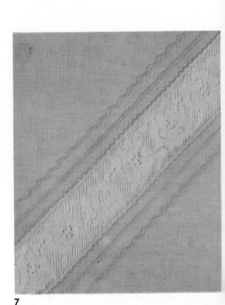

1

2

3

4

5

6

7

the point. Fasten thread ends. Press the dart flat to one side.

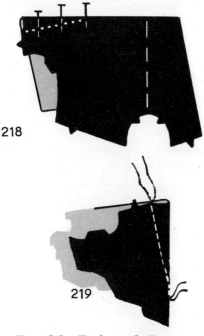

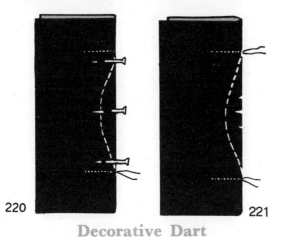

Double-Pointed Dart

Begin stitching at either point, taking several stitches directly on the fold at both points (220). Fasten thread ends. Cut several small clips to the line of stitching in the centre section of the dart to allow it to spread and lie flat (221). Press dart flat to one side.

Decorative Dart

When darts are used decoratively they are stitched on the right side of the fabric and, therefore, should be stitched without any thread ends at the point. To do this, the machine must be threaded with the bobbin thread. Remove the spool thread from the needle and thread the needle with the bobbin, going through the eye in a reverse direction from normal threading. Tie the bobbin thread to the spool thread (222) and wind

the thread on the spool until sufficient bobbin thread, twice the length of the dart, has been threaded on the upper section on the machine. Mark the dart as for the standard dart but fold with wrong sides of the fabric together. Start stitching exactly at the point and continue to wider edge. Re-thread the machine for each dart.

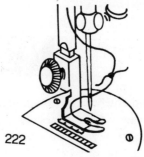

The Dart Tuck

This is often referred to as a "released dart" because fullness is released at the wider end. It is often used in blouses to give shaping at the waistline and fullness at the lower edge. On the wrong side of the fabric, mark the stitching and fold lines and also a short straight line at each end of dart tuck (223). Fold right sides of fabric together on the centre marking, matching stitching lines accurately. Pin or baste in position. Starting at point, take several stitches on the fold and then stitch to wide edge, pivot, stitch straight across the fold edge (224). Fasten thread ends at both ends and press.

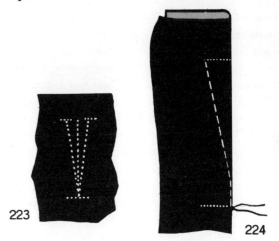

Slash-Gathered Dart

This dart gives added fullness and shaping. Mark on the wrong side of the fabric. Reinforce the point by stitching with a short machine-stitch (14 to 16 stitches to the inch) on the seam line marking (225), approximately $1/2$ inch each side of point; slash to point. Place a row of medium-length machine-stitches (9 to 10 stitches to the inch) on the longer or lower side of dart between the markings for ease of gathering (225). Pull up these stitches until the two edges are the same length. Distribute the fullness evenly. Pin with right

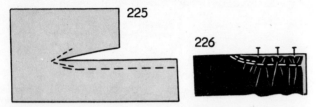

sides together and stitch as for standard dart (218). Press to one side away from fullness (227). If it is an eased dart, steam-pressing into fullness will shrink out the fullness at the line of stitching (228). If it is a gathered dart, press into gathers with point of iron being careful not to flatten gathers. For added reinforcement and decoration, top-stitch through all thicknesses close to seam edge (228).

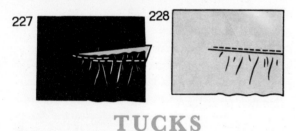

TUCKS

Tucks can be used to hold fullness in place or for a decorative effect. If tucks are part of a pattern design, the pattern will indicate the width and spacing between the tucks. If you are designing your own tucking as a decorative part of a design, you'll have to determine the width you want and space them yourself. First decide where the tucks should be placed on the figure, then how wide and how far apart you want them. They can be used in groups or clusters and in graduated widths. Tucks may be made by hand or machine, using the tucker attachment. Tucking the fabric before cutting the garment section may prove easier since you can work with a straight piece of fabric.

To make tucks, use a tracing wheel and dressmaker's carbon or chalk pencil for marking. Tailor's chalk or tacks do not provide as accurate, sharp lines. Make a gauge by cutting a heavy piece of cardboard several inches longer than the width of the tucks. Mark the width of each tuck by cutting a notch in the cardboard; cut another notch the distance between tucks. Crease or press fabric along the fold lines of

the tucks, using the gauge as a guide. Keep the creases on grain. Hand-sew with a fine running stitch if you do not plan to machine-stitch the tucks (229). Sometimes the fold line of a tuck may be marked by pulling a thread from the fabric.

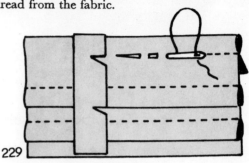

There are several methods of tucking, depending on the effect desired:

Pin Tucks

Small fine tucks usually found in dainty infants' clothing or sheer blouses. After marking and creasing on a single thread, stitch very close to fold edge (230). On sheer, firmly woven fabrics such as organdie, you can pull out a single thread and crease on this line.

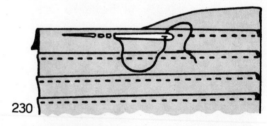

Piped or Corded Tucks

Give additional decoration to a garment since they have the added dimension of thickness. The width of the tuck is determined by the thickness of the cord used. The tuck must be wide enough to encase the cord securely. Measure and mark for tucks. Place cording on the wrong side of the fabric at centre of tuck and form tuck over cord. Sew close to cording with fine running stitches or use the cording foot on the sewing machine. (231)

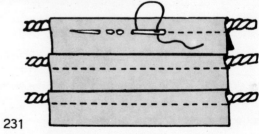

Shell or Scalloped Tucks

A very decorative tuck made by hand. Mark and crease for a straight tuck. On the line of stitching, mark the position for the shell tucks at even distances. Sew the tuck with small running stitches to the first dot. Take an overhand stitch at the dot and pull the thread tightly. Continue across in this manner. (232)

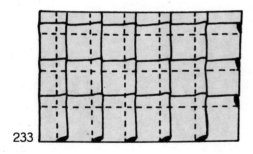

232

Cross Tucking

This type of tucking is done on the fabric piece before the garment is cut. Measure, mark and stitch all tucks on the lengthwise grain of the fabric. Press all tucks to the side in one direction. Measure, mark and stitch tucks on the crosswise grain. Press all crosswise tucks in one direction (233).

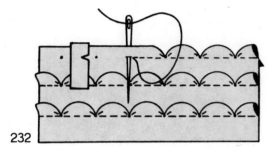

233

Group Tucking with Scalloped Effect

Should be done on the fabric before the garment is cut. Measure, mark and stitch the tucks, placing them close together. Press to one side. Mark the fabric at even intervals in the opposite direction for the crosswise stitching. Stitch across the tucks in the direction they were pressed. Then stitch in the opposite direction, stitching tucks down away from the direction in which they were pressed. Continue stitching, alternating the direction of the tucks in each row. The quilting guide will help to keep the rows of stitching straight and an even distance apart (234).

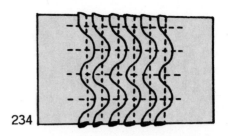

234

Released Tucks

Often used to give shaping to a garment, as well as for decorative effects. Usually they are folded and pinned on the marking lines with the right sides of the fabric together. Starting at the bottom of the tuck, stitch to the top. For reinforcement, pivot at the top of the stitching and stitch straight out to the fold line. Back-stitch and clip threads (235).

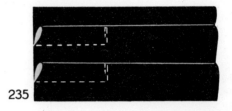

235

PLEATS

Pleats form folds in the fabric and give fullness and shape to a garment. Unpressed pleats are those which do not have the pleat crease line pressed in place and are used to create a rather soft effect. Pressed pleats have the crease line firmly pressed in position the entire length of the pleat. This gives the garment a crisp, tailored look. Usually the pattern will indicate the type of pleat to use, but sometimes it may be left to your discretion. Your choice should depend on the effect you wish and the fabric you're using. For example, a soft drapable fabric which does not retain a crease will be best with unpressed pleats, while a very crisp fabric with little drape to it should have the pleats pressed flat in position. If you select pressed pleats, test your fabric to see how well it will hold a crisp, pressed crease line.

Mark the wrong side of the fabric for pleats with tracing wheel and carbon. If the pleats are to be inverted or box pleats, use one colour for the solid lines which mark the fold and another for the dotted lines which indicate where they meet. This makes it easier to determine in which direction the fold should be laid.

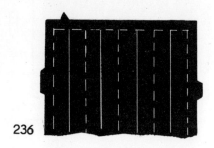

236

After the fabric is marked, place it on a smooth, flat surface, and pin the pleats into position. Be sure they lie smoothly and are on the straight grain of the fabric. Press them into position. Hand-baste (236) each pleat starting at the lower edge and working to the top. Stitching down will stretch the fabric and pleats will not hang straight.

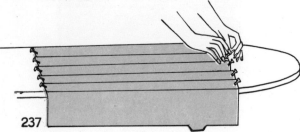

237

When the pleats are to be pressed into position (237), put the hem in the skirt before pressing them. Otherwise, you'll have to remove the crease lines on the hem portion, or they'll be folded in the wrong direction and the hem will be bulky.

Side or Knife Pleats

This type of pleat is the simplest pleat to form. The folded edges either face in one direction around the garment (238) or the direction is reversed only at centre front and centre back pleats.

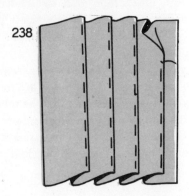

238

Box Pleats

A box pleat is formed by two side pleats which turn toward each other on the wrong side forming a panel on the right side of the fabric (239). McCall's patterns will clearly mark in which direction each fold of the pleat is to go. Follow these guide arrows carefully.

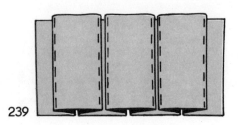

239

Inverted Pleats

A pleat formed by two side pleats which turn toward each other on the right side forming a panel on the wrong side of the fabric (240).

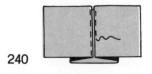

240

Edge-Stitched Pleats

A special finish used to retain a perfect crease (243). It adds a trim look to tailored pleated skirts and holds the pleat in position. It is particularly necessary if the pleating is done on the bias grain of a flared skirt. Simply form the pleats as directed, press and baste in position. Machine top-stitch close to the folded edge beginning at the bottom and stitching to the top. The hem has to be put in the garment before pleats are edge-stitched.

Stitched-Down Pleats

Stitching helps to produce a smooth flat fit over the hipline in a pleated skirt. Baste the pleats in position close to the fold edge through all thicknesses of the skirt, keeping underfolds of pleat free. Measure down from the waistline to the fullest part of the hip, and mark this position evenly on the pleats around the skirt. Top-stitch the pleats close to the fold edge from the hip marking to the waistline (241). Stitching in this direction will retain the proper grain of the fabric and will keep the pleats in proper position. Fasten the threads securely at the hipline on the underside of the garment. Remove the basting and press.

There is also a stitched-down pleat that is stitched on the inside of the pleat so that no top-stitching shows.

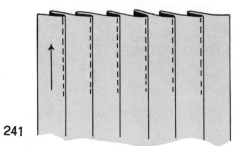

241

Stitched-Down Edge-Stitched Pleats

This type of pleat is a combination of the stitched-down pleat (242), which is also edge-stitched (243). Press and baste pleats in position. Machine top-stitch close to the folded edge beginning at hem edge to marking for hipline where pleat is to be stitched to the skirt. Lift presser foot, pull fabric out slightly and cut bobbin thread only. Rearrange pleat over garment, rewind spool of thread to take up slack and continue stitching along folded edge of pleat up to waistline.

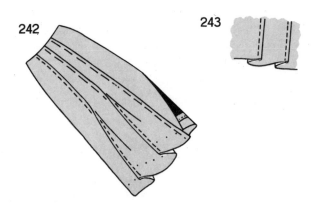

242   243

Accordion Pleats

Accordion pleats are the very tiny pleats made on a straight lengthwise grain of the fabric which spread out in the shape of an accordion fold. These can only be done successfully by a commercial pleating process. The amount of fabric needed for this pleating should be supplied to the commercial pleater. Hem skirt before having pleating done. Check at department stores for this service.

244

Commercially Pleated Fabric

Pleating can often be purchased in skirt lengths, and is usually priced per inch purchased. Make sure you purchase it wide enough to fit over the hip (with pleats lying flat) plus seam allowances (246). Place a row of long stitches (8 to 10 to the inch) across the top of the pleats (245), and gently draw up the bobbin thread, easing it to fit the waistline (246). If you wish, you may have your own fabric commercially pleated. To prepare fabric, allow three times hip measure taken at the widest part. Join all seams but one, and hem the skirt. Finish it after the pleating has been done. Again, check at department stores for this service.

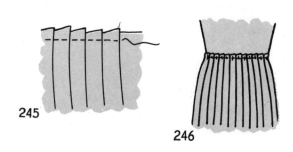

245

246

Cartridge Pleats

Cartridge pleats are round pleats used for decoration (247). A large section of fabric is stitched to a smaller section. The undersection is marked into even spaces. The upper section is marked with the same number of spaces but they are wider. Baste and stitch the upper section to the lower section, matching the marking lines exactly. Do not press.

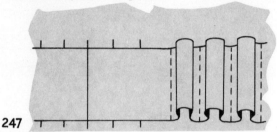

247

Hemming a Pleat with Seam

After the pleat has been made (248), turn up the hem and mark position of hem at seam allowance (249). At that point, clip the seam allowance to the line of stitching. Press seam allowance open in hem. Turn up and hem skirt (250). Press pleat in position.

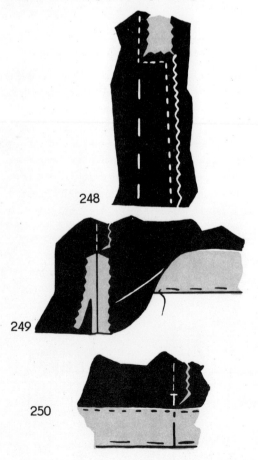

248

249

250

Inverted Pleat with Underlay in a Seam

Stitch seam to marking for pleat and machine-baste below marking. Press the seam open. Pin underlay in position, right sides together, matching edges and seam lines. Stitch the side seams of the skirt and underlay. Press flat. Baste underlay to garment along top seam line (251). Stitch through all thicknesses (252). Remove basting. Hem using the method for hemming a pleat with seam.

251   252

Inset with Inverted Pleat

Stay-stitch on seam line of opening for inset (253a). Clip to the seam line at each point. Turn the seam allowance to inside, using stay-stitching as guide (253b).

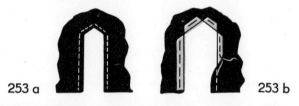

253 a   253 b

Baste close to the edge. Fold and baste the pleat in the inset piece. Place in position on garment matching edges and seam line accurately (253c). Baste in position through all thicknesses. Turn garment to right side and top-stitch close to the edge (253d). Press. Remove bastings.

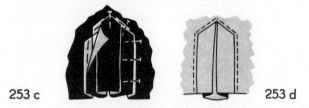

253 c   253 d

GODETS

Godets are flared or pleated inserts used for decorative effect or to give added width to the bottom of a skirt.

Inserting a Godet

Stay-stitch along the seam edges of the godet piece (254a). Reinforce the opening of the garment by stitching on the seam line where the inset is to be joined, taking one stitch across the point (254b). Use a regular machine-stitch for your fabric and matching thread. Slash through the centre of the opening as far as the stitched point. Pin the godet inset to the opening, right sides together, matching the seam lines accurately. The seam allowances on the opening taper from a normal seam allowance width at the bottom edge to almost nothing at the point. Baste together along the seam line (254c). Stitch the seam taking only one stitch across the point. Press the seam allowances to one side toward the main part of the garment.

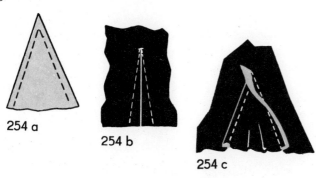

254 a

254 b

254 c

Inserting a Godet with Top-Stitching

Stay-stitch the godet inset section (255a), and reinforce the opening as described above. Turn under the seam allowance of the opening along the seam line, using the reinforcement stitching as a guide (255b). Baste close to the edge and press flat. Pin the godet section in position, right sides up, matching the seam lines of the inset to the folded seam line edge of the garment. Baste the inset in position close to the folded edge. Top-stitch in position through the garment and seam allowances close to the folded edge (255c). Remove the bastings. Press.

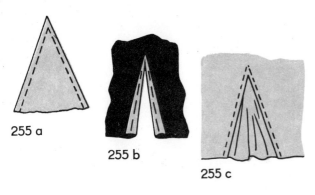

255 a

255 b

255 c

GATHERING AND SHIRRING

Gathering and shirring are perhaps the most popular methods of controlling fullness in a garment. Gathering is one or two rows of stitching drawn up to form very tiny pleats in the fabric. Shirring is three or more rows of gathers.

When either gathering or shirring, it is important that the fullness be distributed evenly throughout the entire area. When pressing, press with the tip of the iron directly into the fullness. Pressing on top will flatten the fullness and spoil the effect.

By Machine

Gathering or shirring by machine is the easiest and quickest method. Adjust the machine to the longest stitch and loosen the top tension slightly if bobbin thread does not pull easily. Place a row of machine-stitching on the seam line for gathering with another line close to it. For shirring, place several rows of stitching under each other about $1/8$ inch apart (256). Pull the top threads through to the wrong side of the fabric and anchor the threads at one end securely around a pin (256). Distribute the fullness evenly by pulling bobbin thread from the other end.

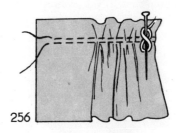

256

By Hand

You can gather or shirr by hand, if you prefer. To gather, fasten the thread securely with several tiny back-stitches. Sew on the gathering line with small evenly spaced running stitches. Pull up the thread and distribute the fullness until the section measures the desired length (257).

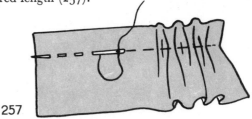

257

Shirring by hand is done the same way, except there are several rows of stitches (258). Be sure stitches are placed directly under one another. After all rows have been stitched, the threads are drawn up at the same time until the section measures the desired length (259). Anchor the threads around a pin at each end of the stitching and distribute the fullness evenly.

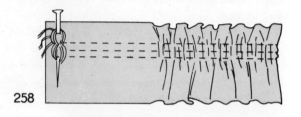

258

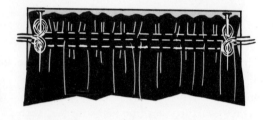

259

On a Large Area

When large sections are to be gathered or shirred, as in a full gathered skirt, divide the section to be gathered into quarters or eighths and mark each with a pin or small clip marking. If the sections will later be attached to a smaller section such as a bodice, also divide the bodice into quarters or eighths. Place two rows of machine-stitches along the top of the section

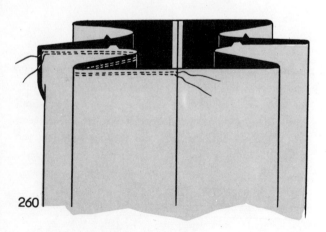

260

to be gathered (260), about $1/4$ inch apart. Use the longest stitch on the machine and loosened tension. Break the stitching at the end of each quarter or eighth section, leaving long thread ends. Pin the section to be gathered to the smaller section, matching the quarter or eighth markings on each. Pull up threads until the two sections measure the same. Fasten threads securely by winding them around a pin. Distribute fullness within each section evenly. If you use heavy-duty thread for the bobbin thread, the construction will be easier because the thread will not break so readily.

With Machine Attachments

The ruffler attachment is also capable of gathering large sections of fabric. Test it on a scrap of fabric; adjust the length of the stitch and tension until you obtain the desired amount of fullness. The longer the stitch, the greater the fullness; the shorter the stitch, the less fullness (261).

261

For shirring large sections, you may wish to use the gathering foot. This distributes fullness evenly and locks it in position as it stitches (262).

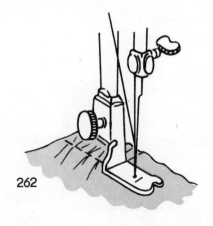

262

With a Stay

Staying the shirring acts as a reinforcement to hold the fullness permanently in position. Cut a piece of sheer fabric, on the lengthwise grain, the length and width of shirred area plus $^3/_8$-inch seam allowance on all sides. Turn under the seam allowances and press. Pin the reinforcement strip to the wrong side of the fabric over the shirred area. Machine in position with a tiny stitch. Instead of cutting a strip of fabric for a stay, you may use woven seam binding (263a). This construction is used for waistline stays in many garments with gathered or pleated skirts.

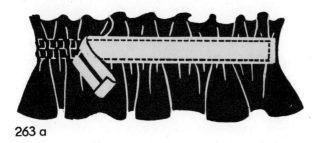

263 a

With Elastic Thread

Elastic thread is often used for gathered effects, and can be used on the machine. Wind elastic thread on the bobbin by hand (263b). Be sure not to stretch the elastic. Use regular thread as the upper thread (263c). Test on a scrap of your fabric, adjusting the length of stitch and tension until you obtain the desired fullness.

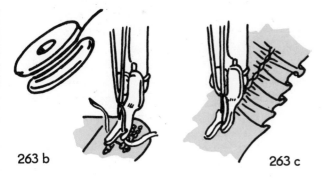

263 b

263 c

With Cord Piping

Shirring can be made with cording, and the cording used as a drawstring type closing. Cut a strip of fabric the length of the fabric to be gathered and the width of the cording plus $^1/_4$-inch seam allowances on all edges. Turn under the seam allowances and press. Place the strip of fabric on the wrong side of the material in the proper position. Stitch one edge of the strip close to the fold edge (264). Run the cording

between the strip and fabric. Stitch close to the cording, using the cording foot. Draw up the cord, pushing the fabric back on the cord for the desired length. Distribute the fullness evenly along the cord (264).

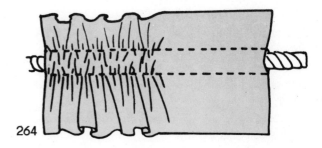

264

Gauging

Gauging is another decorative method of handling fullness. It is done by hand. Fasten thread with tiny back-stitches and taking long stitches on the right side of the fabric and short stitches on the wrong side, place several rows of stitching underneath each other in identical patterns—long stitches under long, short under short (265). Draw up the fullness and folds will form. Distribute the fullness evenly.

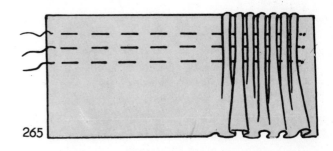

265

FACINGS

Facings are used to provide neat finishes to raw edges in a garment and to support the shape of necklines, armholes, front closings, cuffs, collars, etc. They may be cut in one piece with the garment section or applied separately.

Usually a facing piece is cut on the same grain as the edge it is to finish. For example, if the facing is used to finish and support a front closing which is on the lengthwise grain, the facing should also be cut on the lengthwise grain of the fabric. On a curved edge such as a rounded neckline, the facing should be cut on the same curved grain as the neckline edge of the garment section.

Remember, when cutting facings, if you altered the garment section to which the facing is attached, you will have to alter the facing, too, in exactly the same manner.

There are several types of facings, each requiring slightly different methods of construction. The type of facing needed will either be indicated by a separate pattern piece or the pattern piece will indicate the cut line of the facing, if it is cut in one with the garment section (266). If a garment piece such as a collar is to be faced, you often use the same pattern piece for collar and facing. This will also be indicated on the pattern piece.

Below are listed the most commonly used facings with more detailed instructions for construction than you usually find in pattern instructions.

Facing Cut in One with the Garment Piece

Usually the facing cut in this manner is found on a garment when the edge to be faced is a straight line. Coat fronts often have it, since a fairly heavy fabric is used, and this type of facing eliminates bulky seams at the edge of the garment (266).

The facing is simply folded back on the line indicated by the pattern, and the folded edge pressed. This is done after any necessary interfacings are applied. If you are using a pattern which has a separate facing, and your fabric is fairly bulky, you may wish to cut the facing in the same piece with the garment section. Just be sure the edge to be faced is a straight edge, and your fabric is wide enough for the garment piece. Place the pattern pieces on the fabric, overlapping the seam allowances and matching the

266

seam lines accurately, and cut the two as one piece. The facing is then folded back along the line marked on the pattern for the seam.

Fitted or Shaped Facing

These facings are cut to conform to the edge to be faced. They may vary in width, although usually neckline or armhole facings are $2^5/_8$ inches wide. There will always be a facing pattern piece in a McCall's pattern, if this facing is part of the design. Occasionally, you may wish to change the neckline of a pattern and will need to cut a shaped facing without having the pattern piece. To cut your own shaped facing, place a piece of tissue paper on top of the pattern piece with the altered edge to be faced. Trace the outline of the edge, then measure an equal distance from the outside edge and mark the inside edge. Be sure to mark seam allowances.

In applying fitted facings to a garment, first staystitch the curved edge of the facing (267), following the grain direction. Then the outer raw edge which will not be joined in a seam should be finished (267). The type of edge finish depends upon the fabric being used and the necessary finished appearance of the inside of the garment. For instance, in bulky fabrics you would not want to turn up the edge and stitch it, since this would add unnecessary bulk and leave a ridge when the facing is pressed in place. On unlined jackets the edge of the facing should be very neatly finished, since it is likely to be seen. On lined jackets and coats, where the facing edge will be covered by the lining, no finish is needed. For most fabrics which tend to ravel and are not bulky, the clean finished edge is recommended. First place a row of regular machine-stitching about $1/_8$ to $1/_4$ inch in from the edge. Clip the threads on each end; they do not have to be tied. Turn the fabric over on this row of stitching, and stitch close to this folded edge.

On bulky fabrics which have a slight tendency to ravel, and where the facing will not be seen, place a row of regular machine-stitches $1/_4$ inch from the raw edge. Trim with the pinking shears $1/_8$ inch from the edge.

If your fabric is bulky and tends to ravel rather badly, it is best to finish the edge either with a row of zigzag stitches, using the zigzag attachment (see page 123), or with the zigzag stitch on the automatic machine. If you do not have a zigzag machine or attachment, bind the edge with bias seam binding.

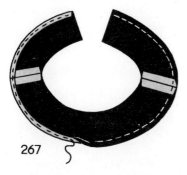

267

269

Neckline and Armhole Facing Cut in One

This facing can be applied completely by machine. Stitch the facing to neck edge of garment (270). Grade seams and understitch seam to facing. Turn facing to inside and press (271). Pin facing to bodice at armhole edges, wrong sides together, seams and notches

After the raw edge of the facing has been finished correctly, pin the facing section to the garment section, matching notches and seam lines (268). Join the two in a plain seam. To stitch accurately around a curved seam, you may wish to place a pin in tape on the bed of the machine used to mark the seam widths (see page 73). The pin will act as a guide for keeping an accurate ⅝-inch seam allowance as you stitch around the curve.

After the seam has been stitched, and the threads secured, the seam should be graded (268). Cut the seam allowance next to the garment the widest (about ⅜ inch), the interfacing, if applied, the narrowest and the facing to about ¼ inch. Cut diagonally across points at corners and clip the curved seam at intervals to the seam line (268).

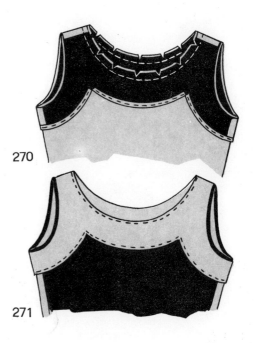

270

271

268

At this point, the facing may be understitched. Understitching holds the facing securely to the seam allowance and prevents it from rolling over the seam edge. It is done on the inside edge, does not show on the right side, and is recommended for neckline edges, sleeve edges, faced sleeveless armholes, collars and cuffs. After the seams have been graded and clipped and the seam allowances pressed toward the facing, top-stitch through the facing and seam allowances close to the seam line.

Turn the facing to the inside and press flat (269). Sew the free edge of the facing to the garment seam allowances with a catch-stitch. (See page 125.)

There are special shaped facings which require slightly different construction than the general directions given above.

matched. If facing extends beyond armhole edge, trim facing off so that edges are exactly even and facing fits perfectly flat (272). This is very important to the appearance of the finished garment. If these seams are not matched accurately the facing will roll out.

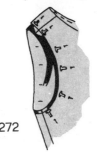

272

Remove pins from armhole edges. Place garment in front of you with wrong side of back uppermost. Turn the underarm area of the facing to the right side of the bodice and match underarm seams, right sides together. Pin in place (273). Working from underarm to shoulder seam and matching notches, continue pinning

273

back armhole to back facing. Roll the facing back and pull the seam to the outside as you pin. Stitch facing to back armhole between underarm and shoulder seams. Grade seams and clip curve at intervals. Turn facing to wrong side of garment and press. Stitch the front facing to the front armhole in this same manner. Understitch the armhole seam starting at the underarm and stitching toward the shoulder on the back and then on the front (274). Catch-stitch facing to underarm seam allowances.

274

Facing Slashed V-Neckline

Stay-stitch neck edges and along each side of slash marking (275). Stitch facing shoulder seams, right sides together, press open and trim seam allowances. Finish outer edge of facing appropriately. Pin the facing to the garment, right sides together along the slash-line markings. Stitch neckline and along each side of slashline marking. Taper stitching at slash line, from $\frac{1}{4}$ inch at neck edge to point; take one extra stitch across point and taper other side. Grade seam allowances, then slash along marking to stitching at point (276). Clip curved neck edge. Turn facing to inside, press, and understitch. Baste close to fold edge,

press, and sew facing to shoulder seam allowances with catch-stitches.

275   **276**

Decorative Facings

These facings are finished on the outside of the garment for decorative detailing (279). Stay-stitch neck edges of bodice and stay-stitch inner and outer edges of facing. Stitch shoulder seams of facing, press seams open, and trim seam allowances. On the garment, the shoulder seams must be reversed under facing to keep the raw edges of seam allowances from showing (277c). Mark position for edge of facing on garment and make a second mark, $\frac{1}{2}$ inch from this, toward neckline. Pin bodice shoulder seams, right sides together (277a), and stitch from armhole to second marking. Fasten thread

277 a

277 c   **277 b**

ends. Clip seam allowance to stitching. Press seams open. Turn bodice to right side and stitch remainder of shoulder seams (277b). Press seams open. Pin and stitch facing to neck edge, right side of facing to wrong side of garment (278). Grade and clip seam allowances. Turn facing to right side. Baste close to fold edge and press. Turn under seam allowance on facing edge, using staystitching as a guide, and baste in position. Stitch in position by hand with slip-stitch or top-stitch by machine close to the edge (279).

278   **279**

Bias-Strip Facing

Stay-stitch edge of garment to be faced (280). Cut strip of true bias fabric (see page 229) the desired width plus seam allowances and desired length. Baste strip to garment edge, right sides together (281), beginning at a seam. Ease bias on inward curves and stretch on outward curves so it will lie flat at inner edge. Stitch the bias together at seam line where bias began and ended. Press seam open. Grade seam allowances and clip at curves (281). Turn facing to

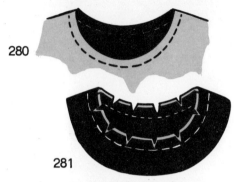

280

281

inside and baste close to fold edge. Turn under raw edge and hem to garment (282).

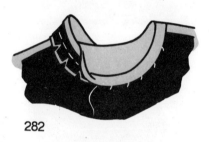

282

Bias-Strip Facing on V-Neckline

Follow same procedure as for Bias-Strip Facing above. However, begin and end strip at point of V, allowing sufficient fabric to join the bias in a seam at the point (283). Press this seam open flat before stitching (284). Clip neck curve at back. Turn under raw edge and hem to garment (285).

283

284

285

Facing with Seam Binding

If the edge to be faced is straight, woven seam binding can be used. Stitch the seam binding, right side up, to the raw edge beginning at a seam (286). Turn under on seam line, press and hem seam binding to the garment (287).

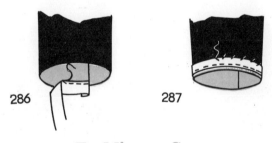

286

287

To Mitre a Corner

There are two methods of folding a mitre depending upon the seam finish. If the facing or trim is applied right side up, the mitre seamline is hand-sewn (289). If the facing or trim is applied and then turned to the wrong side of the garment, the seam is sewn on the wrong side and pressed open (291).

FOLDING MITRED CORNER WITH SEAM FINISHED ON RIGHT SIDE. At the point, fold the fabric with a straight crease from the point even with the edge, and the fabric folded back on itself (288). Then fold a diagonal crease line from the point to inner edge of facing. Slip-stitch the mitre fold together along the diagonal fold (289).

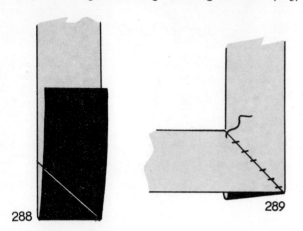

288

289

FOLDING MITRED CORNER WITH SEAM FINISHED ON WRONG SIDE. At the point, fold the fabric with a diagonal crease from the point so that the grain lines are at right angles. Then form a straight crease from the point even with the edge. Stitch the facing together along the diagonal crease line (290). Trim $1/4$ inch from the seam line and press the seam open (291).

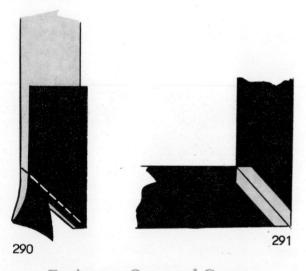

290

291

Facing an Outward Corner

Cut a continuous facing strip on the straight grain of fabric. Pin facing to the garment, right sides together, as far as the corner point (292). Fold and finish mitre as described under "folding mitred corner with seam finished on the wrong side." Continue pinning facing to the garment. Stitch the seam (293). and grade seam allowances, cut seam allowance diagonally across the

point. Turn facing to inside and baste close to the fold edge. Turn under raw edge and hem to garment (294).

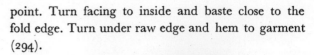

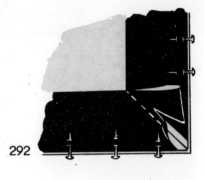

292

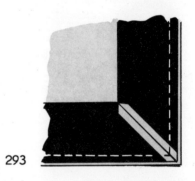

293

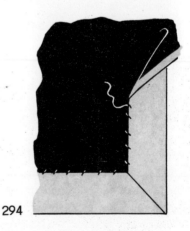

294

Facing an Inward Corner

Pin facing to the garment as far as the corner point (295). Fold the facing in a diagonal crease from the point and then fold a straight crease even with the edge of the facing. Stitch facings together along the diagonal crease marking (295). Trim to $1/4$ inch from stitching line and press seam open (296). Turn facing to wrong side, press and hem to garment (297).

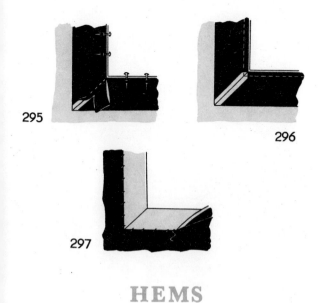

295

296

298

297

HEMS

A hem is a finish for a raw edge which maintains the shape of an article. It may be made in various widths, depending on its placement. In garment construction, it is usually the final step.

Hem in Garment

After finishing all other detailing, allow the garment to hang for at least twenty-four hours before attempting to mark the hem. By letting it hang, the weight of the fabric will cause bias edges to stretch into their normal position, and will prevent unsightly, uneven hems.

MARKING HEM. It is far easier and more accurate to have someone mark the hem for you. Be sure to wear the undergarments and shoes you will wear with the garment. Pin up the front portion of the garment first to find the length which is most flattering for your own figure, within the limits of current fashion. Stand in your normal posture while the person marking the hem moves around you (298). A chalk marker, pin marker, or yardstick may be used. Make pin or chalk markings approximately every three inches around the entire skirt, keeping measuring tool straight and an even distance from the figure for each marking.

To mark a hem yourself, you can use a chalk marker. This is not as accurate as pin marking, but it is much better than trying to turn up the hem by eye or measuring from the top down. Place the marker on the floor and then move slowly around it trying not to twist or pull the garment out of line as you turn. Be

sure to try the chalk on a scrap of the fabric first. Chalk leaves marks on some fabrics that will not come off even with dry-cleaning.

Once the hem has been marked, remove the garment carefully so markings are not distorted. Turn the hem to the inside along the markings and pin in position close to the hemline edge. Baste $1/_2$ inch from the fold edge, removing the pins as you baste. Press the hem lightly in position (299). Measure the hem allowance using a ruler or hem gauge, an even distance from the lower edge, approximately 2 to 3 inches for a straight skirt (300), and 1 to 2 inches for a full bias skirt. Trim the hem allowance evenly along marking. Pin the hem in position matching seam lines first, and placing pins at right angles to the edge.

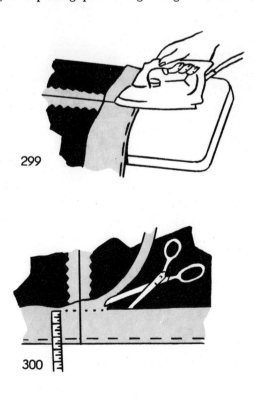

299

300

EASING HEM FULLNESS. When the hem has been turned up, the edge is often fuller than the skirt at the point where it is to be sewn. In order to make the hemline edge even, this fullness should be distributed evenly. Fold back the hem allowance and stitch (approximately 10 stitches to the inch) close to the raw edge from seam to seam. Pin the hem in position at each seam. Draw up the bobbin thread until the hem edge fits the skirt smoothly (301). Distribute the fullness evenly, then steam-press the hem to shrink out fullness (302). Press with the grain of the fabric from folded hemline edge up, never across the hem as this will stretch the fabric. Inserting heavy brown paper between the hem and skirt will keep from making an imprint of hem edge on the right side of the skirt.

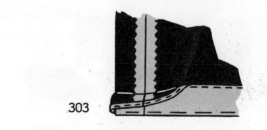

303

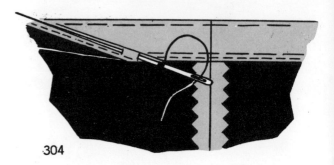

304

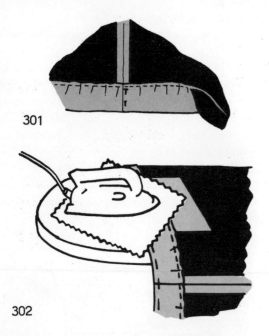

301

302

Types of Hems

The hem finish to use on a garment depends upon the fabric and the style of the garment. Analyse the weight of the fabric. Test its ravelling quality. Become familiar with the types of hems normally used for specific styles.

STITCHED AND TURNED HEM. Use on light-weight, firmly woven fabrics that are not bulky and do not ravel easily. After trimming the hem to an even width, turn under the edge $1/4$ inch (303). Stitch along folded edge, leaving just enough width to slip a needle through the fold when hemming the skirt. Baste upper edge of hem to garment. Use hemming stitch or slipstitch to hold hem in place (304).

HEM FINISHED WITH SEAM BINDING. Used for fabrics that ravel. After trimming hem evenly, put a row of stitching along edge (305). Draw up thread the necessary amount and distribute ease. Stitch seam binding to raw edge. Use woven seam binding on a straight skirt and bias seam binding on a flared skirt. Be sure not to put the binding on too tightly or it will pull and make the hem show on the right side. Slip-stitch hem to garment (305).

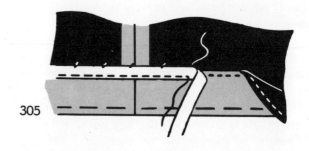

305

TAILOR'S HEM. Used on bulky and heavy fabrics that do not ravel. After trimming the hem to an even width, stitch $1/4$ inch from the edge (306). Pin the hem in the garment at the seams and pull up bobbin thread to ease out any fullness. Shrink out any fullness and pink the upper edge. Baste hem in place $1/2$ inch from the upper edge. Fold upper edge back and sew hem to garment with invisible stitching being careful not to pull the stitches too tight. When the hem is pressed down, the stitches lie between the hem and the garment and are completely invisible. This hem shows less than any other on the right side of the garment.

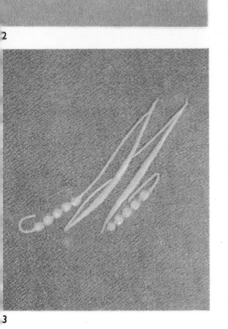

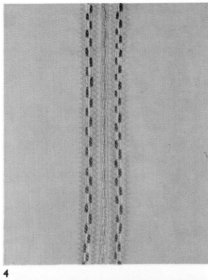

18

AUTOMATIC MACHINE PROCESSES 2

1 Machine embroidery for decorating a variety of garments, and cushions, chairbacks, etc.

2 Felt appliqué with Lurex thread for cushions and chairbacks.

3 Monograms for handkerchiefs, household linen, towels, etc.

4 Matching embroidery for trimmings on garments of all kinds.

5 Appliqué suitable for household linen, aprons, and children's clothes.

6 Machine embroidery, for skirts, sleeves, bodices, and children's clothes.

7 Tape or bias binding with machine embroidery for place mats, cushions, chair seats, etc.

Photograph by courtesy of the Singer Sewing Machine Company Ltd.

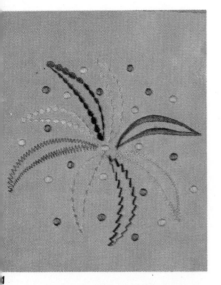

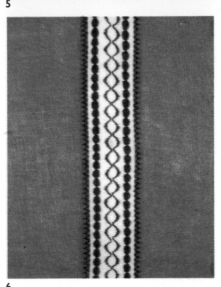

2

5

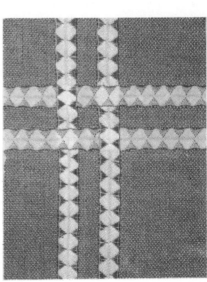

3

6

7

19 Modern methods of dyeing, from the most delicate pastels to the most intense crimsons and purples, provide an unbelievable range of colour shades.

Silk ombré by courtesy of John Lewis of Oxford Street Ltd.

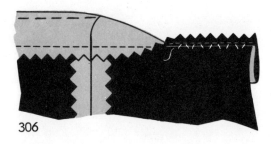

306

DRESSMAKER'S HEM. Similar to the tailor's hem but can be used on almost any type of fabric except sheers or a garment that is to be machine laundered. After trimming hem to an even width, stitch along edge. Draw up the bobbin thread and shrink out the fullness. Hand overcast or zigzag the raw edge if the fabric ravels (307). If the fabric does not ravel, pink the edge. Baste and sew in position with invisible stitching same as the tailor's hem.

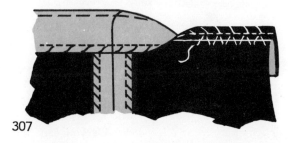

307

CATCH-STITCHED HEM. Used on wool fabrics or velvet when no seam binding is used. This stitch protects the raw edge and holds the hem more firmly than the tailor's hem. However, the more firmly stitched hem may press through to the right side of the garment and show a ridge at the upper edge of the hem. The heavier the fabric, the more it will show. After trimming the hem to an even width, shrink out any fullness at the upper edge so that the hem lies flat, and baste in place (308). Working from left to right attach the hem to the garment with a catch-stitch See page 125 for detailed description of stitch.

308

NARROW MACHINE-STITCHED HEM.
Used on blouses and men's shirts. Stitch ¹/₈ inch from raw edge to serve as a stay and guide. Turn under the

raw edge on line of stitching and then turn under again the same width. Baste and stitch the hem in place. This type of hem may be made with a narrow hemming machine attachment which double-folds and stitches the hem at the same time (309). Follow the instructions provided with the attachment.

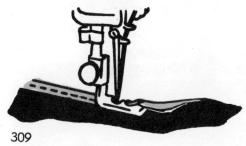

309

NARROW HAND-SEWN HEM. Used on blouses and on sheer or fine fabrics. Turn under the edge ¹/₈ inch and stitch close to the edge (310). Turn under the fold edge the same width and baste. Slip-stitch hem edge to garment.

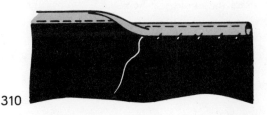

310

HAND-ROLLED HEM. A fine hand-finished hem used on sheer fabric, scarves, sashes, lingerie, etc. Machine-stitch ¹/₈ inch from edge (311). Trim close to stitching. Roll fabric between the thumb and forefinger of the left hand, several inches at a time, and then hem in position with a hemming stitch or slip-stitch or a fine whipping stitch (311). Do not baste.

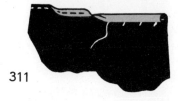

311

QUICK HAND-ROLLED HEM. With this method the hem is rolled by pulling up stitches placed at the upper and lower edges of the hem instead of rolling it between the thumb and forefinger. Machine-stitch ¹/₈ inch from edge and trim close to stitching (312). Turn edge just beyond the stitching. Insert the needle in the turned edge and take a ¹/₈-inch stitch along the fold of hem. Pick up a single thread of the garment fabric directly below this stitch. Carry the needle over the fabric for ¹/₈ inch and pick up another single thread of the garment. Take another stitch directly above in the fold of the hem. Continue taking several stitches in hem and garment and then pull up the stitches. The hem will roll into place and the stitches will be encased in the hem. Note that the stitches must be perpendicular to the edge of the hem and not slanting (312).

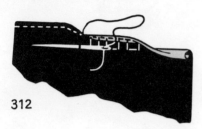

312

NAPERY HEM. This is used for hemming table linens. Napkins have a $1/8$-inch hem and tablecloths about a $1/2$-inch hem. Turn under the raw edge $1/8$ inch and then make a second turn (313). Baste in place and press flat. Fold the hem back against the right side of the fabric at the upper edge of the hem. With a fine needle, overhand the hem to the fabric, taking the stitches close together. See page 126 for instructions for the overhand stitch.

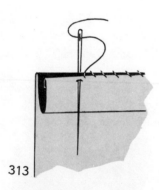

313

HEM STIFFENED WITH WIDE HORSE-HAIR BRAID. Measure and trim hem off evenly, allowing a $1/4$-inch hem allowance at the edge of skirt. Pin two-inch-wide horsehair braid to the lower edge of the skirt, right sides up, overlapping $1/4$ inch (314). Stitch braid in position. Turn hem to inside along edge of braid, placing pins at right angles to edge. Then pin top edge of braid at seams. Draw up the thread on the top edge until horsehair fits smoothly and distribute ease evenly. Pin and baste edge. Attach edge with hemming stitch (315).

314

315

HORSEHAIR BRAID FINISH FOR LACE SKIRT. Measure and trim hem evenly, allowing a $5/8$-inch hem allowance at edge. Turn under hem allowance and baste close to fold edge (316). Pin narrow horsehair braid along hem edge on inside of skirt. Baste through centre of braid. Stitch along each edge of braid through hem allowance and skirt. Remove bastings. Trim off hem edge of lace close to edge of braid (317).

316.   317

FACED HEM. The faced-hem finish is used when the skirt is not long enough for a normal hem allowance or when you want to lengthen a skirt that is too short. Cut a strip of true bias fabric the desired width and length plus seam allowances. Or you can buy a commercial facing especially for this purpose. Measure an even hem on the garment allowing at least $1/2$ inch. Pin bias fabric to edge of hem, right sides together and join ends with plain seam (318). Press seam open. Stitch facing to hem. Turn facing and edge of hem to inside using width of seam allowance for turning line. Baste along fold edge. Pin hem facing to skirt at seams. Ease fullness if necessary and baste in position. Sew hem facing to skirt with hemming stitch or slip-stitch (318).

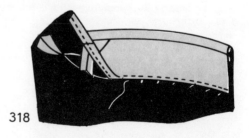

318

Hems with Special Finishing Details
HEM WITH SEAMED PLEAT. After trimming the hem to an even width, clip the seam allowances at the top of pleat to the seamline (319). Trim the

seam allowances in hem section to $^3/_8$ inch. Press the seam open inside hem. Finish hemming the skirt. Press pleat in position (320).

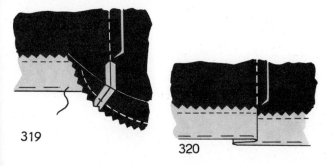

319

320

HEM WITH FACED OPENING.

This finish is used at the bottom of jackets, coats and vents. Hem the lower edge before finishing facing edge. Turn the hem up and finish edge. Stitch hem in position the entire length at the lower edge of facing (321). If the fabric is bulky, trim facing and the hem allowance inside of facing to $^1/_2$ inch (322). Sew the remaining hem in position. Turn facing to inside. Baste close to edge. Slipstitch lower folded edges together and catchstitch inner edge of facing to hem using very small stitches (323).

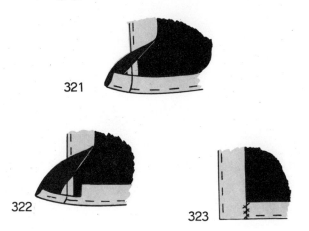

321

322

323

HEM WITH STITCHED MITRED COR-NER.

This finish is sometimes used on dresses but more often on aprons or home furnishing items. Turn the hem allowances to the right side of the garment along marked hemlines. Fold the mitre diagonally from edge point to inner point where edges of hem meet (324). Stitch hems together along diagonal fold. Trim $^1/_4$ to $^1/_2$ inch from line of stitching (325). Press seam open forming diagonal fold at the point. Turn hem to inside. Turn under raw edges of hems and sew to garment with hemming stitch or slip-stitch (326).

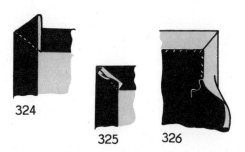

324

325

326

HEM WITH HAND-FINISHED MITRED CORNER.

Fold the hems to the wrong side along hemline. Fold mitre at corner from outer point diagonally to edges of hems. Place fabric flat and trim off corner diagonally $^1/_4$ inch from mitre fold line and point (327). Turn under edge $^1/_4$ inch on diagonal line and $^1/_4$ inch on raw hem edges (328). Turn hems to inside again. Baste edges of mitre in position. Stitch edges of mitre together with tiny whipping stitch. Slip-stitch hem to garment (329).

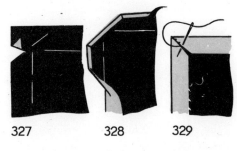

327

328

329

UNDERLININGS

The many uses of underlining are listed in Chapter 3 under "Shaping Materials." Briefly, underlining will help retain the shape of a garment, add to its life expectancy, create fashion effects and provide greater crease resistance.

It is often better to underline dresses, skirts and slacks rather than use a lining. The construction is easier, and the underlining provides a firmer foundation for the garment.

Directions for Underlining

CUTTING. Underlining fabric is cut from the same pattern pieces as the garment sections it will back, and should be cut on the same grain as the garment pieces. Cut the underlining so that the right side of the underlining fabric will show on the inside of the garment.

PREPARING. Trim the underlining along the hemline markings to eliminate bulk at the hem. Transfer the pattern markings to the underlining fabric only, not the garment sections. Pin the two sections together matching notches, seam lines and any construction details. Baste the two pieces together, stitching directionally with the grain (330). Machine-baste through the centre of darts, tucks and pleats. This will eliminate shifting of the two sections during construction.

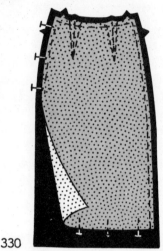

330

MAKING UNDERLINED GARMENT.

Assemble the garment, treating the two layers as one fabric. Turn garment hem allowance over the underlining, and attach hem to underlining only. After the garment is completed, remove the construction bastings.

The bodice front and back are underlined in garments, but the sleeve underlining is sometimes omitted for a set-in sleeve. In bulky fabrics, the armhole seam will be too thick if underlining is used.

LININGS

If you wish the inside of your garments to look as nice as the outside, you may wish to line the entire garment instead of using underlining. Sometimes a skirt section is lined to control stretching.

Linings are also cut from the same pattern pieces as the garment for skirts, dresses and slacks. However, jacket and coat linings are cut slightly different from the garment itself. See Chapter 14 on tailoring for details in cutting a jacket or coat lining.

Again, as for underlinings, cut the lining fabric so that the right side of the lining will show on the inside of the garment. Transfer the pattern markings to both the lining and the garment fabric, since the lining and garment are constructed separately. Follow the sewing

instructions given for the garment when constructing the lining. Pin the lining to the inside of the garment, wrong sides together, matching construction details. Join the lining to the garment along at least one major seam. In skirts and slacks, the lining is basted to the waistline of the garment before the waistband is applied. The seam allowance on the lining is turned under along the placket opening and slip-stitched to the zipper tape (331). Slack linings are attached at the hemline the same as the lower edge of a jacket. (See Chapter 14 on tailoring.) Skirt linings are hemmed separately from the garment and are made slightly shorter than the skirt.

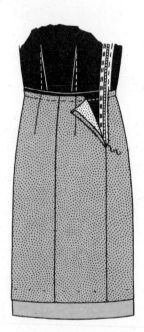

331

If the entire dress is lined, the bodice and sleeve lining can be attached by hand in the same way as for a jacket (see Chapter 14 on tailoring) or the sleeve lining can be machine-stitched to the bodice lining. If the latter method is used, tack the lining to the inside of the bodice at the underarm and shoulder seams with a long loose stitch. When a dress bodice is lined, the neck facing is applied last to give a clean finish to the neckline. Baste the finished lining to the bodice at the neckline and then apply the facing.

The sleeve lining is slip-stitched over the hem of the sleeve. Turn in the seam allowances and slip-stitch bodice lining over the waistline seam and zipper tape to give a clean finish. If the lower edge of the bodice is gathered, then it is best to baste the lining and bodice together at the lower edge. Treating it as one fabric, stitch the waistline seam.

INTERFACINGS

Interfacings are used to give added body to an edge or a construction detail (332). Instructions for applying interfacings are included with instructions for the various sections where interfacings are used. See Collars, Cuffs, Waistbands and Tailoring sections.

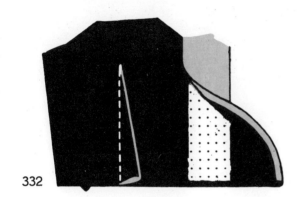

332

INTERLININGS

Interlinings are used to provide additional warmth in a garment and are usually found only in coats (333). We have included instructions for constructing interlining in the section on tailoring in Chapter 14.

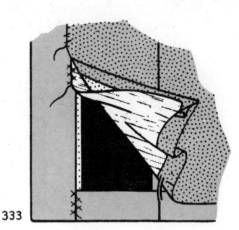

333

CHAPTER 11

DESIGN DETAILS—SLEEVES AND CUFFS, COLLARS AND POCKETS

Working with the smaller design details can be frustrating but interesting. The pieces are usually smaller, the seaming more difficult to handle, and the work must be done with a great deal of precision. However, if you have mastered the basic techniques of sewing, don't hesitate to tackle a set-in sleeve, a French cuff or any style of collar. These details are often what give your garment its individuality.

SLEEVES

A smoothly fitted sleeve is one of the marks of an expert seamstress. A sleeve with unsightly gathers and puckers or one which twists because proper grain lines were not maintained is the sign of the inexperienced and careless.

There are two basic types of sleeves—the set-in or mounted sleeve and the sleeve cut in one with the bodice or unmounted sleeve. The one-piece sleeve, the two-piece sleeve and the puffed sleeve are set into a normal armhole. The shirt sleeve, the dolman sleeve and the raglan sleeve are variations of the set-in sleeve but fit into a deeper or an irregularly shaped armhole. The kimono sleeve is cut in one with the bodice. It can be made without a gusset or with a one- or a two-piece gusset.

All set-in sleeves are cut with a sleeve cap that is larger than the armhole section into which it must fit. The extra fullness or "ease" is necessary for the sleeve to fit over the arm and hang correctly. The home dressmaker must learn to distribute this fullness evenly across the sleeve cap so that it is eased, not gathered. On a McCall pattern special markings make this task easy to do.

One-Piece Set-In Sleeve

PREPARING SLEEVE CAP AND MAKING SLEEVE. Stitch around top of sleeve on the seam line. Use a regulation machine-stitch from underarm to first notch, change to machine-basting stitch between notches and then back to regulation stitch from notch to underarm seam. Stitch the darts or ease in elbow fullness, then stitch sleeve seam.

334

With wash-and-wear and some cottons it is difficult to shrink and ease in fullness. When using a set-in sleeve on such fabrics, mark the $^5/_8$-inch seam allowance around top of sleeve on the wrong side of fabric with white pencil or carbon. Stitch with regulation, machine-basting as outlined above (334), but place stitching $^1/_8$ inch inside seam-line marking around front and back curve of sleeve cap between notches and centre of sleeve cap, tapering from original seam line at notches and back to original seam line at centre of sleeve cap. This reduces the ease but does not change the length of the sleeve cap (335).

335

INSERTING SLEEVE IN GARMENT. Pin sleeve in armhole, matching underarm seams, notches and centre point of sleeve to shoulder seam (336).

Starting at centre, pull up bobbin thread until sleeve cap fits armhole. This gives a more even distribution of fullness and avoids ends of thread wrapped around pins. Pin and baste sleeve firmly in place (337). Shrink

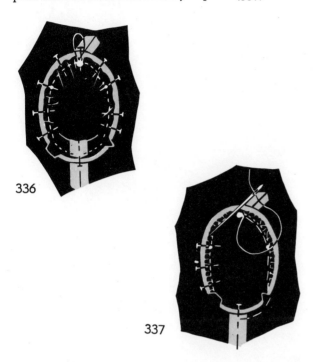

336

337

out the fullness in the sleeve cap by pressing the sleeve and armhole seams together from the sleeve side (338). This shrinks the sleeve cap to the exact size and shape of the armhole. If you take the sleeve out of the armhole and try to shrink out the fullness, there is nothing to stay the shape of the armhole and the fullness may shift with the result that there is too much fullness shrunk out of one-half of the sleeve cap and not enough out of the other half.

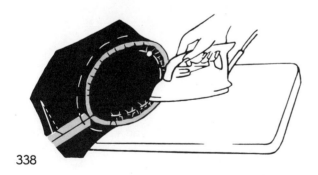

338

Stitch the sleeve into the armhole with the sleeve uppermost on the machine. The seam allowance is turned toward the sleeve at the top and left turned up at the underarm (339).

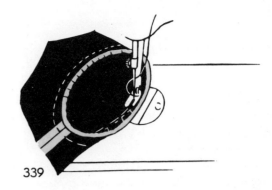

339

FINISHING LOWER EDGE OF SLEEVE.

The elbow darts or fullness can be measured and adjusted before the garment is cut but the sleeve length should be determined after the sleeve is stitched in the armhole. Never hem the lower edge of a sleeve first, any more than you would hem a skirt before attaching it to waistband or bodice. Turn up the lower edge of the sleeve on the finish line indicated on the pattern and baste in place. Try the garment on and look at yourself in a full-length mirror. If the sleeve is not a becoming length, adjust it to suit the proportions of your figure. After correct length has been determined, finish the lower edge with a hem or cuff, depending on the design of the garment.

Two-Piece Set-In Sleeve

This sleeve is found mostly in suits and coats. Both sections of the sleeve are shaped to produce a fitted sleeve. The parts should be joined with a plain seam and pressed (340). After the sleeve is made it is sewn into the armhole in the same way as the one-piece sleeve, and the lower edge finished in an appropriate manner.

340

Puffed Sleeve

Stitch the underarm seam and finish hem edge of the sleeve. Place two rows of machine-basting between markings on the sleeve cap. Place one row on the seam line and the other 1/8 inch into the seam allowance. Pin sleeve into the armhole, right sides together, matching seams, notches and markings. Draw up the bobbin threads evenly until the sleeve fits the armhole smoothly, and distribute the gathers evenly. Holding the sleeve toward you, baste the sleeve in place. Then stitch (341). Press seam at the top of the puffed sleeve away from the gathers and toward the neckline. Press only to the seam line to avoid flattening the gathers (342).

wrong sides together, matching notches and markings and keeping seam lines even at underarm. Ease in the fullness across the cap of the sleeve. There will not be enough fullness to require a gathering thread. Press the seam open and then toward the sleeve. Trim sleeve seam allowance to 1/8 inch. Turn under the raw edge of the shirt seam allowance 1/4 inch and stitch it over the trimmed seam allowance (343). Pin underarm seam of shirt and sleeve, wrong sides together. Make flatfell seam (344). Finish lower edge of sleeve with a cuff or hem as directed on the pattern.

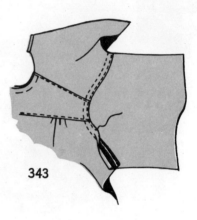

343

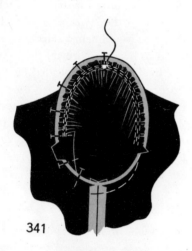

341

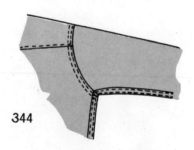

344

342

Shirt Sleeve

The construction of this type of sleeve is quite different from that of the regular set-in sleeve. The cap of a shirt sleeve is more shallow and has much less fullness. A flat-fell seam is used instead of a plain one.

First join the shoulder seams or yoke of the shirt and finish the seams as instructed on the pattern, but do not sew side seams. Pin the sleeve into the armhole

Dolman Sleeve

This sleeve (345) is attached to the bodice before the underarm is stitched because of the deep armhole. There will be very little ease in the cap of the sleeve. Pin the sleeve into the armhole, right sides together, matching notches, markings and keeping seam lines even at underarm. Ease in fullness of sleeve cap so that it fits smoothly. Baste and stitch the sleeve in place (345). Press the seam open, clipping curve at intervals so that the seam will lie flat (346). Pin underarm seam of bodice and sleeve, right sides together. Stitch the seam and press it open. Finish lower edge of sleeve as directed on the pattern.

345

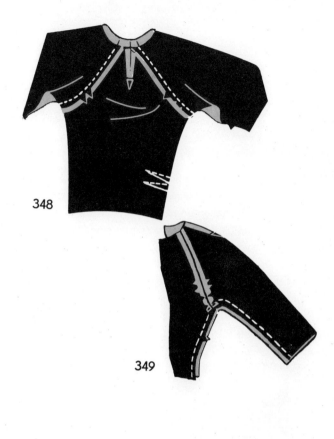

348

349

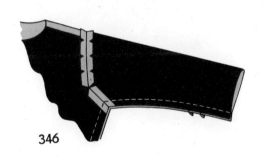

346

Raglan Sleeve

Stitch the shoulder dart of the sleeve (347), and press the dart open. Pin sleeve to bodice front and back, right sides together, matching notches and edges. The sleeve section will require easing when it is joined to the bodice but not enough to require a gathering thread. Stitch the seam and clip curve at intervals (348). Press seam open. Pin the underarm seam of bodice and sleeve, and stitch in a continuous seam (349). Press seam open. Finish lower edge of sleeve as directed on the pattern.

347

Kimono Sleeve without a Gusset

This is the easiest sleeve, so if you are a beginner, look for styles with this sort of sleeve if it is flattering to your figure.

Join the bodice front and back at the shoulder with a plain seam. Press this curved seam open over a tailor's ham to retain the curve. Join bodice front to back at the underarm seam, right sides together, matching notches. Stitch seam and clip curve at intervals. Press seam open. This seam will need reinforcement under the arm, since it will be subject to a great deal of stress in normal body movement. Reinforce it by basting a piece of woven seam binding about $1\frac{1}{2}$ inches long to the inside of the bodice along the curve of the underarm seam. Turn bodice right side out. Stitch $\frac{1}{8}$ inch from the seam, through bodice, seam allowance and seam binding, along both sides and ends (350). Or if you do not wish the stitching to show on the right side, baste the seam binding to the seam line on the inside and stitch it only to the seam allowance on both sides of the seam.

350

Kimono Sleeve with a One-Piece Gusset

The gusset construction is a rather difficult one but the fit of the sleeve is so much better that you should learn how to make it. On the pattern there will be a slash marking at the curve of the underarm. Mark this on the wrong side of the garment section (351). Cut strips of fabric to face this slash, approximately 2 inches wide and 1 inch longer than the marking. Pin and baste facing strip along slash marking, right sides together. Stitch, beginning at edge $1/8$ inch from slash marking and taper to the point (352). Take one extra stitch across point and stitch down other side. Slash on marking to stitching at point. Turn facing to inside

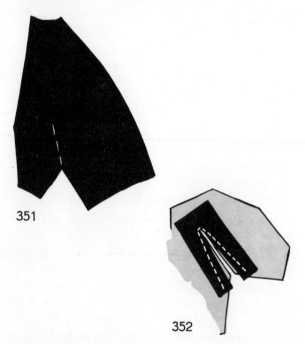

351

352

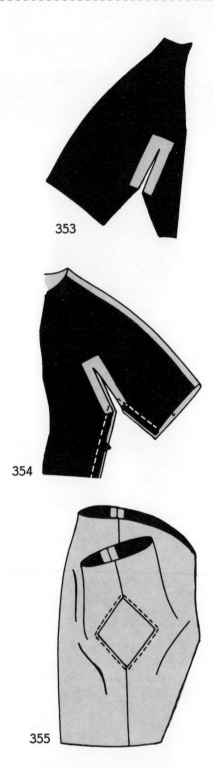

353

354

355

and press flat (353). Pin and stitch underarm seams of bodice and sleeve, matching notches and faced edges accurately (354). Press seam open. Turn bodice to right side. Pin and baste gusset inside opening, right sides up. Lap faced edges of opening to seam line of gusset. Stitch gusset in position by top-stitching close to faced edge of opening (355).

Kimono Sleeve with a Two-Piece Gusset

Cut facing strips. Face slash markings in the same way as for the one-piece gusset (352, 353). Pin and baste front and back gusset pieces to bodice front and back. Place faced edges of bodice over each gusset piece, right sides up, lapping the faced edges to seam line. Top-stitch close to edge (356). Turn bodice to wrong side. Pin underarm seam, matching notches, seam lines for gusset sections and edges accurately (357). Stitch underarm seam of bodice and sleeve in a continuous seam. Press seam open.

356

357

Kimono Sleeve without a Gusset Pattern

If you select a pattern with a kimono sleeve and it does not have a gusset, you may want to add one to give you more ease. Simply mark a diagonal slash line 4 inches long at the highest point of the underarm curve of bodice front and back (358). Cut two facing strips 2 inches wide and 1 inch longer than the slash marking and a $5\frac{1}{4}$ inch square on the straight grain of your garment fabric (359). Follow the instructions given for inserting a one-piece gusset.

358

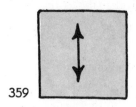

359

CUFFS

Sleeves are often given interest by the use of cuffs. There are many different types, each one creating a definite fashion effect. They may be straight or shaped, closed or open, applied or cut in one with the sleeve.

Turnback cuffs may be applied as separate pieces or are sometimes cut in one with the sleeve and faced. Applied cuffs are either straight or shaped and can be closed or open at the ends. The straight cuff has a fold at the upper edge and fits close to the sleeve. The shaped cuff has a seam at the upper edge and can be curved so that it will flare away from the sleeve. The cuff cut in one with the sleeve can be made with or without an opening. When an opening is used, it may be in the seam.

Cuffs are often interfaced to give them body and firmness. For a straight cuff, cut the interfacing half the width of the cuff or to the fold line; for a shaped cuff, use cuff pattern; for a cuff cut in one with the sleeve, the sleeve facing piece.

Cuffs are applied with a bias facing, a shaped facing or a self-finish.

Straight Cuffs Closed at Ends

Join the seam edges of the interfacing with a lapped seam (360). Stitch seam of cuff (361) and press it open.

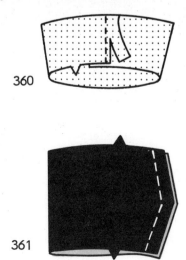

360

361

Baste the interfacing to the inside of cuff with one edge along fold line (362). Slip-stitch to fold line. Fold cuff, wrong sides together, and baste one inch from open edge to hold sections of cuff together until it has been attached to the sleeve (363).

through to the right side of cuff. Turn cuff to right side and press thoroughly while it is flat. Slip-stitch the open ends of the cuff together for $3/4$ inch up from the open edge. Baste layers of fabric together, one inch from the open edge (366).

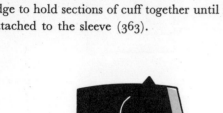

362

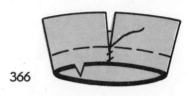

366

Shaped Cuff Closed at Ends

Join the ends of the interfacing with a lapped seam (367). Stitch end seams of each cuff section and press

363

Straight Cuff with Open Ends

Baste the interfacing to the inside of cuff with one edge along fold line. Slip-stitch interfacing to fold line (364). Fold cuff, right sides together, and stitch ends. Trim interfacing close to stitching and grade the seams so that the widest seam is on the edge without the interfacing (365). This keeps seam edges from pressing

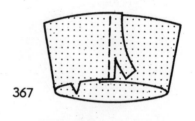

367

368

open (368). Baste the interfacing to the inside of the under-cuff section. Stitch the under-cuff section to the top cuff section at the unnotched edge, right sides together and seams matched (369). Trim interfacing

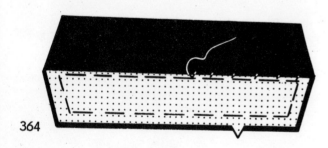

364

369

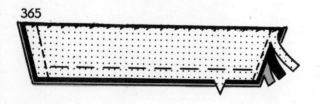

365

close to stitching and grade seam allowances. Turn cuff to right side and baste seamed edge rolling seam slightly to the inside. Baste cuff one inch from open edge (370).

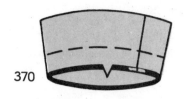

370

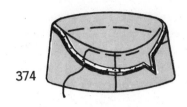

374

Shaped Cuff with Open Ends

Baste the interfacing to the under section of the cuff (371). Place right sides of cuff sections together and stitch at unnotched edges (372). Grade the seams and turn cuff to right side. Baste close to edge, rolling seam

cuff, right sides together, and baste (375). Join ends with a plain seam. Stitch around the lower edge of sleeve through all thicknesses of fabric. Grade seam allowances and press seam toward sleeve. Turn under free edge of bias and hem to inside of sleeve (376). Turn cuff to right side of sleeve (377).

371

375

376

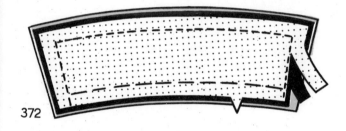

372

slightly to the inside. Slip-stitch the open ends of the cuff together for $^3/_4$ inch up from the open edge. Baste cuff 1 inch from the open edge (373).

377

Cuff Applied with Shaped Facing

Roll the lower edge of cuff toward the side with the interfacing and baste cut edges same as above (378). Baste the cuff to the right side of the sleeve. Join facing, right sides together, with a plain seam, and press seam open (379). Finish unnotched edge of facing with edge-stitching or a finish suitable for fabric. Put facing over

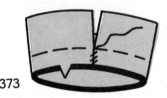

373

Cuff Applied with Bias Facing

Roll the lower edge of cuff slightly toward the side with the interfacing to get the amount of ease necessary to allow the cuff to turn back, and baste the cut edges together (374). Note that the cut edges will not be even. Baste the cuff to the right side of the sleeve. Cut a strip of bias fabric the length of the lower edge of the sleeve plus a seam allowance. Place the bias on top of

378

sleeve and cuff, right sides together, and baste. Stitch around the lower edge of sleeve through all thicknesses of fabric. Grade the seam allowances and press seam toward sleeve. Turn facing to inside of sleeve and press flat. Hem free edge of facing to sleeve (380). Turn cuff to right side of sleeve (381).

the one-inch basting line to keep it free from stitching line (383). Baste the right side of top cuff section and the interfacing to the inside of the sleeve and stitch the seam. Grade the seam allowance and press the seam

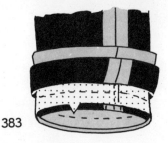

383

toward the cuff. Turn under free edges of under-cuff section $3/4$ inch and hem to seam line (384). Turn cuff up (385).

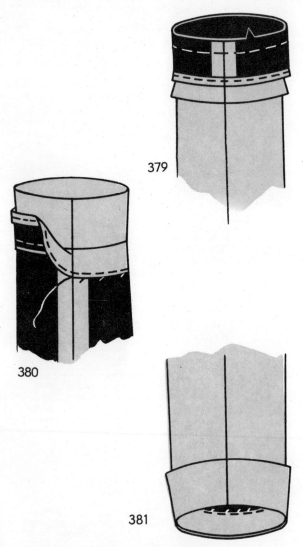

379

380

381

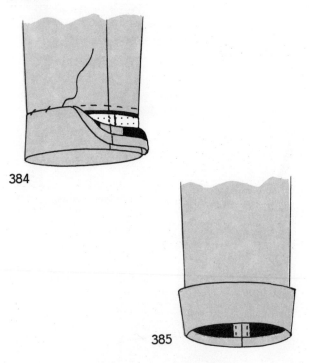

384

385

Cuff Applied with Self-Finish

Edge-stitch the sleeve seam several inches up from the lower edge (382). Turn back the under-cuff section at

Sleeve and Cuff Cut in One with No Opening

Trim off $3/4$ inch from the unnotched edge of the interfacing. Join the interfacing with a lapped seam (386).

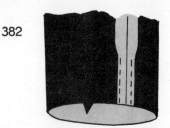

382

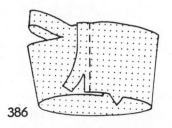

386

Baste the interfacing to the inside of the lower edge of the sleeve and attach the unnotched edge to the sleeve with invisible stitching (387). Stitch facing seam and

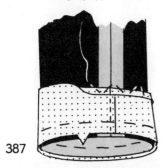

387

press it open. Edge-stitch the unnotched edge of the facing. Baste and stitch the facing to the lower edge of the sleeve, right sides together. Trim interfacing close to stitching and grade the seam allowances (388).

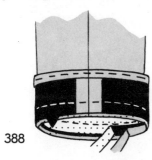

388

Turn facing to inside and baste the edge, rolling the facing seam slightly to the outside. Turn the cuff up and pin it in place. Turn the sleeve to the wrong side and slip-stitch top facing edge to the sleeve (389).

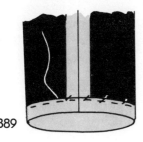

389

Sleeve and Cuff Cut in One with a Slash Opening

Follow the same procedure as for the cuff cut in one with no opening. Stitch the facing to the lower edge of the sleeve (390), right sides together, taking an extra stitch at point of slash to ensure a sharp corner when turned. Slash opening, trim interfacing close to stitching and grade seam allowances. Turn facing to inside and finish in the same way as facing with no opening.

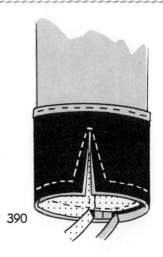

390

Sleeve and Cuff Cut in One with Opening at Seam

Trim off $^3/_4$ inch from the unnotched edge of the interfacing. Baste the interfacing to the lower edge of the sleeve and attach the unnotched edge to the sleeve with invisible stitching (391). Stitch sleeve seam, leaving open below marking (392). Clip to marking and trim interfacing close to stitching. Press seam open.

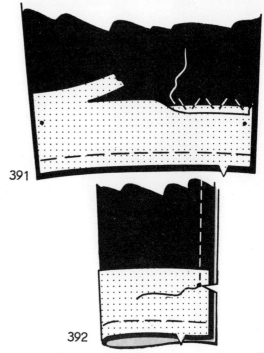

391

392

Stitch the facing seam above the marking, clip to marking and press seam open. Edge-stitch the unnotched edge of facing. Baste and stitch the facing to the lower edge of sleeve, being careful to match notches and markings at the clip (393). Trim interfacing close to stitching and grade seams. Turn facing to inside and finish in the same way as facing with no opening.

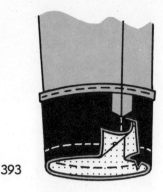

393

Roll-up Sleeve

The true roll-up sleeve has the underarm seam finished with a flat-fell seam and must be made of fabric with no right and wrong side. The lower edge of this straight shirt sleeve is finished in a narrow hem and then the sleeve is turned up twice to give the appearance of a cuff. If the fabric has a right and wrong side, you must cut the sleeve long enough to make a very deep hem. This makes it possible to turn up the lower edge of the sleeve without the wrong side of the fabric showing. Edge-stitch the lower edge of the sleeve (394). Turn the deep hem to the inside and slip-stitch in place (395), then roll up the sleeve.

394

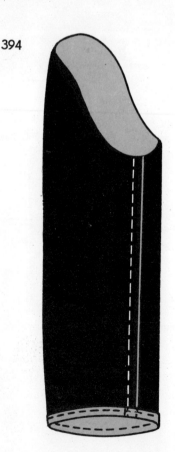

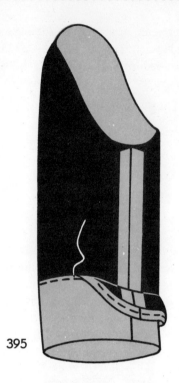

395

Sleeves with Plackets

The full sleeve is finished with a band or shirt cuff which extends down from the lower edge of the sleeve instead of turning back. The French cuff is a double-width shirt cuff folded back and fastened with cuff links.

The interfacing for the band cuff is cut half the width of the cuff to the fold line. The shirt cuff and French cuff interfacing are cut from the cuff pattern. Plackets are part of the cuff construction in these instances, so instructions are included for their application also.

Sleeve with Faced Opening

Apply the facing to opening before stitching underarm seam of sleeve. Turn under and edge-stitch the side and upper edges of the facing piece (396). Pin and baste facing to lower edge of sleeve, right sides together, with centre of facing along slash marking for opening. Stitch along both sides of marking, starting $1/_4$ inch from edge and tapering to point. Take an extra stitch across point to ensure a sharp corner when turned. Double-stitch at point and slash between stitching to point (396). Turn facing to inside and tack corners of facing to sleeve (397).

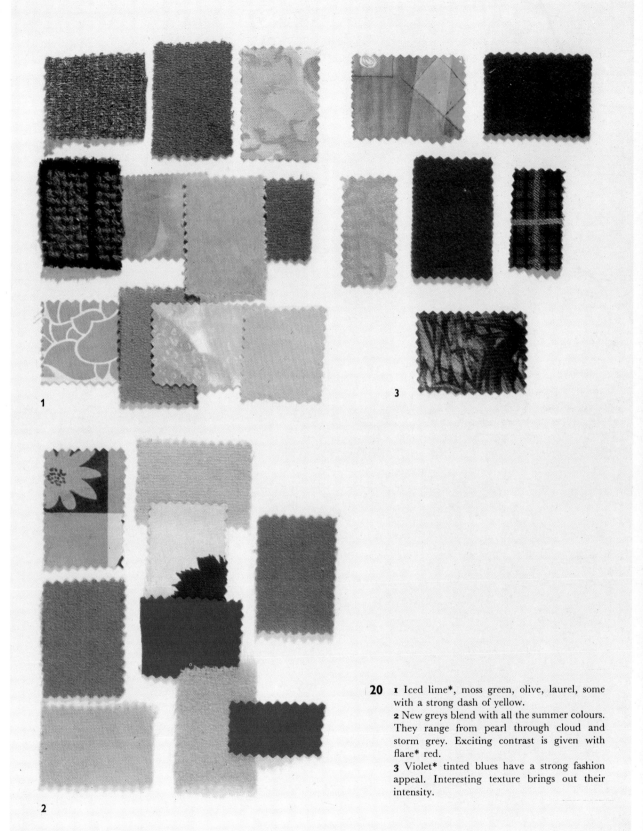

20 **1** Iced lime*, moss green, olive, laurel, some with a strong dash of yellow.

2 New greys blend with all the summer colours. They range from pearl through cloud and storm grey. Exciting contrast is given with flare* red.

3 Violet* tinted blues have a strong fashion appeal. Interesting texture brings out their intensity.

21

1 Scintillating blue, kingfisher* and peacock to clear turquoise — all with a touch of green to give an effect of refreshing coolness.
2 Larkspur*, cornflower*, the intense blue of summer seas and sky, are the ultimate in sophistication when combined with subtle greens.
3 Strong pure colours shown here on ribbon can be used as a guide to colour selection.

*Fabrics by courtesy of members of The British Colour Council. *These are British Colour Council colours*

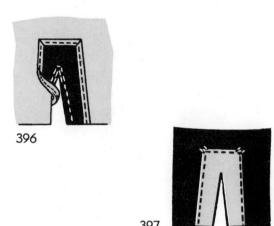

396

397

Sleeve with Continuous Lap Placket

Apply placket before stitching underarm seam of sleeve. Reinforce slash marking with a row of stay-stitching, starting $1/4$ inch from edge and tapering to point (398). Slash on marking to point of stitching. Cut a lengthwise strip of fabric twice the length of the slash and 2 inches wide. Open the slash and spread until line of stitching is straight (399). Pin fabric strip to opening, right sides together. Stitch $1/4$ inch from edge, tapering to end of slash. Press seam away from sleeve. Turn

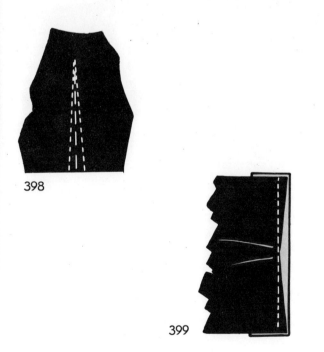

398

399

under the free edge of strip and hem it to the seam line (400). Turn placket to inside along front edge, baste at lower edge and lap over back placket.

400

Sleeve with Faced Lap Placket

Apply placket before stitching underarm seam of sleeve. Cut a facing $3^1/_2$ inches wide and an inch longer than the placket. Turn in the long edges $1/4$ inch and press (401). Pin centre of facing to slash marking, right sides together. Stitch along both sides of marking, starting $1/4$ inch from edge and tapering to point. Take one extra stitch across point. Slash between stitching to point. Turn facing to inside and press seam away from sleeve. Tack and hem the turned-in edges over

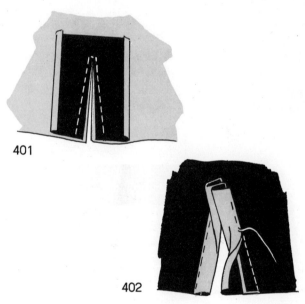

401

402

the seam (402). Stitch upper edges together (403). Turn in front lap at seam and baste at lower edge.

403

Band Cuff

The band cuff can be used with any one of the placket finishes. Stitch the sleeve seam and press it open. Make two rows of machine-gathering at lower edge of

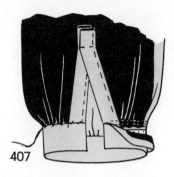

407

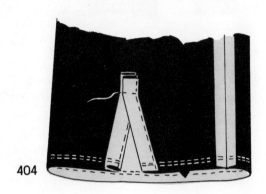

404

sleeve (404). Baste interfacing to inside of cuff at notched edge with one edge at fold line (405). Slip-stitch interfacing along fold line. Fold cuff and stitch ends (406). Trim interfacing close to stitching and

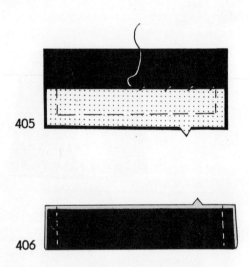

405

406

grade seams. Turn cuff to right side and press. Pull up gathering stitches on sleeve edge to fit cuff. Pin notched edge of cuff to sleeve, right sides together, and adjust gathers evenly (407). Stitch and grade seam. Press seam toward the cuff. On the inside, turn under the free edge and hem over seam (407). Finish cuff with button and buttonhole. (See Chapter 12.)

Shirt Sleeve Placket

Make placket before stitching underarm seam of sleeve. Reinforce slash marking with a row of stay-stitching as for the continuous lap placket (408). Slash to point of stitching. Stay-stitch edges of overlap and underlap. Turn under seam allowances on outer edges using stay-stitching as a guide. Pin underlap to inside of back edge of opening and overlap to inside of front edge of opening (409). Match stay-stitching line of opening to seam lines of overlap and underlap, and stitch seams.

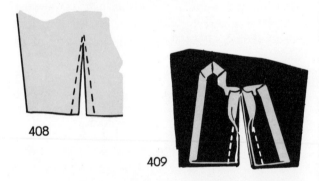

408

409

Press seams toward facings. Turn underlap to right side and stitch turned-in edge over seam (410). Turn overlap to right side and crease at fold line. Baste turned-in edge over seam. Lap placket and baste together at upper edge. Starting at lower edge of sleeve stitch turned-in edge over seam, around point and across top of placket, catching the top edge of the underlap (411). Join sleeve seam with a flat-fell seam. Gather and pleat lower edge of sleeve to fit cuff (411).

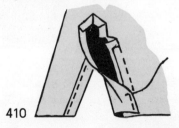

410

411

Shirt Cuff

Baste interfacing to cuff facing (412a). Trim away interfacing seam allowance at upper edge. Stitch cuff to cuff facing, right sides together, leaving upper edge open. Trim interfacing close to stitching and grade seam allowances. Turn to right side and press. Baste and stitch cuff facing to inside of lower edge of sleeve, adjusting gathers evenly. Press seam toward cuff facing. Turn under free edge of cuff and top-stitch over seam on right side (412b). Continue top-stitching around entire cuff. Close cuff with button and buttonhole. (See Chapter 12.)

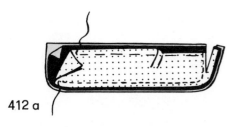

412 a

412 b

French Cuff

The French cuff is made in the same way as the shirt cuff. Before applying the cuff to the sleeve edge turn underlap of placket to the inside (413), and baste at lower edge. Apply the French cuff to the lower edge of sleeve same as the shirt cuff. Make buttonholes in both edges of cuff. (See Chapter 12.) Fold the finished cuff in half and fasten with cuff links or linked buttons (413).

413

Long Tight Sleeve

The long tight sleeve usually has no cuff and the placket opening is closed with snap fasteners, loops and buttons or a zipper. The lower edge of the sleeve is finished with seam binding or a narrow self-facing.

SLEEVE WITH SNAP CLOSING. Cut two strips of woven seam binding one inch longer than opening. Turn under upper edge of one piece of seam binding and stitch to seam allowance of front edge of opening $1/8$ inch from seam line, right sides up (414). Turn seam allowance to inside along seam line and press. Hem edge of seam binding to sleeve (415). Turn under upper edge of other piece of seam binding and stitch to seam allowance at back edge of opening $1/8$ inch from edge, right sides up (415). Clip to seam

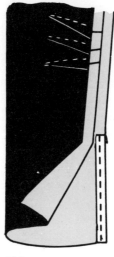

414

415

at top of seam binding of back seam allowance (416). Turn seam binding back along inside edge and press flat. Hem edge to inside of seam allowance. Cut a strip of seam binding ³/₄ inch longer than lower edge of sleeve. Turn under ³/₈ inch on each end of binding and stitch seam binding to right side of lower edge of sleeve (416). Turn seam binding to inside and press flat. Hem edge to sleeve, mitring at corners. Overlap edges of opening to seam line. Sew snaps along opening (417).

SLEEVE WITH FABRIC LOOP AND BUTTON CLOSING. Make fabric tubing or cording and cut in lengths to fit over buttons. (See page 223.) Baste loops to front edge of opening along seam

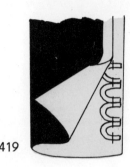

419

416

417

line on right side (419). Cut a bias strip of fabric 1³/₈ inches wide and long enough to face both sides of the opening and the lower edge of the sleeve plus seam allowances. Turn under ends of strip. Baste to front edge of opening over loops (420), right sides together, around lower edge of sleeve and along back edge of opening. Mitre at corners and stitch. Trim seam allowances and turn facing to inside. Turn under edges

420

SLEEVE WITH THREAD LOOP AND BUTTON CLOSING Finish opening and lower edge of sleeve as described above for snap closing. Work thread loops along front edge of opening. (See page 223.) Overlap opening to seam line and mark position for buttons on back edge of sleeve through centre of each loop. Sew buttons at markings (418).

of facing and hem to sleeve (420). Overlap opening to seam line and mark position for buttons along back edge through centre of loops. Sew buttons at markings (421).

418

421

SLEEVE WITH ZIPPER CLOSING. Insert zipper by the slot-seam method given on page 197 (see

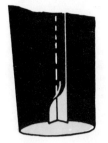

422

423

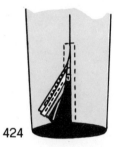

424

diagrams 422, 423, 424 above). To finish the lower edge of the sleeve, cut a strip of woven seam binding $3/4$ inch longer than the measurement of the sleeve and turn under $3/8$ inch on each end. Baste and stitch seam binding to right side of lower edge of sleeve (425). Turn seam binding to inside and press flat. Hem edge to sleeve, mitring at corners.

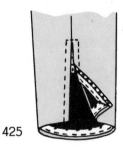

425

SLEEVE WITH VENT CLOSING. Normally vent sleeve closings do not unbutton. Sometimes a bound or worked buttonhole is made for decorative purposes (429), but the buttonhole is never cut through on the facing side. Stitch the sleeve seams leaving extension edge open below marking. Clip seam allowances

to marking at top of extension of undersleeve. Press seams open. Turn up lower edge of sleeve at hemline and baste. Attach hem to sleeve with invisible stitch-

426

ing (426). Turn under extension of upper sleeve along seam fold line and press. Catch-stitch edge to hem allowance (427). Lap upper sleeve extension over

427

undersleeve, matching edge markings for opening. Catch-stitch in place along hem allowance and baste permanently to undersleeve extension above hem (428). Turn sleeve to right side and sew buttons in position on upper sleeve through all thicknesses (429).

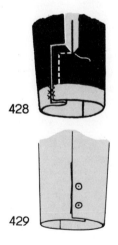

428

429

COLLARS

The collar is about the most important part of any garment, and must fit well. Although there is a variety of collar designs and shapes, construction-wise they all fit into one of three groups—round, pointed, or collar and undercollar cut in one.

All collars except the detachable ones are normally interfaced to give them needed body and shaping. The type of interfacing to select will depend upon the design of the collar and the fabric used. For help in selecting the proper interfacing, consult Chapter 3 on shaping materials.

Flat collars, or those which have only a slight roll, normally have the upper and undercollar cut from the same pattern piece. The interfacing is also cut from this piece and on the same grain as the collar sections. When interfacing small flat collars in a smooth, light- or medium-weight fabric, you may wish to try iron-on interfacing. This is placed face down on the wrong side of the collar and pressed in position until it is bonded to the fabric. This eliminates the need to stitch interfacing to the collar, but is not really successful for use on coarse, heavy fabrics or for tailored garments.

Collars which have a decided roll need two separate pattern pieces—one for the top and one for the under-collar. The undercollar is slightly smaller than the top section, to allow the top collar to roll properly. The interfacing is cut from the undercollar piece.

When the top and undercollar are cut in one piece, to be folded in half to form the collar, the interfacing is cut only half the width of the collar pattern piece or to the fold line.

If you are using sheer fabric, cut the interfacing from the top collar pattern piece and baste the inter-facing to the top collar section. This prevents the seam from showing through the sheer collar when it is finished.

In some patterns, especially suits and coats, there is a separate pattern piece for the interfacing. This inter-facing is cut on the bias with a seam at the centre back so that both sides of the collar are cut on the same grain and will roll the same. This type of collar is discussed in detail in the chapter on tailoring.

Round Collar

Baste interfacing to wrong side of undercollar (430). Stitch two sections of collar, right sides together, leaving neck edge open (431). Trim interfacing close to stitching and grade seam allowances so that the widest seam is on the edge without interfacing (432). This will keep the seam edges from pressing through to the right side. Clip small notches to seam line in outward curve. Press seam open, using the tip of the iron. Turn collar to right side. Understitch the seam allowance to the undercollar section (433). Press collar flat and baste around the outer edge (434).

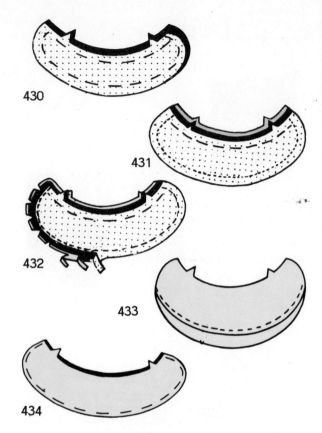

Pointed Collar

Baste interfacing to wrong side of undercollar (435). Stitch two sections of collar, right sides together, leaving neck edge open (436). Start at neck edge, stitch to point, take one diagonal stitch at point and continue stitching. Grade seam allowances same as for round collar. Cut diagonally across points (436). Press seam open. If you have a point presser, slip collar over board

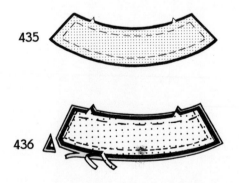

to press seam open. Turn collar to right side and pull out the corners, using fine needle. Understitch the seam allowance to undercollar, stitching as far into the points as possible (437). Press collar flat and baste around the outer edge (438).

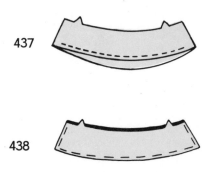

437

438

Collar and Undercollar Cut in One

Baste interfacing to wrong side of undercollar with one edge on fold line. Slip-stitch interfacing to collar on fold line (439). Fold collar in half, right sides together, and stitch side edges (440). Trim interfacing and grade seam allowances as for round collar, trim diagonally across points at fold edge. Turn to right side, pull out corners and press. Baste around outer edges (441).

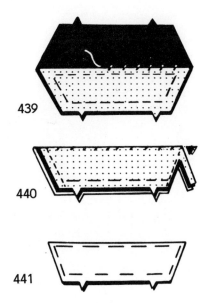

439

440

441

It is best to attach the collar as soon as possible so that neckline does not become stretched while working on the garment. Collars are applied with a bias facing, a back and front facing, or without a back facing. There are special instructions for applying the collar when the facing has a slash opening, fits on a V neckline, or if collar is two-piece. All of these methods are described in detail below.

Collar Applied with a Bias Facing

Pin and baste collar to neck edge of bodice, right sides

up, matching notches, centres and markings (442). Finish outside edge of facing in manner appropriate for

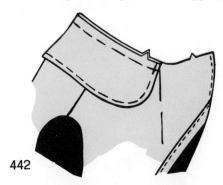

442

the fabric. Turn facing to outside at fold line and baste at neck edge. The facing will overlap the ends of the collar. Cut a bias strip $1/2$ inch wide and baste to neck edge over collar, lapping bias about $1/2$ inch over facings (443). Stitch entire neck edge. Grade seam allowances and clip curve at intervals. Turn facings to

443

inside. Press seam allowances toward bodice. Turn in free edge of bias facing and hem to bodice (444).

444

Collar Applied with Front and Back Facing

Pin and baste collar to neck edge of bodice, right sides up, matching notches, centres and markings (445). Join back and front facings, right sides together, with a plain seam (446). Press seams open. Finish outer edge of

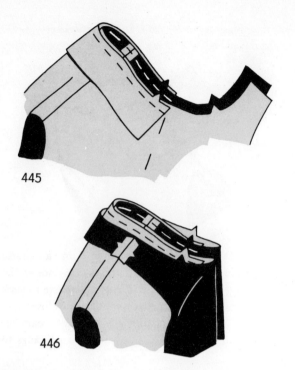

445

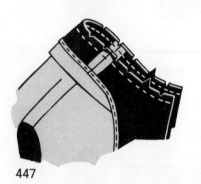

447

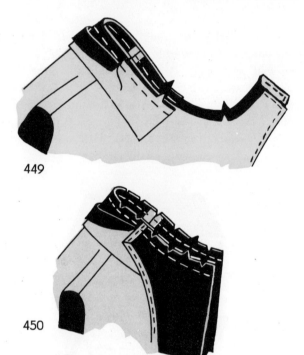

446

Collar Applied without a Back Facing

Finish shoulder and outer edge of facing in manner appropriate for the fabric used. Pin and baste collar in position, right sides up, from front edge to shoulder seam, match notches and markings (449). Clip top collar seam allowance at shoulder seam. Pin the undercollar only to the back bodice neck edge between the shoulder seams, leaving the top collar free (449). Baste in position. Stitch the entire neck edge as basted, leaving the top collar free across the back. Grade seam

449

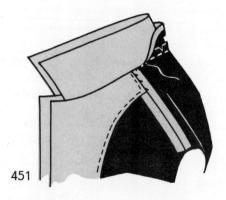

facing in manner suitable for fabric. Pin neck edge of facing to neck edge of bodice, matching notches and centres. Stitch entire neck edge (447). Grade seam allowances and clip curve at intervals. Press seam allowance toward facing and understitch to facing. Turn facing to inside and press. Tack facing at shoulder seams of bodice (448).

450

allowances and clip curve at intervals (450). Turn facing to inside and press, pressing back neck seam allowance up toward collar and front seam allowance down. Turn under seam allowance of top collar and slip-stitch to back seam line (451). Slip-stitch shoulder edge of front facing to shoulder seam allowance of bodice.

448

451

Collar Applied to a V-Neckline without Centre Front Seam

Reinforce point of neckline with a row of stitching along seam line (452). Slash seam allowance at point to stitching. Baste collar to right side of neck edge, matching notches, centres and markings (453). The ends of the collar must meet at the exact centre front. Note that when the seam line at the front edge of the collar is matched to the centre front of the bodice, the ends of the collar seam allowance extend over the seam line on the other side of the V neckline (453). The slash at the point of the V makes it possible to separate the V enough to attach the collar without catching the end of the collar in the seam line. Stitch front and back

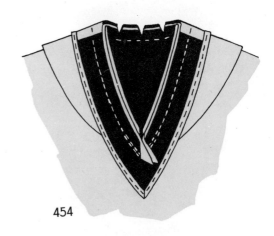

454

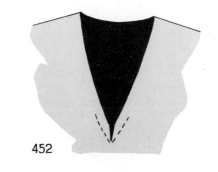

452

455

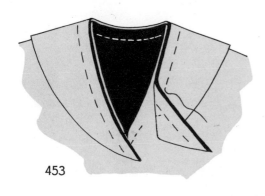

453

facings at shoulder seams and press seams open. Finish outer edge of facing in a manner suitable for the fabric (454). Reinforce the point of the neckline with a row of stitching and clip to stitching line. Baste facing over collar, right sides together, matching notches and centres, and keeping ends of collar free (454). Stitch entire neck seam and grade seam allowance. Press seam toward facing. Understitch facing to seam allowance. Turn facing to inside and tack facing at shoulder seams (455).

Collar Applied to a V-Neckline with a Centre Front Seam

Stitch centre front seam of bodice to seam line marking at neck edge (456). Clip to seam line at end of stitching. Stitch bodice back to bodice front at shoulder seams (456). Press seams open. Baste collar to right side of neck edge, matching notches, centres and markings. The ends of the collar seam allowance extend over the seam line on the other side of the V neckline (457), the same as in the V-neckline without centre front seam. The open seam above the clip at the point of the V makes it possible to separate the V enough to attach the collar without catching the ends of the collar in the

456

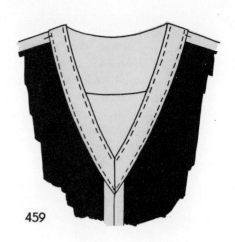

459

457

seam line. Stitch centre front seam of facing to seam-line marking at neck edge. Clip to seam line at end of stitching. Stitch front and back facings at shoulder seams and press seams open. Finish outer edge of facing in a manner suitable for the fabric. Baste facing over collar, right sides together, matching notches and centres, and keeping ends of collar free (458). Stitch entire neck seam and grade seam allowances. Turn facing to inside and press seam toward facing. Under-stitch facing to seam allowance. Tack facing at all seams (459).

Collar Applied with a Slash Opening

Pin and baste collar to neck edge of bodice, right sides up, matching notches, centres and markings (460). Place the front seam line edge of the collar at the stitching line for the slash opening. The ends of the collar seam may overlap at neck edge, depending on the width of the slash opening at top, but this will not interfere with stitching the seam. Stitch back facing

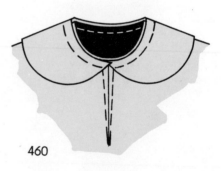

460

to front facing at shoulder seams. Press seams open. Finish outer edge of facing in a manner appropriate for the fabric (461). Baste facing in place, right sides together, matching notches, seams and slash markings. Stitch entire neck edge and along both sides of slash markings, tapering at point (461). Take an extra stitch at point. Slash opening to stitching, grade seam allowances and clip curve at intervals. Press seam toward

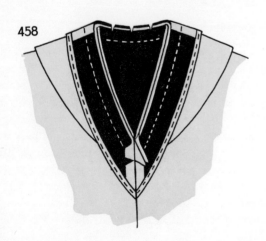

458

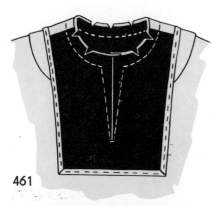

461

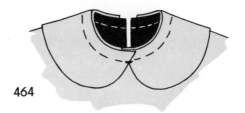

464

462

facing. Understitch facing to seam allowance, stitching as far into corners as possible. Turn facing to inside and press. Tack facing to shoulder seams (462).

This general information can be applied to these specific types of collars:

Peter Pan Collar

This is a round flat collar, and can be one- or two-piece. It is attached to the neck edge with a bias or fitted facing (465).

465

Convertible Collar

Any collar that can be worn open or closed at the neck. It can have a seam at the outer edge, or can be cut all in one with a fold at the outer edge. It can be attached to the neck edge with or without a back facing. The back facing is used when the neckline stands away from the neck (466, 467).

Applying a Two-Piece Collar

Construct same as a one-piece collar. Tack ends together at seam line at centre front, to hold in place while collar is being attached. Note that ends of collar overlap above seam line (463). Baste collar to neck edge, right sides up, matching notches, centres and markings (464). This kind of collar can be attached with a bias facing or a back and front facing, depending on the pattern and the design.

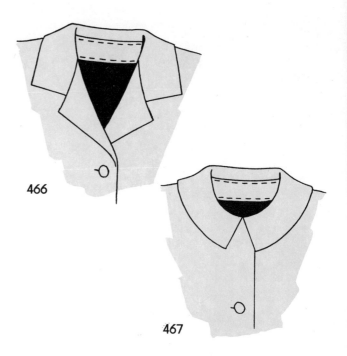

466

467

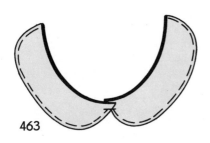

463

Sailor Collar

This is a wide, square collar at back (468), and comes to a V in front (469). It can be applied to a V-neckline with or without a centre front seam.

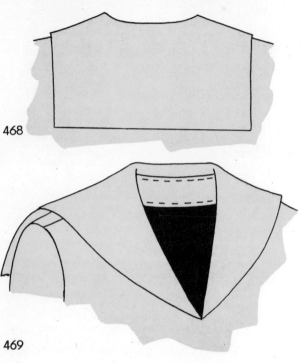

468

469

Shirt Collar

Construct collar section as for pointed collar (470). Topstitch around outside edges of collar $1/4$ inch from

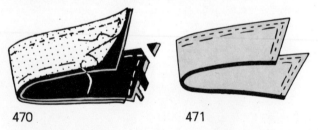

470   471

edge (471). Cut interfacing for collar band from collar band pattern. Baste interfacing to inside of undercollar band section (472). Turn in lower edge of outer collar band section at seam line and baste. Trim seam allowance to $1/4$ inch. Baste one section of collar band on each side of collar, right sides together, matching notches and markings. Stitch seam continuing to ends of collar band (472). Grade seam allowances and clip

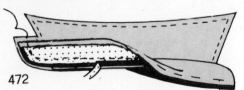

472

curve at intervals. Turn collar band down and press. Stitch interfaced section of collar band to inside neck edge of shirt (473). Grade and clip seam allowance, and press seam toward collar band. Baste turned-in edge of collar band over seam and top-stitch, continuing to stitch around collar band close to edges.

473

Shawl Collar

Mark seam allowance on wrong side of fabric where neck and shoulder seams meet on bodice back. Use a chalk or pencil and mark several inches on either side

474

of point (474). Stitch centre back seam of collar, right sides together (475), and press seam open. Lap and

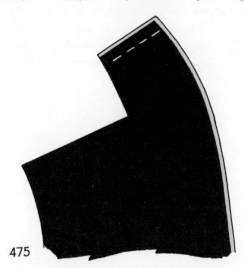

475

stitch centre back seam of interfacing, and trim close to stitching (476). Baste interfacing to inside of bodice front and collar. Reinforce corner at neck and shoulder on bodice front with a row of machine-stitching on seam line through interfacing (476). Slash to stitching

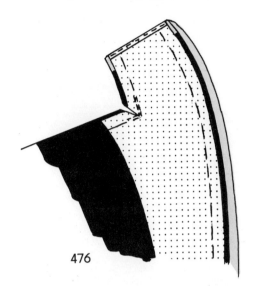

476

line at corner. Pin front and back together at neck and shoulder seams, match centres and reinforced corners to marked point on bodice back (477). Trim interfacing close to stitching and grade neckline seam. Clip curve at intervals and press seam toward collar. Press

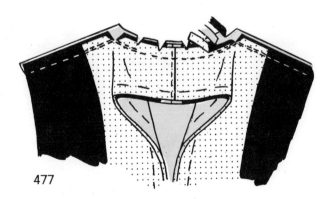

477

shoulder seams open. Stitch centre back seam of collar and facing (478). Press seam open. Reinforce corner at neck and shoulder with a row of machine stitching on seam line. Slash to point of stitching (478). Turn under neck and shoulder edge of facing at seam line and baste (479). Finish outer edge of facing in a way

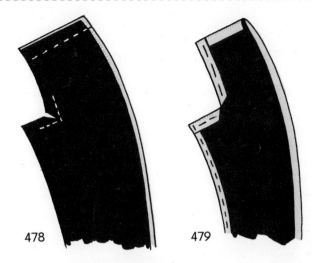

478   479

suitable for the fabric. Stitch collar and facing to bodice, matching centres and notches. Grade seams and trim interfacing close to stitching (480). Clip curve at intervals and turn facing to inside (481). Baste outer edges, rolling seam slightly to the underside on collar and to the inside on front edge. Press. Baste and slip-stitch over back neck seam line. Slip-stitch shoulder edge of facing to shoulder seam allowance of bodice (481).

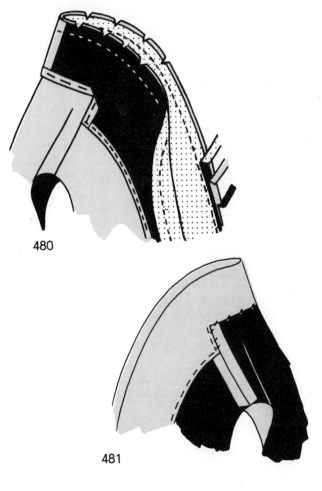

480

481

Tie Collar

A narrow straight collar that stands up from the neck edge and ties at centre front. It is used on a round neck with a lapped front closing. Finish the edge of the front facing in a manner suitable for the fabric. Turn the facing to the right side and stitch neck edge from fold to centre front (482), or marking for end of collar. Clip neck seam at end of stitching and trim seam allowance (482). Turn facing to inside and baste facing to neck edge beyond clip. Baste interfacing to inside of tie

482

collar with one edge on fold line (483). Slip-stitch interfacing to collar at fold line. Interface the full length of the collar and tie section for a tailored bow. For a soft bow, omit interfacing in the tie section (483). Interface collar section to centre front marking. Baste interfacing edge of tie collar to neck edge, right sides together, matching centre backs, notches and markings. Stitch neck edge between clips. Fold ends in half lengthwise with right sides together and stitch along edge and across ends (483). Trim interfacing close to stitching and grade seams. Turn to right side. Turn under free edge of tie collar between clips and slip-stitch to neck edge (484).

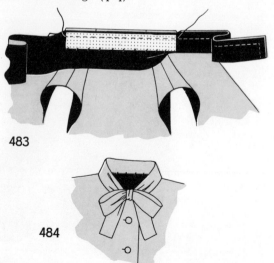

483

484

Band Collar

A narrow straight collar that stands up from the neck edge same as the tie collar, but stops at the centre front and has no tie ends (487). When the collar fits close to the neck it is applied in the same way as the tie collar. If the band collar is used on an open neckline, it is applied with a front and back facing (485, 486).

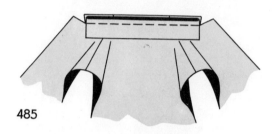

485

486

487

Turtle-Neck Collar

A wide true bias band that stands up from the neck edge and then rolls back over the neckline seam. If the collar is stretched as it is applied to the neckline, the collar will roll higher and fit close to the neck. If the collar is eased as it is applied to the neckline, it will roll less and stand away from the neck. Baste interfacing to inside of collar with one edge along fold line (488). Slip-stitch interfacing to fold line. Fold collar lengthwise, right sides together and stitch ends. Trim interfacing close to stitching and grade seams; turn

488

and press. Baste interfaced edge of collar to right side of neck edge, matching centres and notches (489). Stitch seam. Clip curve at intervals. Press seam toward the collar. Turn under free edge of collar and hem over neckline seam (490).

Detachable Collar

The detachable collar is never interfaced. Stitch two sections of collar together, leaving neck edge open. Trim seams, clip curve at intervals and turn to right side. Press and baste outer edge. Use commercial cotton bias tape or cut a bias binding 1 inch wide and stitch to neck edge of collar in a narrow seam (492). Turn in the ends and free edge of binding and hem along seam line (493). Collar can be basted to neck edge, or attached with snap fasteners.

489

492

490

493

Top Collar Applied to Attached Collar

This would be used when applying a velvet collar to a coat or suit. Turn under all seam allowances of the top collar and baste (491). Baste top collar over the attached collar matching neck edges and centres. Slip-stitch all edges of top collar in place.

POCKETS

Pockets are functional and often decorative as well. There are three types—the patch pocket which is stitched to the surface of the garment, the set-in pocket for which a special opening is made in the garment, and the pocket set into a seam in the garment. Follow the directions on your Easy Sewing Guide sheet for specific directions as to when the pocket should be applied and for any special construction details for that pattern design.

Transfer the pattern markings for the exact placement of the pocket to the wrong side of the fabric. Pin-mark the pocket location and try on the garment to be sure that this is the correct and most flattering placement for your figure.

491

Patch Pockets

For pockets that are to be applied to the right side of the garment, baste-mark the location of the pocket on the right side of the garment.

If a patch pocket is applied in a fabric that should be matched, such as printed, checked, or plaid fabric, be sure to cut the pocket so it will match the fabric design on the garment exactly at the place the pocket is to be applied.

UNLINED PATCH POCKETS. Turn under the raw edge $1/4$ inch at the top of the pocket (494). Edge-stitch close to the folded edge. Turn down the top of the pocket on the right side along the fold-line marking. Beginning at hem fold, edge-stitch around the entire pocket along the seam line (494). Fasten thread ends at the tops of pocket. Trim the seam allowance from $1/4$ to $3/8$ inch and clip points diagonally at top corners (495). For square-corner and pointed pockets, cut diagonally across the corners in order to mitre the seam allowances. For rounded pockets, cut small notches in the seam allowance on curved edge (496). Turn the top hem allowance to the wrong side. Press in position. Turn under the seam allowances along the

line of stitching (497). On square-corner and pointed pockets, fold mitres in the seam allowances at the corner points (497). Press seam allowances flat. Baste around the pocket close to the edge. If you wish the hem allowance to be top-stitched in position, turn pocket to wrong side and stitch close to the folded hem edge. Fasten thread ends by tying them on the wrong side of pocket. Pin the pocket, right side up, to the right side of the garment, matching corners of pocket to markings accurately. Baste in position. Top-stitch pocket in position close to edge, starting at upper edge of pocket (498). The top corners may be reinforced by stitching a tiny triangle of fabric at the corner on wrong side. Fasten thread ends securely. Remove bastings and press. If the pocket is to be used mainly for decoration and you do not wish the stitching to show, slip-stitch the pocket in position with tiny, fine stitches.

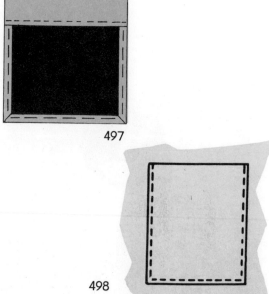

497

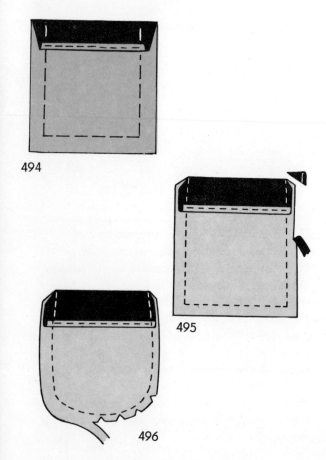

494

495

496

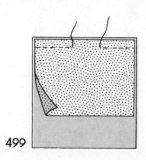

498

LINED PATCH POCKET. Stitch the right side of the lining to the right side of the pocket at the upper edge, leaving an opening at the centre of the seam (499). Press seam toward lining. Fold pocket at seam

499

2

3

1

22 **1** Sparkling pink*, vivid and exciting, the ideal contrast to basic colours — grey, black, dark green and fawn.
2 Pink accented with yellow gives a peachy coral glow. These are intensely flattering shades.
3 Buttercup, citrus yellow*, golden corn and honey. These attractive shades of yellow are redolent of summer sunshine.

23 Part of the fun of making clothes is choosing unusual combinations of colour and texture. The gorgeous selection in the shops makes co-ordinating easy, and gives real satisfaction in creating an exclusive ensemble. All the materials in this picture are 100% cotton.

Photograph by courtesy of The Cotton Board.

line, right sides together (500). Baste and stitch lining to pocket around outer edges (500). Grade seam allowances and turn pocket to right side through opening. Baste close to edges rolling seam slightly toward the lining. Slip-stitch the opening and press pocket flat (501). Pin and baste the pocket to the right side of garment matching edges of pockets to markings accurately. Top-stitch or slip-stitch in position (502), in the same manner as for unlined patch pocket.

503

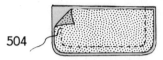

504

505

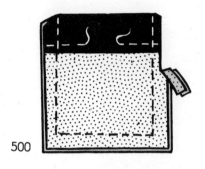

500

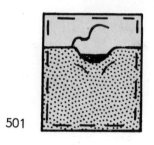

501

the lining (505). Press flap. Pin and baste right side of flap to right side of garment about $^3/_4$ inch above pocket or at markings. Stitch in place and fasten ends of thread securely. Trim seam allowance of flap section to $^1/_8$ inch (506). Turn in edge of lining section and ends diagonally so they do not show when flap is pressed down. Stitch turned-in edges of lining (507), and press flap down.

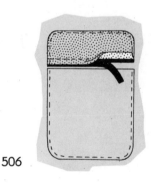

506

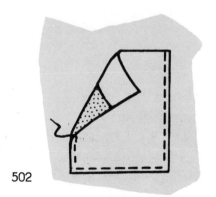

502

PATCH POCKET WITH FLAP. Construct and apply pocket as for lined patch pocket (503). Stitch lining to flap, right sides together, leaving upper edge open (504). Grade seam allowance and turn to right side. Baste close to edges, rolling seam slightly toward

507

Set-In Pockets

The set-in pocket is made by cutting an opening in the garment, and the construction is similar to that of a bound buttonhole. There are three types of set-in pockets—welt, flap and bound. The welt pocket has the extension covering the opening extending above the pocket (516). The flap pocket has the extension turned down over the opening (526). The bound pocket has an even width binding on either side of the opening (534). The bound pocket can be made of one or two pieces, and sometimes the binding is corded.

Pockets are cut of self-fabric in light-weight materials. In heavy fabrics, the pocket is cut of lining material and the area near the opening is faced with self-fabric.

WELT POCKET. Baste-mark position of the pocket on the right side of the garment (508). Fold the fabric strip for welt in half lengthwise, right sides together, and stitch ends (509). Trim seam allowance, turn to right side and press flat. Pin welt to right side of garment, with fold edge down and raw edge along bottom of marking for opening (510). Baste along seam

511

512

513

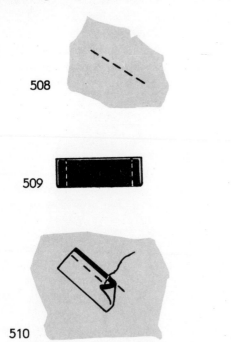

508

509

510

line. Pin one pocket section to garment, right sides together matching markings for opening accurately (511). Baste in position. Turn garment to wrong side. Stitch all around slash on seam line (512). Slash between stitching and clip diagonally into corners. Draw pocket piece through slash to wrong side (513),

and baste around opening (514). Press welt section up over opening. On wrong side, baste second section of pocket over the first section (515). Stitch pocket section together around all outside edges. On the right side, slip-stitch the seamed edges of welt to the garment with tiny, invisible stitches or top-stitch close to edge of welt (516).

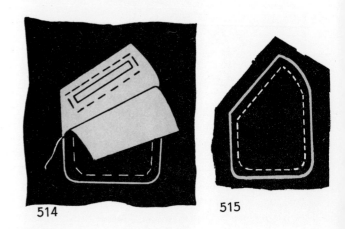

514

515

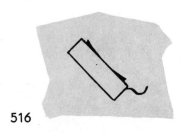

516

FLAP POCKET. Baste-mark the position for pocket opening on the right side of the garment (517). Stitch facing to flap section leaving upper straight edge open (518). Grade seam allowances and turn flap to right side. Baste close to edge, rolling seam slightly to facing side. Top-stitch close to finished edges if desired. Pin flap to right side of garment, with raw edge along top of marking for opening (519). Baste

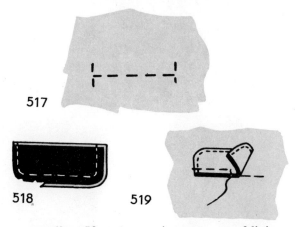

517

518   519

along seam line. If pocket sections are cut of lining fabric, cut two pieces of garment fabric about $2^1/_2$ inches wide to fit the top of the pocket sections (520). Turn in the lower edge and stitch fabric piece over lining with upper edges matched. Trim away the

lining fabric under the applied fabric pieces (521). Transfer markings for slash opening to one of these applied fabric pieces. Place this section over pocket opening, right sides together, and markings matched (522). Turn the garment to the wrong side and stitch around slash on seam line (523). Note that corners are not square; lower ends taper slightly so that they do not show when flap is pressed down. Slash between stitching lines and clip diagonally into corners. Draw

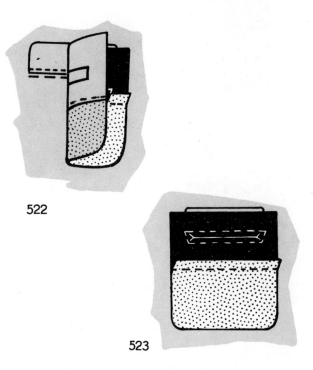

522

523

pocket piece through slash to wrong side. Fold up the fabric section of pocket, forming a welt at bottom edge of opening wide enough to fill the space and marking pleats at ends on inside (524). Stitch welt in position close to seam line at lower edge of opening. On inside,

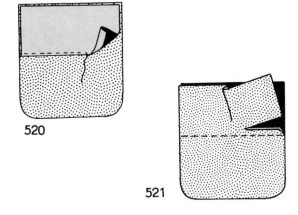

520

521

524

stitch ends of welt, catching small triangles and pleats (525). On the right side, press the flap section down

525

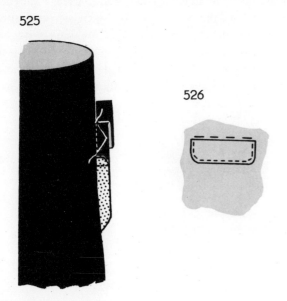

526

over the welt (526). Turn garment to wrong side and baste second section of pocket over the first section (527). Trim second section so that edges are even. Stitch together all edges of pocket. For a simulated patch pocket, stitch garment to pocket on right side. Add another row of stitching ½ inch outside the first row and across the top of the flap (528).

527

528

ONE-PIECE BOUND POCKET. Baste-mark the position for pocket opening on the right side of the garment (529). Be sure the marking is exactly on a single yarn of the fabric if the pocket opening is to be straight. Cut a piece of fabric 1 inch wider than the opening and twice the depth of the finished pocket plus 1 inch to allow for the binding (530). Measure 1 inch down from the centre of the piece and mark the line for the opening the same width as pocket opening. Place the pocket section on the garment, right sides together, with the shorter pocket section below opening. Match markings accurately and baste together along opening. Stitch ¼ inch from each side of opening and across ends. Slash through centre of

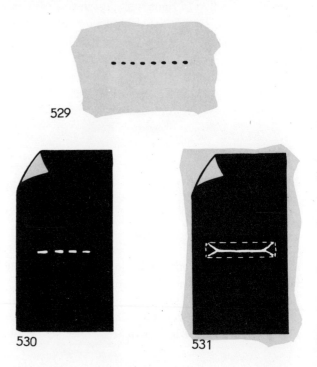

529

530   **531**

marking and cut diagonally into corners to line of stitching (531). Draw the pocket through the slash to the wrong side (532). Bring folded edges together forming an even binding on each side of opening on

532

533

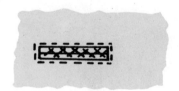

534

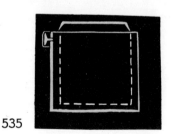

535

right side and inverted pleats at ends on wrong side (533). Catch-stitch the centre folds of bindings together on the right side and stitch around pocket opening close to binding (534). On the inside, press the upper section of pocket down and stitch the pocket sections together around outer edges (535). Remove catch-stitching and press the finished pocket.

TWO-PIECE BOUND OR PIPED POCKET. Baste-mark position for pocket opening on the right side of fabric (536). If pocket opening is on straight grain, be sure marking is along a single yarn of the fabric. Cut two strips for binding on straight grain of fabric. If fabric is plaid or check, the strips can be cut on the bias to give a decorative effect to the

pocket. Cut strips 1 inch wide and 1 inch longer than the opening. For bound opening, fold the strips of binding in half lengthwise, wrong sides together and press (537). If pocket opening is to be corded, fold the strip of binding over the piping cord and stitch close to piping cord with special foot on sewing machine. Baste the binding strips to the right side of the garment with the raw edges exactly along the marking for the opening (538). If the pocket sections are cut from lining fabric, cut a strip of garment fabric 2 inches wide and the length of the top of the pocket. Turn under lower edge and baste over one lining piece with upper edges even (539). Stitch lower edge of strip to pocket section

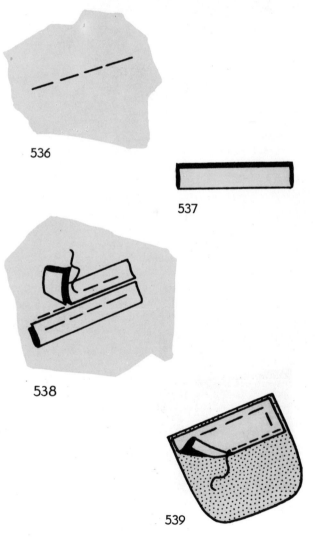

536

537

538

539

and trim away lining under self-fabric (540). Baste the pocket sections over the binding, right sides together and raw edges meeting at marking for opening (541). The pocket section with the self-fabric facing is placed above the opening. Turn garment to wrong side. Stitch $1/4$ inch above and below the marking for opening,

toward centre of opening and catch-stitch edges together (544). On the wrong side of garment, press the upper section of the pocket down over the lower section. Stitch the pocket together at outer edges being sure to catch the binding and triangular pieces at ends of opening (545). Remove catch-stitching and press.

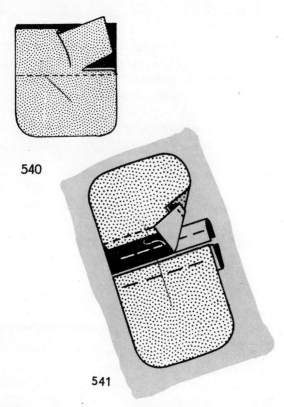

540

541

544

keeping both lines of stitching exactly the same length (542). Fasten ends of thread securely. Slash through the centre on marking and cut diagonally to the ends of stitching. Draw pocket sections through the slash opening to the wrong side (543). Press binding strips

545

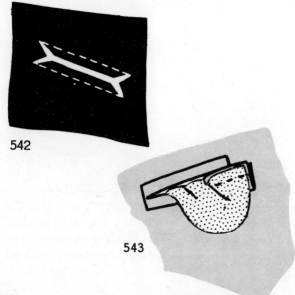

542

543

POCKET SET INTO A SEAM. The pocket set into a seam can be any pocket in which the opening falls along a seam line of the garment. In heavy fabrics, this pocket is cut of lining fabric and faced with self-fabric same as the set-in pocket.

SIDE-SEAM POCKET. Stitch side seam, leaving it open between markings for pocket (546). Fasten threads securely at ends of stitching. Machine-baste seam between markings. Press entire seam open. Pin one section of pocket to garment front seam allowance, right side together (547). Stitch $3/8$ inch from edge between markings and grade seams. Press seam

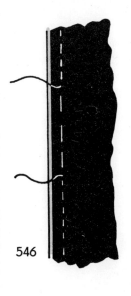

546

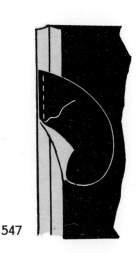

547

$^3/_8$ inch from edge (549). Clip back seam allowance at top and bottom of pocket to stitching line and press pocket section toward front (550). Baste and stitch outer edges of pocket together. Remove machine-basting at seamline opening.

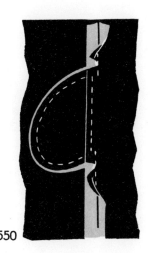

550

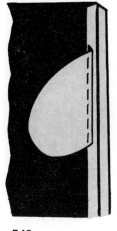

548

open and understitch seam to pocket section. Press pocket section toward the front of garment (548). Pin other pocket section to back seam allowance and stitch

FRONT HIP POCKET. Apply the pocket before side seams of the skirt are joined. This type of pocket should be interfaced to give the proper shape and support to the uper edge of the pocket (551). Cut the interfacing from the pattern piece for the pocket facing. Baste interfacing to inside of skirt front. Baste

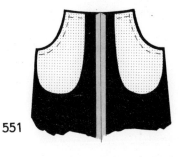

551

and stitch pocket facing to right side of skirt front. Trim interfacing close to stitching (552), grade seams and

549

552

clip curve at intervals. Turn facing to inside, press and understitch seam to facing (553). Lap front over side and pocket section to markings and pin in place (554).

554

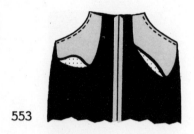

553

Note that the pocket stands away. On the inside, stitch side and pocket section to facing along curved edge to form the pocket (555). Baste pocket to skirt front at side seam and waistline. Continue constructing skirt.

555

CHAPTER 12

IMPORTANT CLOSINGS

One of the most vital steps in garment construction is closing the gaps—joining bodices to skirts, inserting zippers, making buttonholes. Give these areas the same attention and care as you do the rest. A badly inserted zipper, a messy buttonhole, even an insecurely sewn button can almost ruin the look of the garment.

The method you use to close up gaps depends on the garment design. There may even be times when you want to change the closing suggested by the pattern. On very bulky or pile fabrics, you may decide to substitute another type of closing for bound buttonholes, which are difficult to manipulate in these fabrics. Machine-worked buttonholes or perhaps heavy hooks and eyes will suffice. If you are in a hurry and wish to avoid making long rows of buttonholes for the back closing of a garment, you may recut the back opening a bit and insert a zipper without ruining the looks of the garment. As you sew, you'll find the methods which you like best, both in appearance and ease of application. The pattern will show the best type to use, but you should be familiar enough with all types to be able to substitute when feasible.

JOINING BODICES AND SKIRTS

The most common gap you'll close is that between the bodice and skirt. The waistline is usually the joining point.

Waistlines

In fashion, waistlines wander from just below the bust to the hip. However, the waistline of most garments fits smoothly and comfortably at the natural waistline. There is usually from $1/4$ to $3/8$ inch ease allowance in the normal bodice length to allow for movement and comfort. A bloused bodice will have more length.

To test for the correct bodice length and fit, put the bodice on over the undergarments you will be wearing. Pin the side opening with wrong sides of fabric together. Tie a heavy string around your natural waistline, adjusting it until it feels comfortable (556). If there is too much fullness in the bodice, or the side opening will not close, you need to adjust the fit of the waistline (556). To determine the correct length, move slightly until the bodice does not pull. Chalk-mark the waistline of the bodice along the bottom edge of the string.

556

Be sure the waistline of the skirt is the same size as the waistline of the bodice and that darts are in corresponding positions with seam lines matching. Pin the bodice and skirt, right sides together, at the waistline. Match notches, centre fronts and backs, side seams and construction darts, pleats, or gathers accurately. Baste. Try on the garment and check the fit and comfort of the waistline.

All waistlines should be stayed to prevent stretching. In most garments, a piece of woven seam binding stitched into the seam is sufficient. Woven seam binding is also used in the waistline of a lined jacket. Some garments require a firmer stay or an inside belt of grosgrain ribbon. This kind of stay is used to support a very full or heavy skirt as well as to hold a bloused top in place.

WOVEN SEAM BINDING STAY. Cut a piece of woven seam binding the length of your waist measurement plus seam allowances. Baste centre of seam binding over waistline seam on the skirt side (557). Stitch seam through all thicknesses. Press seam toward bodice.

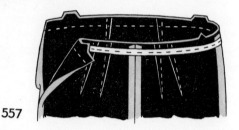

557

If skirt is gathered, apply the waistline stay to the skirt before it is attached to the bodice (558). Press the seam toward the bodice. If bodice is gathered, apply stay to bodice and press waistline seam toward skirt. When both skirt and bodice are gathered attach the waistline stay to the bodice side and then apply the skirt. Press the seam open.

558

See Chapter 14 for attaching a waistline stay in a lined suit jacket.

INSIDE BELT OF GROSGRAIN RIBBON. Cut a piece of grosgrain ribbon 2 inches longer than your waist measurement. Be sure to take a snug waist measurement. Turn under the ends ¹/₄ inch;

make a ½-inch hem on one end and a 1-inch hem on the other (559). Sew a hook in the centre of the 1-inch hem and an eye on the end of the ½-inch hem. Sew the grosgrain ribbon through the middle to the waistline seam of the garment, easing the seam to the ribbon if necessary. Place the hook and eye directly under the placket opening and leave the ribbon free for an inch on either side of the placket (560).

An inside grosgrain ribbon belt is also used to stay the waistline of a princess dress or any garment without a waistline seam. Tack the ribbon at all seams. Place the hook-and-eye closing directly under the placket opening.

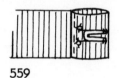

559

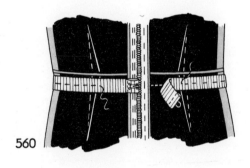

560

WAISTLINE FINISHES

Waistbands

The waistband should fit snugly at the natural waistline and lap front over back at the side closing. If closing is at centre back then the band laps left over right or the same direction as the lapped zipper application. Close waistband with hooks and eyes or a worked buttonhole and button.

The upper edge of the skirt should be ¹/₂ or ³/₄ inch larger than the waistband. This fullness is eased in to allow for the curve of the hip. The waistband is usually cut on the lengthwise grain of the fabric. For wool fabric, place the seam line of the inner edge of the waistband on the selvage and eliminate the seam allowance (561). The selvage finish on the inside of the band is less bulky than a turned-in seam.

561

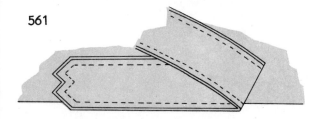

If you are cutting your own waistband without a pattern, cut a piece of fabric the length of your waist measurement plus about 3 inches for seam allowances and overlap and twice the finished width plus seam allowances.

Waistbands are interfaced to give body and prevent stretching. Cut the interfacing half the width of the waistband pattern or to the fold line. Baste the interfacing to the inside of the edge of waistband to be stitched to skirt with other edge along lengthwise fold. Slip-stitch interfacing to fold line (562).

562

When applying a waistband, it may be slip-stitched on the inside so that no stitching shows, or it may be top-stitched. Wide waistbands are stiffened with belting or boning to keep them from rolling over at the upper edge. In a very heavy fabric, the waistband can be cut of a single thickness of wool and backed with grosgrain ribbon to reduce the bulk.

SLIP-STITCHED WAISTBAND. Fold waistband lengthwise, right sides together (563). Stitch ends and along extension for lap at back edge. Trim interfacing close to stitching and grade seams. Clip to stitching at end of extension. Turn band to right side and press. Pin interfaced edge of band to *outside* of skirt, right sides together (564). Match notches, centres and markings. Ease skirt to band and stitch. Trim interfacing close to stitching and grade seam. Press seam toward band. Turn under free edge of band. Slip-stitch over seam on inside, enclosing raw edges (565). If selvage edge has been used, slip-stitch the selvage to the seam line.

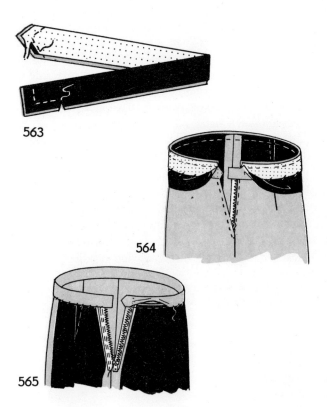

563

564

565

TOP-STITCHED WAISTBAND. Fold waistband lengthwise. Stitch and turn ends of band same as for slip-stitched waistband (563). Pin right side of waistband to *inside* of skirt, matching notches, centres and markings (566). Ease skirt to band and stitch. Trim interfacing close to stitching and grade seam. Press seam toward band. Turn under free edge of band and baste over seam on right side of skirt. Top-stitch through all thicknesses (567), and continue top-stitching around all edges of waistband, if desired.

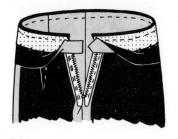

566

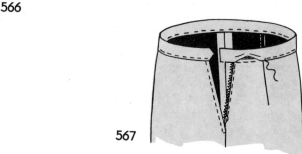

567

BONED WAISTBAND. Cut 6 pieces of feather-boning the width of the waistband. Push back the covering on the boning and cut off $3/4$ inch of the boning on one end (568b). Baste boning to inside of waistband on the side without the interfacing with trimmed edge of boning at seam line (568a). Place one piece at the side seam and one at the back edge of the placket opening. Place the other pieces $1^1/_2$ to 2 inches on either side of the centre front and centre back marking. Stitch through tape on both sides of the boning. Belting can be substituted for the boning. Stitch ends of band and apply it to the outside of the skirt as for the slip-stitched waistband. The boned waistband should never be top-stitched. Trying to stitch over the ends of the boning will break the machine needle.

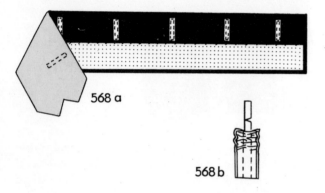

568 a

568 b

WAISTBAND BACKED WITH GROS-GRAIN RIBBON. Allow only a seam allowance beyond the fold line at the upper edge of the waistband pattern when cutting the fabric waistband. Cut the interfacing half the width of the waistband pattern. Trim off the $5/_8$-inch seam allowance at the ends and lower edge of the interfacing. Baste interfacing to inside of waistband. Turn in the seam allowance on all edges of the waistband and baste over the interfacing (569). Lap waistband over upper edge of skirt to seam line and baste, matching centres, notches and markings (570). Ease skirt to waistband. Top-stitch band to skirt and continue stitching around all edges of band. Baste grosgrain ribbon to inside of waistband turning in ends of ribbon to match ends of waistband. Slip-stitch ribbon to inside of band (571).

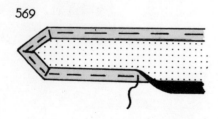

569

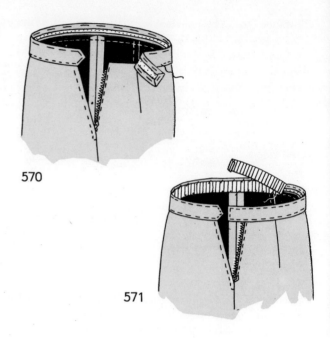

570

571

PLACKETS

Plackets are openings in a garment usually put there for the purely practical purpose of allowing one to get in and out of a garment. Most plackets are closed with zippers, but there are some designs and garments that require a placket finished with buttons, hooks and eyes or snap fasteners. Nylon tape is the newest closure on the market.

Zippers

Zippers are made with metal or nylon chains. The nylon chain is lighter-weight and more flexible than the metal chain. The automatic locking slider locks at any point on the chain. There are six basic types of zippers and it is important that you select the one designed for your particular purpose.

SKIRT ZIPPER. Open at the top; comes in 7- or 9-inch lengths to take care of any skirt opening.

DRESS ZIPPER. Closed at the upper edge with a bridge top stop; comes in 10-, 12- and 14-inch lengths. Use the longest length in tight-fitting dresses.

NECKLINE ZIPPER. Open at the top; used for necklines, sleeves, housecoats or underarm blouse plackets. It is made in lengths every inch from 4 through 10 inches, every two inches from 10 through 24 inches, 30-inch and 36-inch.

SEPARATING ZIPPER. Open at both ends;

designed for use in coats and jackets that have to open down the front. This type is available in a light-weight chain in lengths every two inches from 10 through 20 inches and a heavy-weight chain in lengths every two inches from 14 through 24 inches.

TROUSER ZIPPER. Comes in just one length

—11 inches. This is the only zipper that can be cut to fit the placket. The zipper is cut after it is inserted in the garment so be sure to read the directions carefully before cutting. The extra-wide tape allows for the double stitching necessary in the application. The slider is specially made to withstand frequent commercial pressings.

LOOSE COVER ZIPPER. Has a heavier chain

and is put on a stronger, wider tape for use in loose covers and pillows. It is made in 24-inch, 27-inch, 30-inch and 36-inch lengths.

Zipper applications sometimes prove a bit difficult for beginners. They are really easy if the correct procedures are followed, and the zipper or cording foot is used on the machine. Never try to insert a zipper without this attachment. You'll risk breaking the machine needle, perhaps damage the machine, and it's doubtful that the zipper will look trim once it's in the garment.

There are various zipper applications depending on the placement of the zipper in the garment, and the type of garment. Excellent directions for various applications are usually furnished with any packaged zipper you purchase. However, there may be times when you will wish to change the type of application or you may purchase zippers with no accompanying instructions. Generally zippers are centred in a slot seam or hidden in a lapped seam.

Most zippers are inserted into seams. The placket or seam opening for the zipper should be $1/4$ to $3/8$ inch longer than the metal teeth or nylon coils of the zipper. *Don't include the top seam allowance, if there is one, in this measurement.* Stitch the placket opening closed with a machine-basting stitch (8 to 10 stitches to the inch) on the seam line. Stay-stitch the seam allowances of the placket $1/4$ inch from the seam line in the direction of the grain. If the seam allowance is less than $5/8$ inch, stitch woven seam binding to the edges, right sides up.

SLOT SEAM APPLICATION. This type of

application is used at necklines, sleeves, centre back or centre front seams and under inverted or box pleats. Machine-baste seam for placket (572) and press seam open.

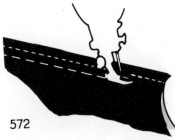

572

Attach zipper foot to the sewing machine. Adjust to right-hand side of needle (573). Open zipper, keeping the pull tab up. Place face down on pressed open seam with bottom stop of zipper at start of basting for opening. With the teeth of one side of zipper on the seam line, stitch to the seam allowance close to the teeth from bottom to top of zipper (573). *Sew through tape and seam allowance only.* Adjust zipper foot to left-hand

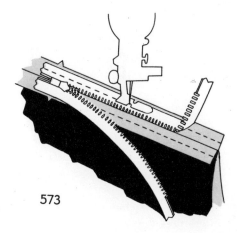

573

side of needle (574). Match the other side of teeth to seam line and stitch zipper tape *to the other seam allowance in same manner,* beginning at turned-up pull tab. Sew through zipper tape and seam allowance only. Close

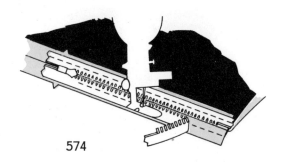

574

the zipper by pulling up the pull tab. Spread the garment flat and stitch the zipper to the garment, starting at top of zipper, down one side, across the bottom, and up the other side (575). Sew through zipper tape, seam allowance and garment. Be sure to stitch an even distance from the teeth so that the stitching on the right side will be even from the seam. Some people prefer

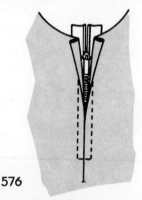

575

to do this final top-stitching from the right side of the garment on the slot seam application. They feel that it is easier to get the two sides exactly even. Either way is correct, so choose the one which gives you the best results. Press and remove machine-basting (576).

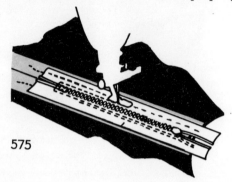

576

Finish outer edge of facing in appropriate manner. Stitch facing to neck (577) or sleeve edge of garment, grade seam and clip curve at intervals. Understitch seam allowances to facing. Press facing down over zipper tape. Turn under raw edges of facing and slip-stitch over zipper tape (578). Sew a hook and eye above zipper (579).

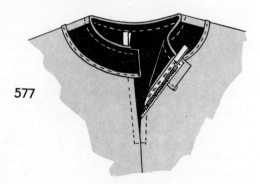

577

578

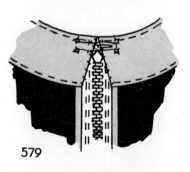

579

If facing has been applied before the zipper, machine-baste seam together with facing turned up so as not to catch it in the seam (580). Apply zipper as described above. Trim zipper tape off at neckline seam (581). Remove basting. Press facing down over zipper tape. Turn under raw edges of facing and slip-stitch over zipper tape (581). Sew a hook and eye above zipper.

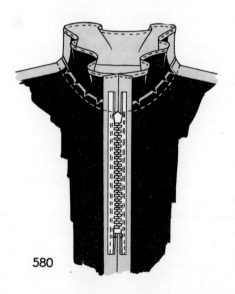

580

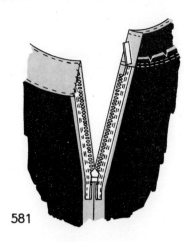

581

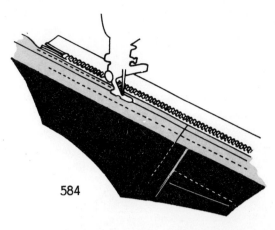

584

LAPPED SEAM APPLICATION FOR DRESS PLACKET.

This type of application is used primarily in the side seam of a dress or in any placket that falls in the middle of a seam. Baste the seam for placket by machine (582) and press open. Attach zipper foot to machine and adjust to right-hand

Spread garment flat and turn zipper face down over front seam allowance. Note the small pleat in seam allowance at top and bottom of placket (585). Starting at seam line, stitch across bottom of zipper, up the front side and across the top. Stitch an even distance from the teeth, sewing through zipper tape, seam allowance

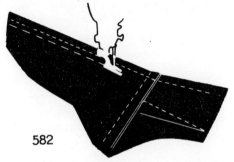

582

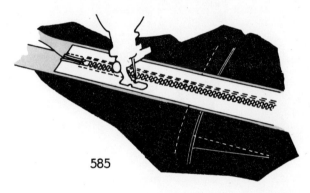

585

side of needle (583). Open zipper and place face down *on back seam allowance.* Match the bottom of zipper to beginning of machine basting with teeth on seam line. Stitch zipper to seam allowance close to teeth from bottom to top (583). *Sew through zipper tape and back seam aliowance only.* Adjust zipper foot to left-hand

and front of garment. The stitching line should be as close to folded edge as possible (586). Press and remove machine-basting.

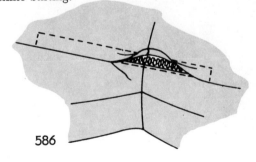

586

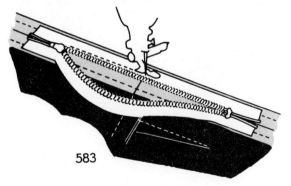

583

of needle. Close zipper and turn face up. Press fabric away from zipper forming a fold in back seam allowance along zipper (584). Stitch from bottom up through seam allowance and tape close to zipper.

LAPPED SEAM APPLICATION FOR PLACKET OPEN AT ONE END.

This type of application is used in skirts, necklines, centre back or centre front seams. Fashion-wise, the lapped application is more popular than the slot seam for back neckline or the long back zippers. The lapped application conceals the zipper better than the slot seam during normal movement of the body. Use the same method as the lapped application for dress placket but eliminate stitching across the top of the zipper.

Finish outer edge of facing in appropriate manner. Stitch facing to neck edge of garment, grade seams, clip curve at intervals. Understitch seam allowance to facing. Press facing down over zipper tape. Turn under raw edge of facing and slip-stitch over double-stitched side of zipper tape. Clip and trim facing on lapped side of zipper as shown. Turn under raw edges and slip-stitch over zipper tape. Sew a hook and eye above zipper.

If facing has been applied before the zipper, machine-baste seam together with facing turned up so as not to catch it in the seam. Apply zipper as de-

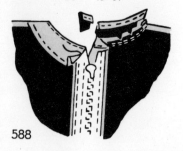

587

scribed above. Trim zipper tape off at neckline seam (587). Remove basting. Press facing down over zipper tape. Clip and trim facing on lapped side of zipper as shown (588). Turn under edges of facing on both sides and slip-stitch over zipper tape. Sew a hook and eye above zipper (589).

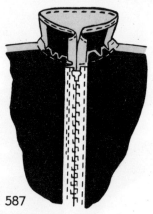

588

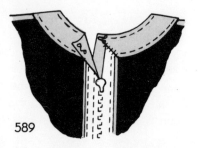

589

HAND-FINISHED APPLICATION OF A ZIPPER.

The finest couturier garments have hand-finished zippers. This gives a professionally finished appearance to the garment. It is preferable for many fabrics, such as velvet, velveteen, fleece, lace or sheer fabrics, when top-stitching is either difficult or unsightly. It is quite simple to do, and you should try it on your finer garments. It can be used with either the slot or lapped application. Complete all machine-stitching on the inside seam allowances of the garment. Spread garment flat with zipper face down (590) and baste to garment instead of the usual top-stitching in the last step. Turn garment to right side. Sew zipper in place by hand with a half-back or prick stitch using basting as a guide line (591).

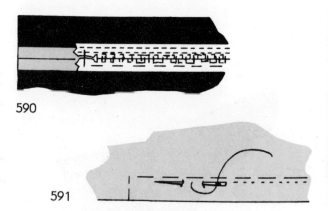

590

591

APPLICATION IN A FACED OPENING.

Slip-baste finished opening edges together (592). Place

592

open zipper face down on wrong side of garment with bottom stop of zipper at lower end of opening (593). Baste one side of zipper to the garment with the teeth on the seam line. Turn under the end of tape at neck edge (593). Close the zipper and baste other side of tape to garment, turning under the tape at neck edge.

24 Simplicity and elegance should be the aim in choosing accessories. This combination of texture and colour is as interesting as it is original.

Handbag, scarf, brooch and gloves by courtesy of Woollands of Knightsbridge, London.

25 Colourful, attractive and easily cared for, these are a few of the wide variety of materials giving lasting wear for lively youngsters of all ages. John's blazer is of a wool and cotton mixture flannel, trousers of 100% woollen flannel. Phillip's jacket is 100% Harris tweed, trousers of all cotton corduroy, shirt 100% cotton poplin. Carol wears a coat of woollen velour. Veronica's dress is of 100% washable woollen material proofed and guaranted against shrinkage by the Dylan process.

Tony's sports jacket is of Irish tweed, trousers of Terylene and wool flannel.

Renée has a Viyella blouse under a tunic of 55% Terylene and 45% wool worsted.

Joan's party dress is made from one of the Horrockses range of cotton prints.

593

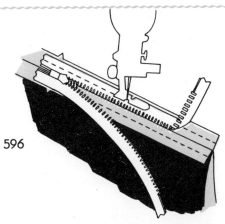

596

Attach zipper foot to machine. Turn garment to right side and top-stitch down one side, across bottom and up the other side of zipper. Remove the bastings and sew hook and eye at neck edge above zipper (594).

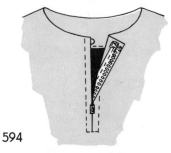

594

APPLICATION IN A KNIFE-PLEATED SKIRT. Plan pleats so that seam falls on the inner edge of a pleat. Insert zipper before skirt is pleated. Stitch seam to marking for placket opening and fasten threads securely. Baste seam for placket by machine and press open (595). Attach zipper foot to machine

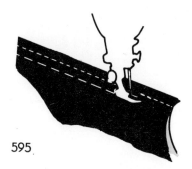

595

and adjust to right-hand side of needle. Open zipper and place face down *on back seam allowance*. Match the bottom of zipper to beginning of machine-basting with teeth on seam line (596). Stitch zipper to seam allowance close to teeth from bottom to top. *Sew through zipper tape and back seam allowance only.* Adjust zipper foot to left-hand side of needle. Close zipper and turn face up. Press fabric away from zipper, forming a

fold in back seam allowance along zipper. Stitch from bottom up through seam allowance and tape close to

597

zipper (597). Turn zipper face down over front seam allowance. There will be a small pleat at lower end of placket (598). Starting at seam line, stitch across bottom of zipper and up the front side. *Sew through zipper tape and front seam allowance only.* Make pleats in skirt

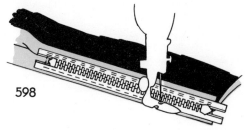

598

and press. Baste pleats at upper edge leaving pleat over placket opening free (599). Remove machine-basting from placket opening.

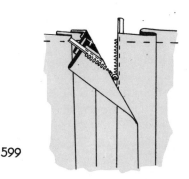

599

APPLICATION IN A BOX-PLEATED SKIRT.

Plan pleats so that the seam with placket opening falls between two box pleats (600, 601). Stitch seam to marking for placket opening and fasten thread securely. Machine-baste placket opening and press seam open. Insert zipper in seam by either the slot

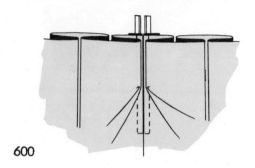

600

(600) or lapped (601) application before skirt is pleated. The application you choose is a matter of personal preference since both are used in ready-made garments. After the zipper application is completed, make the pleats in the skirt. The zipper will be concealed under the folds between two pleats.

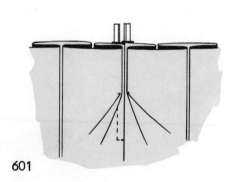

601

APPLICATION IN A WELT SEAM.

Apply the zipper before completing the welt seam. Make a plain seam to marking for placket opening and fasten thread securely. Machine-baste seam for placket opening and press seam open (602). Apply zipper as directed for lapped seam application normally done in a skirt placket. To complete the welt seam, trim the front seam allowance to $1/4$ inch (602). Clip the back seam allowance to the seam line at bottom of zipper and press seam allowance toward the front over trimmed seam allowance. Stitch close to the raw edge in line with stitching line for zipper (603).

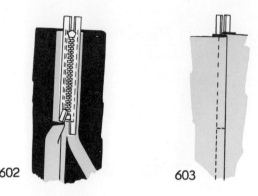

602   603

APPLICATION IN A FLAT-FELL SEAM.

Before seam is stitched, cut a facing of self-fabric on the lengthwise grain 1 inch wide and the length of the placket opening. Pin the facing to the front seam allowance, right sides together, along placket opening (604). Place end of facing in line with marking for placket opening. Stitch in a $1/4$-inch seam. Turn facing to inside and press (604). Stitch the flat-fell seam to the marking for placket opening, wrong sides together. Press seam toward back. Clip the back seam allowance to marking for placket opening and trim back seam allowance below placket to $1/8$ inch (604). Turn under

604

front seam allowance in line with facing and top-stitch to garment close to folded edge (605). Fasten thread

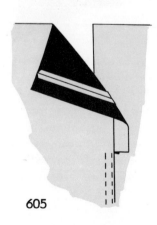

605

securely at end of placket. Turn garment to wrong side and continue clipping the back across the flat-fell seam

606

to the last row of stitching (606). Machine-baste placket opening together along seam line of facing (607), and press seam open. Apply zipper as directed

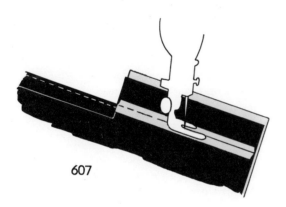

607

for lapped seam application. Remove machine-basting and open zipper. Top-stitch the front edge of the placket to meet top-stitching on flat-fell seam (608).

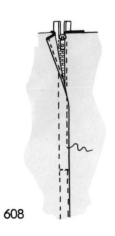

608

APPLICATION IN A SKIRT OF RE-VERSIBLE FABRIC. The flat-fell seam application can be used if your fabric is light-weight. However, most reversible fabrics are too bulky for that extra facing piece. For heavy reversible fabrics it is important to note that the flat-fell seams must be made on the inside of the fabric so that the zipper can be inserted without the extra facing. Stitch the flat-fell seam to the marking for placket opening, right sides together (609). Press seam toward front. Clip the seam allowances to marking for placket opening and trim front seam allowance below placket to $1/_8$ inch. Turn under back seam allowance and top-stitch to garment close to folded edge (610). Fasten thread securely at end of placket. Machine-baste placket opening

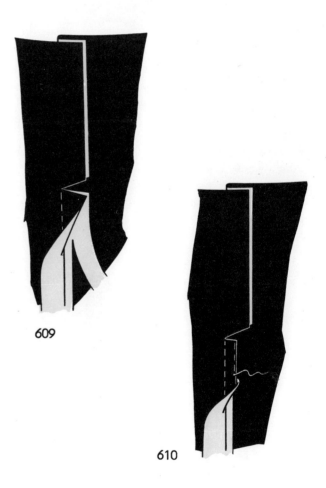

609

610

together along seam line. Apply zipper as directed for lapped seam application. Trim off seam allowances on both sides even with edge of zipper tape (611). Sew the zipper tape to the back of the garment with a very fine slip-stitch, being careful that it does not show on the right side (611).

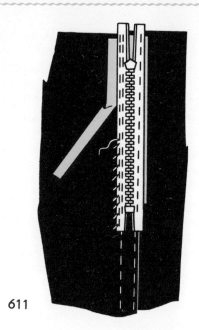

611

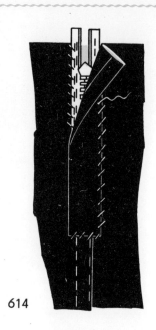

614

When the skirt is worn on the reverse side, the zipper application will be on the right hip instead of the left. It is necessary to make a self-fabric shield to hide the zipper tape when the skirt is worn on this side. Cut a piece of skirt fabric $2^1/_2$ inches wide and the entire length of the zipper tape plus a $^1/_4$-inch seam allowance. Fold in half lengthwise with reverse side of fabric together and stitch in a $^1/_4$-inch seam (612). Press seam open and match to centre of piece. Stitch across one end in a $^1/_4$-inch seam (613). Turn to

APPLICATION IN A REVERSIBLE SKIRT OF TWO FABRICS.

Stitch seams of one skirt fabric, leaving open above marking for placket on left side. Stitch seams of second skirt fabric, leaving open above marking for placket on right side. Press seams open and fasten thread securely at ends of openings. Machine-baste placket openings in both skirts. Attach zipper foot and adjust to right-hand side of needle. Open zipper, keeping pull tab up. Place face down on placket seam allowance of first skirt with bottom stop of zipper at end of opening. With the teeth of one side of zipper on the seamline, stitch to the seam allowance, close to teeth, from bottom to top of zipper (615). *Sew through tape and seam allowance only.*

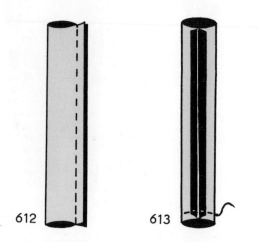

612　　　613

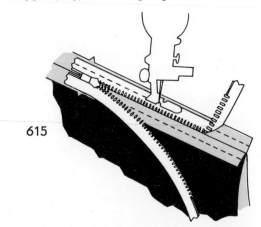

615

outside and press. Centre the piece over zipper tape. Sew to garment along bottom and front edge of zipper tape with a very fine slip-stitch (614). Press.

Adjust zipper foot to left-hand side of needle. Match the other side of teeth to seam line and stitch zipper tape to the other seam allowance in same manner beginning at turned-up pull tab. *Sew through zipper tape and seam allowance only* (616). Close zipper. Spread the

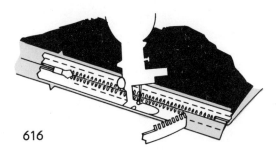

616

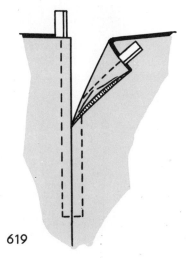

skirt flat and machine-baste the zipper to the garment starting at top of zipper, down one side, across the bottom and up the other side. *Sew through zipper tape, seam allowance and skirt* (617). Match seams of both

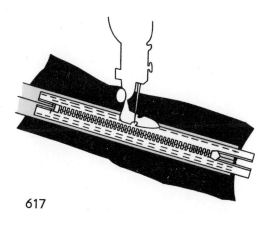

617

619

APPLICATION IN A KNIFE-PLEATED SKIRT OF REVERSIBLE FABRIC. Plan your pleats so that all the seams fall in the centre of the upper underfold of a pleat. The pleats must be at least 1 inch deep to conceal the zipper tape. The flat-fell seams must be made on the inside of the fabric because of the zipper application. Insert the zipper before making the pleats. Stitch the flat-fell seam to the marking for placket opening, right sides together. Press seam toward front. Clip the seam allowance to marking for placket opening and trim front seam allowance below placket to $1/8$ inch (620). Turn under

skirts at placket opening with wrong sides of skirts together and baste (618). Using regular machine-stitching, stitch along machine-basting down one side, across the bottom and up the other side of zipper.

620

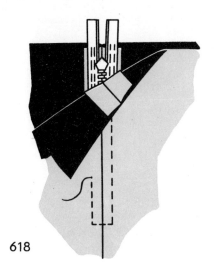

618

back seam allowance and top-stitch to front, close to folded edge. Fasten thread securely at end of placket. Machine-baste placket opening together along seam

621

line (621). Apply zipper as directed for slot seam application. Trim off seam allowances on both sides even with edge of zipper tape (622). Make pleats in skirt and press; baste pleats at upper edge (623).

622

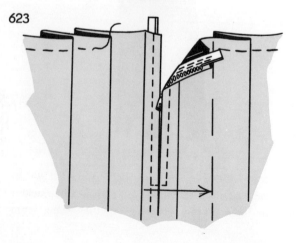

623

When the skirt is worn on the reverse side, you will be able to look into the pleat containing the placket, so it is necessary to make a self-fabric shield to hide the zipper tape. Cut a piece of skirt fabric $2^1/_2$ inches wide and the length of the zipper tape extending below the waistline seam plus a $^1/_4$-inch seam allowance (624). Fold in half lengthwise with reverse side of fabric together and stitch in a $^1/_4$-inch seam (625). Press seam open and match to centre of piece. Stitch across one end in a $^1/_4$-inch seam. Turn to outside and press. Turn in $^1/_4$-inch seam at open end and slip-stitch together

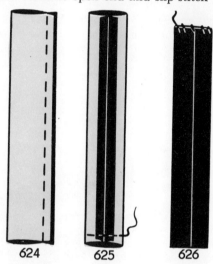

624   625   626

(626). Centre piece over zipper tape. Sew to garment along bottom and front edge of zipper tape with a very fine slip-stitch (627). Upper edge of shield will remain free. On a 1-inch pleat, the shield will be even with the folded edge of the pleat, while on a deeper pleat the shield will not reach to the edge of the pleat. Remove machine-basting from placket opening.

627

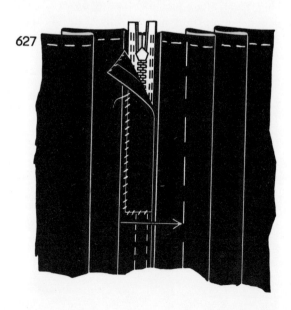

APPLICATION IN FLY FRONT OF SKIRT. Turn under right skirt front along fold line for overlap and baste close to edge (628). Press. Reinforce lower corner of placket opening on left skirt front with a row of stitching along seamline (629). Clip seam allowance diagonally to seam line at corner. Turn under seam allowance along side and lower edge of

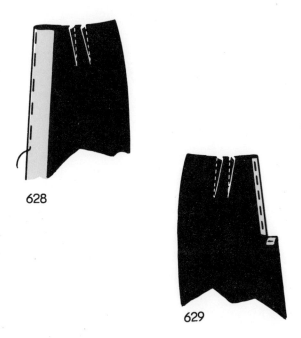

628

629

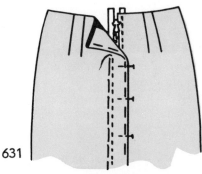

631

underlap piece in half lengthwise, wrong sides together, and press (632a). Baste underlap to left side of placket behind zipper, matching seam edges on wrong side (632b). Turn to right side of garment and fold back front overlap. Using zipper foot, stitch across bottom and left side of zipper through all thicknesses over first row of stitching.

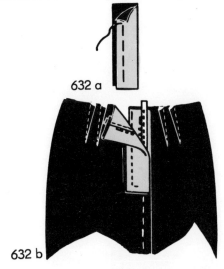

632 a

632 b

placket and baste. Press. Place left skirt front over zipper with side edge of placket along zipper chain and lower edge of placket at bottom of zipper (630). Baste and then stitch close to edge, using zipper foot. Work-

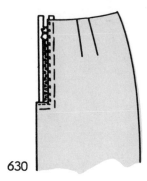

630

ing from right side of garment, lap right skirt front over left skirt front, matching centre front markings accurately and baste (631). Baste to zipper tape above placket opening. Top-stitch entire length of fly front through all thicknesses, using zipper foot. Fold

APPLICATION IN FLY FRONT OF TROUSERS. Be sure you are using the specially constructed trouser zipper. Face the left side of fly placket (633). Clip curve at intervals and press seam. Make the right fly shield and press it (634). Attach zipper foot to machine and adjust to right-hand side

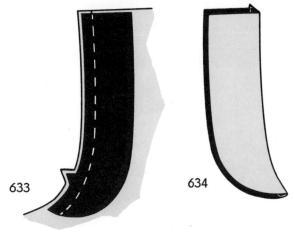

633

634

of needle. Place closed zipper face down on opened-out facing with right edge of tape matched to facing seam and bottom stop at seam allowance of facing. Allow any extra length of the zipper to extend above the waistline edge. Double-stitch the left side of tape to

edge over right zipper tape and baste. Baste fly shield behind zipper, matching seam edges on wrong side (637). Stitch from right side close to zipper teeth through all thicknesses. Join crotch seam. Clip curve at intervals and press seam open. Make a bar tack

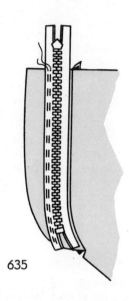

635

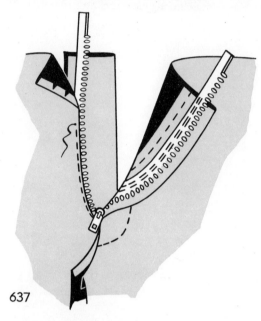

637

the facing (635). Turn left fly facing to inside at seam line and baste. Stitch inner edge of facing to front, keeping end of unstitched, right zipper tape free (636). Clip right front seam allowance to stitching. Open

at bottom of fly (638). Open zipper. Attach waistband to garment. The waistband acts as a top stop for

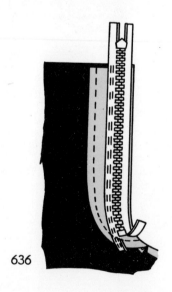

636

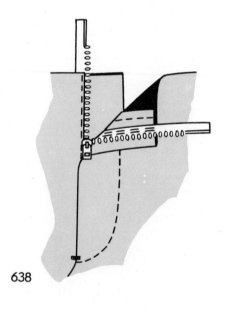

638

zipper. Turn in right side of fly placket at seam line and baste. Clip curve at intervals and to seam line at lower end of placket opening and press. Lap placket

the zipper. Now it is safe to cut off the excess tape extending above the waistband seam allowance. Cut between metal teeth at edge of seam allowance (639).

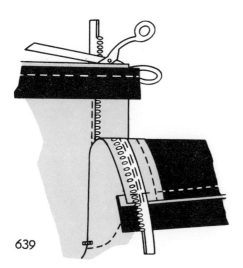

639

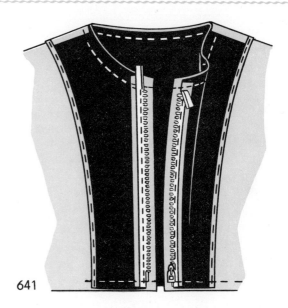

641

APPLICATION OF SEPARATING ZIPPER.

Finish outer edge of facing in manner suitable for fabric. Make a chalk line on outside of front edge facing $1/4$ inch inside of seam line (640). Place open zipper face up on outside of facing with edge of teeth at chalk line. Stitch close to teeth, using zipper foot (640). Attach other side of zipper to other side of facing in same manner. If garment has a collar, baste the collar

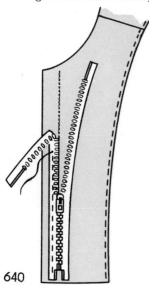

640

to the right side of neck edge. Stitch facing to garment at neck and lower edge, right sides together. Note that zipper tape is not stitched in with the neckline seam (641). Separate the zipper. Grade seam allowances and clip curve at intervals. Turn facing to inside and press zipper toward centre front. Turn in seam allowance on front and press. On the inside, match edge of zipper teeth to front edge of garment and baste in place (642). Stitch along edge of facing through all thicknesses, using zipper foot. Stitch other side of zipper to the

other side of front in same manner. Close the zipper and press the application (643).

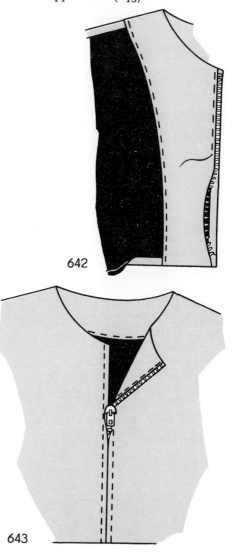

642

643

See Chapter 16 for application of loose cover zippers.

Plackets without Zippers

The placket without a zipper must always be faced, bound or hemmed to finish the edges. This type of placket is usually found either on infants' and children's clothes or in a sleeve opening. However, some sheer dresses have snapped plackets because a zipper might be too bulky or will show through the fabric.

TWO-PIECE PLACKET. Used in side or back seam of a dress. Stitch the seam to markings for placket opening and fasten threads securely. Machine-baste placket closed. Press seam open and then remove basting. Cut a piece of bias fabric $1^3/_4$ inches wide and $1^1/_4$ inches longer than the placket opening. Stitch piece to front edge of opening, right sides together, in a $^3/_8$-inch seam (644). Turn under raw edge of facing and slip-stitch to front of garment. For the

644

underlap, cut a piece of bias fabric $2^1/_2$ inches wide and $1^1/_4$ inches longer than the opening. Stitch piece to back edge of opening, right sides together (645). Turn under raw edge of facing, fold through centre and slip-stitch over seam line. Lap front facing over back facing and stitch ends together. Clip back seam allow-

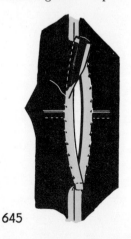

645

ance to seam line at ends of placket and press flat. Sew a hook and eye at the waistline and snaps on rest of placket opening (646).

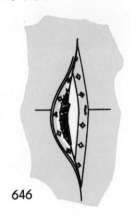

646

CONTINUOUS LAP PLACKET IN A SEAM. Stitch the seam to marking for placket opening and fasten thread securely. Clip seam allowance to stitching line at end of placket (647). Cut a lengthwise piece of fabric $2^1/_2$ inches wide and twice the length of the opening. Stitch one edge of piece to edges of opening, right sides together, in a $^5/_8$-inch

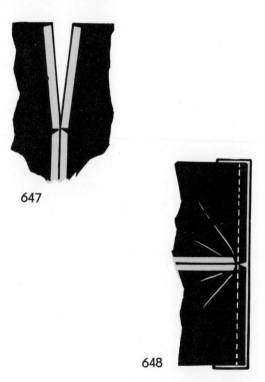

647

648

seam (648). Trim seam and press toward facing. Turn under free edge of facing and hem over seam (649). Turn placket to inside along front edge and baste at upper edge. Lap over back placket.

649

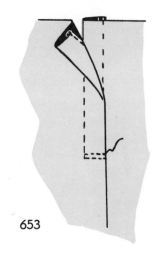

653

HEMMED PLACKET IN A PLEAT. Slash garment on the straight grain of fabric the desired length of placket. Clip diagonally ¹/₄ inch on both sides of point of slash (650). Turn in ¹/₄ inch on each side of

See page 168 for description of placket finishes used in sleeves.

Nylon Tape Closure

Nylon tape closure is excellent for fastening buckleless belts, waistbands in wrapped or adjustable-waist garments, jacket fronts, loose covers, pelmets and valances. Once you start using it, you will find numerous other uses for it. It is, however, too bulky to use in place of a zipper in a dress or skirt placket or in light-weight garments

The tape comes in 1-inch widths (654), and you purchase it by the yard or in packaged lengths. When preparing the tape for application, close it and cut to the desired length, press flat with a warm iron. It doesn't really matter which side of the tape is sewn to the underlap or overlap, but usually the fleece side is put on the section that comes in contact with the body. It is softer than the burr side and less apt to cause irritation.

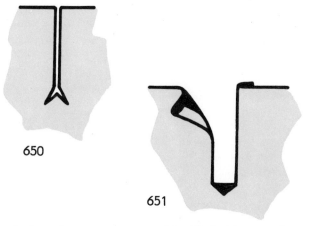

650

651

slash and press to wrong side (651). Turn under a ¹/₂-inch hem on each side of slash and stitch (652). Lap

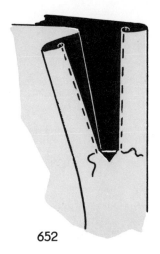

652

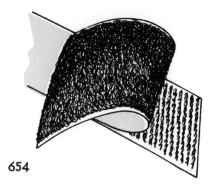

654

APPLICATION WITH TOP-STITCHING

the hems forming pleats. Stitch across lower end of placket through all thicknesses to hold pleats in place (653).

Separate the two sides of tape. Pin the fleece side, right side up, to facing side of overlap. Place ¹/₈ inch in from the folded edge (655). Machine-stitch around outside edges of tape through all thicknesses. Lap closing,

centres and markings matched. Centre the burr side
of the tape, right side up, directly under the fleece side
of tape (656). Pin the burr side of tape to the underlap
and stitch around outside edges of tape through all
thicknesses.

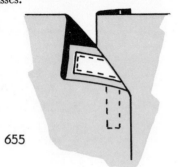

655

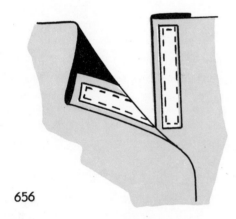

656

APPLICATION WITHOUT TOP-STITCHING. ·Separate the two sides of tape.

Before facing is attached to the garment, pin fleece side
of tape, right side up, to right side of facing. Stitch
around all sides of tape (657). Apply facing to garment

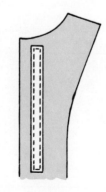

657

(658). Lap closing, centres and markings matched.
Centre the burr side of the tape, right side up, directly
under the fleece side of tape. Stitch the burr side to the
underlap through all thicknesses.

658

For a fly-front effect, make one row of stitching
through all thicknesses along inner edge of tape (659).

659

APPLICATION ON A WAISTBAND. Sep-
arate the two sides of tape. Before making waistband,
pin fleece side, right side up, to facing side of front edge
of waistband (660). Centre tape between seam line and
fold line. Stitch to waistband facing around all sides
of tape. Apply waistband to skirt. Lap waistband (661).
and pin burr side of tape to back underlap, right side
up, directly under fleece side of tape. Stitch burr side
to back edge of waistband through all thicknesses.

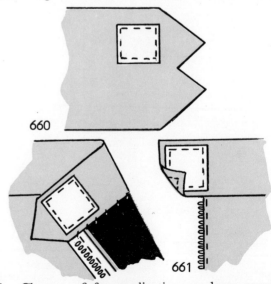

660

661

See Chapter 16 for application on loose covers
and valances.

BUTTONHOLES

Buttonholes can "make" or "break" a garment. There is nothing more discouraging than a well-made garment with unsightly buttonholes. Before making the buttonholes on your garment, practice. Make a test on a scrap of the same fabric. In this way you can decide whether you are using the correct method to obtain the effect you want.

The size and spacing of the buttonholes is indicated on patterns requiring buttonholes, but you may have to change the spacing if you use a size button other than the one suggested in the pattern, or if you alter the section in which the buttonholes are placed. If you use a bigger button, you may want to make fewer buttonholes and space them farther apart. The reverse is true if you use smaller buttons. When you change the size of the buttons, be sure to check the width of extension beyond the centre marking of your garment. The extension should be one-half the diameter of the button plus $1/4$ to $1/2$ inch. Increase or decrease the width of your extension accordingly, if you change the size of the buttons. If you alter the length of the garment, re-space the buttonholes evenly, retaining the placement of the first and last buttonhole markings on the pattern.

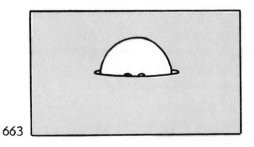

663

and worked. Bound buttonholes have the edges finished with fabric while worked buttonholes have the edges finished with thread. All areas containing buttonholes should be interfaced. Bound buttonholes are made through the garment and interfacing before the facing is applied. Worked buttonholes are made through garment, interfacing and facing after garment is finished.

Mark horizontal buttonholes on the crosswise grain of fabric, vertical ones on the lengthwise grain. Each buttonhole should be the same length and an even distance from the centre marking. Transfer buttonhole markings from pattern to wrong side of garment; then hand- or machine-baste through fabric so markings appear on the right side. Mark the length of buttonholes with a row of vertical basting at each end (664). Mark the position of buttonholes with basting between these two lines.

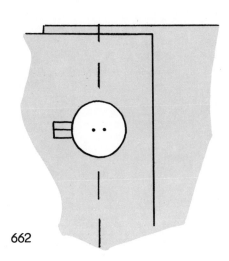

662

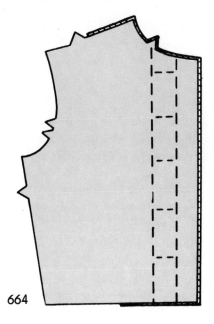

664

Buttonholes must be at least $1/8$ inch longer than the diameter of the button (662). When the button is thick and bulky, the buttonhole must be even larger. Some buttons are difficult to measure because of their shape. The simplest way to determine the correct size buttonhole for a specific button is to cut a slit in a scrap of fabric and adjust the length until the button slips through easily and smoothly (663).

There are two general types of buttonholes—bound

The type of buttonhole to be used on your garment will usually be indicated on your pattern. Bound buttonholes are generally used on garments which are dry-cleaned and worked buttonholes on man-tailored or washable garments. The various kinds of bound and worked buttonholes which you may wish to use are outlined here.

Bound Buttonholes

Bound buttonholes require some practice before they are fully mastered. You should try all of the following methods and select the one you like best and find easiest to do. If you are making a number of buttonholes, prepare a long strip of fabric and then cut in pieces 1 inch longer than the finished buttonhole.

ONE-PIECE BOUND BUTTONHOLE. Cut a piece of fabric on lengthwise grain, 1 inch wide and 1 inch longer than the finished buttonhole. Mark the centre of the piece (665). Bring the long edges to the centre marking, wrong sides together, and press (665).

665

Place folded piece over buttonhole marking on right side of garment (666). Baste centre of piece to buttonhole marking with cut edges up. Adjust machine to

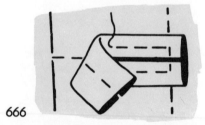

666

approximately 12 stitches to the inch and stitch round buttonhole $1/8$ inch from centre on each side and across ends (667). Start the stitching at the middle of one side and end by overlapping several stitches. Count the number of stitches across the ends to keep all buttonholes a uniform size. Cut along marking at centre for $1/4$ inch and then slash diagonally to the corners. Turn

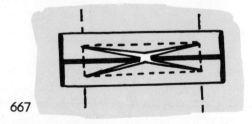

667

piece to wrong side through opening (668). The folded edges will form even bindings along each side and meet

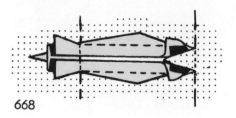

668

at the centre of the opening. On outside, fold garment back over buttonhole and stitch triangular ends to ends of binding to form strong, square corners (669). Catch-stitch edges of binding together (670) and press.

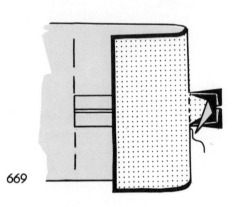

669

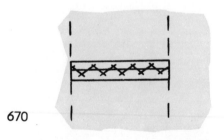

670

To finish buttonhole after facing has been attached to garment, the buttonhole must be cut through the facing. Baste facing to the garment around each buttonhole (671). Slash facing same as buttonhole opening. Turn in edges of facing and hem to stitching. Remove basting and press.

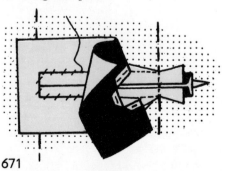

671

To finish buttonholes on loosely woven or very bulky fabric, the opening in the facing can in turn be faced with a light-weight fabric. Cut a piece of this fabric 1 inch wide and 1 inch longer than buttonhole. Mark exact position of buttonhole on the facing (672). Open out facing and baste piece to facing only, right sides together, with centre of piece over buttonhole marking. Stitch $\frac{1}{8}$ inch from marking and across ends forming a rectangle the size of the buttonhole. Slash along centre of buttonhole marking and clip diagonally

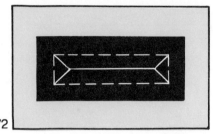

672

into corners. Turn piece to wrong side of facing and press flat. Fold facing back on garment and baste around buttonhole. Hem finished edges of facing to buttonhole binding along the stitching (673). Remove basting and press.

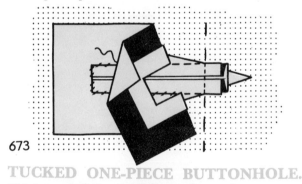

673

TUCKED ONE-PIECE BUTTONHOLE.

This buttonhole is very similar to the regular one-piece buttonhole but the extra fabric beyond the tucks allows for blending of seams. In the one-piece buttonhole the seams are all the same width and may make a ridge when pressed in a heavy fabric.

Cut a piece of fabric $1\frac{1}{2}$ inches wide and 1 inch longer than the buttonhole marking. Mark the centre of the piece with a basting thread (674). Fold one edge of the piece $\frac{1}{4}$ inch from the centre basting and stitch a $\frac{1}{8}$-inch tuck. Fold and stitch the same kind of tuck on the other edge of the piece. The tuck stitching

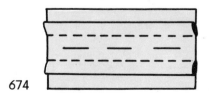

674

lines will be $\frac{1}{4}$ inch apart. If you are making a number of buttonholes, prepare a long strip and then cut in pieces 1 inch longer than the finished buttonhole. Baste tucked piece to right side of garment with centre basting matched to buttonhole marking. Stitch along lines of tucking between vertical bastings (675). Fasten threads securely at ends of buttonholes. Cut along

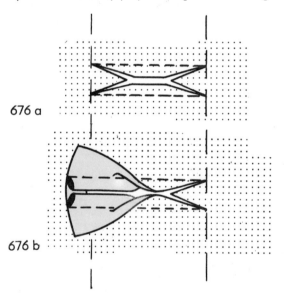

675

marking at centre for $\frac{1}{4}$ inch and then slash diagonally to the corners (676a). Turn piece to wrong side

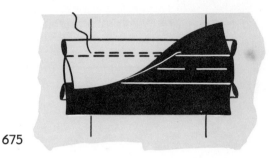

676 a

676 b

through opening (676b). Stitch triangular ends to ends of binding (677). Catch-stitch edges of binding together and press. Cut buttonhole through facing and finish by one of the methods described under the one-piece bound buttonhole.

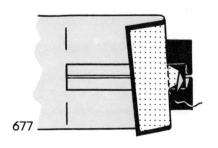

677

TWO-PIECE BOUND BUTTONHOLE.

Cut two pieces of fabric on lengthwise grain for each buttonhole $^1/_2$ inch wide and 1 inch longer than finished buttonhole. Fold the pieces in half lengthwise, wrong sides together, and press. Stitch close to raw edges (678). Place the two pieces on right side of garment, with raw edges on the buttonhole marking (679). Stitch $^1/_8$ inch from raw edges between vertical bastings the length of the buttonhole. Don't stitch

678

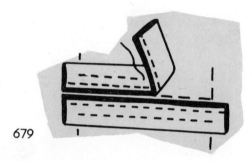

679

across the ends. Fasten threads securely at ends of buttonhole. Cut along marking at centre for $^1/_4$ inch and then slash diagonally to the corners (680). Turn pieces to wrong side through opening. Stitch triangular ends to ends of binding to form strong, square corners (681). Catch-stitch edges of binding together and press. Cut buttonhole through facing and finish by one of two methods described under the one-piece bound buttonhole.

680

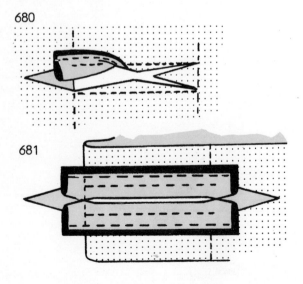

681

CORDED OR PIPED BUTTONHOLE.

Place additional basting-line markings $^1/_8$ inch above and below the buttonhole marking line. Extend the basting lines 1 inch beyond the buttonhole marking (682). Cut a strip of fabric $1^1/_4$ inches wide. Fold fabric over fine cording or soft string. Stitch close to cording, using the cording foot attachment on the machine (683). Cut the cording in pieces 1 inch longer than the

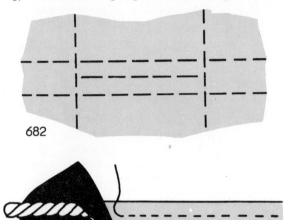

682

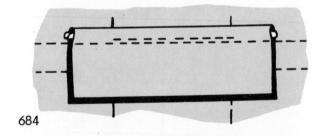

683

length of the finished buttonhole. Pin one piece to right side of garment with stitching line of cording matched to upper basting line (684). Baste in place with seam allowance toward centre. Stitch the length of the buttonhole, using extended basting lines as a

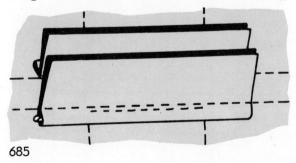

684

guide. Baste and stitch other piece of cording to lower basting mark with seam allowance toward centre (685).

685

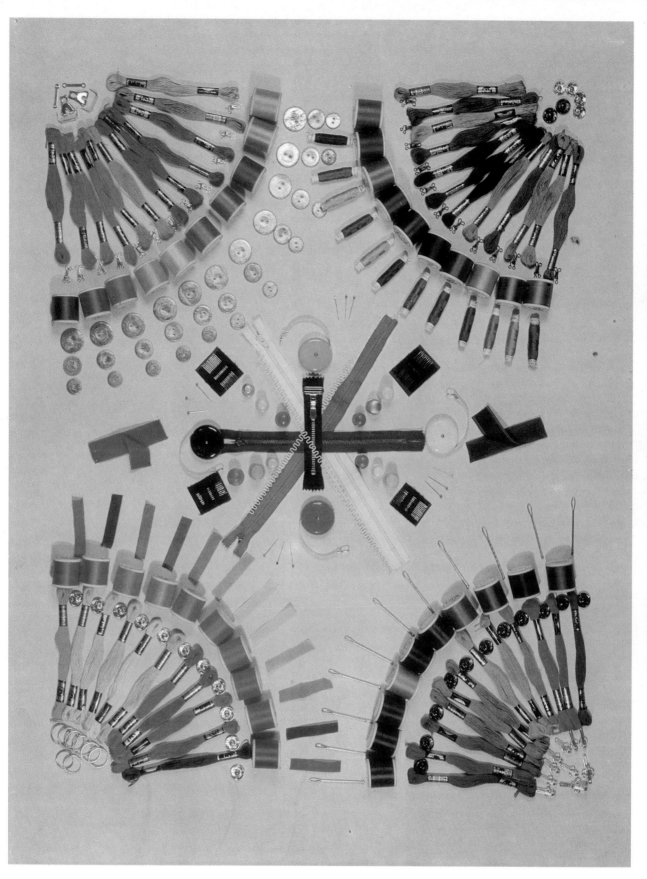

26 There is an enormous choice of colours in sewing threads, silks, zips, needles, and other essentials which will equip you to sew any colour and type of material in the best possible way.

Haberdashery by courtesy of John Lewis of Oxford Street Ltd.

27 The haberdashery department of a large store
is a treasure house of colourful and attractive
aids to dressmaking. Trimmings such as these
add a personal touch of individuality to any
garment.

*Haberdashery by courtesy of John Lewis of Oxford
Street Ltd.*

Fasten the threads securely at ends of buttonhole. Cut along markings at centre for $1/4$ inch and then slash diagonally to the corners (686a). Turn pieces to wrong side through opening (686b). Stitch triangular ends to ends of cording to form strong, square corners (687). Catch-stitch edges of cording together and press. Cut buttonhole facing and finish by one of two methods described under the one-piece bound buttonhole.

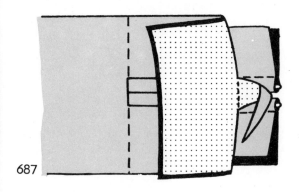

686 a   686 b

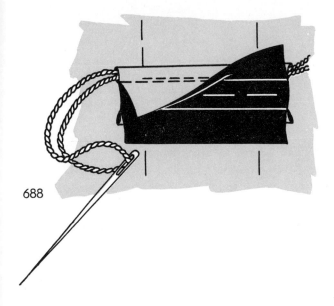

687

The tucked one-piece buttonhole can also be corded. Thread a darning needle with wool yarn and draw two

strands of yarn through each tuck before cutting and finishing the buttonhole (688).

BUTTONHOLE IN A SEAM.

Mark position for buttonholes on the seam line. Stitch seam, leaving openings between buttonhole markings (689). Fasten threads securely at each end of buttonholes. If the facing has a corresponding seam line, stitch facing

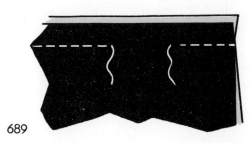

689

section in the same manner. Match the two openings and slip-stitch the folded edges together around the buttonhole opening (690). If the facing section does not have a seam, cut the buttonhole through facing and finish by one of two methods described under the one-piece bound buttonhole.

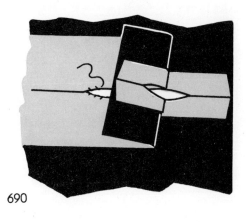

690

Worked Buttonholes

MACHINE-WORKED BUTTONHOLE.

Machine-made buttonholes save many hours of work and give excellent results. The automatic machines make buttonholes without an attachment, but for the standard machine it is necessary to use a buttonhole attachment (691). Follow the manual with your machine or attachment for specific instructions for making buttonholes. Always test the buttonhole first on a scrap of your fabric.

688

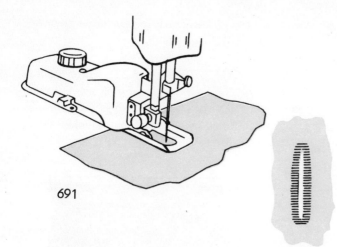

691

shape and down the side of slash (693). Hold the edge being worked away from you. Put needle up through slash, bringing it out to front of fabric beyond stay-stitching. Carry thread from eye under point of needle from right to left. Pull the needle through the fabric and down, drawing the stitch tight so twist or knot is at the cut edge of the buttonhole. Work from left to right keeping stitches close together an even distance apart. At the inner end, make several stitches across slash for bar tack (694). Work blanket stitches over threads, taking stitches through fabric and over threads. Hold the edge being worked to-ward you; bring the needle out of the cloth and over the loop of thread. Work from left to right.

HAND-WORKED BUTTONHOLE. Use matching thread, silk thread or buttonhole twist and a slender needle which will allow you to make fine, close stitches. After marking the position of button-holes, place a row of machine-stitching 1/16 inch from slash line on both sides (692). This holds the three layers of fabric together besides serving as a guide for the handstitches. Cut along the marking, using one thread of fabric as a guide.

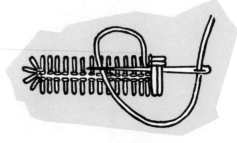

694

Vertical worked buttonholes are used on front clos-ings with no crosswise strain. They are made the same as the horizontal buttonhole except that both ends are finished with a bar tack (695).

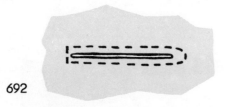

692

The horizontal worked buttonholes are secured with a bar or fan-shaped stitches at the ends. Usually they have a fan at the edge nearest the centre marking and a bar at the inner end to prevent stretching. Beginning at inner end, work buttonhole stitches down one side of slash, around point with stitches spread in a fan

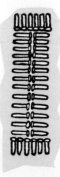

695

The tailored worked buttonhole has an eyelet at the end of the buttonhole and is used on men's clothing and top coats. After the buttonhole is marked, punch a hole at the outer end with a stiletto (696). Cut on line for buttonhole and overcast edges of buttonhole

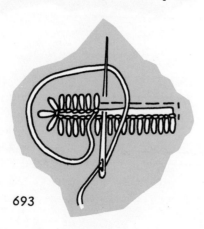

693

696

and eyelet. Work the buttonhole stitches from right to left over a cord (697), and finish inner end with a bar tack (698). The cord makes a very strong buttonhole which will wear better than the regular buttonhole.

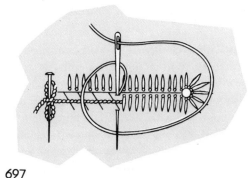

697

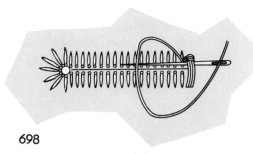

698

EYELETS. Small worked eyelets are often used in belts, or for threading ribbon or drawstring in garments. We suggest that you machine-work them, using the special eyelet template provided with the buttonhole attachment, if you have one. If you want to hand-work the eyelets, mark a small circle on the fabric the size you wish it to be. Baste on the marking to serve as a reinforcement and guide (699). Punch a hole in the centre, using a stiletto. Work over the edge with blanket stitches or buttonhole stitches (700), keeping them close together and even, shaping the eyelet as you work. If you insert the stiletto from the right side every few stitches, it will keep the fabric edge turned under and help shape the eyelet.

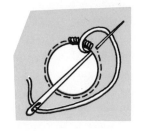

700

BUTTONS

Buttons may be used for decorative effect on a garment, as well as to serve a functional purpose. Select buttons which are suitable to the garment design and the colour and texture of fabric. If the garment design is quite intricate, select a fairly simple button. If the garment is quite plain, then perhaps a decorative button would provide just the right touch. Also, you must consider the figure size when selecting buttons. A very large figure can take fairly large buttons, but the petite figure would be overpowered by big 3-inch buttons.

Buttons come in two different types—the sew-through type with holes, or the shank type which is attached to the garment from the underside of the button. These can have metal, cloth or self shanks.

Buttons are made of various materials—fabric, leather, bone, shell, jet, glass, metals and plastics. There are also inexpensive button forms which can be covered quickly and easily in the garment fabric. These are available at any notions counter, and complete instructions for covering are included in the package. Select the size which is right for your garment, and use the pattern in the package to cut the fabric covering.

To determine the placement for buttons, overlap the closing to the correct position and pin closed. Place a pin through each buttonhole at centre front marking. Slip the pin through each buttonhole as you separate the closure. The centre of the button is placed at the point marked by the pin (701).

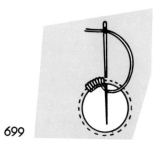

699

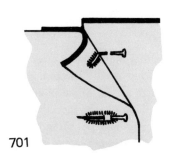

701

Buttons are sewn to the garment with heavy-duty thread or buttonhole twist. If you cannot match your fabric with one of these, wax regular thread with beeswax to make it stronger. Use a double thread and a small knot. Buttons used for decorative purposes can be sewn close to the garment, but all other buttons need a thread or metal shank to allow the button to ride smoothly in the buttonhole. The thread shank holds the button away from the garment enough to allow for the thickness of fabric at the buttonhole. The bulkier or heavier the fabric, the longer the shank needs to be.

If the underside of your garment will not show, sew the button through all thicknesses of fabric. On coats and suits or any other garment that might be worn open, sew the buttons through fabric and interfacing but not through the facing.

Sew-Through Buttons

Take several small stitches on right side of garment to secure thread at point where button is to be placed. Bring needle through button and back into fabric, inserting a heavy pin, toothpick or matchstick over the button under the first stitch to allow for a thread shank. Continue sewing through fabric and button until button is secure (702). Remove the pin and pull button to top of threads evenly. Bring thread to right side of fabric and wind tightly around the stitches under button to form a shank. Fasten thread securely on underside with several stitches.

702

Shank Buttons

Buttons with a thin metal shank do not need a thread shank (703a). Bring needle through fabric and shank then back through fabric. Make small stitches at right angles to buttonhole so that metal shank will line up with buttonhole rather than spread open the end of the buttonhole. Continue sewing through fabric and

shank until button is secure (703b). Fasten thread on underside with several stitches.

703 a   703 b

Buttons with a cloth or self-shank will need to be sewn on with an additional thread shank (704). These shanks are bulky and will spread the buttonhole and are usually not long enough to allow the garment to button without pulling. Take several stitches on right side of garment at point where button is to be placed. Holding your forefinger between the button and the garment, bring the thread through the shank and back into the fabric. The forefinger holds the button away from the fabric as you continue sewing through fabric and shank until the button is secure. On the last stitch, bring the thread out of the button and wind thread tightly around the stitches to form the thread shank. Fasten thread securely on underside with several stitches.

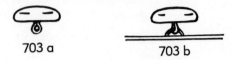

704

Removable shank buttons are used on uniforms and overalls. Mark position for the button and make a small eyelet in the garment (705a). Place metal shank through eyelet and fasten on underside with a special shank pin made for attaching these buttons (705b) or a small safety pin.

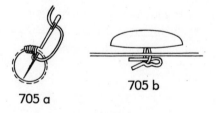

705 a   705 b

Stayed Buttons

When buttons are sewn to a single thickness of fabric or where there is a great deal of strain on the button, a reinforcement or stay is needed. A small patch of fabric or woven seam binding is used under a single thickness of fabric. A small button is used to stay the underside of buttons where there is great strain. Place square of fabric or small button on inside of garment under button and sew in place through button, garment and stay using the same method as for the sew-through button (706).

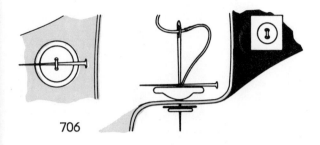

706

Link Buttons

These are used on French cuffs. Determine the length needed between the buttons. Holding the two buttons apart the desired distance, insert thread through both buttons several times (707). Fasten securely. Form a bar tack between buttons by making blanket stitches over the threads. Keep stitches close together.

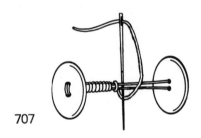

707

OTHER FASTENINGS
Snap Fasteners

Snap fasteners range in size from 000, the smallest, used on sheer fabrics, to number 10, the largest, used on coarse heavy fabrics. Snaps are used to hold fabrics together where there is little strain on the garment. They give a neat flat closure. Place them close enough together to prevent the opening from gaping. Mark position for snaps on the overlap. The ball part is generally sewn to the overlap and the socket part to the underlap of the closure. Fasten thread on marking for snap and sew the ball section on with overhand stitches through each hole. Carry thread under snap from one hole to the next (708). Sew snap through facing and interfacing being careful not to have any stitches

show on the right side of the garment. After stitching ball section securely in place, lap the closure. Place pin through centre hole of ball section and mark position for socket section. Then place a pin through centre hole of socket section to hold it in position while sewing it on. Attach in the same manner as the ball section.

Hammer-on snaps are used on children's clothes and sportswear. These are easily and quickly applied according to the instructions on the package.

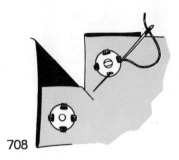

708

Hooks and Eyes

There is a very wide range of sizes to suit all weights of fabrics. They give a more secure fastening than snap fasteners and are often combined with snaps. Use a straight bar eye section when the edges of the closure overlap or a round eye section when the edges just meet. In place of either of the eye sections, a thread loop may be used. It gives a less conspicuous closing on a garment to be worn open at times or above a zipper.

Mark the position of the hook and eye. The hook is sewed to the overlap or to the right-hand side of the closure if edges just meet (709). Take several small stitches in the fabric at the marking for the hook to secure the thread. Place the hook about $1/_8$ inch from the edge of the closure and sew to the underside of the overlap with overhand or buttonhole stitches around the holes. Stitches should not show on the right side of the garment. Take several stitches across under the end of the hook and through the facing to hold it securely.

The bar eye should come just under the bend of the hook section when the garment is lapped and the curve of the bar eye should face toward the outer edge of the closing. Sew in position with an overhand or buttonhole stitch around the holes (709).

709

The round eye must extend beyond the edge of the garment (710). Sew in position with an overhand or buttonhole stitch around the holes. Take several stitches across the sides of the eye and through the facing to hold it securely. Round eyes are sometimes inserted in the seam between the facing and garment so that only the metal eye extends beyond the seam.

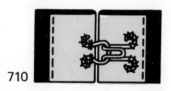

710

Thread eyes are made of matching thread so that they are inconspicuous. Sew two strands of thread on the underlap at the point where the eye is to be placed (711). Work over these strands with a blanket-stitch, using needle eye first (712). Bring the needle under the strands and through the loop formed by the stitch.

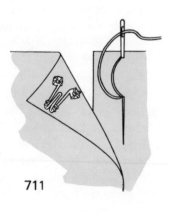

711

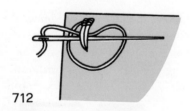

712

Lingerie Strap Holders

Use narrow tape or ribbon, about 2 inches long. The opening should always be placed toward the neck edge.

Turn under one end of tape and sew to inside of shoulder seam allowance. Turn under free end of tape and sew one part of snap to it. Sew other part of snap to shoulder seam allowance (713).

713

French Tack

This is used to hold two parts of a garment together loosely, as at the lower edge of a coat to hold the lining to the hem. Fasten the thread in one section of the garment and take a stitch in the other section (714). Take several stitches between the two sections, holding the fabric apart the desired amount. Work over the threads with a blanket stitch keeping them even and close together (715).

 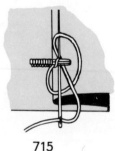

714   715

Chain Tack

This could be substituted for the French tack. Using a double thread, fasten the thread securely in one section. Take a short stitch to form thread loop (716). Hold needle with right hand. Slip thumb and first two fingers of left hand through loop and pick up needle thread (717). Pull thread through first loop forming a new loop (718). Continue in this manner keeping chain loops an even size until the chain is the desired length (719). Place needle through last loop and pull thread through to form knot. Fasten thread in other section of fabric with tiny back-stitches.

Thread Loops

This type of fastening is most often found at the neck edge of a convertible neckline so that the closing will be inconspicuous when the collar is left open. Use buttonhole twist, silk thread or elastic thread. The button size determines the length of the loop (720). They are worked the same as thread eyes (721). Lap closing and sew button under thread loop.

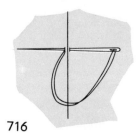

716

717

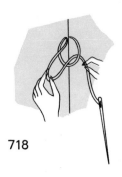

718

719

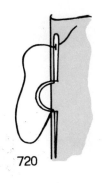

720

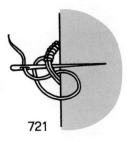

721

Fabric Loops

Cut a strip of bias fabric the desired width of loop plus seam allowances (722). Fold in half lengthwise, right sides together, and stitch, leaving ends open. Do not trim seam allowance. This seam allowance forms the filler for the tubing. Attach a strong thread to one end of tube at the seam. Draw the thread through the tubing with a bodkin or heavy needle inserted eye first (723). Continue pulling end of tube through tubing to turn to right side. Determine the length of loops needed to slip over the button smoothly.

To apply loops in seam, cut loops to correct length plus seam allowance (724). Mark spacing and size of loops on brown paper and sew loops to paper. Stitch loops and paper to right side of garment along opening. Tear paper away. Apply facing (725, 726), and sew buttons to other side of closure (727). To apply loops to a finished edge, use a long strip of tubing. Mark position for loops on garment. Determine size of loop needed for button and mark off even lengths on tubing for the loops. Sew to garment between loops with an overhand stitch. Sew buttons to other side of closure.

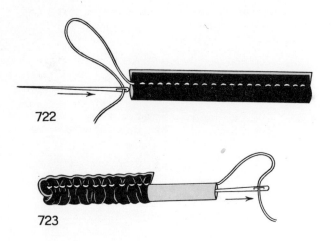

722

723

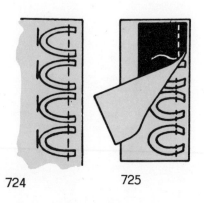

724   725

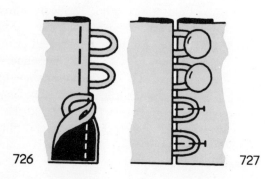

726   727

Corded Loops

Cut a bias strip the necessary width to cover cording plus seam allowances and the desired length (728). Cut a piece of cording twice the length of the bias. Sew end of bias strip to centre of cording. Fold right side of fabric over cording and stitch, using a cording foot. Trim seam allowance and draw enclosed cording out of tubing. This will turn bias inside out and pull free cording into tubing (729). Use the covered cording for your loops. They can be applied in a seam or to a finished edge in the same way as the fabric loops.

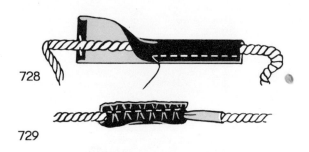

728

729

Corded Frogs

These may be made from cording or braid trim. Draw design for frog on brown paper with button loop long enough to slip over button smoothly (730). Pin and baste cording face down to paper, following pattern (731). Sew cording securely together where cording meets or crosses (732). Remove frog from paper and place face up on garment so that loop extends beyond front edge. Slip-stitch frog securely to garment from underside. Overlap edges of garment, centres matched and mark position for button. Sew button under loop (733).

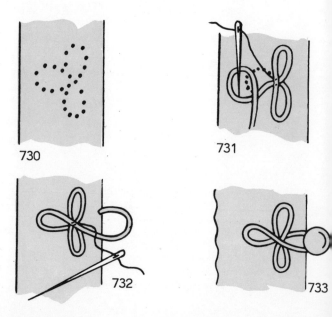

730

731

732

733

BELTS

Belts can add a professional finished look to many garments, so select belts with care. Choose the type which is best suited to your garment and your figure. Remember, the wider and more conspicuous the belt, the more attention you will draw to your waistline. This is fine if you have a tiny waist, and don't mind looking a little shorter and wider. If your waist is anything but waspish, a narrow belt of the garment fabric is your best choice. You should investigate the kits available for making belts. Kits are available for various widths, both straight and contour, and usually have buckles with them which can also be easily covered with the garment fabric. They are quite simple to use, and excellent instructions for making the belt and buckle accompany each kit.

All self belts should have stiffening to keep them neat and in shape. The commercial beltings are the best stiffening to use for straight belts, since they are cut to standard widths and can be purchased by the yard. If you cannot find a commercial belting in the width you need, use a heavy interfacing or canvas. For a softer backing, you may wish to try grosgrain ribbon. Be sure to shrink the ribbon before using it in the belt, since it shrinks about 3 inches to the yard.

To determine the proper width belt for a garment, you may want to cut a sample belt of brown paper and try it to see the effect on the garment. Cut several in various widths to find the one which is most flattering.

When a buckle is used on a belt, the belt should be about $1/8$ inch narrower than the inside measurement of the buckle. The belt should be cut about 6 inches longer than the waistline measurement to allow for overlap, attaching the buckle and seam allowances. Wide belts must be made longer than the waist measurement. For any belt over 1 inch wide, add $1/2$ inch in length for every additional inch in width.

The popular tie belts are quite easy to make. You may want to make one for a dress which doesn't include one in the pattern. To determine the length, tie a string or ribbon around your waist, and cut it the length you think best. Use this as a guide for the length of your tie belt.

Belt with Belting

Commercial belting gives the most professional looking belt and never loses its shape even after repeated laundering or dry-cleaning. Cut fabric on lengthwise grain 6 inches longer than waistline measurement and twice the width of the finished belt plus $1/2$-inch seam allowances (734). Cut the belting the same length as the fabric minus seam allowances at the ends. Cut one end to a point. Fold belt fabric lengthwise, wrong sides together, and press a crease through the middle. Mark a $1/2$-inch seam allowance along the lower edge of the

734

belt fabric. Baste the belting to the wrong side of the fabric seam allowance with one edge of belting along the marking and a seam allowance extending on each end (735). Turn in the upper edge of the belt fabric

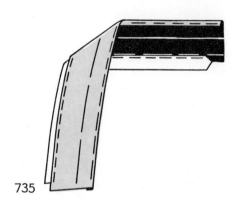

735

$5/8$ inch. Baste and press. Place the belt right side up. Fold up the edge with the $5/8$-inch seam allowance on the centre crease line and fold the edge with the belting down over it so that the belting covers the belt (736). Stitch around point (737). Do not catch the belting in this line of stitching. Trim seam allowances and cut

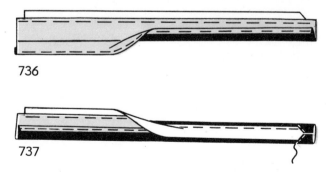

736

737

a cross point. Turn to right side, encasing belting in the belt. Note that the folded edge does not come to the lower edge of the belt on the inside (738). This keeps both edges of the belt the same thickness. Slip-stitch the folded edge to the belt. Do not try to top-stitch a belt with commercial belting. It is difficult to do, and there is danger of breaking the machine needle. On very heavy fabrics, the selvage edge can be used instead of the $^5/_8$-inch turn-under as a finish on the wrong side.

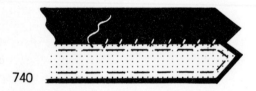

738

Attach the buckle to the straight end of the belt (739). Pierce holes and work eyelets in the pointed end of the belt if the buckle has a prong.

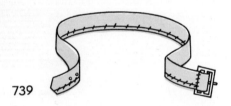

739

Belt with Interfacing

Interfacing makes a much softer belt than belting. Cut fabric on lengthwise grain 6 inches longer than waistline measurement and twice the width of the finished belt plus seam allowances. Cut the interfacing half the width of the belt. Bast interfacing to inside of belt with one edge along centre of belt (740). Tack interfacing to belt fabric along centre marking. Fold belt in half

740

lengthwise, right sides together. Stitch, leaving an opening for turning (741). Trim interfacing close to stitching and grade seam allowances. Turn to right side and slip-stitch opening edges together. Baste around edges and press. Top-stitch all edges if desired (742). Attach buckle to straight end and work eyelets in pointed end if buckle has a prong.

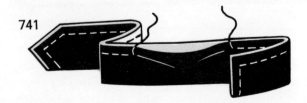

741

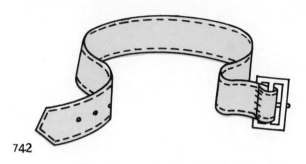

742

Belt with Grosgrain Ribbon Backing

Grosgrain ribbon is used with very heavy fabric to reduce bulk, to finish the back of novelty braid and ribbon belts or to face the back of any fabric belt if you are short of material. Cut pre-shrunk grosgrain ribbon 6 inches longer than your waistline measurement. For fabric belts cut a piece of interfacing the same length as ribbon and $^1/_4$ inch wider. Omit interfacing on ribbon or braid belts. Cut fabric on lengthwise grain the same size as the interfacing with $^3/_8$-inch seam allowances. Cut a point at one end of the fabric and interfacing. Baste interfacing to inside of fabric (743). Turn all edges of the fabric belt over interfacing and baste (743). Press. Top-stitch around belt, close to edges. Cut one end of the ribbon in the same shaped point as the fabric belt. Turn in ends of ribbon and baste (744). Baste the ribbon to the inside of fabric belt, wrong sides together. Ribbon will be narrower than belt so edges cannot show. Slip-stitch ribbon to inside of belt (745). Attach buckle to straight end of belt and work eyelets in pointed end if buckle has a prong.

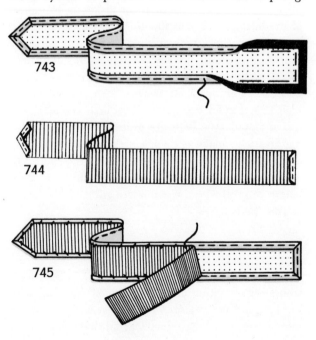

743

744

745

Tie Belt

A tie belt, without stiffening, becomes a string in no time. Stiffening in the waistline section keeps it smooth and leaves the ends soft for a tie or bow. Cut fabric on lengthwise grain, the waistline measurement plus the desired length for tie ends and twice the width of the finished belt plus seam allowances. Cut a piece of commercial belting 1 inch shorter than the waistline measurement and shape both ends (746). The belting cut shorter than the waistline measurement allows space to tie the knot and the curved ends allow the fabric to crush at the knot. Fold fabric in half lengthwise,

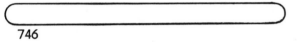

746

right sides together. Stitch, leaving an opening at centre back (747). Trim seam, turn and press. Insert belting through opening, matching centre of belting to centre of belt (748). Slip-stitch opening edges

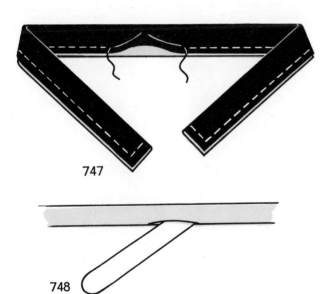

747

748

together (749). It is not necessary to tack the belting. It will not shift if the belt has been made exactly the same width as the belting.

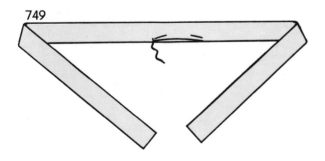

749

Cummerbund

In order for a cummerbund to fit smoothly to the body and conform to its shape, it should be cut on the bias. Cut a bias piece 10 inches in width and the necessary length, plus 1 inch for seam allowances and overlap (750). Turn under the lengthwise edges $^1/_4$ inch and

750

stitch. Turn under a $^3/_4$-inch hem on lengthwise edges and press. Fold the cummerbund crosswise to find the centre and then mark a line 1 inch from the centre

751

on the back section. The back section of the cummerbund must be smaller than the front to fit the figure properly. Open out hem. Make three rows of machine basting $^1/_4$ inch apart at marking and three rows $^1/_2$ inch from each end between hem folds (751). Draw up

752 a

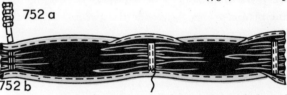

752 b

gathers to desired width and fasten ends of thread securely. Cut two pieces of featherboning the length of the pulled-up gathers plus seam allowances. Push back the tape covering the boning and cut off the seam allowance from the boning (752a). Fold tape over ends of boning and sew in place (752b). Sew boning to inside of

753

cummerbund over gathers in middle and at back edge. Fold hem back in place covering ends of boning. Tack hem to featherboning but leave rest of hem loose to allow bias to stretch as the cummerbund fits snugly

754

around the waistline. Stitch woven seam binding to ends (753). Turn seam binding to inside, turn in ends and slip-stitch in place. Lap front over back and fasten with hooks on the front and bar eyes on the back (754).

BELT BUCKLES

Buckles are decorative as well as functional and should be correct in colour and style for the design and fabric of the garment. They are made from bone, metal, plastic or fabric. There are several types of buckle forms you can have covered or cover yourself with fabric to match your garment. These are very easy to do and the instructions come with the buckle form. Buy the correct size buckle for your belt. The inside of the buckle should be slightly wider than the finished belt width.

755   756   757

A plain buckle (755) is attached by folding the straight end of the belt over the bar section of the buckle. Turn the straight end to the inside of the belt and stitch in place either by hand or machine.

A buckle with a prong (756, 757) requires an oblong opening at the straight end of the belt. Using a stiletto, punch two holes about $1/4$ inch apart near the straight end of the belt (758). Cut between the holes to form the oblong opening (759). Finish edges of opening same as eyelet. (See page 219). Insert prong through opening and turn the straight end to the inside of the belt. Stitch end of belt in place by hand or machine (760).

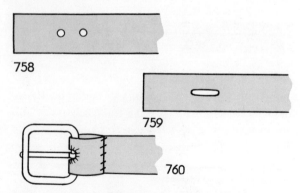

758

759

760

All buckles with a prong require eyelets at the pointed end of the belt. Thread eyelets can be worked in the fabric or metal eyelets may be used. The metal

eyelets come with all covered belt kits, and instructions for applying them are included. However, the metal eyelets are too thick and clumsy for use in fine fabrics.

BELT CARRIERS

Belt carriers are used to hold belts in position at the waistline. They may be made from narrow tubes of fabric or from thread. Make them $1/8$ to $1/4$ inch longer than the width of the belt so that the belt can slip through easily.

Fabric Belt Carriers

Make a length of tubing (761), as for fabric loops, page 223. Cut pieces the desired length plus a small seam allowance at each end. Turn under at the ends and pin in position on garment, centring over waistline seam. Stitch ends to garment and fasten thread securely (762).

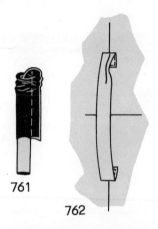

761

762

Thread Loop Belt Carrier

Mark position for ends of thread loops on garment. Fasten thread on underside of garment, bring to right side, and take a small stitch at marked position on right side. Loops are worked the same as thread loops for buttons (763, 764).

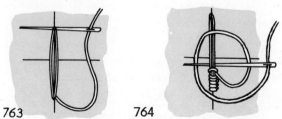

763   764

Chain Stitch Belt Carrier

This is worked the same as a chain tack, page 222.

CHAPTER 13

THE PERSONAL TOUCH

You can be your own designer and give an air of individuality to an outfit changing a plain one into something distinctive, by adding a touch of trimming to your costume. Browse through magazines and study ready-to-wear and then develop your own ideas.

However, before you begin the actual trimming, a word of caution. There is a general tendency to overdo trimming, so keep your trimmed design simple and make it look like a part of the original garment design. Use it to call attention to only one part of the garment instead of trimming collar, cuffs, hem and belt, so that the effect is confusing and you look shorter and, in turn, broader. Trim the neckline if you want to emphasise a pretty face; the belt if you are proud of a tiny waistline; the hem if you possess shapely legs.

There are a myriad of ways to trim a garment. Bindings, braids and embroidery are just a few. Select the one which is appropriate for the style of the costume and the fabric and be sure it enhances the design. If it doesn't, the trimming should be removed immediately. A plain costume is in better taste than an overly ornate one.

BINDING

Binding used in construction to finish and strengthen a raw edge may also add a decorative trim to a garment. In some cases, it may replace a facing at neckline and armhole edges, or be used to finish front closings, collars, cuffs and seams. Binding may be cut by hand and applied as single or double binding, or it may be purchased as commercial bias tape or binding.

The commercial bias binding is already folded for application, either in single-fold, which is a straight strip with the lengthwise edges folded under and pressed, or double-fold, which is a single-fold strip with an additional centre fold pressed in it.

Preparing Binding

CUTTING BIAS STRIPS. Straighten the fabric on both the lengthwise and crosswise grains. Fold the fabric diagonally with the lengthwise grain parallel to the crosswise grain. The diagonal line of the fold is the true bias. Cut along this diagonal fold. Measure and mark the desired width of the strips, evenly spaced, parallel to the diagonal (765). Cut on these marked lines. The gauge mentioned on page 62 will make the cutting of bias strips easier.

765

JOINING BIAS STRIPS. To join strips, place two strips right sides together and at right angles to each other so that a diagonal seam will be on the straight grain of the fabric (766). Overlap the corners of the strips so that the edges are exactly even at the seam line. Stitch seam and press open (767). Cut off points that extend beyond the edge of strip.

766

767

JOINING AND CUTTING CONTINUOUS BIAS STRIPS. If you have a great amount of bias to cut into strips, you will find this method less time consuming. Take a long rectangular piece of fabric. Fold the fabric diagonally at both ends and from opposite corners for true bias. Cut along both diagonal folds. The centre strip, shaped as a parallelogram, will be a long strip of true bias fabric (768). Mark the desired width of the strips on this piece of true bias fabric, beginning at one diagonal end. Join ends of fabric, right sides together with one strip width extending beyond edge at each side. Stitch seam and press open (769). Begin cutting on marking line at one end and continue in a circular manner.

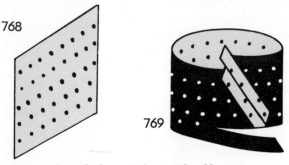

768

769

Applying Bias Binding

SINGLE BIAS BINDING. Determine the desired width of the finished binding. Cut a true bias strip of fabric that is twice the desired finished width plus the two seam allowances. Pin binding to garment right sides together, so centre of binding will fold over edge of garment and ends. Join at a seam of the garment. Stretch the bias on inside curved edges and ease the bias on outside curves. Stitch the ends of the binding, right sides together, with a plain seam. Press seam open. Stitch binding to seam line of garment. Fold binding over edge of garment, turn under raw edge of binding and hem to stitching line (770).

To finish binding on the right side, stitch binding to inside of garment. Fold binding to right side and slip-stitch or top-stitch in place.

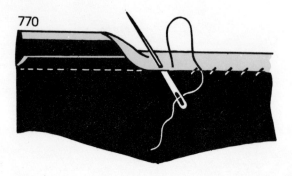

770

DOUBLE BIAS BINDING. If the fabric is sheer, it is best to use double bias binding so that raw edges will not show through the binding. Cut a true bias strip of fabric that is six times the desired finished width. Fold it in half, wrong sides together. Press. Stitch raw edges of binding over seam and hem fold to stitching line (771).

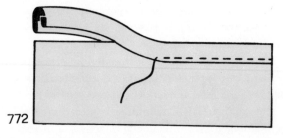

771

COMMERCIAL BIAS BINDING. The single-fold binding is applied in the same manner as the single bias binding. Double-fold binding is folded with one edge slightly narrower than the other (772). The double-fold binding can be slipped over the edge of the garment with the fold line directly on the edge of the section to be bound. Place the narrower side on the right side of the garment so that you will be sure to catch the binding on wrong side as it is stitched. Baste the binding in position. Join the binding by overlapping the ends at a seam and slip-stitch the ends together. Machine-stitch from the right side, close to the edge of the binding.

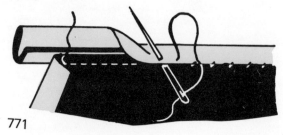

772

MACHINE BINDER ATTACHMENT. The binder can be adjusted to various widths of binding. Follow the instructions given in your manual which accompanies the attachment. When using the attachment, top-stitching will show on the right side of the binding (773).

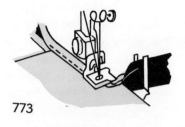

773

Special Problems in Applying Binding

In working with binding there are certain areas which can cause a little difficulty if the binding application is not handled correctly. Corners need special attention.

BINDING OUTWARD CORNER. On an outward corner, such as the point of a collar, or the corner of a jacket, stitch the binding to the point; allow enough binding at corner to mitre. Do not catch fold allowed for the mitre in stitching the binding (774). Sew binding to rest of the edge. Turn bias to inside. At the corner, turn the binding over the edge forming a mitre to the point on both sides of binding (775). Turn in the edge and slip-stitch binding in position on the wrong side of the garment.

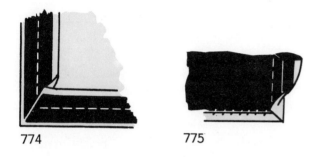

774   775

BINDING INWARD CORNER. Apply the binding to the edge, drawing bias tight at corner. Leave needle in the fabric at point, raise presser foot and pivot to turn corner (776). Continue stitching binding to rest of edge. Turn binding to inside and form a mitre at the corner on both sides of binding. Slip-stitch along the fold of mitre to hold it permanently. Turn in the edge and slip-stitch binding in position on wrong side of garment (777).

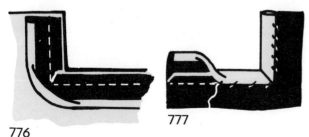

776

777

BINDING SCALLOPS. To apply bias binding to scalloped edges, ease the bias around the full curve of scallop and stretch at inner point (778). Turn binding over the raw edge and form mitres at the inner corners on each side of binding (779). Slip-stitch binding in position on wrong side of garment.

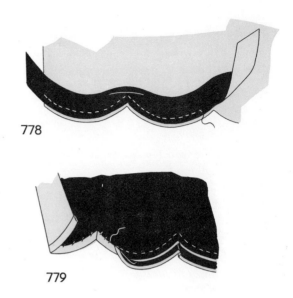

778

779

BANDS

Bias Bands

Make a paper pattern the exact shape of the band to be applied. Cut a crinoline stay from this pattern. The stay keeps the bias band an even width and makes it much easier to apply. Cut a bias strip of fabric twice the finished width of the band. Working on the ironing board, centre the crinoline stay on the wrong side of the fabric band. Hold in place with a row of pins through the centre of the stay, shaping the bias band to fit the stay as you work (780). Turn the raw edges of the bias band over the stay and steam-press in place. Baste the raw edges of the band over the centre of the stay with diagonal stitches. Baste the band in position. From the wrong side of the garment, sew both edges of the band in place with a tiny back-stitch (781). Check as you work to be sure stitches are not showing on the right side.

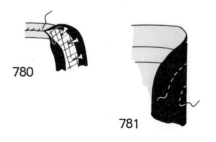

780

781

FRILLS

Frills are a strip of fabric or lace gathered or pleated at one edge. It may be purchased commercially or you may make your own.

Making Frills

To make frills cut a strip of fabric on lengthwise grain the desired length and width plus hem allowance and seam allowance. To determine the desired length of the strip for the frill, first measure the exact length of the edge of the garment to which the frill is to be attached. Next determine the amount of fullness you desire in the frill. Usually a frill is 2 or 3 times fuller than the edge to which it is applied. A wide frill should have more fullness than a narrow one to keep it from looking skimpy.

Turn under and hem the lower edges of the frill by hand or machine (782). Make two rows of machine-basting along upper edge, one on the seam line and one $1/8$ inch inside seam allowance. Use heavy-duty thread or buttonhole twist on the bobbin thread to keep the thread from breaking when the gathers are pulled up.

782

783

If you have a large area to gather it also helps to gather the piece in sections rather than on one continuous thread. Do not pull up the gathering threads until you are ready to apply the ruffle to the garment (783).

The ruffler attachment on the sewing machine can be used to gather or pleat the upper edge. Test on a scrap of fabric, adjusting the attachment according to the directions in the manual, until you obtain the desired fullness. The ruffler attachment will stitch the frill to the section of the garment at the same time the fullness is being gathered or pleated.

Although a frill is usually made of a single thickness of fabric, it can be made double. Cut a strip of fabric twice as wide as the width of the frill plus the seam allowance. Fold the fabric strip in half and treat as a single thickness.

Frill Applied in a Seam

Pin the ruffle to one of the pieces to be joined in the seam, right sides up, matching seam lines. Pull up the gathering threads and adjust the fullness evenly to fit the space. Baste in place. Pin the second section over the frill, right sides together, matching seam lines. Stitch the seam and grade the seam allowances (784). Press seam allowances away from the frill.

784

Frill Extending From an Edge

This occurs in collars, cuffs and edges of facings. Pin the frill to the garment or one section of the collar or cuff, right sides together, matching seam lines. Pull up the gathering threads and adjust the fullness, allowing a little extra fullness at corners. Baste in place, tapering frill at ends (785). Pin the facing or second section over the frill. Stitch seam and grade seam allowances. Turn facing to wrong side, leaving frill free (786).

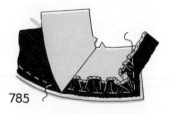

785

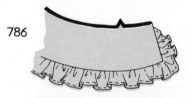

786

Frill Applied with Bias Strip

Pin frill to garment, right sides together, matching seam lines. Pull up the gathering threads and adjust the fullness evenly. Baste bias strip over the frill and stitch the seam (787). Grade seam allowance. Press seam allowance and bias strip toward garment and away from frill. Turn in edge of bias strip and hem to garment.

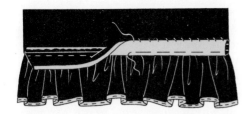

787

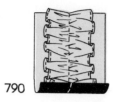

790

Frill Applied with Heading

Turn under the upper edge of frill the desired width of heading plus a seam allowance. Make two rows of gathering, one along seam line, the other just above. Pin frill to under fabric, right sides up, matching seam lines. Pull up the gathering threads and adjust gathers evenly. Baste and stitch seam with frill side up through all thicknesses (788).

PIPING

Piping is made by covering cord with bias fabric. It can be set into a seam or used as a surface trim. The bias fabric for covering the cord is cut and joined in the same way as for binding.

Piping in a Seam

Encase cord in a bias strip of fabric and stitch close to cord with a cording foot (791). Baste piping to right side of garment with stitching line along seam line of unfinished edge. Baste facing over and stitch seam with a piping foot (792). Grade seam allowances and press seam away from piping.

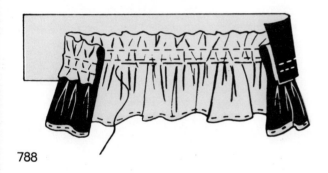

788

Circular Frill

Cut frill in circular form the desired width plus hem and seam allowance. The smaller the inner circle the fuller the frill will be. Seam frill pieces together for desired length with a flat-fell, French or plain seam. Stay-stitch the inner edge of the seam line. Turn under and hem the lower edge by hand or machine. Clip to the stay-stitching on upper edge so it will lie flat (789). Pin and sew in position.

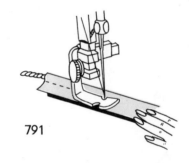

791

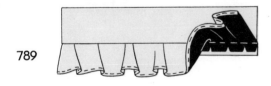

789

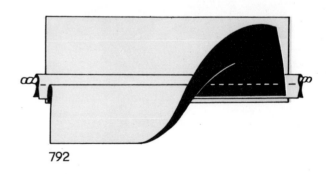

792

Double Frill

Cut frill the desired width plus hem allowances on both edges. Finish both edges with a narrow hand or machine hem. Place a gathering thread through the centre of the frill. Pin centre of frill to stitching line for frill on the garment, right sides up. Pull up gathering thread and adjust gathers evenly. Top-stitch frill to garment along line of gathering stitches (790).

Turned Piping

This type of piping is used for buttonhole loops, ties and other surface trims. Cut a piece of cord twice the length of the strip of bias fabric. Attach one end of the bias strip to centre of the cord (793). Fold right side of bias strip over cord and stitch, using a piping foot.

Trim seam. Pull the encased cord out of the tubing (794). This will automatically turn the bias to the right side and pull the free cord into the bias tubing. Cut off the extra cord.

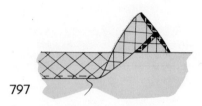

793

794

BRAID

There is a wide variety of novelty braid on the market but all can be applied by one of these methods.

Narrow Bias Braid

Soutache and other narrow bias braid can be used to outline the lines of a design. It is applied by hand or by machine using a braiding foot (795). Follow directions given in machine manual. If braid pulls up, place paper under fabric and sew through it. Tear paper away after stitching is completed.

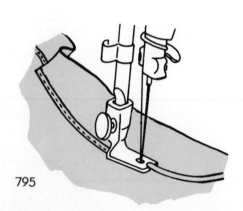

795

Flat Braid

These braids come in a number of widths and are used mostly as a border trim. They are applied with hand- or machine-stitching along both edges of the braid (796).

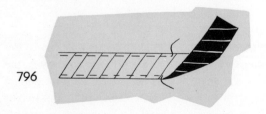

796

READY-FOLDED BRAID. These braids are of a woven bias construction so that they can be shaped to fit around a curved edge. The braid is already folded so that it can be easily applied as an edge finish (797). The top edge is always folded slightly narrower so that the underside is sure to catch when stitching. Shape the braid with a steam iron before basting it to a curved edge. Stretch the folded edge to fit around an outward curve and stretch the open edge for an inward curve. Stitch in place by hand or machine.

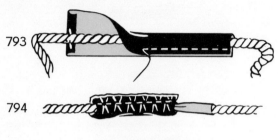

797

RIC RAC. Ric rac braid can be used as a piping, an edging or to outline a design. When used as a piping (798), the edge of the garment is lapped and stitched over the ric rac so that just half of the ric rac shows, forming a point design. As an edging, the ric rac is lapped and stitched over the edge of the

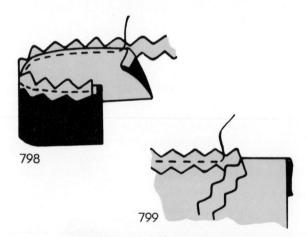

798

799

garment so that both pointed edges of the ric rac are visible (799). If used to outline a design, the ric rac is placed over the pencil or chalk marking for the design and stitched through the centre (800).

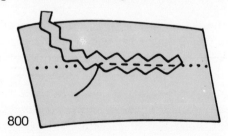

800

FRINGE

Fringe is an edge trim made from threads of the fabric or from yarn. The kind of fringe used depends on the effect you wish to create. The fringe made by drawing threads of the fabric is very fine while fringe made from yarn can be heavy and bulky, depending on the weight of yarn used. Ready-made fringe can also be purchased by the yard.

Self Fringe

Be sure edge of fabric to be fringed is cut on a single thread of the straight fabric grain. Mark the depth of fringe on the fabric and stay-stitch this line with zig-zag or straight machine-stitching. Ravel the threads of the fabric to the line of stay-stitching (801).

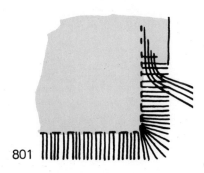

801

Knotted Fringe

Cut a piece of cardboard the desired depth of fringe. Wind yarn around it. Cut at one edge (802). Count the number of yarns depending on the weight of fringe you wish to make. Insert a crochet hook through fabric and pull yarn through forming a loop (803). Draw yarn ends through loop and pull tight. Continue pulling groups of yarn through fabric, keeping each group the same size and an even distance from the edge.

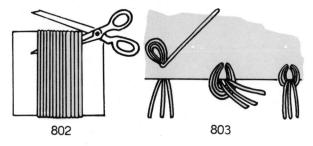

802   803

Ready-Made Fringe

This comes with a heading and can be applied to a shaped edge, while fringe made by drawing a thread must always be on a straight edge. The ready-made

fringe (804) can be top-stitched to the garment as a border or edging, or it can also be applied with a facing. When a facing is used, baste the fringe to the edge of the garment, right sides together, with seam line of fringe along seam line of garment. Baste facing over fringe and stitch seam. Grade seam allowance and turn facing to inside.

804

TASSELS

The tassel is used as a finish for the end of a tie or a cord. Cut a piece of cardboard the desired depth. Place a piece of yarn across top of cardboard and then wind yarn around cardboard to desired fullness. Tie the top firmly with the piece of yarn placed at the top of the cardboard (805). Wrap yarn around the top end several times and tie to hold strands together. Trim cut ends evenly (806).

805

806

POMPONS

The pompon is made on circular pieces of cardboard. It can be used just as an ornament or can be substituted for a button trim. Cut two circles of cardboard the size of the pompon required. Cut a smaller circle out of the centres about a quarter of the size of the original diameter. Put the discs together and cover with wool (807a), threading wool through hole.

When the centre circle is full, cut the strands round outside edge (807b). Wind a strand of wool very tightly between the cards several times and tie, leaving the ends for attaching the pompon. Pull off discs and fluff out pompon, trimming uneven ends (808).

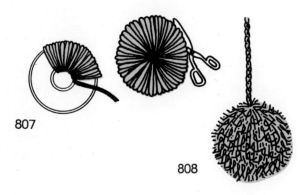

807

808

BEADING

Beading is a very effective trim but tedious to do. It should be done after the garment is completed. Mark the outline for design on the right side of the fabric with chalk. Wax the thread with beeswax to prevent the thread from twisting and breaking.

Beads Applied Singly

Working from right to left, sew each bead on individually with a back-stitch following along the line of the design. Be sure to fasten all ends of thread securely (809).

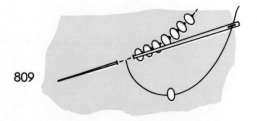

809

Beads Applied on a Thread

Tiny beads can be strung on a heavy thread. The thread holding the beads is then whip-stitched to the garment along the line of the design. A whip-stitch must be taken between each bead (810).

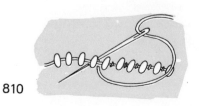

810

SEQUINS

Sequins, like beads, are applied after the garment is finished. Machine-stitching will break the sequins near the seam. Mark the design on the right side of the fabric with chalk.

Sequins Applied Singly

Sequins sewed on singly are usually applied with a small bead in the centre. Fasten the thread on the wrong side of the fabric. Bring the needle through centre of sequin and bead and back down through the centre of the sequin (811). Fasten thread in the fabric.

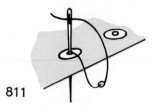

811

Sequins Applied in a Row

Working from right to left, bring needle through the fabric and the centre of the sequin. Take a back-stitch in the fabric and draw up thread until sequin is flat against the fabric (812). Continue sewing on the sequins in this manner so that the edges of the sequins are overlapped.

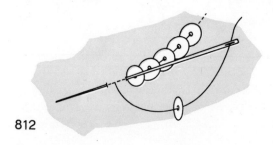

812

APPLIQUÉ

Appliqué is the method of applying a design of one fabric to a second fabric. A motif may be selected from a printed fabric or the design can be traced on the fabric. It may be applied by hand or machine.

Hand Appliqué

Machine-stitch around the outside of the design (813a). Cut out the design to be appliquéd, allowing a $1/8$-inch seam allowance beyond the row of machine-stitching (813b). Turn under the edges of the piece along the line of stitching and baste. Press the piece so that it lies perfectly flat before it is basted in position (813c). The design may be applied with a blanket or buttonhole stitch or by slip-stitching (813d).

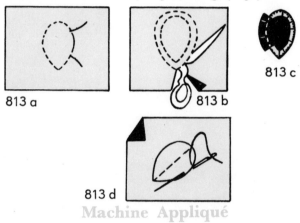

813 a   813 b   813 c

813 d

Machine Appliqué

Cut out the design of the appliqué, leaving a $1/4$-inch margin around edges (814a). Pin the design to the fabric to which it is to be applied and machine-stitch in place along the seam line. Trim close to stitching. Cover raw edge and machine-stitching with a very close zigzag or satin stitch (814b).

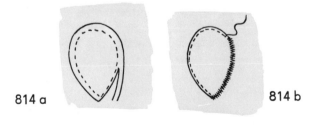

814 a   814 b

Bias Tape Appliqué

This is particularly suited to making monograms. Transfer the design markings to the fabric. Turn under the cut edge of the tape and pin single-fold bias tape along the markings (815). Stretch tape around outside curves, ease around inside curves and mitre corners. Turn in end of tape and slip-stitch or machine-stitch tape in position (816).

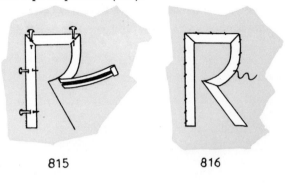

815   816

LACE

Lace can be used as an edging, as insertion or to make an entire garment. Due to the delicate, open construction of lace, special construction techniques are required.

Lace Edging

Lace edging has one straight edge which is applied to fabric or insertion. All edging should be gathered slightly before it is attached.

GATHERING LACE EDGING. Draw up heavy thread in upper edge of lace, gathering to desired fullness. Secure ends of thread by winding around pins. Adjust fullness evenly (817).

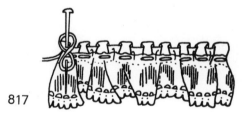

817

LACE EDGING APPLIED TO HEMMED EDGE. Gather edging the desired amount. Place lace on right side of finished hem. Working from right to left, sew lace to fabric with a close whip-stitch (818).

818

LACE EDGING APPLIED TO ROLLED EDGE.

Gather edging the desired amount. Hold fabric toward you; roll edge of fabric and join edge of lace in one operation. Sew from right to left with a small, even whip-stitch (819).

LACE EDGING APPLIED TO INSERTION.

Gather edging the desired amount. Place lace over insertion, right sides together. Working from right to left, whip-stitch the straight edges together (820).

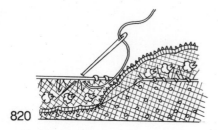

LACE EDGING APPLIED BY MACHINE.

Gather edging slightly. Lap the straight side of the edging over the edge of the fabric, right sides up. Join with a machine zigzag stitch (821).

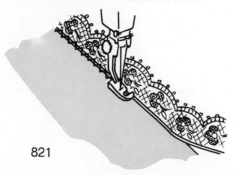

LACE EDGING WITH A MITRED CORNER.

Pin edging around corner of fabric allowing enough for mitring. Fold the edging at corner, forming a mitre (822). Cut away excess lace and whip edges together by hand or with a machine zigzag stitch (823).

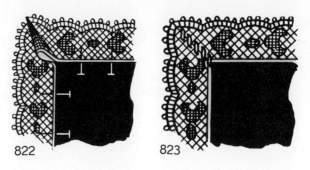

Lace Insertion

Lace insertion has both edges finished in the same way. They can be either straight or scalloped. The straight insertion is usually set into fabric or between fabric and lace edging. The scalloped insertion can also be used as a flat edge finish.

LACE INSERTION APPLIED BY HAND.

Baste insertion to right side of fabric. Sew both edges of the insertion to the fabric with a fine hemming stitch (824). Cut away fabric under the lace, leaving enough so that edges of the fabric can be rolled and whipped in place (825).

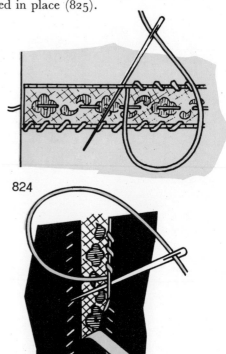

LACE INSERTION APPLIED BY MACHINE.

Baste insertion to right side of fabric. Sew both edges of insertion to fabric with a machine zigzag stitch (826). Cut away the fabric under the lace, and trim close to stitching (827).

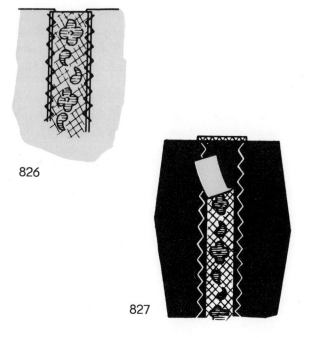

826

827

embroidery floss or buttonhole twist in a matching or contrasting colour.

SADDLE STITCHING. Take short stitches through the garment and facing an even distance from the edge. The stitches on the top side are longer than the stitches on the underside (829).

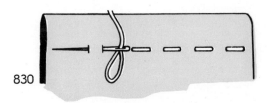

829

GLOVE STITCHING. This is done in the same manner as the saddle stitch but the stitches on the top and underside are equal in length (830).

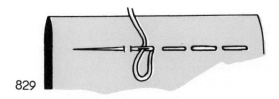

830

SCALLOPED INSERTION USED AS FLAT EDGE FINISH. Lap and baste insertion over unfinished edge of fabric, right sides up. Sew edge of insertion to fabric with a zigzag stitch. On the wrong side, trim fabric close to stitching (828).

828

PRICK STITCHING. Take short half-back-stitches in which only two or three threads of the fabric are picked up. Pull each stitch tight (831).

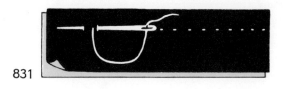

831

DECORATIVE STITCHES

Decorative stitches or stitching should add to the finished appearance of a garment. Such trimming usually carries the eye to the one area and makes it the centre of interest.

Hand Edge-Stitching

Saddle, glove and prick stitches are all decorative hand top-stitching used to outline the edges of a garment. These are usually done with several strands of

Machine Edge-Stitching

Machine-stitching used to trim the edges of a garment can be placed close to the edge or as much as $1\frac{1}{2}$ inches from the edge, depending on the effect you wish to create. You may use a single row of stitching or a number of rows. Keep stitching an even distance from the edge and the rows an even distance apart if there is to be more than one row of stitching. This top stitching must be straight or it will spoil the appearance of your garment.

Tacks

Tacks are decorative thread reinforcements used on the right side of the fabric at ends of pockets, seams and pleats. They can be made of buttonhole twist or embroidery floss. The bar tack is the least conspicuous and is used mostly on tailored garments or men's clothes. The arrowhead and crow's-foot tack are more decorative and very attractive when well made.

BAR TACK. Take several long stitches through fabric, across ends of opening (832a). Cover these strands with overhand stitches close together, picking up a few threads of the fabric at the same time (832b). Finish ends of bar tack with small bar tacks at right angles to it (832c, 832d).

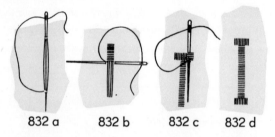

832 a   832 b   832 c   832 d

ARROWHEAD TACK. Mark the triangular outline for the tack on the right side of the fabric with chalk or basting stitches (833a). Start by bringing needle out at lower left-hand corner and take a small stitch across upper corner from right to left. Insert the needle at lower right-hand corner and bring needle out at left corner just inside first stitch (833b). Continue placing stitches close to each other in this pattern around the triangle until the entire area is filled in (833c, 833d).

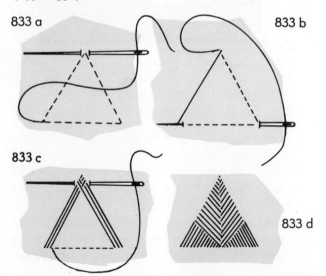

833 a   833 b

833 c

833 d

CROW'S-FOOT TACK. Mark outline of tack with chalk or basting stitches on the right side of the fabric. Bring needle out at lower left-hand corner and take a small horizontal stitch across upper corner from right to left (834a). Insert the needle at lower right-hand corner and take a small diagonal stitch across the point from left to right. Insert the needle at lower left-hand corner and take a small diagonal stitch across the point from left to right (834b). Continue placing stitches close to each other in this pattern around the triangle until the area is filled in (834c, 834d).

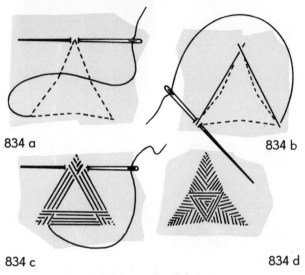

834 a   834 b

834 c   834 d

Hemstitching

Hemstitching is made by drawing out threads of the fabric. It must always be done in straight lines following the grain of the material. The different kinds of hemstitching are formed by grouping the threads of the fabric in various ways.

Mark the hem width and then draw out the required number of threads above the hem marking. Turn up the hem and baste it along the line where the first thread was drawn (835). Use regular mercerised sewing thread for hemstitching.

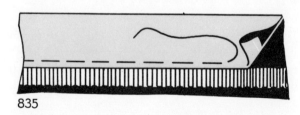

835

SINGLE HEMSTITCHING. Work from left to right with wrong side of fabric uppermost. Bring needle out at the edge of hem. Pick up the desired number of threads on needle, passing needle from right to left.

Take a tiny stitch in the hem just to the right of the threads you have encircled (836). Pull the sewing thread tight around the drawn threads. Continue in this manner.

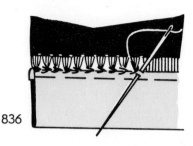

836

DOUBLE HEMSTITCHING. Make single hemstitching along the hem edge (836). Turn work around and repeat the same stitch taking a tiny stitch through the fabric along the inner edge. Pick up the same groups of threads with each stitch to form straight bars between the edges (837).

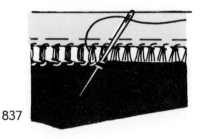

837

DIAGONAL HEMSTITCHING. Make single hemstitching along the hem edge, picking up an even number of threads with each stitch. Turn work around. Pass the needle around half of the first group of threads and half of the second group of threads and then through fabric making a zigzag line of bars (838).

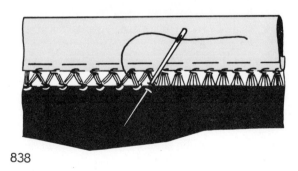

838

Faggoting

Faggoting is a decorative joining of two finished edges with buttonhole twist or heavy embroidery floss. This open-work stitch can be used on curved or shaped areas.

Turn under the raw edges of the two pieces of fabric to be joined. Press. Draw two parallel lines on a piece of brown paper, the desired distance apart. Baste the edge of the fabric to the paper along the lines marked, right side up. Work from the top of the design down.

CRISS-CROSS FAGGOTING. Bring needle to the right side of the material through the fold at the upper-left corner. Take a diagonal stitch across to the other side bringing the needle up through the fabric. Pass the needle under the thread and take a diagonal stitch on the other side. Continue stitching in this manner (839). Remove paper when faggoting is completed.

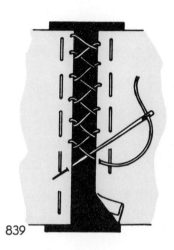

839

LADDER OR BAR FAGGOTING. Take stitches from left side to right side straight across (840). Wrap thread around needle several times and bring needle out at left again. Slip needle between fold along edge and bring out to start next stitch. Continue making stitches in this way. Remove the paper when completed.

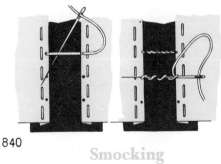

840

Smocking

Smocking is a decorative way of holding fullness in even folds. It should be done on the fabric before the garment is constructed. There are two methods of smocking—regular and English smocking.

In regular smocking the transfer is stamped on the right side of the fabric, and the pleats and gathers are made as the dots of the smocking pattern are picked up. English smocking has rows of gathering thread run through rows of evenly spaced dots stamped on the wrong side of the fabric. These dots are pulled up to gather the material into evenly spaced pleats. The decorative smocking stitches are then worked on the right side of the fabric on top of the pleats. Gathering threads are removed after smocking is done. The same smocking stitches can be used in both types of smocking. Use six-strand embroidery floss for all smocking.

OUTLINE STITCH. Work from left to right (841). Bring the needle to right side of fabric at dot 1. Place thread above needle. Insert needle in fabric under dot 2. Pull up the thread so that fold is made. Continue in this way making one stitch at each dot (842).

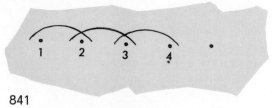

841

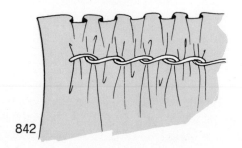

842

CABLE STITCH. Working from left to right (843), bring the needle to right side of fabric at dot 1. Put thread above needle. Insert needle in the fabric under dot 2 and bring it out. Draw up the thread. For second stitch, hold the thread below needle and make a stitch at dot 3. Hold the thread above needle for stitch at dot 4. Continue across the row in this manner (844).

843

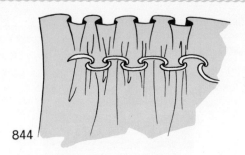

844

DOUBLE CABLE STITCH. Work a second row of cable stitches under the first, placing thread above and below the needle in opposite directions (845, 846).

845

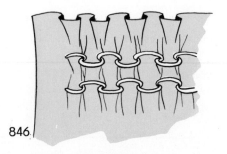

846

HONEYCOMB OR SEED STITCH. Work from left to right on two alternating rows of dots (847). Bring the needle up to right side of fabric through first dot on top row. With thread above needle, take a small stitch at dot 2 and another at dot 1. Draw together tightly. Insert needle at dot 2, carry thread under fabric and bring it out at dot 3 on the row below. Keeping thread below needle, pick up dot 4 and dot 3 in the same manner as dot 2 and dot 1. Insert needle at dot 4, carry thread under fabric and bring out at dot 5 on the top row. Continue working in this manner, alternating the stitch from one row to the other until completed (848).

847

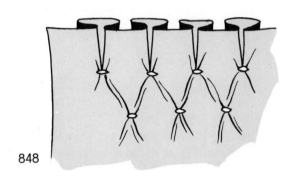

848

DIAMOND OR CHEVRON STITCH. This

looks like the honeycomb stitch except that the thread
between the rows is carried on top of the fabric instead
of under the fabric. Work from left to right on two
alternating rows of dots (849). Bring the needle up to
right side of fabric through first dot on top row. With
thread above needle, take a small stitch at dot 2. Draw
together tightly. Take a stitch at dot 3. With thread below needle, take a stitch at dot 4 and pull the thread
tight. Take a stitch at dot 5. With thread above needle,
take a stitch at dot 6. Draw together tightly. Continue
in this manner alternating from one row to the other
(850).

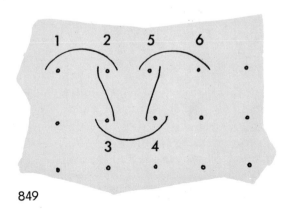

849

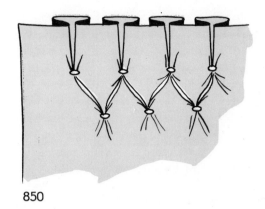

850

TWO-STEP WAVE STITCH. This is done

with six dots in each wave group (851.) Working from
left to right, bring the needle up at left of dot 1. Take
a stitch through dot 1 with thread above needle. Pull
down, drawing thread tight. Take a stitch through dots
2 and 3 with thread above needle and pull down after
each stitch. Take a stitch through dot 4 with thread
below needle and pull up. Take a stitch through dots
5 and 6 with thread below needle and pull up after
each stitch. Pick up dot 1 of next group with thread
above needle and pull down. Continue in this manner
until design is completed (852).

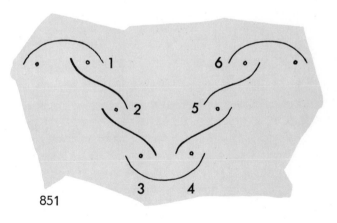

851

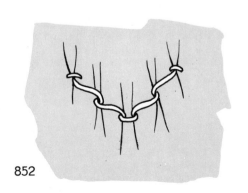

852

THREE-STEP WAVE STITCH. This is done with eight dots in each wave group (853). Working from left to right, bring the needle up at left of dot 1. Take a stitch through dot 1 with thread above needle. Pull down, drawing thread tight. Take a stitch through dots 2, 3 and 4 with thread above needle and pull down after each stitch. Take a stitch through dot 5 with the thread below needle and pull up. Take a stitch through dots 6, 7 and 8 with thread below needle and pull up after each stitch. Pick up dot 1 of next group with thread above needle and pull down. Continue in this manner until design is completed (854).

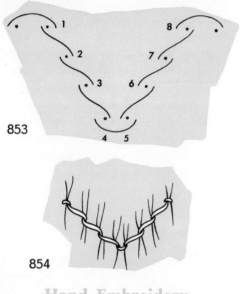

853

854

Hand Embroidery

There are a great variety of hand-embroidery stitches. These stitches may be used individually or combined with other stitches to form a more elaborate design.

When doing hand embroidery, mark the design on the right side of the fabric. Always use embroidery hoops to hold the fabric firm and keep it from puckering as stitches are pulled tight. Fasten the threads with tiny back-stitches instead of using knots.

RUNNING STITCH. Working from right to left, pick up several small stitches on the needle. Draw the thread through the fabric. Continue in this manner, keeping the stitches an even size and length (855).

855

TWISTED RUNNING STITCH. After completing the running stitch, working from left to right, overcast the stitches with thread of matching or contrasting colour and weight. Use a blunt-end needle and run it under each stitch but do not catch any of the fabric. This gives the effect of a twisted cord (856).

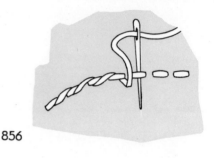

856

STEM OR OUTLINE STITCH. Working from left to right, bring thread through to right side of fabric. Take a back stitch $1/4$ inch away. Take a second back-stitch, bringing needle out close to last stitch. Continue in this manner, keeping stitches even. For the stem stitch the thread is placed below the needle (857); for the outline stitch the thread is placed above the needle.

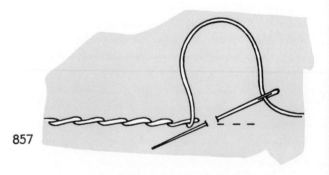

857

STRAIGHT OR SPOKE STITCH. This is a single flat stitch used to form flowers, stems, leaves (858).

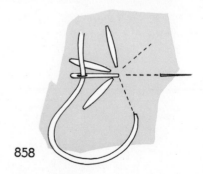

858

SATIN STITCH. This makes a smooth covering for regular- or irregular-shaped spaces. Carry the thread across the design and take a stitch under the fabric, bringing the needle out at the starting point. Keep the stitches even and very close together. For a more raised effect, the design should be padded with tiny running stitches in the opposite direction from the satin stitch to be applied over it (859, 860).

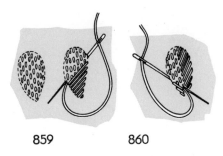

859   860

HERRINGBONE STITCH. This is the same as the catch-stitch used in sewing. Work from left to right along two parallel lines. Bring the needle out at lower left corner. Take a stitch through fabric from right to left on top line. Then take a stitch through fabric from right to left on bottom line so that the thread between the two parallel lines is slanted. Keep stitches an even length and an even distance apart (861).

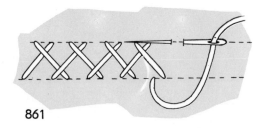

861

CROSS STITCH. Work from left to right along two parallel lines. Make first half of crosses by taking diagonal stitches with needle straight and point down (862). Complete entire row forming half of the cross stitch. Then work from right to left, filling in the second half of the cross in the same manner (863). Keep stitches even.

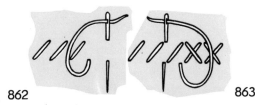

862   863

BLANKET STITCH. Working from left to right, bring needle out on marked line or at edge of the fabric. Hold thread down and take a stitch, pointing needle toward you with thread under needle. Draw needle through loop that has been formed (864a). Stitches may be even length and distance apart or grouped and spaced according to the desired effect. Keep stitches or groupings even (864b, 864c).

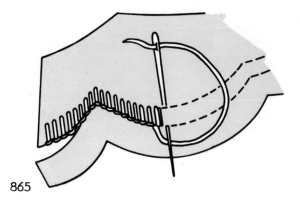

864 a   864 b

864 c

SCALLOPED EDGE. Outline the scallops with small running stitches. Working from left to right and holding lower edge of scallops toward you, work blanket stitches between the outline stitches. Keep stitches very close together and even. Trim fabric away close to scallops after embroidery is completed (865).

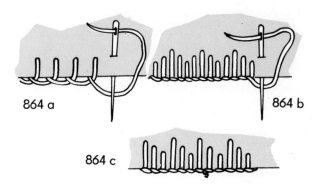

865

FEATHER STITCH. This is a blanket stitch made at an angle. Working from top to bottom, bring needle out at beginning of marking. Hold thread down and take a slanting stitch to the right, and a little below this spot. The needle will be pointing to the left. Pull the needle through the fabric and over the thread. Carry thread to the left and make a similar stitch with needle pointed to the right. Continue alternating the stitches from right to left, keeping them evenly spaced (866). This stitch can be varied by marking several blanket stitches on each side.

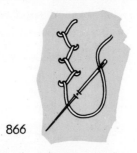

866

CHAIN STITCH. Work from right to left. Bring needle to right side of fabric. Insert needle in fabric at almost the same point and take a stitch, looping thread under the point of needle. Pull up the thread, forming a loop. Put needle back into fabric inside loop, close to emerging thread. Take another stitch with thread around and under point of needle. Continue, keeping stitches and loops even (867).

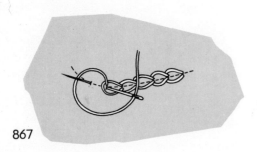

867

LADDER STITCH. A double row of dots is used to mark the ladder stitch. Working from top to bottom, bring needle out at top left-hand dot. Hold thread down. Take a slanting stitch from top right-hand dot to second left-hand dot, passing needle over the thread. Pull up thread forming a loop. Take another slanting stitch from second right-hand dot to third left-hand dot. Pass needle over the thread and form the next loop by pulling up the thread. Continue in this manner, working down the dots from right to left (868).

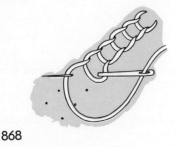

868

FLY STITCH. This is an open chain stitch made in the shape of a V. Working from left to right, bring needle to right side of fabric at a point which will be the top of the left side of the V. Hold thread down, insert needle at the top of the right side of the V and bring it out at the base of the V. Pull the needle through the fabric and insert the needle below the base of the V to hold the loop in place (870).

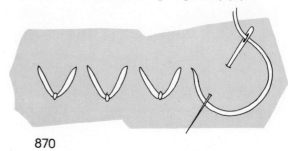

870

LAZY DAISY STITCH. This is a detached chain stitch radiating from a centre point to form petals of a flower. Bring needle to right side of fabric at centre of flower. Holding thread down, insert needle as close as possible to the starting point (871). Take a long stitch the length of the petal to form a loop. Pull the needle through the fabric and take a short stitch to hold the end of the loop in place. Bring needle back to centre to start the next petal (872).

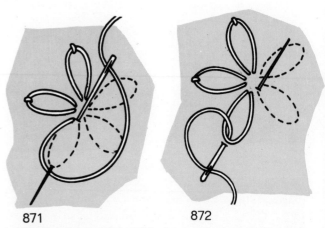

871   872

SEED STITCH. This is a very tiny chain stitch tightly drawn and scattered in all directions to fill an open area (873).

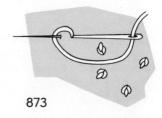

873

FRENCH KNOT. Bring needle to right side of fabric at point knot is to be placed. Wind thread around needle two or three times (874). Holding thread firmly around needle, insert needle in fabric as closely as possible to the point it emerged (875). Pull thread to wrong side. The more times the thread is wrapped around the needle the heavier the French knot will be.

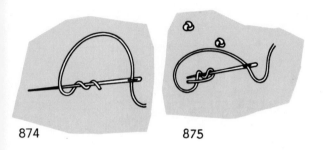

874   875

BULLION STITCH. This stitch is similar to the French knot in construction. The thread is wrapped around the needle four or five times and the needle is inserted a short distance from the point it emerged. It is used mainly for embroidering roses (876).

876

COUCHING STITCH. Use a single or double cord of either matching or contrasting colour to follow the line of the design. Working from right to left, catch the cord down firmly by bringing thread over cord and through fabric with evenly spaced stitches (877).

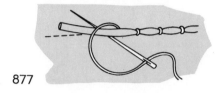

877

Machine Embroidery

Machine embroidery can be done with attachments on your straight-stitch machine or by a zigzag machine. Follow the directions in the booklet supplied with the sewing machine. Always make a test sample first on your fabric. Test thread, pressure on the presser foot and tension. Practise using the machine until you are adept at handling the machine for decorative stitching.

You can follow designs provided with the pattern or make your own designs. Transfer markings for the design to the right side of the fabric and do the embroidery on the right side of the material.

To embroider designs on sheer fabric you may need to baste a piece of tissue or organdie to the wrong side of the fabric under the design to keep the fabric from slipping and pulling. If tissue is used, tear it away after embroidery is completed. If organdie is used, trim it close to stitching after embroidery is completed.

CHAPTER 14

TAILORING TALK

One of the biggest events in the life of a seamstress is the day she appears in a beautifully tailored suit or coat of her own making. She has a perfect right to be proud. Tailoring is not a hard task, but it is an exacting one. It takes time and attention to detail to tailor well, but the extra effort is rewarded by the overwhelming sense of pride one takes in turning out a truly high quality garment.

Before you attempt any tailoring, you should have an ideal in mind. You should know what constitutes a good coat or suit. If you are going to spend the extra time it takes to tailor, you want the garment to have a professional appearance.

Examine better ready-to-wear tailored garments. If possible, visit a tailor's shop and examine the garments he makes. Note how thin the edges of the garments are, even where you would expect to find thick, bulky seams. Notice, too, how the edges of the lapels curl toward the body, never outward. Seams are flat and straight with no puckers. Linings are loosely tacked to the seams so they don't interfere with the drape of the garment. Buttons are carefully sewed on with an ample shank so they won't pull on the buttonholes. The collars and lapels roll smoothly. Only by recognising good tailoring in a garment, can you attempt to become an expert tailor.

TAILORING EQUIPMENT

Tailoring requires some additional equipment besides that needed for dressmaking. You will need a tailor's ham, wooden clapper, point presser, needle board and a seam roll. (See page 61.) If you plan to do quite a bit of tailoring, you may want to invest in one of the heavy tailor's flat-irons. The extra weight of the iron helps produce the sharp tailored edges you want.

The secret of fine tailoring is actually in the pressing and moulding of the garment, so keep your pressing equipment handy. You will use it just as often as your machine.

FABRICS FOR TAILORING

Tailoring is a building and moulding process. It is best to select a fabric which can be easily moulded through steaming, shrinking and pressing over shaping mat-

erials. Wool is the best selection since it shapes and shrinks so beautifully. A medium-weight wool with a spongy texture and an unfinished or napped surface such as tweed or flannel will be best for your first tailored garment. They are easier to shrink and shape and will not shine readily when pressed. Avoid the worsteds such as covert, gabardine or anything with a hard finish. These are difficult to shrink and press. Save plaids, checks, stripes and very heavy coatings until you have had some experience in tailoring. The patterned materials create problems in matching and very heavy coatings tend to slip under the presser foot of the machine when stitching several thicknesses of fabric.

Linings

Linings are subject to more wear and stress than the actual garment fabric. Select a lining fabric that is durable, opaque, colourfast to perspiration, capable of being dry-cleaned and in a colour which harmonises with the colour of the garment. Select a smooth-finished

28   Designs such as this are great fun and surprisingly
easy to do. Only originality and a few hours of
experimentation with your machine are needed
to achieve outstandingly artistic results.

*Photograph by courtesy of Singer Sewing Machine
Company Ltd.*

29 Use your skill in sewing to transform your bathroom into a colourful luxurious room such as this one.
Cotton poplin and terry-towelling are used for the curtains, shower curtains, cushion and floor covering.

Photograph by courtesy of The Cotton Board

fabric which is easy to slip in and out of. Fabrics most frequently used are silk crêpe, soft satin, silk taffeta, surah, rayons or synthetics of similar construction.

Aluminium-backed lining fabrics will provide additional warmth without weight. These are available in crêpes and satins and a few have both the aluminium and a laminated backing which gives greater warmth to the garment than those without the laminated backing.

Interfacing

For any tailoring, you will need interfacing fabric to give firmness and shaping to the garment and to reinforce collar, cuffs, buttonholes, buttons and hems. For tailoring woollen garments, use a weight of hair canvas that is suitable for the weight of your fabric. This same hair canvas or pre-shrunk muslin is used to interface sleeve and jacket hems. For tips on selecting the proper interfacing, check the chart in Chapter 3.

Interlining

For heavy coats which need additional warmth, you will want a lining plus an interlining. Make it of special interlining material. There are several good commercial interlining fabrics on the market, and these are listed in the shaping materials chart on page 40.

Patterns will give the proper yardages for garment fabric, interfacing, interlining and lining. Most suits will have lining fabric listed only for jackets. If you wish to line the skirt also, purchase additional yardage equal to the yardage needed for the skirt. If skirt yardages are not listed separately on the pattern, then measure the length of the skirt and buy lining yardage equal to two skirt lengths.

Pre-Shrunk and Grain Perfect

Be sure that all fabrics you use are pre-shrunk and that they are grain perfect. Check our suggestions in Chapter 7 for fabric preparation. In tailoring it is even more essential to the good looks of the garment than it is in dressmaking for grain lines to be perfectly straight. The garment simply will not mould and shape correctly if grain lines are not maintained on all fabrics.

Notions

Select all the notions needed for the garment before you begin any construction. Usually you will need seam binding, zipper, silk or mercerised sewing thread, buttonhole twist, $1/4$-inch twill tape, buttons, hooks and eyes and snaps. Check pattern envelope carefully for special items such as cording, braid or weights which may be needed for your garment. Shoulder pads are optional.

THE PATTERN

Your first suit or coat should be an important item in your wardrobe for years to come. After all, if you are going to spend the time and effort required to tailor well, you will want a garment you can wear for more than the current season. Select a basic suit in classic style. Avoid the extreme styles which may become dated. Select the suit design which is most flattering. Buy the pattern in your correct figure type and size.

Suit and coat patterns are both purchased in the same figure type and size as your dress patterns. DO NOT buy a larger size. The correct amount of ease for proper fit has been included in the pattern and it is not necessary to allow extra.

Adjust the suit pattern, just as you do your dress pattern. If you need to narrow the shoulders, then do so using the same method as outlined for narrow shoulders in a dress, page 80. It is never necessary to allow extra for pads. Shoulder pads today are used to correct figure faults such as one low shoulder or sloping shoulders. Adding extra pad allowance to your pattern only creates a worse alteration problem.

If you are in doubt about your alterations, then make the suit in muslin, just as you made your basic pattern. Remember that muslin will not drape in the same way as wool fabric. Additional minor alterations will have to be made in the wool fabric but the muslin will be very helpful if you have a number of major alterations. Be sure to allow sufficient ease in the muslin for the weight of the fabric, interfacing and lining.

TAILORING A SUIT
Cutting and Marking

After all necessary pattern alterations have been made, lay out the pattern following the diagrams on pattern guide sheet. If the fabric has a nap, cut it with the nap running down and place all pattern pieces in the same direction. Material with a pile is usually cut with the pile running up for a rich effect. Plaids should be matched both crosswise and lengthwise. Use the same line of the plaid for centre front and centre back. Diagonal-weave fabrics should be cut with the diagonal running from the left side toward the right in the front and from the right to the left in the back.

Cut and mark the fabric following the same procedure as suggested for dressmaking on page 103. Be careful to cut and mark accurately. You may find when cutting a double section that the under fabric is cut slightly larger than the upper section of fabric, because shears slip slightly due to the thickness of the material. Check each section, and trim so that the two are identical in size with the pattern.

If the wool is a very soft or stratchy one, you may wish to underline each section with china silk or the lightest weights of commercial underlining. Cut from the same pattern pieces used for the suit, and mark these carefully. If an underlining is used, you will not have to mark the suit fabric, except for placement of trims, centre front and back and grain-line positions. These markings are best done by hand-bastings.

The pattern usually has separate pattern pieces for interfacing sections. If for some reason these pieces do not accompany the pattern, then cut them from the jacket pieces. Mark the cutting lines on the pattern. On the pattern front, mark the width of the facing from hemline along the front edge (878). Then mark a short line 3 inches below the armhole (878). Draw a curved line from the underarm marking to ½ inch wider than the facing width at the front edge. On the back, mark a line from 3 inches below the underarm

curving up to 4 to 5 inches below the centre back neckline (879). Cut interfacing on the same grain as the suit fabric, using the marked pattern pieces.

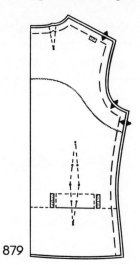

879

Be sure to make all the alterations on the lining pattern pieces that you made on the jacket pattern. If you wish to line a suit, and no lining pattern is given, you can make a lining pattern by using your jacket pieces. On the front pattern piece (880), extend the cutting line $1\frac{1}{4}$ inches beyond the marking for front facing. The lining overlaps the front facing $\frac{5}{8}$ inch and the other $\frac{5}{8}$ inch gives seam allowance for turning

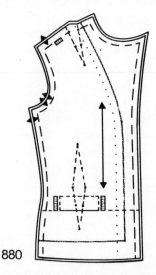

880

under the raw edge. On the back pattern piece (881), extend the cutting line $1\frac{1}{4}$ inches beyond the marking for the back facing. The back of the lining section has a pleat at the centre back to keep the lining from pulling during wear. Fold the fabric and place the centre back marking $\frac{3}{4}$ to 1 inch beyond the fold to allow for the back pleat. Cut lining along the hemline marking at

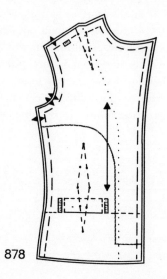

878

the bottom of the jacket. The sleeve is cut the same as the suit sleeve except that it is cut off at the hemline marking (882).

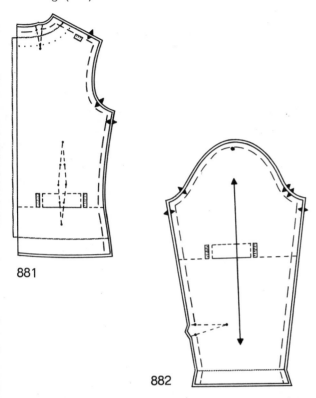

881

882

If you plan to line the skirt completely, use the skirt pattern pieces, and cut the lining fabric identical to the skirt sections. For underlinings, use the skirt pattern and cut off at the hemline marking. For partial lining or underlining over the hip area in front and back, use the skirt pattern pieces and cut about 18 inches in length or to the top of the back pleat.

Be sure to mark all fabric pieces accurately. Transfer all markings to the wrong side of the suit fabric, interfacing and lining fabric; when underlining is used the right side of the fabric is marked.

If the garment is underlined, pin the two sections—fabric and underlining—wrong sides together. Stay-stitch together at each seam allowance. Baste together through centre of darts, other construction details and along hemline edge.

Darts

Stitch all darts and construction details, following the pattern guide sheet. Do not baste and press the darts expecting to stitch them later. It is next to impossible to do a good job of stitching a dart point after it has been basted and pressed even lightly. If darts are wide,

trim them to $5/8$ inch, or in bulky fabrics, narrow darts can be slashed open through the centre to within $1/2$ inch of point. On curved darts, such as waistline darts, clip to stitching line at centre of dart but only after jacket has been fitted and all alterations are complete.

883

Pressing of darts should be done over the tailor's ham (883). Use the wide part of the ham for shaping and moulding the bustline and hip, carefully shrinking the areas at the ends of the darts. Place heavy brown paper between the dart and the body of the suit to eliminate the impression of the dart showing on the right side. Press front darts toward the centre front, underarm darts down, back darts toward centre back, sleeve darts down. If the darts were trimmed or slashed through the centre, press open forming triangle folds at the points.

Press on the wrong side of the fabric, using a damp cloth. The home steam iron does not give enough steam for tailoring—an additional damp press cloth is needed. A dry wool press cloth under a damp cheese-cloth is helpful for problem materials that shine.

Make all darts in the interfacing by slashing darts along the centre marking and overlapping the edges of the slash to the dart stitching line. Stitch along the dart seam markings with a straight machine-stitch or small catch-stitch. Trim the seam allowances on each side of the dart, close to the line of stitching (884). Press the darts, placing interfacing over tailor's ham to retain the shaping.

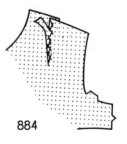

884

Seams

Mark the seam allowance on the neck and front edges of the interfacing with chalk or pencil (885, 886). Baste the interfacing to the jacket front and jacket back pieces (887, 888).

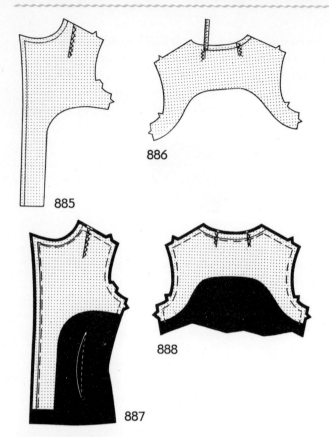

885

886

887

888

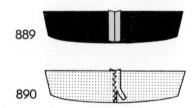

889

890

Machine-baste the shoulder and underarm seams for an accurate fit. Press seams open lightly. Join the sleeve seams following the guide sheet directions. Press the seams lightly on the wrong side and hand-baste the sleeves in the armhole. Stitch the undercollar at centre back seam (889). Join the seam in the undercollar interfacing by overlapping the seam allowances and matching the seam lines. Stitch along the seam line with straight stitch or small catch-stitch through both thicknesses of fabric. Trim seam allowance close to stitching (890).

Mark seam allowances on the undercollar interfacing with chalk or pencil (891). Baste the interfacing to the undercollar (892) and then baste the undercollar

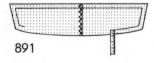

891

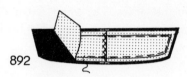

892

to the neck edge. If shoulder pads are to be used, pin them in position.

First Fitting

Try the jacket on, right side out over the undergarments, completed skirt and blouse or sweater you will be wearing with the suit. Also, put on the shoes you plan to wear with the garment. Overlap the jacket closing, matching the centre front basting markings. Pin together at buttonhole markings.

Check the fit and the grain lines of the jacket carefully. In adjusting the fit of the jacket, be sure to allow sufficient ease over and above the normal ease for the lining.

Check the following places for the correct fit and make any necessary adjustments.

☐ Centre front and back markings should be in the middle of the figure and perpendicular to the floor.

☐ Grain line markings across the chest and sleeve cap should be straight and parallel to the floor.

☐ Grain line marking in centre of sleeves should be straight and perpendicular to the floor.

☐ The front darts should be straight and pointed toward the fullest part of the bust.

☐ The back darts should be straight and pointed toward the shoulder blades.

☐ Underarm seams should be straight and in the middle of the figure.

☐ Shoulder seams should be straight and lie smoothly across the top of the shoulder.

☐ Sleeve armhole should fit smoothly and comfortably and lie across the end of the shoulder point.

☐ The centre sleeve dart should fall at the tip of the elbow.

☐ The widest part of the waistline dart should fall at the natural waistline.

☐ The collar should fit smoothly and hug the neck.

Check the length of the sleeves and jacket and mark the correct length.

Pin in any necessary adjustments on the right side of the jacket. Remove the bastings and make the necessary adjustments. Try the jacket on again, and re-check until all necessary alterations have been made. Make only one adjustment at a time, as correction of one may affect the fit of another.

Construction Details

Once the jacket is correctly fitted, check the position of the *buttonholes* (893). The waistline buttonhole is usually at the natural waistline and the buttonholes equally spaced. Mark the roll line on the undercollar and lapel. Check the length of the sleeves and length of the jacket again. Adjust length to suit your particular figure.

893

If there are any *decorative details*, such as pockets or trim, check to be sure these will be in the correct and most flattering position of the figure.

Make bound or corded buttonholes through the suit fabric and interfacing, following the procedure given on pages 214—216. Follow guide sheet for construction of pockets or other trim.

Stitch the seams and trim interfacing close to stitching on shoulder and underarm seams (894). Press straight seams open over seam roll (895) or flat on the board. Curved seams should be placed over the tailor's ham and pressed.

Pressing the garment as you sew is essential to the final appearance of the suit. Don't depend on one final pressing by a tailor to give a professional look to your suit—it won't. Press each seam before crossing it with another seam.

Now you are ready to *shape the roll of the lapel*. Baste the interfacing to the jacket front along the roll line and remove the bastings at the outer edge of the lapel (896). Roll the lapel over your hand with the interfacing on top. This makes the underpart of lapel a little smaller than the interfacing and keeps the corners of the lapel from rolling up. Starting just inside the roll line, work parallel rows of padding stitches $1/2$ inch apart through the interfacing and fabric (897). Use matching silk thread and be sure to catch only one thread of the suit fabric each time. Pad-stitch only to the seam line. Shape both lapels in the same manner.

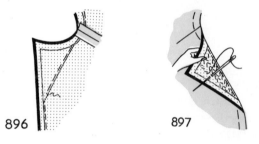

896   897

Always *stay the front edge* of the jacket with $1/4$-inch pre-shrunk twill tape to prevent stretching (898). Trim away the seam allowance of the interfacing at front and neck edge to the centre front. Baste tape to front edge of the jacket along the seam line and across the neck edge to the centre front. Slip-stitch outer edge of tape to seam line and inner edge to interfacing only.

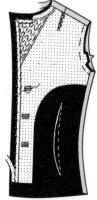

898

Baste interfacing to *undercollar* along roll line, remove basting at outer edges of undercollar (899). Holding undercollar over the hand to create desired slight roll,

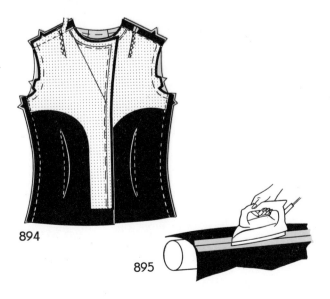

894

895

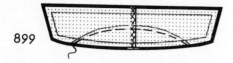

899

pad-stitch from roll line to neck edge and then from roll line to outer edge of undercollar. End pad-stitching at seam line (900). Trim away the seam allowance of interfacing on all edges except the neck edge (901).

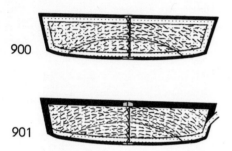

900

901

Attaching the collar is one of the most important steps in the construction of a suit. Be very accurate in matching all notches, centres and any other markings. Pin and stitch undercollar to neck edge of jacket, right sides together (902). Trim interfacing seam allowances at neck edge close to stitching. Trim fabric seam allowance and clip along neckline curve to stitching. Press

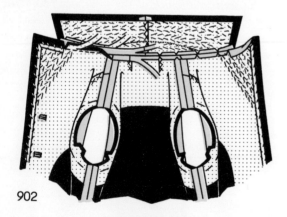

902

seam open, placing neck edge on the tailor's ham to retain shape of neckline (903).

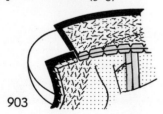

903

Join back facing to front *facing* at the shoulder seams (904), and stitch top collar to the facing (905). Trim seam allowance and clip to stitching line. Press seams open.

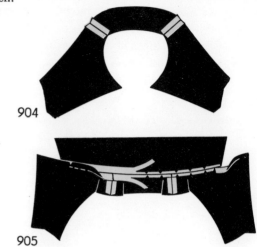

904

905

Turn jacket right side out. Pin facing and top collar to jacket, right sides together (906). Ease top collar to undercollar and front facing to lapel to allow collar and lapel to roll and lie smoothly. Baste together, being very careful to have seams match at the point where collar and lapel join. Stitch across hemline at lower edge of front facing, up front edge, around the lapel and to centre back of collar. Stitch the other side of the jacket in the same manner, overlapping stitches at centre back of collar for about $1/_2$ inch. This keeps roll of lapel and collar the same on both sides. Do not catch tape in the seams.

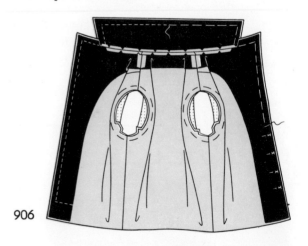

906

Trim across lower edge of jacket to within 1 inch of inner edge of front facing (907). Grade seam allowances. Trim seam allowance of front facing narrower than suit fabric as far as roll line on lapel. Then reverse, trimming suit fabric closest to stitching. This will place the wider seam allowance nearest to the outside and prevent ridges from showing. Clip to point where collar and lapel meet, and trim diagonally across outside corners of hem, lapel and collar (908).

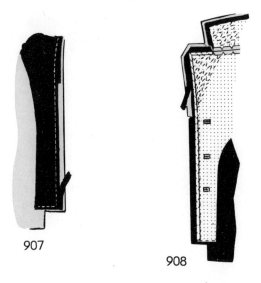

907

908

Press seams open first in order to form flat, smooth edges. Use the point presser to open seams in corners and areas difficult to reach (909). Turn the facing and

909

collar to the inside of jacket. Roll the seam edge very slightly to the inside below the roll line on the front edge. Turn the seam edge above roll line and around collar slightly to the underside. Using silk thread, baste in this position so that seam edges will not show (910).

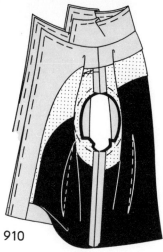

910

For the first time, it is necessary to press on the right side of the garment. This is known as *top-pressing*. For best results, use a damp cheesecloth over a dry wool press cloth. Top-press from the underside of the lapel and collar. From the end of the roll line to the hem, turn and top-press from the facing side. Start with a rather damp press cloth to produce steam. Remove press cloth immediately and pound seam edge with a wooden clapper to flatten the seam. It may be necessary to repeat this several times, depending on the fabric. After the crease line on the edge has been firmly established, remove the silk basting threads and give the edges a final pressing on the needle board to remove the basting marks. Use the damp cheesecloth and the dry wool press cloth with the needle board to protect both sides of the fabric.

Slip-stitch the *back neckline* seam allowances together. Baste the facing to the interfacing (911). Tack facing to interfacing with invisible stitching to within 5 inches of the lower edge. *Finish bound buttonholes* on facing side of front (912).

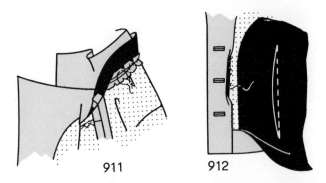

911

912

Stitch around top of *sleeve* on seam line to ease in fullness. Use a regulation machine-stitch from underarm to first notch, change to machine-basting between notches and then change back to regulation stitch from notch to underarm seam. Ease and shrink out fullness at the elbow. If darted at elbow, press darts down. Stitch the sleeve seam and make any changes necessary. Press seams open.

Set sleeve in armhole, right sides together, holding wrong side of jacket up toward you and looking into armhole. Pin sleeve in position, matching notches, seams and other markings. Starting at centre point of sleeve, pull up bobbin thread until sleeve cap fits armhole. Distribute ease evenly. Pin every half inch and baste firmly. Press the sleeve and armhole seams together from the sleeve side, shrinking out any fullness in the sleeve cap. This shrinks the sleeve to fit the armhole without distorting the shape of the sleeve cap.

Second Fitting

Fit the jacket for the second time. Pin in shoulder pads if they are to be used. Recheck all the points checked in the first fitting. Also check the sleeves carefully to be sure the shoulder line is correct and that there is enough ease to allow for moving and raising the arms. Make any necessary alterations, rebaste and try the jacket on again. Recheck the sleeve length to be sure that it has not changed.

Stitch the sleeve into the armhole with the sleeve uppermost under the machine. Press the seam lines together from the sleeve side the same as when shrinking out fullness. Turn the seam allowance at the top of the sleeve into the sleeve; the underarm seam is left turned up. For heavy fabrics, clip seam allowance at notches and press seam open over cap of sleeve.

Turn the sleeve and jacket *hems* up along the marked lines (913). If the hem is an uneven width, trim hem allowances evenly. Baste close to the edge. Press the hems up and shrink out any fullness. Remove the basting. Cut strips of true bias interfacing fabric or muslin for the jacket and sleeve hems. Cut $1/_2$ inch wider than the hem allowances and the length of the lower edges plus seam allowance. Baste interfacing inside hems with one edge at lower edge of hem and other extending $1/_2$ inch beyond hem edge. On jacket front, overlap end of bias strip at interfacing and tack. Use invisible stitching to attach bias strip to jacket (914). Attach hem to bias strip with the same stitch. Fasten the raw edge of the front facing to the hem with a very fine catch-stitch (915).

Lead *weights* may be used at the seams to give a better hang to the garment. Encase the weight in a small piece of lining fabric (916), and attach to the top of the hem at the seams (917).

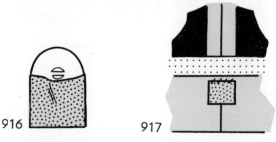

916   917

If *shoulder pads* are to be used, try on the jacket and adjust the pad to the proper position. Pin the pads securely from the right side of the garment. On the inside the pads must go under the facing. Clip the stitches holding the facing in place, slip the pad under the facing. Attach the pad loosely but firmly to the shoulder seam and to the armhole seam at each side (918). Tack facing to the pad.

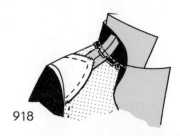

918

A *waistline stay* of woven seam binding will keep the waistline from stretching. Pin the seam binding in position along the waistline of the jacket, beginning and ending at the facing edge. Catch-stitch the seam binding to the jacket at facing edges, darts and seam allowances (919).

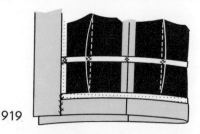

919

When the design of a jacket calls for *edge finishing* such as saddle stitching, glove stitching, prick stitching or machine top-stitching, it is done at this time. Reverse the top and bottom stitches at the roll line of the lapels and around the collar.

Press the jacket completely before the lining is attached. Remove all bastings except the one marking

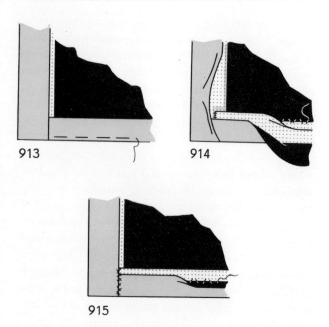

913   914

915

the centre front. Allow the garment to dry thoroughly. If you wish to have the garment professionally pressed, have it done before applying the lining.

The *buttons* are attached after the final pressing. Heavy thread or buttonhole twist is the most satisfactory thread for sewing on buttons. If these are not available in a matching colour, mercerised or silk thread can be substituted by first waxing it with beeswax. Follow the procedure on page 219 for marking the position and attaching the buttons.

Tailoring Collar and Lapels by Hand

The person who has had some experience in tailoring may wish to try constructing the collar and lapels by hand. This is not as difficult as it sounds at first. It takes a little longer, but the professional appearance of your finished garment makes it well worth the extra time. Once you have mastered the technique, you will never want to go back to the machine method.

After the lapel has been pad-stitched, stay-stitch the front and entire neck edge on the seam line (920). Trim off the interfacing at the stay-stitching. Tape the front and neck edge to the centre front as directed on

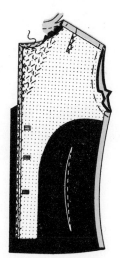

921

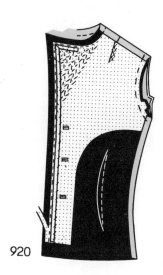

920

corners (921). Follow the directions on page 253 for pad-stitching the undercollar. Stay-stitch all edges and finish same as the lapel and neck edges. Press the undercollar and let it dry thoroughly (922).

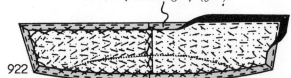

922

Pin the undercollar to neck edge of jacket—right sides together. Whip-stitch the two finished edges together (923), catching the rows of stay-stitching in your stitches (924). Keep stitches close and pull them tight. Press seam over tailor's ham.

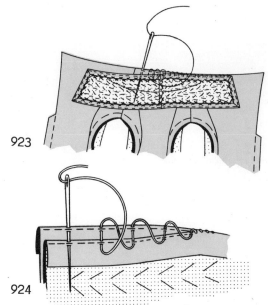

923

924

Stitch back facing to front facing at the shoulder seams (925). Stay-stitch on seam line of the lapel and neck edge above the roll line. Clip at roll line; trim the seam above clip to $^3/_8$ inch. Turn in the seam

page 253. Clip front seam allowance to stay-stitching at beginning of roll line. Trim the fabric seam allowance above clip on lapel and neck edge to $^1/_4$ inch. Turn in the seam allowance on the line of stay-stitching and baste. Clip curved areas, mitre and trim out corners so that seam lies flat. Catch-stitch the seam allowance to the interfacing. Press thoroughly—the edge should be completely flat with no thick spots at the

925

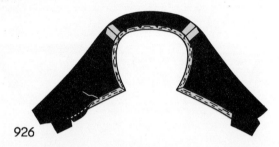

926

927

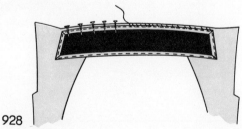

928

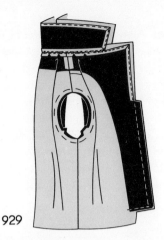

929

930

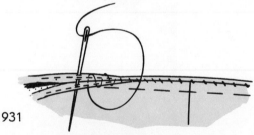

931

allowance just beyond the stay-stitching, clipping at curved edges, and baste with silk thread (926). Press, being sure that the crease line on the edge is well established. Stay-stitch all edges of top collar on seam line. Trim seam to ³/₈ inch. Turn in the seam allowance just beyond the stay-stitching, mitre at corners and trim out excess fabric. Baste in place and press (927).

Pin top collar to neck edge of facing, right sides together (928). Use a small, tight whip-stitch to sew the two finished edges together and press over the tailor's ham.

Turn jacket right side out. Stitch facing to jacket, right sides together below the roll line (929). Grade seam allowances and press seam open. Turn facing to inside and roll seam slightly to the inside. Baste in

position and top-press. Pin the top collar over the undercollar and lapels, wrong sides together (930). The top collar and lapel should extend beyond the undercollar, then the seam edge will never be able to roll up and show on the right side. Baste and slip-stitch the edges together with a very fine stitch (931). Remove bastings and top-press with a damp cheese-cloth and a dry wool press cloth over a needle board.

This method leaves the corners of the collar and lapel much flatter and thinner than it is possible to get with the machine application.

LINING A JACKET

If the garment to be lined was altered in any way, make the corresponding changes on the lining, but never make the lining smaller than the garment. Stay-stitch the armholes and back neck on the seam line (932, 933). Machine-stitch waistline and back neck darts. Press waistline and back darts toward centre. Clip darts to stitching if necessary to make them lie flat. Stitch the underarm seams and press them open. Baste the pleat in the centre back of the lining, press to the right (934).

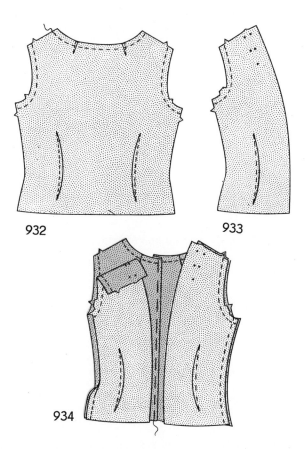

932   933

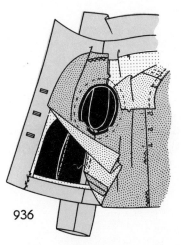

936

Turn under the seam allowance along the front of the lining. Lap and pin the lining over the front facing, easing slightly over the bustline (937). Baste and slip-stitch to within 3 inches of the hemline. Baste front shoulder seam allowance of lining to back shoulder

934

Turn lining to right side. Lap front shoulder darts to stitching line and catch-stitch halfway down from the top (935). Catch-stitch the back pleat for about $1^1/_2$ inches at the neckline, waistline and at the hemline. Press entire lining.

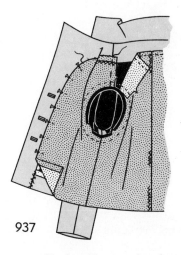

937

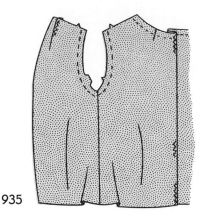

935

seam allowance of jacket. Turn under the seam allowances of the back lining section at neckline and shoulder seams. Clip the seam allowance to the stay-stitching at the neckline to make it lie flat. Lap and baste the neck edge of back lining over the lower edge of the back facing and the shoulder along shoulder seam line of front lining (938). Slip-stitch in place. Baste the lining to the jacket around the armholes, just outside the seam, close to stay-stitching (939).

Open the jacket and place flat on a table with the wrong side up. Pin lining to the jacket down the centre back, wrong sides together. Match the underarm seams of the lining to the corresponding seams of the jacket; tack together with a long, loose stitch to within 3 inches from the hem (936).

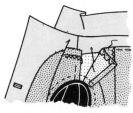

938

939

The lining of a jacket is always attached to the hem-line. Baste the lining to the jacket about 5 inches above the hem. Turn under a seam allowance at the lower edge of the lining and lap over hem of jacket about $^1/_2$ inch (940). Pin and slip-stitch in position. The extra length in the lining forms a fold at the hem and prevents drawing. After the hem is finished, press the fold down and finish slip-stitching front edges to the facing.

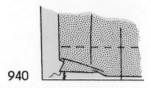

940

Stitch sleeve seams same as for the jacket. Press seams open. Stay-stitch on seam line of the underarm section between the notches and place one row of machine-gathering on the cap of the sleeve (941). Turn under the seam allowance at top of sleeve, clip underarm section to seam line to allow it to lie flat.

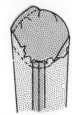

941

To attach the sleeve lining, turn sleeve and lining inside out. Match corresponding seams and tack together with a long, loose stitch (942). Leave 2 inches free at the armhole and 3 inches free at the lower edge. To turn the lining over the sleeve, place your hand inside the lining, catch the lining and sleeve at the bottom and pull through.

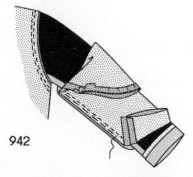

942

Lap the lining over the armhole seam allowance to stay-stitching, ease the fullness and pin and baste in place. Slip-stitch the lining in the armhole with a very small stitch (943). Finish lower edge of sleeve lining same as lower edge of jacket lining.

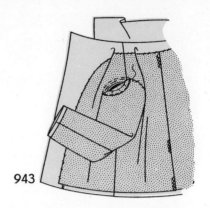

943

TAILORING A COAT

A coat is tailored in the same way as a suit with one exception—the lower edges of the coat and lining are finished separately.

If no lining pattern is given and you are using the coat pattern pieces to cut the lining, follow directions for the jacket on page 250 but DO NOT cut off the hem allowance on the coat lining.

A coat may need to be lengthened, so it is unwise to trim off the fabric at the lower front facing as is done on a suit. Open the facing and continue the hem across the lower edge. Pink the upper edge of the hem on materials that do not fray, overcast or zigzag edges of materials that fray. Attach the hem and interfacing with invisible stitching same as the jacket (944). The interfacing may or may not extend above the hem. If the interfacing extends above the hem, the hemline will show less on the right side.

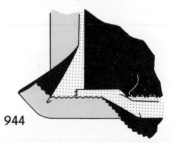

944

Turn facing back, slip-stitch the lower edges together and catch-stitch the inner edge to the hem (945). The lining is hemmed separately and should be about $^3/_4$ inch shorter than the coat. Finish slip-stitching front edges to the facing, and fasten lining to hem with 1-inch French tacks at seams.

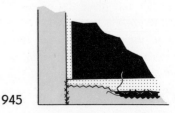

945

Some expensive ready-to-wear slim coats have the entire back underlined with a light-weight hair canvas. This helps the coat keep its shape and gives added warmth to a mid-season coat. Cut the hair canvas the same as the coat back pattern, but cut off at the hemline. Make darts in underlining same as darts in interfacing (946). Stitch and press darts in coat back. Baste underlining to wrong side of coat back, stay-stitching seam allowances together and baste along hemline edge. Treat as one fabric and construct coat in the same way as usual.

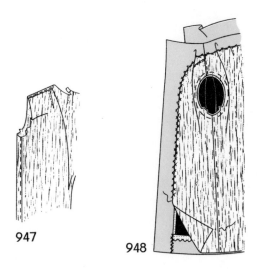

947

948

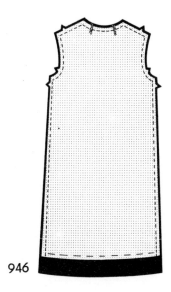

946

Construct and insert body of the lining in the same way as for a jacket except for the lower edge. Hem the lining over the lower edge of the interlining. Finish slip-stitching front edges (949) to the facing and fasten lining to hem with 1-inch French tacks at seams.

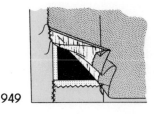

949

An interlining is used in most winter coats for added warmth. Cut interlining from lining pattern, making any alterations that were made on the coat. Trim off the interlining at the hemline of the coat and sleeve. Interline the entire one-piece sleeve but only the upper section of a two-piece sleeve. Omit pleat in back of interlining.

There are two ways of attaching an interlining. The interlining can be stitched in with the lining seams, but this may be bulky. The other method is to apply the interlining before the lining.

Slash, lap and stitch the darts same as the interfacing (947). Lap and stitch the shoulder and underarm seams same as the darts. Trim seams to remove bulk. Trim off seam allowance at front and back neck edge. Pin interlining to inside of coat. Baste side seams loosely together to within 3 inches of hem. Baste the armhole seam allowances together. Catch-stitch interlining to facings to within 3 inches of hem (948).

Stay-stitch interlining to sleeve section of lining along sides and across sleeve cap (950). Trim away interfacing seam allowances close to stay-stitching. Treat as one fabric and insert the sleeve lining in the usual manner.

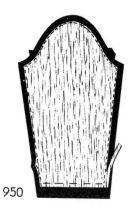

950

THE THREE R'S — REPAIRING, REMODELLING, REMAKING

Even though you may not be interested in making all or some of your own clothes, there are certain techniques of sewing that you should learn in order to keep yourself well groomed. And there are many things you can do to make ready-made clothes fit better. We no longer mend and darn the way our grandmothers did; the emphasis on what we mend has changed. It is no longer practical to darn socks; in fact the new stretch socks cannot be darned. However, there are a variety of repairs that are necessary to good grooming. Modern living has still found no escape from the loose button, the pulled-out hem, the broken strap or the cigarette burn in a new garment. That "stitch in time" does wonders for one's personal appearance.

LOOSE FASTENERS

Buttons

Taking the time to sew on a loose button will save losing the button and having to replace a whole set. Regular sewing thread is not strong enough to hold buttons. Heavy-duty thread or buttonhole twist is best, but if these are not available in a matching colour, then wax your sewing thread with beeswax to make it stronger. If the button has dropped off, be sure to remove all the old threads from the fabric before restitching the button. See page 220 for detailed directions for sewing on the different kinds of buttons.

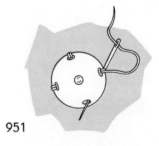

951

Hooks and Eyes

Take several small stitches under the hook to secure the thread. Take small overhand stitches around each hole being careful that the stitches do not show on the right side of the garment (952). Carry the needle to the hook end and take several stitches across the end of the hook to hold it securely (952). The eye is sewn in position by taking overhand stitches around each hole. If it is a round eye, take several stitches across the sides of the eye to hold it securely. A round eye is used when

Snap Fasteners

A loose snap fastener can be sewn firmly in place by taking a few stitches over the edge of each hole. Carry the thread under the snap from one hole to the next (951). If the snap has come off completely, remember that the ball section is sewn to the upper part of the closing and the socket section to the under part. See page 221.

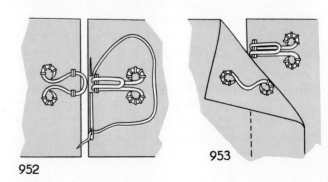

952

953

the closing just meets and the bar eye is used when the closing is lapped (953).

RIPPED SEAMS

In Garments

When the thread of a machine-stitched seam in a garment breaks, it can be repaired by hand or machine. Hand-stitches are usually used if the ripped seam is in an area difficult to reach by machine or if a machine is not available. Turn the garment to the wrong side and clip the loose threads close to the fabric. To repair by hand, begin about $1/2$ inch from the opening and take tiny back-stitches along the original seam line (954). Continue about $1/2$ inch beyond the opening

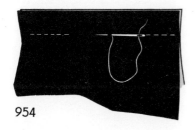

954

(955). To repair by machine, adjust the length of stitch to correspond with that used on the rest of the seam. Follow the original seam line and let the new stitching overlap the old about $1/2$ inch on either side of the opening. Pull threads to one side and tie ends in a double knot before clipping. Press the seam.

955

In Gloves

Gloves are made with a wide variety of seams. When repairing a glove seam, duplicate the original stitching as accurately as possible, using a matching thread (956, 957). Gloves that are stitched on the inside should be turned to the wrong side for mending. Try to follow the original seam line and use the same needle holes. The new stitches should overlap the old ones at both ends of the opening. Fabric gloves are frequently made with the seams showing on the right side. If the seam is made with small running stitches, then the same kind of hand-stitches should be used to repair the seam (956).

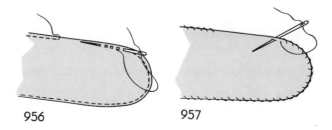

956   957

PULLED HEMS

The hems of all garments are under constant strain and are subject to catching. The thread in hand-sewn hems can break very easily. Remove a few stitches from each end of the ripped area so that the ends can be fastened. Either knot the threads or take a few back-stitches to fasten the ends. Replace the hem in the ripped area with the same kind of stitch used in the original hem. Press the hem after it has been repaired.

RIPPED PLEATS

It is a very common problem to have the stitching break at the top of a pleat in a narrow skirt. When this happens, clip the broken threads close to the fabric and restitch. Sometimes, if there is fabric under the pleat it is wise to raise the pleat to allow more room for walking. To raise the pleat, turn the skirt to the wrong side and pull out the stitches the desired distance above the end of the original pleat (958). Tie the ends in a double knot and then thread them into a needle and take a few back-stitches along the seam to secure the ends. Press the pleat to remove the old stitching marks.

If the fabric has been pulled or torn at the end of the pleat, it will have to be reinforced. Restitch the pleat from the inside of the skirt, as directed above. On the right side, embroider an arrowhead or a crow's-foot tack at the end of the pleat (959). See page 240 for detailed directions for making these tacks.

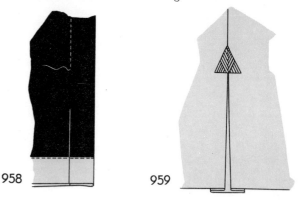

958   959

LINGERIE REPAIRS

Broken Shoulder Strap

If the top of the garment is made of a double thickness of fabric, the shoulder strap should be placed between the two layers of material. Insert the strap deeply enough that it cannot pull out easily again (960). Sew along the original stitching line with a tiny back-stitch extending beyond the strap on both sides (961). If the strap has been attached to lace or a single thickness of fabric, take tiny hemming stitches along the turned-in end of the strap and along the top edge of the lace or fabric so the strap will be secured in two places (962).

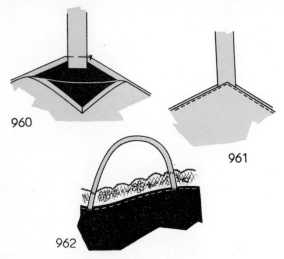

Broken Faggoted Seams

Remove several stitches from either end of the break and fasten the ends with several tiny stitches on the wrong side of the garment. Baste a strip of brown paper under the section that is to be refaggoted (963). With buttonhole twist, working from the top down, replace the broken stitches. See page 241 for detailed directions for making the various faggoting stitches. Use the stitch which matches the faggoted seam in your garment.

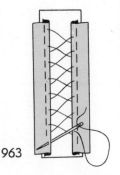

Replacing an Elastic Waistband

Remove the old elastic, noting the way in which it was applied so that you can replace it the same way. Cut a piece of elastic the measurement of your waistline plus $1/2$ inch for lap or joining. Divide the waistline of the garment into halves, quarters and then eighths and mark each division with a pin. Divide the piece of elastic to be applied in halves, quarters and then eighths and mark the same way. Match the markings on the elastic to the markings on the garment. Lap the ends of the elastic and stitch securely (964). Distribute the fullness evenly between the pins. Stretch the elastic as you stitch so that the fabric passes under the presser foot of the machine without any gathers or puckers (964). As the elastic springs back into place, it gathers the fabric. Regular machine-stitching can be used but a zigzag stitch will be stronger on elastic with the same number of rows of stitching as was used on the original elastic.

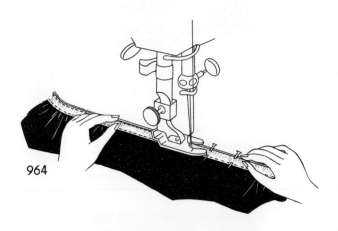

Replacing Elastic in a Casing

Look for an opening in the casing. If there is none, rip the stitching enough to remove the old elastic. Cut a new piece of elastic the desired length plus $1/2$ inch for lapping. Run the elastic through the casing with a bodkin or a safety pin (965). Sew the ends of elastic securely and replace the stitching in the casing (966).

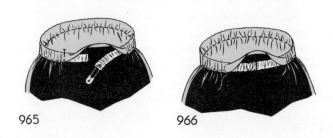

30 The bold use of pattern and colour gives an immediate impression of trapped sunshine and warmth, which is particularly attractive in a bedroom. A new bedcover and curtains can alter a room entirely, and give an enormous sense of achievement.

Photograph ana Crestaline flooring in orange, white and honey by courtesy of Nairn-Williamson Ltd. Fabrics by courtesy of Donald Bros.

31 The use of wool in this room setting shows the great versatility of wool as a furnishing fabric. An appearance of luxury and warmth is created by its texture and depth of colour. All materials used here are washable.

Panorama furnishing fabric range by courtesy of Charterhouse Fashions Ltd.

Replacing a Suspender

Old suspenders should be removed by opening the seam line at the lower edge of the garment. Slip the new suspender in place and sew with two rows of machine-stitching (967). Bring the facing down over the suspender and sew it in place with machine-stitching or small zigzag stitches (968).

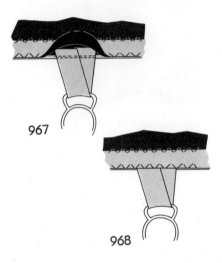

967

968

REWEAVING

This is a job that requires great skill and patience. If it is done well, there is no visible sign of mending. Study the weave of the fabric carefully so that you will be able to duplicate it exactly (969). Working under a magnifying glass is most helpful. Use an embroidery hoop to hold the fabric taut. You can only use threads ravelled from the fabric for reweaving. Working from the right side of the fabric, fill in all the lengthwise threads weaving them several stitches into the body of the fabric to hold them. Weave in the crosswise threads to match the original weave of the fabric. Steam-press the area after you finish, and the mend should be completely invisible.

969

INVISIBLE PATCHING

This is an easy way to mend a hole in a loosely woven fabric and is not quite as tedious as reweaving. Determine the size of the patch needed. Cut a piece of fabric from the hem or some part of the inside of the garment, 1 inch larger all around than the desired patch. The lengthwise threads of the patch and the garment must be matched as well as any design in the fabric. Ravel out the threads on all sides of the patch until it is the

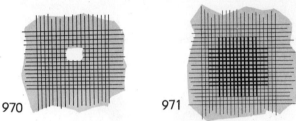

970

971

exact size needed (970). Place the fabric in an embroidery hoop and lay the patch right side up over the hole (971). Baste the patch in place. Beginning at one corner, pull the ravelled threads through to the wrong side with a crochet hook (972). Follow the weave of the fabric in drawing the threads through. If the fabric is a plain weave, the edges of the patch will be even,

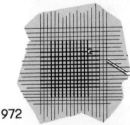

972

otherwise the edges of the patch will be uneven. After all threads have been pulled through, turn the garment to the wrong side. Take tiny hemming stitches close to the spot where each ravelled thread was pulled through. These stitches should not show on the right side (973). Clip the ends of the ravelled threads about $1/_4$ inch from the fabric. Steam-press the area after the patch is finished.

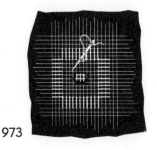

973

REPLACING
A BROKEN ZIPPER

When the chain of a zipper is broken or damaged, there is no way to repair it other than to replace the entire zipper. Examine the application carefully before removing the broken zipper. It is important that the new zipper be put in the same way. Remove the old zipper and all the threads. In a skirt, open waistband about 1 inch on either side of the placket (974). Baste the opening together along the original seam line and press the seam open. Insert the new zipper according to detailed directions given in Chapter 12, depending upon the type of application used in your garment.

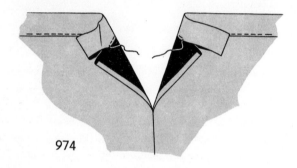

974

REPLACING
A LINING

Occasionally a lining will become worn or damaged while the outside of the garment is still in good condition. It is practical to replace a lining if there is at least another season's wear in the garment. The original lining can be removed and used as a pattern (976). Before ripping the old lining apart, mark key construction points on it so that it will be easier to assemble the new lining. With chalk or a pencil, mark a horizontal line across the seam at the following

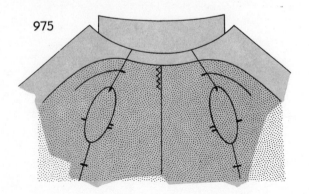

975

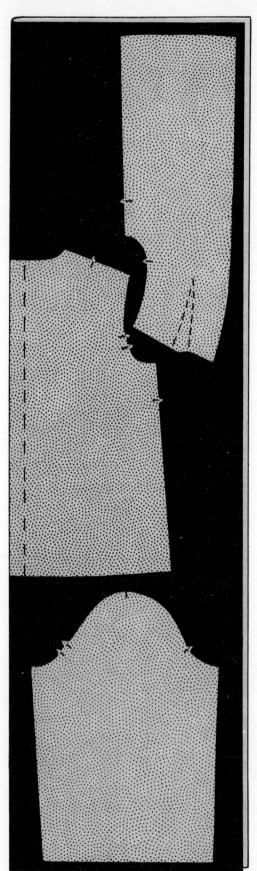

976

places: underarm seam about 4'' below the armhole, midpoint of the armhole front and back, point where shoulder seam joins cap of sleeve, and point where front dart joins back shoulder seam (975). Rip lining apart and press all the pieces out flat. Pin the pieces on the new fabric, placing the centre back on a fold. With chalk or a pencil, mark accurate $5/_8$-inch seam allowances on all pieces, make notches at the key construction points marked with the horizontal lines and mark the centre back pleat and front shoulder dart (976). Cut out the lining. Assemble lining pieces and attach the lining to the garment according to the directions given in Chapter 14.

GARMENT ALTERATIONS

Most of us cannot walk into a store and buy clothes without needing some alteration to attain a perfect fit. If a garment requires major alterations, it is not wise to buy it. Shoulder and neckline alterations are difficult to make and should be avoided. However, lengthening and shortening or adjusting a waistline or hipline are simple alterations and do much to improve the appearance of a garment.

Shortening or Lengthening a Skirt or Dress

Rip out the original hem. If seam binding has been used, remove it and pick out all the threads. Working from the wrong side, press out the crease mark of the hem. (See Chapter 8 for suggestions on how to press various fabrics.) Press out the seam binding.

Try on the garment with the shoes and foundation garment you intend to wear with it. Decide how far from the floor the finished skirt should be. With a yardstick or hem marker, have someone pin an even line parallel to the floor at this point. Turn hem up on marked line and baste about $1/_2$ inch from the folded edge. A hem should be $2^1/_2$ to 3 inches wide. Mark the width of the hem by measuring up from the folded edge with a ruler or hem gauge. Cut along marking.

Finish the cut edge of the hem the same as it was finished before. If there is excess fullness at the upper edge of the hem, place a row of machine basting $1/_4$ inch from the cut edge. Pin the hem at the seams of the skirt and pull up the bobbin thread to ease in the full-

ness until the hem fits flat on the skirt. Adjust fullness evenly and shrink out the excess.

After the cut edge has been properly finished, baste the hem in place and stitch by hand. See Chapter 10 for detailed directions on various hem finishes.

Facing a Skirt

When a skirt has to be lengthened and there is not sufficient fabric to turn up a new hem, the skirt will have to be faced. Rip out the hem and pick out all the threads. Press the hem thoroughly so that there is no crease line showing. Skirt facings must be bias. If you have matching fabric, cut a true bias strip the length of the lower edge of the skirt plus seam allowances. When matching fabric is not available, commercially packaged skirt facing can be purchased in cotton or taffeta in a variety of colours. Start at a seam and pin facing to lower edge of skirt, right sides together. Join bias on the straight grain (977). Press seam open. Stitch facing to lower edge of skirt and

977

press seam open. Understitch the seam allowance to the facing. Turn facing to inside using the seam allowance width as the turning line. Baste along folded edge. Turn under the upper edge of facing and stitch close to edge. Slip-stitch facing to skirt (978).

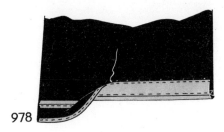

978

Adjusting Back Pleat When Skirt Is Shortened

A pleat in the back of a skirt must be open at least 4 inches to be of any value. Be sure to check this when shortening a skirt. If there is fabric under the pleat, it is very easy to rip the pleat up the desired amount and tie the threads on the wrong side to finish the end of the pleat (979). If it is impossible to raise the pleat, it is best to stitch the pleat shut entirely. Your skirt will look better without a pleat than with a skimpy useless one. Mark a $5/_8$-inch seam allowance beyond the stitching line (980) and trim off the extra fabric. Press the seam in the same direction as the other seams of the skirt (981).

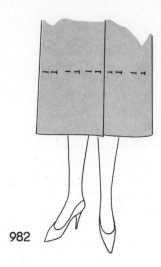

982

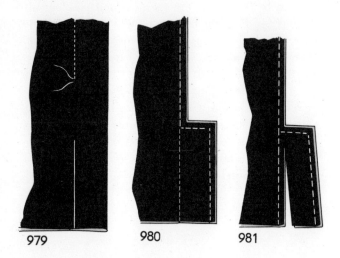

979   980   981

Shortening or Lengthening a Coat

If the fabric is trimmed out under the facing at the front corner, it will be impossible ever to lengthen the coat. If it has not been trimmed, rip out the hem in the coat and the lining. Pick out all the threads and press out the crease line in coat and lining. See Chapter 8 for pressing directions for various fabrics.

Try on the coat with the shoes you intend to wear with it. Attach the coat to the lining with a row of pins placed about 12 inches from the lower edge of the coat. This allows room to hem the coat and the lining and still holds the two layers together so that you won't end up with the lining hanging longer than the coat. Decide on the proper length for the coat and have someone pin a line parallel to the floor at this point with a yardstick or hem marker (982). A coat should be hemmed about 1 inch longer than you wear your dresses. Remember that a very heavy, bulky fabric will always be a little shorter than it was marked after the hem has been turned.

The lower edge of a coat and lining are finished separately. Hem coat first. Rip the lining from the front facing for 6 to 8 inches to allow room to turn the hem on the front facing. Turn up the hem and facing on the new line and baste close to folded edge. Coat

hem is 2 to $2^1/_2$ inches; the lining hem is 2 inches. Lap and button the coat and check the lower edge to be sure that one front corner does not hang longer than the other. It is easier to adjust this now than to discover it after the hem has been finished. Using a ruler or hem gauge, mark the width of the hem. Cut on this marking. Continue the hem the same width on coat and facing. If the hem does not fit smoothly, place a row of machine-basting $1/_2$ inch from the cut edge. Pin the hem at the seams and pull up the bobbin thread to ease in any fullness. Steam-press to shrink out the extra fullness. Finish the upper edge of hem the same as it was finished before. Baste the hem in place and stitch by hand. See Chapter 10 for details on hem finishes. Turn the front facing back, slip-stitch the lower edges together and fasten the raw edge to the hem with a very fine catch-stitch (983).

The lining should be about $3/_4$ inch shorter than the coat. Turn up the lower edge and baste along the fold. Mark and trim hem and even width. Turn under the edge $1/_4$ inch and stitch. Baste hem and slip-stitch in place. Slip-stitch front edges of the lining to the facing and fasten lining to coat hem with 1-inch French tacks at seams (983).

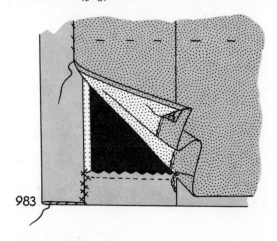

983

Adjusting Sleeve Length

Sleeves can be shortened without too much trouble. Take out the hem or remove the cuff, depending on how the sleeve was finished. Remove all the threads and press the lower edge flat. Decide on the correct sleeve length, then measure up from the lower edge and mark a line around the sleeve. Cut the sleeve off a seam or hem allowance below the marking, depending on the way your sleeve is to be finished. Finish the lower edge of the sleeve in the same way that it was finished originally.

A sleeve with a hem can always be lengthened by letting down the hem or even facing it if necessary. However, if the sleeve is finished with a cuff, it is usually not possible to lengthen it.

Shortening a Coat Sleeve

Baste around the sleeve below the elbow to hold the sleeve and lining together. Turn the sleeve wrong side out and open the lining at the lower edge. Rip out the hem of the sleeve and press the crease marks out of the lining and sleeve (984). Mark the new sleeve length. Turn up the hem on the marking and baste close to lower edge (985). Mark the width of new hem same as the original one and cut along the marking. Press, then remove basting. Baste interfacing inside hem with one edge at lower edge of hem. Use an invisible stitch to attach hem edge to interfacing. Attach interfacing to sleeve with the same stitch.

Turn sleeve lining up so that it is about $^3/_4$ inch shorter than the sleeve. Cut the lining off, leaving a seam allowance beyond the fold line. Lap the lining over the sleeve hem and slip-stitch the lining in place.

Lengthening a Coat Sleeve

Baste around the sleeve below the elbow to hold the sleeve and lining together. Turn the sleeve wrong side out; open lining and remove sleeve hem. Press the old crease line out of the sleeve and lining. The hem can be let down or faced, depending on the amount of length needed. If a facing is to be used, apply it same as for a skirt. Baste interfacing to inside of hem or facing with one edge at lower edge of hem. Attach hem to interfacing and then sew interfacing to sleeve with same invisible stitch (985). If lining is not long enough to reach the top of the hem, then it is necessary to add a strip of fabric to the lower edge of the sleeve

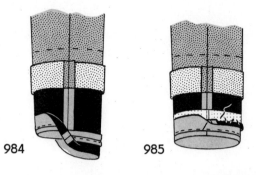

984   985

lining (985). Turn up lower edge of lining so that it is about $^3/_4$ inch shorter than the sleeve. Lap lining over the upper edge of the sleeve hem and slip-stitch in place (987).

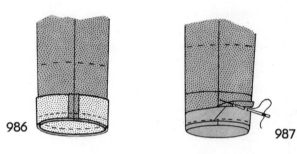

986   987

Shortening a Belt

When a belt is too long, never shorten it by punching an extra eyelet. This only leaves a long ungainly end, and the new eyelet will never match the original ones exactly. Take your waist measurement over the garment to be belted. Remember that a belt for a bulky fabric suit or coat always has to be a little longer than the belt for a soft silk dress. Remove the buckle. Measure the belt from the centre eyelet to the buckle end and mark waistline measurement. Punch two holes about $^1/_4$ inch apart on either side of marking (988). Cut an oblong opening between the two holes for the prong of the buckle (989). Insert prong through the opening and turn end of belt to inside. Cut off extra length and stitch end of the belt in place (990). On leather belts or other fabric that is difficult to stitch, use a thumbtack to punch holes for the needle.

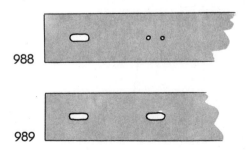

988

989

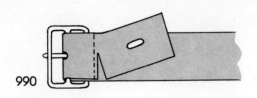

990

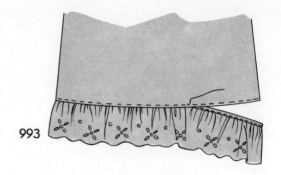

993

Shortening a Slip

If a slip needs to be shortened only a slight amount, you can do it by taking several small pin tucks around the lower edge or just above the lace or frill (991). This adds a decorative touch and can be done by hand or machine. Any large adjustment in length will have to be made by cutting off the lower edge. Be sure to allow enough for a narrow hem finish. A tailored slip is usually finished with just a narrow hem. If the slip is finished with lace or a frill, this has to be removed and restitched to the lower edge.

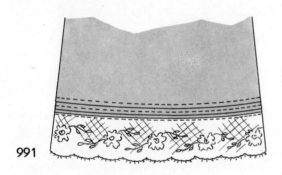

991

Lengthening a Slip

A band of lace or a frill can be stitched to the lower edge of a slip to give added length. Lace is lapped over lower edge finish on the slip and stitched in place (992).

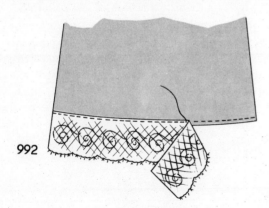

992

The finished lower edge of the slip should be lapped and stitched over the binding on purchased frilling (993).

Shortening a Skirt from the Waistline

A skirt that is too tight in the hipline or has some decorative detail at the lower edge can be shortened by raising from the waistline. Pin a tuck just below the waistband, raising the skirt the necessary amount (994). The width of the tuck tells you how much the skirt should be shortened. Rip off the waistband, remove the zipper and cut off the top of the skirt the amount to be

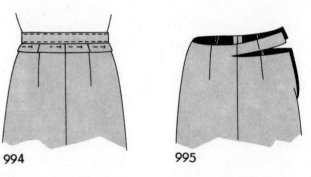

994   995

shortened (995). Try on the skirt and pin in the darts and side seams until the skirt fits smoothly (996). Restitch the darts and seams, tapering the new stitching into the old. Remove the old stitching and press seams open and darts toward the centre. Replace zipper

996

according to directions given in Chapter 12. Replace the waistband, duplicating the original method of application, and sew on the hooks and eyes.

Shortening a Bodice

Short-waisted people very often find that the waistline seam of a dress falls below their natural waistline. When this happens, take out the zipper and rip the waistline seam. Try on the bodice and pin placket closed. Tie a cord or tape around your waistline and mark a new waistline seam with pins or chalk along the lower edge of the cord (997). Pin and baste the skirt to the bodice along the markings for the new waistline seam, matching centres, seams and darts. Stitch the new waistline seam and trim off the extra fabric after you have tried on the dress and are sure the seam is in the correct place (998). Replace the zipper according to directions given in Chapter 12.

be taken in or let out. Remove the zipper and open the waistline seam. Divide the total amount of the adjustment by the number of darts and seams (1001, 1002). Make the same amount of alteration on each seam and dart on the skirt and bodice. Taper the new lines of stitching into the original stitching, then remove the old threads. Press seams open and darts toward the centre. When a garment is let out, be sure that the marks of the original seam line are pressed out completely. Baste skirt to bodice, matching centres, seams and darts. Try on the dress again to check the fit above and below the waistline. Stitch the waistline seam and replace the zipper according to directions in Chapter 12.

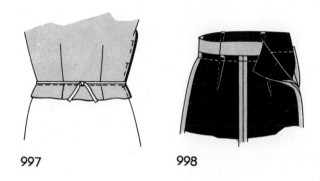

997   998

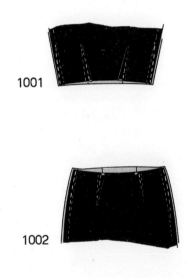

1001

1002

Taking In or Letting Out a Waistline

A waistline can usually be nipped in without too much trouble (999, 1000). However, if the waistline is tight, before buying the garment check to be sure there is enough fabric in seams and darts to let out. Try on the garment and determine how much should

999

1000

Taking In the Hipline

The curve of the hipline varies with each individual, so it is a very common problem to need slight adjustments at this point. It is not usually necessary to take off the waistband or open the waistline seam, but the zipper will have to be removed if it falls in the side seam. If you have very straight hips, the seam line on most skirts will have too great a curve over the hip. Try on the garment and pin out the extra curve or bulge in the seam (1003). Make the same adjustment on both sides of the skirt to keep it balanced. Restitch the seam line, tapering into the old stitching. Remove the original stitching and press seam open. Replace the zipper according to directions in Chapter 12.

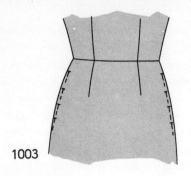

1003

Letting Out the Hipline

When a skirt is tight in the hipline, the adjustment becomes a greater problem. First, before buying the garment, check to see that there is enough fabric in the seams to let out. Remove the zipper and open the hem. Press side seams together so that they will be easier to restitch accurately. Determine the amount of extra fullness needed and let out each side seam half this amount (1004). Restitch the side seams, tapering from the original seam line near the waist to the hipline, and then continue stitching down the side to the lower edge. Letting the skirt out the same amount from the hipline to the lower edge retains the original shaping and proportions of the skirt. Press seams open, replace the zipper and hem.

1004

Sometimes fabric is left under a wide centre-back pleat. If there is not enough fabric to let out the side seams, this wide pleat can be opened. Restitch the centre back seam tapering from the original stitching line near the waist to the amount needed at the hipline. Continue stitching parallel to the centre back seam from hipline to top of pleat. Never let the back pleat out just in the hip area. This gives a very unattractive line and the skirt will always have a seat even if it is lined. Machine-baste from top of pleat to lower edge, parallel to the old crease line (1005). Remove the original stitching and press out the marks of the orig-

inal seam and pleat. Press the pleat in the same direction as before and remove the machine-basting. Tie the threads at the end of the pleat and take a few back-stitches in the fabric to secure the threads. Turn up the hem and stitch it in place again.

1005

Adjusting for Sway-Back

Wrinkles across the back of the skirt just below the waistline indicate that the skirt should be raised across the back. This is a very common alteration for people with a sway-back. Rip the waistline seam across the back. Raise centre back of skirt $1/2$ to $3/4$ inch and taper to side seams. Baste back waistline seam and try garment on to check fit. Side seams should hang straight and back of skirt should fit smoothly without wrinkles. Restitch and press back waistline seam (1006).

1006

Adding a Gusset to a Kimono Sleeve

A tight kimono sleeve can be eased by adding a gusset, if extra fabric is available. Measurements and complete directions for doing this without a pattern are given on page 163.

CHAPTER 16

THE DECORATOR'S TOUCH

Decorating a home can be fun, and it is especially so when one knows how to sew. A pillow, a bedspread, a loose cover can transform the mood, the personality, and even the seasonal fitness of a room. You can make your home the right background for the new you. Browse through magazines to get ideas. Look around the shops for interesting fabrics. Use your sewing know-how to give your home the custom look.

DECORATIVE CUSHIONS

Cushions are so easy to make, and so effective as a decorating tool, that everyone should know how to make them. They can provide wonderful colour accents to "spark" room decor, giving the room a completely new look. Variations on the cushion theme are limitless. Let your imagination soar. Put all of those designer hopes to work. Combine unusual fabrics and trimmings in a variety of shapes. Seams may be trimmed with piping, ruffling, lace or fringe. Tassels, buttons or embroidery can be used to give a decorative touch to the cushion top. Recently, hand-smocked cushions have been extremely popular. Notice how many different effects can be produced by a few simple smocking stitches.

Inner Cushion Form

When planning your cushions, consider the inner construction. Special forms can be purchased or made. If you wish to buy a form, you should do so before you make the covering so it will be the correct size. Forms of solid foam rubber, synthetic foam or ticking filled with down or kapok are easy to use. It is also possible to buy foam by the yard which you can shape as you wish.

If you decide to make your own form, cut fabric in the desired size and shape. Muslin can be used for the inner cushion covering but ticking or a downproof fabric must be used if the cushion is to be stuffed with feathers. Use a $1/2$-inch plain seam to sew pieces together and leave a 3-inch opening in one seam. Stuff to desired fullness with synthetic stuffing, kapok, nylon stockings, clippings or down. Turn in raw edges of opening and sew together with close overhand stitches.

If down from an old cushion is used, open one corner of the covering and pour water on the feathers. The damp feathers can be transferred to the new covering without filling the room with down. Be sure that the opening is securely stitched shut and then place the new cushion in the spin drier to fluff-dry the feathers. Remove the cushion as soon as it is dry. Do not let the drier run a full cycle.

Cushions without Boxing

Cushions can be made with or without an insertion of piping or trimming between pieces. If piping cord is to be used, this should be made before pieces are put together according to directions on page 233. Also, if applied decoration is being used, such as smocking, quilting, or appliqué, it should be done before construction begins.

Measure pillow from seam to seam. The cover should be snug but not tight. Add $1/2$-inch seam allowance to each edge. Join the two pieces with a plain seam (1007). If piping or trimming is to be used as an edge finish, stitch it to one section before making the plain seam. Leave an opening wide enough to insert the pillow form. Slip-stitch the edges of the opening together after the cushion has been put in place. Or, if fabric will need to be laundered or dry-cleaned frequently, it is wise to close the opening with a zipper so that the cover can be removed easily.

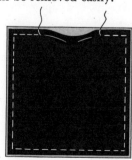

1007

Boxed Cushions

Solid foam forms are easiest to use for box cushions. Measure the cushion, length and width, as well as the depth of the boxing and its circumference. Cut two identical pieces for the top and bottom and a strip of fabric for the boxing. To each edge, add $1/_2$-inch seam allowance (1008). Pin-fit the covering fabric over the cushion, and stitch as for a seat cushion, described on page 297.

If a soft filling is used, the inner pillow should be packed very tightly.

1008

CURTAINS

In choosing fabric and style for curtains consider first your needs for light, air and privacy. Do you want to frame the view or hide it? Then appraise the windows in relation to the room. Should the windows appear higher or wider to make the room seem to be in good proportion? Perhaps two windows should be treated as one. Sometimes curving folds will do more to enhance a room than straight ones. Should there be a valance? Check outside effect. How will the style and fabric appear in relation to the exterior architecture? Will your home look friendly and inviting? Browse through magazines for information about new style trends. After you have done a thorough research job, select the style and fabrics that you like best, that are suited to your needs and flatter your decor.

Curtain Fixtures

After you have decided upon the style of curtains which will best suit your rooms, your next step is to find the correct fitment to support them. There are two basic kinds of rods for curtains: *stationary rods* (1009), which hold draperies in one place; and

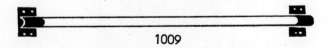

1009

traverse rods (1010), which allow curtains to be opened and closed.

1010

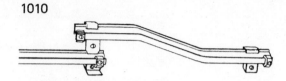

You can buy rods and brackets to fit or to increase the width and height of curtains beyond the actual size of the windows. They are also available to fit round curves and corners of all kinds. Curtain fitments are made in brass, decorative coloured aluminium and plastic. The latter have the advantage of being noiseless and non-rusting. Special screws are supplied for use on different wall finishes and there are many types of rings and hooks for attaching curtains to their rods. Look around the shops and compare the wide variety of fitments available and you are bound to find one to fit your particular requirements.

Attach rods to the wall or window frame and you are ready to begin.

Window Measurements

Before you can begin to make your curtains, you have to decide how long and how wide they should be. The finished length is the distance from the rod to the lower edge of the finished curtain (1011). Curtains should begin and end with a structural part of the window or

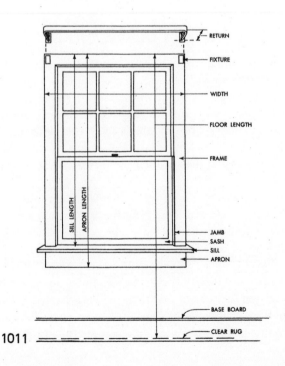

1011

wall. They begin at the ceiling, window top or beneath a cornice and end at the sill, apron, skirting or floor. The finished width encompasses the length of the curtain rod, including the part that curves into the wall (the return) plus the amount of the centre overlap.

Fabric Measurement

To work out the total length of one panel, take the measurement you have decided on for finished length of curtain and add to it the allowance for heading and hem. If patterned fabric is used, one extra pattern repeat must be added for matching.

For total fabric width you must decide on the amount of fullness you want. For very full, sheer curtains, multiply the finished width by three. When using medium- or heavy-weight fabrics, reduce the amount of fullness by multiplying the finished width by two or two and a half. To this amount, add allowance for seams or side hems on each panel.

HEM ALLOWANCES.

Before the final yardage can be decided, you must make some decisions about hem width. Hem allowances will vary with the fabric used. Average hem measures are given here. For further information, check specific instructions for the type of curtain and heading you decide to make.

Top Hem Allowances

Straight hems (used with rings
   loops): .... $1^{1}/_{4}$ to 4 inches
Casing with heading .... 3 inches
4-Cord shirring .... $4^{1}/_{4}$ inches
Pleating .... 4 to 5 inches
Ready-made pleating or
   Rufflette tape .... $^{1}/_{2}$ inch
Scallop .... $4^{1}/_{4}$ inches (or
                       depth of scallop
                       plus $1^{1}/_{4}$ inches)

Bottom Hem Allowances

	Single Hem	Double Hem
Glass Curtains	$3^{1}/_{4}$ in.	6 in.
Café Curtains	$2^{1}/_{4}$ to $3^{1}/_{4}$ in.	4 to 6 in.
Curtains	4 to 5 in.	7 to 9 in.
Frilled Curtains	$^{1}/_{4}$ inch (first, subtract width of frill from finished length; then, allow $^{1}/_{4}$ inch hem)	

Before you decide on the exact yardage to buy, consider the advantages of a double hem. In sheer fabrics, the turned-under raw edge will not show when light shines through the curtain. The extra weight of the double hem will make draperies hang better. Extra fabric is available to let down if shrinkage occurs, or if curtains are moved to another window. With these decisions made, take out paper and pencil and work out yardage you need. Remember the width of your fabric will influence the amount needed.

Cutting the Fabric

Accuracy is extremely important when cutting out curtains. Press the fabric to remove wrinkles and crease marks. Lay fabric on a large smooth surface with right side up. Check grain line carefully. It is as important to have the grain line perfect in curtains as it is in clothes. They will not hang properly otherwise.

Decide in which direction the pattern or pile should go. All fabric lengths should run in the same direction.

PATTERNED FABRIC.

It is important that the design be properly placed so that the effect will be pleasing (1012). On long curtains, an unbroken pattern repeat should be at the finished top of the curtain since a broken repeat will be less noticeable at the floor. On short curtains, the bottom repeat is more noticeable and so should not be broken.

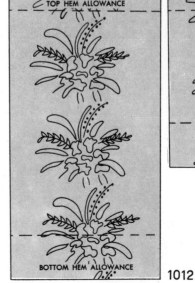

1012

MEASURING. Mark finished top edge. Mark top hem allowance above this line. Draw a thread to make a straight line, and cut on this line.

Measuring from the finished top edge, mark the length of the finished curtain. From this line, add hem allowance. Draw out a thread to make a straight line for cutting. After cutting, check grain line. Straighten fabric if necessary, following directions on page 97.

Cutting Additional Panels

Place fabric right side up on cutting surface. Then put cut panel right side down on fabric. Match design carefully. Be sure the designs run in the same direction, using the cut panel as a pattern for cutting the other lengths.

After cutting, follow directions for specific types of curtains. You will find headings treated separately, since most types of headings may be used on all types of curtains and draperies.

Fine Window Curtains

This type of curtain hangs straight from the rod, against the window. If used alone, decorative headings may be applied. If another curtain or drapery is used over the sheer curtain, the top finish is a simple casing and heading.

After determining the finished length, add $3\frac{1}{4}$ inches for bottom hem (6 inches, if double) and $2\frac{3}{4}$ inches for top heading and casing (5 inches, if double). The width of the curtain is decided by the fabric. If the material is not too sheer, $2\frac{1}{2}$ times the finished width will be attractive on sheer fabrics, 3 times the finished width will create a more pleasing effect. Allow $\frac{1}{2}$ inch for seam allowances and 2 inches for each double side hem.

After cutting the panels, join them with tiny French seams (1013). Turn double hems in the sides, 1 inch deep (1014). Press and machine-stitch using 8 to 10 stitches to the inch.

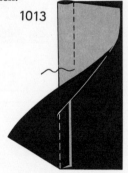

1013

1014

For top hem, follow directions on page 282 for plain casing with heading. Many fabrics used for glass curtains tend to stretch with hanging. To overcome this, hang curtains on rod for several days. Then make a 3-inch hem, preferably double. To make a 3-inch double hem, turn 3-inch fold to underside. Press. Turn another 3-inch fold, making the hem double (1015). It may be stitched by machine or hemmed by hand.

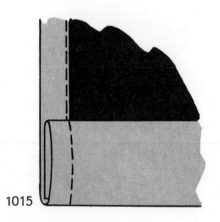

1015

Frilled Curtains

Curtains with frilled edges are the favourite of all informal window treatments. They are generally made of crisp light-weight or sheer fabrics and are tied back to the edge of the window frame. More formal frilled curtains are also possible. The formal types hang straight from the curtain rod and are made of softer fabrics, such as pongee, ninon and silks.

In determining the finished length of the curtain, subtract the width of the frill that falls below the bottom edge of curtain body but add 3 inches for top casing and heading and $\frac{1}{4}$ inch for lower edge. For width, allow $2^1/_2$ to 3 times the finished width, adding $^1/_2$ inch for seam allowance joinings, 1 inch for double hems for outer side edges, and $^1/_4$ inch for centre side hems or seams.

A strip should be cut 2 to 3 times the finished length and width of the curtain. A fuller frill gives a more luxurious, expensive look. Although the strip can be cut on the lengthwise or crosswise grain, the lengthwise grain is preferred. If necessary, the strips should be joined with a tiny French seam. A small hem is used to finish the raw edges. When the frill is attached to the body of the curtain with a heading, both edges are hemmed, but when the frill is attached to the curtain with a seam only one edge must be hemmed. Using the narrow hemmer attachment will simplify this task a great deal.

It is also easier to use the ruffler attachment when making frills. Directions for making frills are found on page 232.

FRILL WITH HEADING. On the body of the curtain, measure 3 inches down from top edge. Do not apply ruffles above this point (1016). Make a $^1/_8$-inch double hem on bottom and centre-side edges of curtain body. With right sides up, pin gathering stitches on ruffle to stitches on hem. At corners, allow enough extra fullness to make frill fall gracefully around corner. Stitch on gathering line. Be careful not to catch in folds of the fabric.

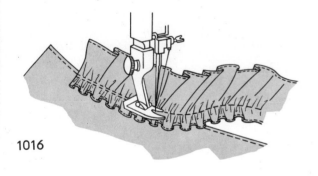

1016

FRILL WITHOUT HEADING. Place frill on top of curtain body, wrong sides together and stitch $^1/_4$ inch from edge. Press seam toward curtain. Turn ruffle back over curtain, right sides together. Press fold formed along edge of seam allowance. Stitch along first row of stitching, enclosing the raw edges as in a French seam (1017).

To finish curtain body, make a $^1/_2$-inch double hem on outer edge. Begin at the top of curtain body and

continue to lower edge of ruffle. At top edge, make a casing and heading as shown on page 281.

1017

FRILLED VALANCE. Sometimes a frilled valance is used with frilled curtains. The finished length of the frill valance is the same as the finished width of the curtain body. Finish both edges of the strip with $^1/_8$-inch double hems. After making the ruffle, pin line of gathering stitches to top row of stitching for casing. Stitch on this line (1018).

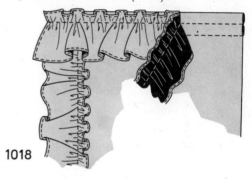

1018

FRILLED TIE-BACKS. To determine size of tie-back, hang curtains on rod. Put tape measure around curtain, as if it were the tie-back, to get the desired effect. Add 1 inch to this measurement for seam allowance.

TIE-BACK WITH ONE FRILL. Cut $2^1/_2$-inch-wide band the necessary length. Stitch the frill to the band with a plain seam along one long edge beginning and ending $^1/_2$ inch from ends. With right sides together, stitch ends of band together with $^1/_2$-inch plain seam. Turn band to right side. Turn in free edge of band and pin to ruffles along gathering line. Top-stitch along folded edge (1019).

1019

TIE-BACK WITH FRILL ON BOTH SIDES OF BAND. Cut two bands, each $1^1/_2$ inches wide. To one of the bands, pin frill along one edge, right sides together. Pin second band in place along frill, right side down. Stitch across ends and down length of band (1020). Turn band right side out and press. Second frill is applied as for one frill tie-back.

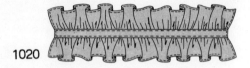

1020

Café Curtains

Café curtains may be made in many variations. You may use two or more tiers in the same or varying lengths (1021). You may use a café curtain on the bottom half of the window only and combine it with a valance of full-length over-curtains. Almost any heading may be used.

First, attach café rods and brackets to window frame, or rod and sockets to inside of window frame. If there are horizontal wood strips between the panes of glass in the window, the rod (or rods) should be mounted even with one of the strips.

Check the measurement for each tier carefully. For the bottom tier, measure from top of rod to sill or apron. Add $2^1/_2$ to 3 inches for bottom hem (6 inches for double hem on sheers). Add the necessary amount, depending upon heading used, for the top hem allowance. For upper tiers, measure from rod which will hold tier to rod directly below it. Add 3 inches for overlap, $2^1/_2$ to 3 inches for lower hem (6 inches if double hem is used) and the necessary amount for top hem allowance, depending on heading used.

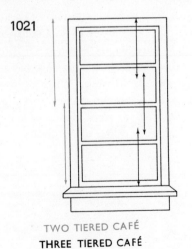

1021

TWO TIERED CAFÉ
THREE TIERED CAFÉ

In order for the curtains to fall in pleasing folds, allow at least two times the finished width of the curtains. Add $1^1/_2$ inches for each side hem (2 inches for double hem) and $1/_2$-inch seam allowances if joining seams are necessary.

Finish the side and lower edges with appropriate hems. Use special heading for top of each tier. Various types are described on page 282.

Window Curtains

Curtains may be lined or unlined. Unlined curtains are used in informal treatments. They are made of light- or medium-weight fabrics which are attractive on both sides. Loosely woven fabrics are very effective when unlined, when the sun shines through, casting shadow within the room.

Lined Curtains

Lined curtains are made of medium- to heavy-weight fabrics. The lining provides additional weight, causing the fabric to hang in deeper, more formal folds. Linings also protect curtain fabrics from dust and from sun-fading, presenting a more attractive appearance from the outside of the house.

Before cutting out the curtains determine the length and width of each piece. To finished *length*, add:

- 1 inch for heading or the amount that will extend above the rod
- Plus 4 inches for the top hem
- Plus bottom hem: single—5 inches; or double—9 inches.

If deep pleat of pinch pleating tape is used, no top hem is needed. Allow only $1/_2$-inch seam allowance for attaching the tape.

For *width:*

- Allow 2 to $2^1/_2$ times the finished width for regular curtain fabrics, and 3 to 4 times the finished width for very sheer fabrics
- Add $1^1/_2$ inches for each side hem (1 inch for hem and $1/_2$ inch for seam allowance)
- Add $1/_2$ inch for seam allowances to join lengths of fabric for multiple-width curtains.

Cut out curtains according to instructions on page 275.

To join fabric lengths, clip or cut off selvages and press. Pin fabric lengths together, carefully matching patterns. It is often best to slip-stitch edges together for perfect matching. Stitch and press seams open.

FINISHING UPPER EDGE OF LINED CURTAINS. Place stiffening on inside of curtain fabric with upper edges even and ends 1½ inches from side edges of curtain. Stitch along lower edge of the stiffening (1022).

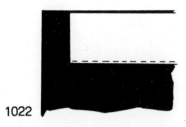

1022

Turn top hem to inside along edge of stiffening (1023).

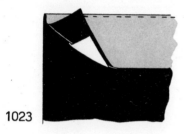

1023

When deep pleat or pinch pleating tape is used, lap the tape ½ inch over the top edge of the drapery,

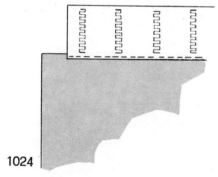

1024

right sides up. Top-stitch in place (1024). Then turn the tape to the inside and stitch along lower edge of tape through all thicknesses (1025).

1025

If Rufflette tape is to be used follow directions given on page 280.

Preparation of a Lining

LINING WIDTH. For multiple-width curtains, lining fabric must be the same width as the fabric. Curtains made of a single fabric width may use a lining fabric 4 inches narrower than fabric width.

CUTTING. Cut lining 4 inches narrower than curtains. For multiple-width curtains cut 2 inches off each side edge so that fabric and lining seams will match (1026).

Cut lining 1½ inches shorter than the finished length of the curtain. This allows 2½ inches at the bottom (2 inches for hem and ½ inch turn-in) and ½-inch seam allowances on top and both side edges.

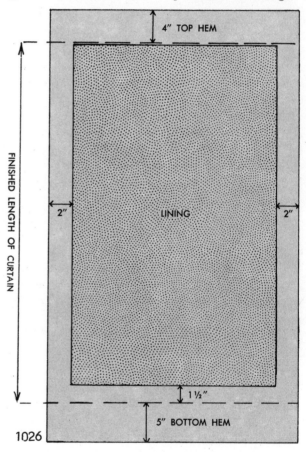

4" TOP HEM

FINISHED LENGTH OF CURTAIN

2" LINING 2"

1½"

5" BOTTOM HEM

1026

JOINING LINING LENGTHS. Match width of lining lengths to corresponding widths of curtain lengths. Lining and curtain seams will be matched together. Stitch lining seams. Trim seam allowances to ½ inch. Press open.

Turn in ½ inch at upper and lower edge of lining and press.

Turn up and stitch a 2-inch hem at lower edge of lining.

JOINING LINING TO CURTAIN. Place lining over curtain right sides together. Pin both side edges of lining and curtain together. Start folded top edge of lining $3^1/_2$ inches down from the top of the curtain. Stitch in a $^1/_2$-inch seam (each side). Clip seams every 3 to 4 inches and press open (1027).

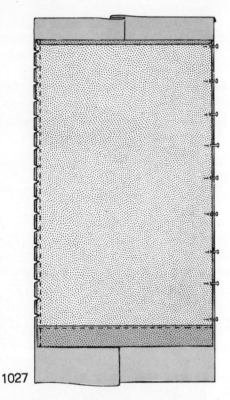

1027

Turn inside out and centre lining over curtain. Pin seams of lining and curtain fabric to give a multiple-width curtain. Press. There will be a 1-inch side hem of curtain fabric showing on either side of the lining. Turn in the edge of the side hem above the lining. Mitre the top corner and slipstitch the side hem in place. Pin the top edge of the lining over the lower edge of the top hem or pleating tape. Slipstitch the lining to the top hem or pleating tape (1028).

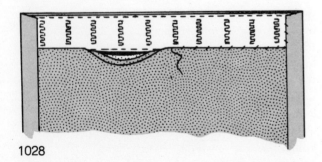

1028

To make pleats without pleating tape follow directions on page 283.

TO ATTACH RUFFLETTE TAPE. Two types of Rufflette are available giving gathered or pleated effects.

In both cases first form hem (1029) then baste Rufflette tape to this so that the tape just covers the lower raw edge, turning in the ends of the tape. Make sure the tie ends are left free at each end. Machine stitch the Rufflette tape in position close to the edge and finish off carefully. Slip hem or machine stitch the remaining open side edges of the hem (1030).

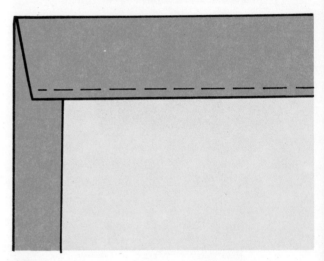

1029

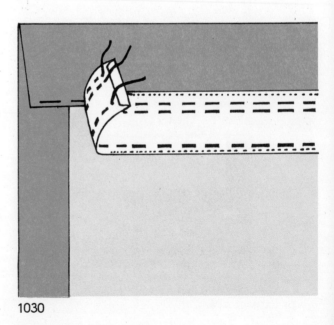

1030

FINISHING LOWER EDGE OF LINED CURTAINS.

Allow curtains to hang for several days before finishing lower edge. It is much more accurate to turn and adjust the hem after the curtains have been hung. The fabric of your curtains will affect the finished length. Heavy fabrics will hang straight and some may stretch longer, while crisp, light-weight fabric will billow out and may require slightly more length.

Finish the lower edge in a single or double hem according to the allowance planned. For a single hem, turn in the edge and turn hem up the correct width

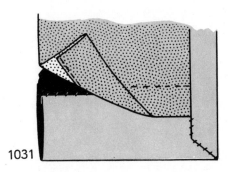

1031

(1031). For a double hem, turn up the edge one-half the amount allowed and then turn the same width a second time. Slip-stitch hem in place (1032).

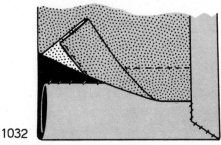

1032

Turn in the edge of the side hem below the lining. Mitre lower corner and slip-stitch the side hem in place.

The lining hem hangs free from the curtain hem and overlaps the top edge by about 2 inches. The lining hem is held to the curtain hem with a French tack every 12 to 14 inches.

Unlined Curtains

To measure:
- To finished *length*, add 1 inch for heading or the amount that will extend above the rod
- Plus 4^1/$_2$ inches for the top hem
- Plus bottom hem: single—5 inches; or double—9 inches.

If pleating tape is to be used, no top hem is needed. Allow only ^{1}/$_2$-inch seam allowance for attaching to the tape.

For *width:*

Allow 2 to 2^1/$_2$ times the finished width for regular drapery fabric and 3 to 4 times the finished width for very sheer fabrics. Add 1^1/$_2$ inches for each side hem (1 inch for hem and ^{1}/$_2$ inch for turn-in). Add ^{5}/$_8$-inch seam allowances to join lengths of fabric for multiple-width draperies.

Follow cutting directions on page 275.

TO JOIN FABRIC LENGTHS.

Clip or cut off selvages and press. Pin fabric lengths together, carefully matching patterns. Stitch and press seams open. Pinking seams is a satisfactory finish for most fabrics but sheer fabrics that ravel may need to be French-seamed. Extensive seam finishing on these long seams will cause puckering.

TO FINISH UPPER EDGE OF UNLINED CURTAINS.

Place stiffening on inside of curtain fabric ^{1}/$_2$ inch from upper edge with ends 1^1/$_2$ inches from side edges of (1033). Stitch along lower edge of stiffening. Turn top edge of curtain over stiffening and press. Turn top hem to inside along upper edge of stiffening. Stitch along lower edge of stiffening through all thicknesses (1034).

When pleating tape is used, finish same as for lined curtains, page 279.

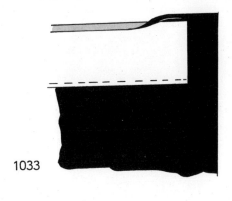

1033

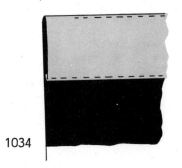

1034

TO FINISH SIDE EDGES OF UNLINED

CURTAINS. Turn in side edges $1/2$ inch and press. Turn in 1 inch for a hem and mitre upper corners. Pin in place. Slip-stitch or machine-stitch hem to within 6 inches of finished length (1035).

To make pleats without pleating tape, follow directions on page 283.

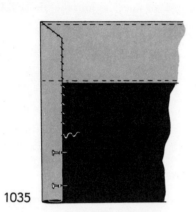

1035

TO FINISH LOWER EDGE OF UNLINED

CURTAINS. Finish lower edge in a single or double hem same as for lined curtains, page 281. After hem is turned up, continue side hems to the lower edge. Mitre corners at lower edge and stitch in place (1036).

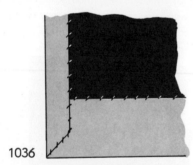

1036

Headings

Headings give an attractive finish to the top of curtains. There are many different types which can be used in a variety of ways. Some are straight, while others may be pleated and scalloped.

PLAIN CASING WITH HEADING. A hem is placed in the top edge of the curtain. After the rod casing has been stitched, the part above the rod is called a heading. In deciding on the width of the hem, determine the width of the heading. To this add one half the distance around the rod, $1/4$-inch ease, and $1/4$-inch seam allowance.

After the hem has been made, place rod inside hem along stitching line. Put a few pins above the rod to mark the width of the casing (1037). Remove rod. Stitch along marked line. When the finished curtain is slipped on the rod the effect will be of a small frill above the rod.

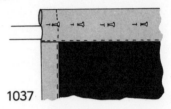

1037

LOOPED TOPS. Straight or shaped bands of fabric, decorative tape or braid can be used for making loops. Sew loops to top of straight hem or attach with facing to seam at top edge (1038). If you wish, sew only one end of loop and attach other end in a decorative way, using a button and buttonhole.

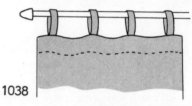

1038

FOUR-CORD SHIRRING. When this heading is used, the total fabric width should be 3 times the finished width. At top edge, turn down fabric $4^1/4$ inches to the wrong side and press. Turn under the raw edge $1/4$ inch and press.

Mark lines for cording beginning at stitching line. Place a mark $1/4$ inch from stitching for the first cord, then marks at 1 inch and $1^1/4$ inches for second cord; at 2 inches and $2^1/4$ inches for third; 3 inches and $3^1/4$ inches for fourth. A $3/4$-inch space is left between cords.

Use piping cord of $1/8$-inch diameter. Buy four times the total fabric width plus four feet. Insert the cord in hem against the stitching. Stitch on marked line using piping and zipper foot. Stitch on the second marked line. Insert cord and stitch on third line which is just above cording. Continue in this manner until the four rows of cording have been inserted (1039).

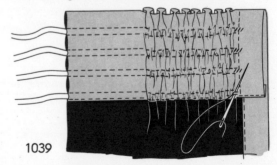

1039

Stitch down one side (1039), across cords, to hold them securely in place. Pull up cords from opposite end to desired length, distributing fullness evenly. Stitch across ends to hold cording securely.

PLEATED HEADINGS. This is the type of heading used on curtains. To keep the pleats standing upright, a stiffening fabric such as crinoline or buckram must be used. A 4- to 5-inch top hem is pressed into place with the raw edge turned under $1/2$ inch. Cut stiffening the same width as the top hem. Open hem and place edge of stiffening inside the tuck-under fold of the hem. Stitch along edge of fold (1040). Turn hem back into place with stiffening inside. Pin hem into place. Press and stitch (1041).

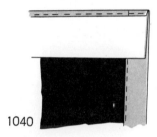

1040   1041

To determine the size and placement of pleats, you must first know the amount of fabric you have for pleating. To get this figure, subtract from the total fabric width the finished width of the curtain. There should be an uneven number of pleats on each panel and each pleat should fall in graceful folds. Try pleating a piece of fabric to see how deep the pleats should be. Here is an example of how this is done:

You have 40 inches to pleat. You want each pleat to be about 5 inches deep. Divide 5 inches into 40 inches. You will have eight pleats. But, you want an uneven number of pleats; so divide seven pleats into 40 inches. Each pleat will be almost $5^3/_4$ inches deep. You decide that your pleat will be too bulky.

The efore, you try dividing nine pleats into 40 inches. Each pleat will be a little less than $4^1/_2$ inches. You try making a $4^1/_2$-inch pleat. This looks better than the $5^3/_4$-inch pleat. And so nine $4^1/_2$-inch pleats is your selection (1042).

To mark the place for the pleats along the top of the curtain, measure in, from the outer side edge of the curtain, the distance that the rod curves into the wall. This is where the outermost pleat will be. Mark the $4^1/_2$-inch width of the pleat.

The innermost pleat will be 2 inches in from the centre side edge of the drapery; again mark the $4^1/_2$-inch width of the pleat.

The third pleat is centred between the two outside pleats. The rest of the pleats are evenly spaced between the centre pleat and each side edge pleat. Be sure to mark the width of each pleat.

Form the pleat by pinning the markings for each pleat together with the folded width of the pleat on the right side. Stitch the markings together on the right side, from the top edge to $3/_4$ inch below the heading (1043).

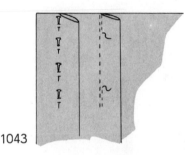

1043

You are now ready to make the type of pleat you desire.

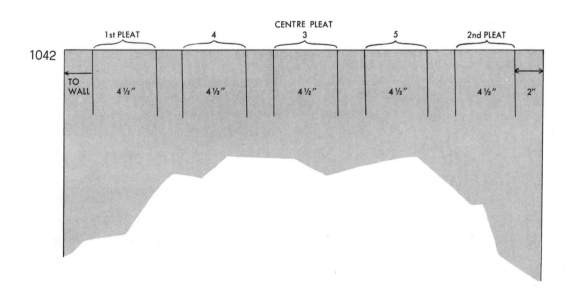

1042

1st PLEAT   4   CENTRE PLEAT   5   2nd PLEAT
                    3

TO WALL   4½"   4½"   4½"   4½"   4½"   2"

FOLDED PLEATS. Leave pleats as they are. Press and attach to rod with rings or loops (1044). These are not suitable for heavy fabrics.

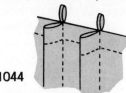

1044

BOX PLEATS. Find centre of pleat fold (1045). Pin to stitching that holds fold in place. Now, there are folds of equal width on either side of the stitching line. Press. Sew pleats into place, tacking from wrong side.

If the rod will show, use rings or loops at the top centre of each pleat. If the rod is to be covered, attach hooks to wrong side of pleat.

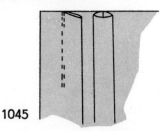

1045

PINCH PLEATS. Divide fullness of pleat fold into three equal, smaller folds. Baste top and front edges of folds together. Press. Machine-stitch across the folds at the bottom of the heading (1046).

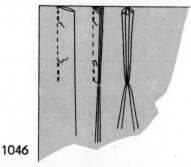

1046

FRENCH PLEATS. Divide fullness of pleat fold into three equal, smaller folds. At the bottom of the heading, sew by hand through the three pleats on the right side of the fabric. Pull thread up tight and fasten securely (1047). Top edge of heading is not pressed into pleats.

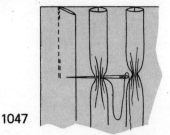

1047

PLEATING TAPE. Stiffening in the top hem is not necessary when pleating tapes are used. Leave only $1/2$-inch allowance above the finished top edge. Place top of tape across top edge of fabric, right sides up, with tape overlapping about $1/2$ inch of fabric (1048). Pin and stitch. Turn tape to wrong side and press. Turn under raw edges of tape at side hems and pin lower edge of tape to fabric. Stitch only along the bottom edge of tape (1049). Insert hooks in pockets. Pleats are made automatically. For sheer fabrics, make double hem on top, the width of the tape, to prevent tape from showing through.

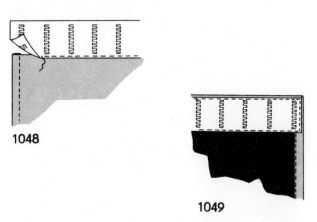

1048

1049

PINCH PLEATING TAPE. This is a type of Rufflette tape made with regularly spaced pockets into which special four-prong hooks are inserted at regular intervals. Stitch pinch pleating tape to the curtain as Rufflette tape (directions on page 280).

SCALLOPED HEADINGS. The width of top hem and interfacing depends upon depth of scallop used. There should be an even number of scallops on each panel. For a 3-inch scallop, allow $4\frac{1}{4}$ inches for top hem. Make hems on side and bottom edges of curtain (1050.) Fold top edge down $4\frac{1}{4}$ inches on the right side of the fabric. Pin and press in place.

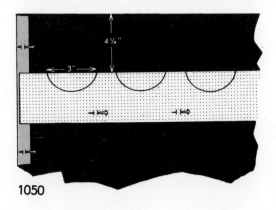

1050

Draw scallop pattern on interfacing strip. Be sure the number of scallops, the size and the space between them, form a pleasing look in proportion to the curtains. Pin interfacing to wrong side of the fabric along folded top edge. Then pin along lower edge of interfacing. Using a small stitch, stitch along scallop markings on interfacing. Cut scallops out, ¼ inch from stitching. Clip seam allowance (1051). Turn hem to wrong side. Press scallops evenly along seam. Turn edge of hem under ¼ inch. Press and stitch (1052).

Other decorative shapes can be made in the same manner. Attach loops or rings to points of scallops.

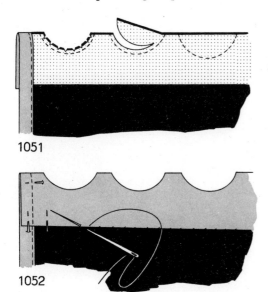

1051

1052

SCALLOPS WITH PINCH PLEATS. No special pleating tape is available for making scalloped pinch pleats, but the same effect can be obtained by using interfacing and making the scallop markings as above but ensuring that the space between each scallop is wide enough to allow for the pinch pleating. If necessary small sections of ordinary pinch pleating tape can be used between each scallop as below (in addition to the interfacing in this case).

1053

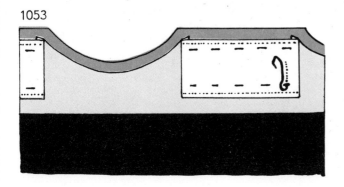

Weights

Weighting will make your curtains hang more evenly. Weighted tapes and lead weights are available in many sizes (1054a, 1054b).

1054 a   1054 b

SMALL SHOT INSIDE FABRIC CASING

This type of weighting is sold by the yard. It is most satisfactory when used on medium- to light-weight fabrics. Cut weighting strip as long as the width of the curtain. Lay inside the bottom fold of the hem. Turn under the raw edges at the ends of the casing, forcing out the last piece of shot if necessary. Tack inside each side corner of the hem. Further tacking is unnecessary, as its own weight will hold it in place as the curtain is hanging. Remove before washing.

INDIVIDUAL LEAD WEIGHTS. Individual weights are used on heavier fabrics. You may buy sew-on or pin-on weights. For lined curtains, cover weight with lining fabric. Attach at top of fabric hem on the wrong side, underneath lining hem. Place one weight near each side hem. For longer, heavier curtains, use one weight opposite each fixture which attaches curtains to the rod. For unlined curtains, cover weight with curtain fabric and fasten to lower hem on the wrong side.

TO COVER WEIGHTS. Cut two pieces of fabric in the shape of the weight, leaving ¼-inch seam allowance on each side. With right sides facing, stitch around three sides, with scant ¼-inch seam. Trim seam close to stitching. Turn right side out. Drop weight into pocket. Finish last side, turning edges in and stitching by hand.

Another very satisfactory method is to cut one piece of fabric the size of the weight, with ¼-inch turn-under on each side. Turn under edges a scant ¼ inch and press. Place patch on curtain and sew by hand around three sides. Drop weight into pocket. Sew fourth side.

Anchoring Curtains

At the outside edge of the curtain, sew plastic rings to the top and bottom corners. Screw a cup hook into the wall where each corner of curtain should meet the wall. Hook rings on curtain into cup hooks. This will hold curtains in place.

PELMETS

Pelmets should blend in style and fabric with the curtains and with the room decor. They conceal the curtain track and help to balance the proportions of the window or to connect several windows treated as one. The depth of the pelmet depends on the height of the window, usually one-sixth to one-ninth the length of the curtain.

Firm buckram is necessary to hold the pelmet stiff and straight. Cotton flannel is often used for interlining. Pelmets may be taped and hung from curtain rods or taped, nailed or drawing-pinned to existing wooden pelmets or other fixtures.

Tape a piece of heavy paper to the curtain rail or wooden pelmet. Determine the depth and shape of the pelmet design. Using the paper as a pattern cut the buckram to the measurements of the finished pelmet. Cut interlining and fabric to the same shape leaving 1-inch seam allowance on each edge. Cut lining leaving $1/_4$-inch seam allowance.

Baste interlining to the wrong side of the fabric, then place interlining against buckram. Turn 1-inch seam allowance over the buckram. Clip and notch edges as required for curves. Catch-stitch raw edges to the buckram. Pin lining to back of buckram, turning raw edges under $1/_2$ inch. Slip-stitch to turned edge of curtain and interlining (1056). Sew hooks or loops to the back of the finished pelmet for attachment to pelmet fixture if required.

There is a special buckram which obviates sewing fabric to the buckram. It is moistened and the fabric can be ironed into position.

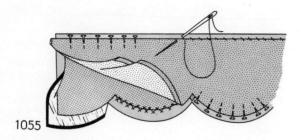

1055

VALANCES

Valances are shortened versions of the curtains with which they are used, and are usually made all in one piece. They may be unlined, lined or interlined, depending upon the weight of the fabric used.

First, determine the depth desired. Add 2 inches for the hem and the amount necessary for the heading. Work out the fullness and construct, following directions for the corresponding type of curtain. The only difference is in the depth and in the depth of the bottom hem.

BEDSPREADS

Bedspreads are fun to make. Begin with a few rules and then let your imagination run free. Directions for basic types of spreads are given here. Combine them and trim them; the variations are endless.

Important Measurements

Begin by taking measurements when the bed is made up with blankets and sheets in place, since these will increase the size of the bed. Measure top length, top width, side overhang, foot overhang, head overhang, depth of top mattress, top of box spring to floor and "returns" at head overhang (1056). With these measurements, it is possible to make any type of spread.

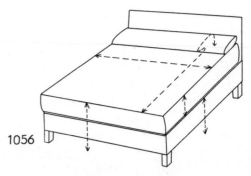

1056

The term "return at head overhang" is one used in discussing beds with headboards. It is an extension of the side treatment at the head end. It rounds the corners and runs 6 to 10 inches in along the headboard, holding the side overhang in place. The return is also used on beds without headboards, when the head end is against the wall.

To the measurements, add $1/_2$ inch for each seam allowance and 2 inches for hems. The bottom hem should clear the floor by $1/_2$ to 1 inch. If the pillow is to be covered by the spread, add 30 inches to the top length measurement to allow for pillow covering and tuck-in. In planning the yardage requirements, the full width of the fabric is always placed down the centre of the bed. Any piecing necessary is done on either side. This may increase the yardage required.

All bedspreads described here are for beds with headboards only. If your bed has a footboard, do not add foot overhang. Allow only for tuck-in at foot. If you do not have a headboard, add head overhang.

Throw-over Bedspread

To determine size, use this formula:

Total length = Top length + foot overhang + head tuck-in + hems (2).

Total width = Top width + side overhang (2) + seam allowance (4) + hems (2).

Cut one length of fabric and place it, full width, down the centre top of the bed. Join side sections of equal length to centre section. Cording can be inserted in the seams, or braid and fabric bands added for decorative effect (1057).

Corners may hang in points or be rounded. Finish edges with hem, piping or a novelty trim.

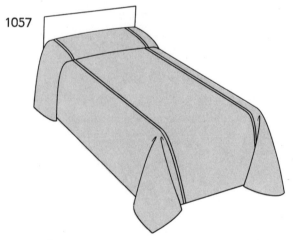

1057

Three-Section Tailored Spread

To determine size, use this formula:

Top section:

Length = Top length + foot overhang + head tuck-in + hems (2).

Width = Top width + $\frac{1}{2}$-inch seam allowance on each side (+ 2 seam allowances if top piecing is required).

Side sections:

Length = Top length + head tuck-in + hems (2).

Height = Side overhang + hem (1) + seam allowance (1 ").

Place centre section down top of bed. Piece side to cover top section, if necessary. Leave $\frac{1}{2}$-inch seam allowances at side edges of top.

Hem side overhang sections at bottom and at foot end. Join side overhangs to top section, starting at the head end with plain seam. Foot overhang and side sections will just meet at the foot corners of the bed. Hem side and bottom edges of foot overhang. Hem edge at head of bed.

These spreads are lined, because the underside shows at the open corners (1058).

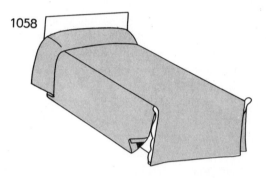

1058

Fitted Spread with Box-Pleated Corners

To determine size of top section:

Length = Top length + seam allowances (2).

Width = Top width + side seam allowances (2) + seam allowances for piecing, if necessary (4).

Place full width of fabric down centre of bed. Piece sides, if necessary. Cut off excess at side edges, leaving $\frac{1}{2}$-inch seam allowance. If lining is used, cut to exactly the same measurements as the fabric sections. Pipe edges around sides of top section, if desired (1059).

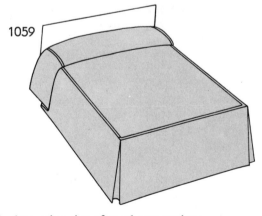

1059

To determine size of overhang section:

Sides: (Cut 2, on lengthwise grain).

Width = Top length + 3 inches for pleats (2) + seam allowance (2).

Height = Side overhang + seam allowance (1) + hem (1).

End, or Foot Overhang: (Cut 1, on crosswise grain).

Width = Top width + 9 inches for pleat (2) + seam allowance (2).

Height = Foot overhang + seam allowance (1) + hem (1).

Front Returns: (Cut 2, on crosswise grain).

Width = 12″ for return + 9″ for pleat (1) + seam allowance (1) + side hem (1).

Height = Head overhang + seam allowance (1) + hem (1).

If overhang sections are to be lined, cut height of lining $1\frac{1}{2}$ inches shorter than bedspread fabric.

Join side sections to end section with $\frac{1}{2}$-inch seams. Press open. Lay out joined sections on a flat surface.

From seam, measure 3 inches into side section and mark. Pin a fold on this line. Measure into end section from seam, 3 inches and 9 inches. Mark each point. Pin a fold on the 9-inch mark. Bring pinned folds together to meet on the 3-inch line on the end section. This is your box pleat. The seam is at the inside turn of the pleat. Repeat on other seam. Press pleats.

Hem inside edges of front returns and join returns to side sections. Make pleats as before, measuring 3 inches into the side overhang, 3 inches and 9 inches into the front returns. Finish hem on overhang and join overhang to top section.

Fitted Spread with Mock Pleats at Corners

Cut spread as for spread with box-pleated corners, except—do *not* add pleat allowance. Instead, add 4 inches to end overhang, 4 inches to each side overhang, and 2 inches to each front return section. Turn

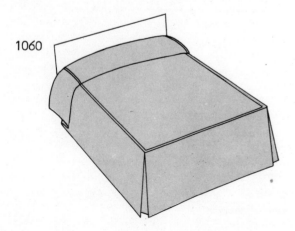

1060

back a 2-inch fold to the wrong side on each side end. Turn in raw edges and hem. Hem bottom edges of all overhang sections (1060).

1061

Cut four strips for backing pieces, 7 inches wide and the height of the overhang sections. On each piece, make $\frac{1}{2}$-inch side hems and 2-inch bottom hem. Make centre fold down each backing piece.

Place one side edge of end-overhang section on top of the backing, against centre fold, matching bottom hems. On the other side of the centre fold, place the adjacent edge of the side overhang, matching bottom hems. Overhang sections should meet exactly, and completely cover the backing piece (1061). Stitch overhang pieces to backing, a scant $\frac{1}{2}$ inch from the top edge. Repeat for other side and end corner, then for sides and front returns. Join overhang to top section.

A decorative touch may be added by using a different fabric for the backing pieces.

Other Fitted Bedspreads

Overhang sections for fitted spreads may be varied in many ways: they may be pleated all around, made with spaced pleats, gathered, gathered with frills, etc.

Boxed Spread with Frill Attached

Make top of spread, as in fitted spread. Pipe edges. Make boxing:

Height = Depth of top mattress + seam allowances (2).

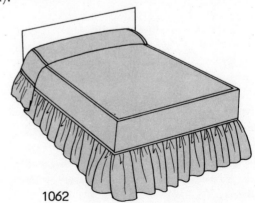

1062

Side lengths (2) = Top length + seam allowances (2).

Head and foot lengths = Top widths + seam allowances (2).

Join all corner seams. Apply cording to lower edge of boxing.

Make frill:

Height = Distance from top of box spring to floor + seam allowance (1) + hem (1).

Length = Twice the distance to be covered by the dust ruffle.

Join lengths together with $^1/_2$-inch seam allowances and press seams open. Hem bottom edge and inside edges of returns. Gather along top edge. Join skirt to lower edge of boxing. Join top edge of boxing to top section of spread (1062).

The attached flounce may also be made with inverted box pleats at the corners, with pleats all the way around, or with grouped pleats.

Frills may be added to gathered skirt and to lower edge of boxing.

Bed Valance for Divan

This type of covering is placed between mattress and springs (1063).

For the strip which covers side of box springs, cut strips 5 inches wide. The length will follow this formula: Top lengths (2) + top width (1) + 8 inch return (2) + seam allowances for joining seams.

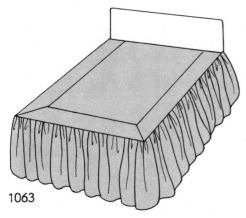

1063

Join strips together. Place around top edges of the box spring, wrong side up. Outer edge should extend $^1/_2$ inch beyond the edge of the box spring. Mitre corners. Press seams.

For the centre piece, cut muslin to fit across the top of the box spring, inside the fabric strips. Allow $^1/_2$-inch seam allowance on all sides.

Pin muslin to facing strips, starting at the foot edge and working to the head on each side. Hem muslin across the head edge, between front returns. Stitch muslin to facing strips with $^1/_2$-inch seam. Press seam open.

Replace muslin and facing on top of box spring, right side up.

For valance: Cut strips for flounce.

Height = Distance from top of box spring to floor + hem (1) + seam allowance (1).

Length will be determined by the type of flounce.

Valances may be pleated or gathered, in any variation desired. First, hem bottom edge. Gather or pin pleats in skirt, and stitch across top of skirt to hold fullness in place. Pin, then stitch valance to top section covering box spring.

The valance may be attached in other ways. A pleated flounce may be applied to box spring with twill tape. Allow $2^1/_2$ inches extra on the height of the flounce. Stitch pleats into place both at the top edge and 2 inches down from the top. Stitch twill tape along pleated top edge. Pin flounce to box spring, gathering in fullness of tape at the corners. With strong thread and curved needle, whip tape to box spring.

Gripper snap tape provides a flounce that will detach easily for washing. Sew socket edge to box spring $2^1/_2$ inches in from the edge. Stitch ball side to wrong side of flounce at the top edge of $2^1/_2$-inch allowance. Snap flounce into place.

Coverlet

To determine size, use this formula:

Length = Top length + depth of top mattress (2) + hems (2) + overlap (2 to 3 inches on each end).

Width = Top width + depth of top mattress (2) + hems (2) + overlap (2 to 3 inches on each side) + seam allowances, if piecing is necessary.

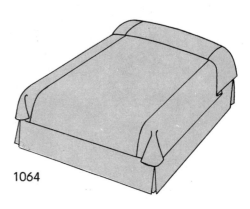

1064

Lining: Cut to same measurements as fabric.

Place full width of fabric down centre top of bed.

Join side sections to achieve required width. Edges will extend 4 to 5 inches below top of box spring on all sides (overlap + hem allowances). If piping fringe, or other edging is to be used, stitch to right side of fabric.

Pin lining to coverlet, right sides together. Match side piecing seams of lining to corresponding seams in fabric. Stitch around sides and foot of coverlet. Turn coverlet right side out. Press. At head, turn in raw edges and slip-stitch together (1064).

Other Spreads to Use with Bed Valance

The coverlet is actually a shortened version of the throw-over spread. You may make any type of top spread desired, following directions given for the full-length spread. Change only the height of the overhang. For the top spread, the overhang equals the depth of the top mattress plus 2-to-3 inch overlap over the box-spring. Allow 2 inches for hems. If scalloped or other shaped patterns are made on the edge of the overhang, a stiffening fabric and lining should be used.

PILLOW COVERS

Pillow Sham

Measure length and width of pillow over the fullest parts. Add 1 inch to both measurements.

For top pillow section cut to measured length and width. Stitch trimming, if any, around edge of top section, right sides together. For bottom section cut to measured width. To length, add $3^1/_2$ inches. Fold section in half lengthwise. Cut on fold. Make 1-inch hem

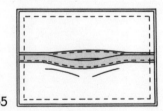

1065

on both cut edges. Overlap hems $1^1/_2$ inches. Pin overlap together on wrong side (1065).

Pin top and bottom sections together, right sides facing. Stitch around edges. Take pins from overlapped hems at centre of bottom section. Turn sham

right side out. If desired, snap fasteners may be sewn on overlapped opening, but it is not necessary.

Decorative edge trimmings such as frills, fringe, cording, fabric bands, lace, eyelet can be used.

Separate Pillow Cover Sewn to Spread

The width of the pillow cover is the same as the width of the spread (1066). Seams are placed to match seams in spread. Side edges are finished in the same manner as on the spread. The pillow cover is lined if the spread is lined.

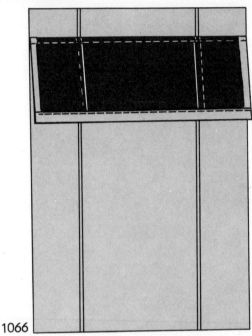

1066

The pillow cover must be long enough to go over the pillow, to tuck in under the pillow and to tuck in at the headboard. To this length, add 3 inches for hem and seam. Make 2-inch hem at top edge of pillow cover. Finish side edges.

With right sides together, pin bottom edge of pillow cover to spread, about 12 inches from the head edge of the bed. Stitch on pinned line, across entire width. Turn under raw edge of pillow cover, and stitch again.

Place pillow over seam line. When pillow cover is drawn up over the pillow, it appears to be tucked in underneath.

Bolster Roll

To determine size of inner form, cut a rectangular piece of heavy muslin or sailcloth, four times the desired height of the pillow, by top width of bed plus 8 inches.

Stitch long edges together. Gather around the edge of one end, and pull gathering up tight to close the end. Fasten securely. Turn tube right side out. Pack tightly and evenly with stuffing material. Close open end same as the first end.

For the cover, measure inner form for correct length and circumference. Allow ½ inch for seams. Join long edges (1067). Cut two fabric circles to fit over end sections, adding ½-inch seam allowance all around.

Stitch one end section to the tube section. Turn right side out. Insert inner form. Stitch other end section to tubing by hand (1068).

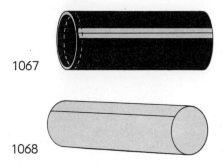

1067

1068

Bolster covers may be made in any shape in this same manner. The tubing, cut to the correct circumference, will take the shape of any inner form. Only the end pieces are changed. Their shapes are determined by pin-fitting the fabric to the inner form.

LOOSE COVERS

If you have time and enjoy precision work, making loose covers will give you a great deal of satisfaction. It is always fun to see a "new chair" take shape.

Fabric Required

The following chart shows the amount of fabric needed for various types of loose covers. Remember these are *average* measurements, for *average*-size chairs and *average*-size prints.

In measuring, figure the yardage required for each section of the chair. Ample allowance must be made for centring the decorative motif on each section. With 54-inch fabric, reduce yardage five per cent.

Begin by pinning the fabric to each section of the chair. Place the fabric right side up if there is a pattern or design to be matched. Solid-coloured fabrics can be placed wrong side up on the chair. This eliminates the step of having to unpin and turn the seams for stitching after loose cover is fitted.

Place the design so it blends to best advantage with the pattern on surrounding pieces. Be sure the grain line is straight.

Pin the fabric to each section of the chair, beginning at the centre of the section, then pinning out toward the seam lines. The fabric should fit smoothly and snugly at every point. As you fit each section according to the following instructions, mark the seam lines,

YARDAGE CHART FOR LOOSE COVERS

		Yardage				
		48″ Wide		36″ Wide		
Type	No. of Cushions	Plain	Pattern	Plain	Pattern	Cording or Trimming
Armchair	1	$7\frac{1}{2}$	$8\frac{1}{2}$	$11\frac{1}{2}$	$12\frac{1}{2}$	18
Wing Chair	1	8	$8\frac{1}{2}$	12	$13\frac{1}{2}$	18
Ottoman	0	2	$2\frac{1}{2}$	3	$3\frac{1}{2}$	6
Sofa (settee) (6—7′)	2—3	14	$15\frac{1}{2}$	21	23	36
	1	$13\frac{1}{2}$	15	$20\frac{1}{2}$	$22\frac{1}{2}$	33
Day Bed	2	$14\frac{1}{2}$	16	20	21	40
Cushion	1	$1\frac{1}{4}$	$1\frac{3}{4}$	2	$2\frac{1}{4}$	5

following the construction lines of the chair. Cut away the excess fabric, leaving 1-inch seam allowances.

Pin-Fitting and Cutting Loose Covers

INSIDE BACK. Remove chair cushion. Place fabric right side out on the inside back section. Centre design, then pin from centre out to seam lines (1069). At top seam, make a 2-inch fold. Pin. Then pin fabric back across top boxing. Allow 1-inch seam allowance beyond back seam. Cut off excess. Cut through centre of 2-inch fold.

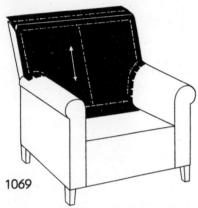

1069

At the crevice at the bottom of the inside back, allow 5 inches for tuck-in allowance. Cut off excess. At the side seams, allow 1-inch seam allowance. Where inside back is joined to curved section of arm, shape around top of arm, clipping seam allowances where necessary. Mark seam line. Where chair back and arm are separated, allow 5-inch tuck-in.

SEAT. Smooth fabric over seat. Pin from centre out. Allow 5 inches for tuck-in at back and side edges of seat (1070).

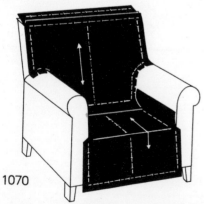

1070

At seat front, bring fabric down over the spring-edge and pin down the front of the chair. Cut off excess fabric at bottom edge, 2 inches below the skirt line.

OUTSIDE BACK. Centre design on chair back with straight of material running up and down (1071). Pin from centre out. At top edge, pin seam line to top boxing. Leave 1-inch seam allowance. At side seams, leave 1-inch seam allowance, and cut away excess. At bottom edge, leave 2-inch allowance.

SIDE BACK (above arms). Grain line runs from top to bottom. Centre the design, then pin from the centre out. Mark seam lines. Pin to top boxing, inside and outside back pieces. Allow 1-inch seam allowance.

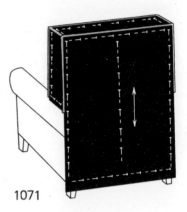

1071

FRONT ARM SECTIONS. Place design on front arm section. Grain line should run up and down. Pin from centre out. Mark seam lines. Allow 1-inch seam allowance. Remove from chair.

Front arm sections must match perfectly. Lay cut piece, right side down, on right side of fabric. Match design and cut second piece, using the first as a pattern. Trace seam line to second part.

INSIDE TOP ARMS. Grain line should run from front to back. Centre design on top of arm. Pin from centre out. Mark front seam. Allow 1-inch seam allowance. Mark back seam. Allow 1-inch seam allowance where arm and chair back are joined. Allow 5-inch tuck-in where arm and chair back are separated.

At bottom of inside arm, allow 5-inch tuck-in at seat crevice. Cut away excess and remove piece from chair. Cut second inside top arm section, by matching cut piece to design on fabric and tracing seam lines, as for arm fronts.

Pin both arm pieces to chair. Make sure that design is centred evenly, matching on both sides. Pin from centre out. Check marked seam lines.

1072

OUTSIDE ARMS. Straight of grain should run up and down, along front edge. Pin from centre out. Smooth fabric under curve of arm top. Mark seam line. At bottom edge, cut away excess 2 inches below the skirt line.

All pieces should now be pinned together, except at tuck-ins (1072). Check to see that grain line runs straight on all sections, and that all pinned seams are tight-fitting and as straight as possible. If slight changes must be made, you have $1/_2$ inch extra in each seam allowance with which to make changes. Then, trim seam allowance to $1/_2$ inch on all seams except zipper seam.

MARKING. On the chair, spread seams open, one at a time. Make chalk marks between layers along pinned lines. Marks will be on the wrong side of the fabric (1073).

At 2- to 3-inch intervals, make straight lines across seams (1074). On curved areas, make cross lines 1 inch apart. These "notch" marks will help in matching seams together again.

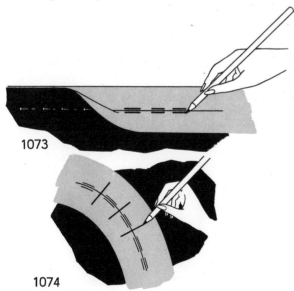

1073

1074

Sewing Loose Covers

On each section of the loose cover, you will stitch the inside (plain) seams first, then the piping seams.

(*a*) To make self-covered bias piping, see page 233

(*b*) To apply piping to the loose cover:

The piping is applied to the right side of the fabric. The raw edges of the piping are placed toward the raw edge of the fabric piece. Stitch piping to the marked seam line of one piece of the fabric, using a piping foot on your machine. Place the second piece of fabric over the piece with the piping, right sides together, and pin the seam. Place the piece with the piping uppermost on the machine and stitch just inside your first row of stitching (1075). The two rows of stitching strengthen the seam and prevent the piping from slipping as it may if you try to stitch piping and seam all at once (1076).

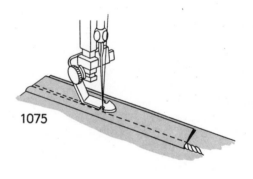

1075

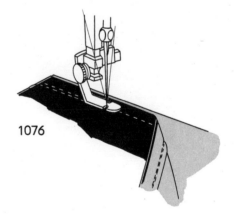

1076

BACK SECTIONS. Remove only the pins joining arm sections to inside, outside and side back sections. Remove back from chair, pins still in place. Straighten seams along pinned line and correct markings. Remove pins.

Right sides together, matching seam lines and notches, stitch top boxing to top of side back, with plain seam (1077). Press seam open. Put section on chair. Check seam placement.

1077

INSIDE BACK. Stay-stitch top edge and upper corners, and curved lines where inside back meets arm of chair (1078). Stitch piping along seams which join inside back to side back and top boxing. Pin piped edge to top boxing and side backs on marked seam lines, matching notches. Use machine-stitching on piping for stitching guide lines.

1078

OUTSIDE BACK. Stay-stitch across top and upper corners. Attach piping (see page 293) around side and top seams (1079). Pin outside back to top boxing and side back, matching seam lines and notches. Stitch one side and top edge. On other side, where zipper will be inserted, stitch from upper corner

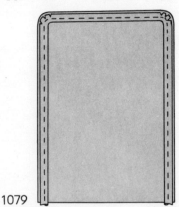

1079

down to top of placket opening, depending on length of zipper to be used.

Return whole back section to chair. Check for fitting on all seams and adjust where necessary (1080).

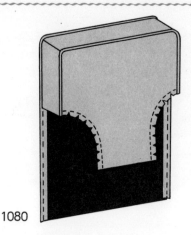

1080

ARM SECTIONS. Remove arm sections, still pinned, from the chair. Check and straighten seams. Remove pins. Stay-stitch back of inside top arm section (where seams join to back section) (1081). Join inside top and outside arm sections with plain seam. Press seam open.

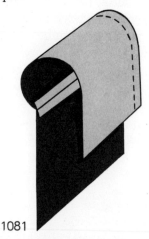

1081

Stay-stitch around edges of front arm section. Stitch piping to side and top edges (1082). Baste front arm section to outside and inside top arm sections. Check fitting on chair. Stitch on basting line. Put arm section back on chair, and check fitting again (1083).

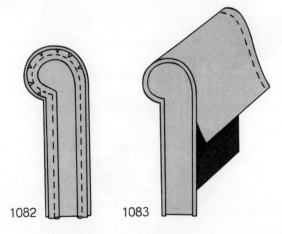

1082   1083

Join arm to back sections (1084). On zipper side, remove arm and back sections from chair. Pin top arm to side back on marked seam line, matching notches. Stitch.

Pin inside top arm to inside back on marked seam lines, to area where tuck-in allowance begins. Stitch, running seam down to edge of tuck-in allowance. Join edges of tuck-in allowance.

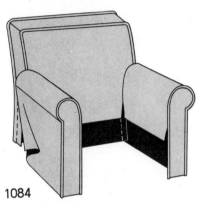

1084

INSERTING ZIPPER. Be sure to use a loose cover zipper with wider tape. Trim the piped seam allowance to $^1/_2$ inch along placket opening (1085). Place the open zipper face down with top end of zipper at lower edge of loose cover. (If you are putting a skirt on your loose cover the top end of zipper should be 1 inch from floor. Insert zipper after skirt has been attached.)

1085

Match edge of tape to edge of piped seam allowance. Attach zipper foot and adjust to right-hand side of needle. Stitch close to zipper teeth. Turn in seam allowance on other side of placket opening and press. Turn loose cover to outside and close zipper. Lap folded edge of placket opening over zipper teeth to piped seam line. Stitch across the end and down the side of the zipper to give the appearance of a lapped application (1086.)

Now, join the other arm sections to the inside and side back. Then, join outside arm to outside back section (1087).

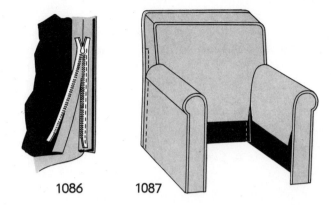

1086   1087

SEAT SECTION. With plain seams, join front arm sections to spring edge section of seat. Join tuck-in allowance on the sides of the seat section to tuck-in allowance at bottom of arm section. Stitch side edge of tuck-in allowances up to the end of the seam, joining front arm and spring edge. Join tuck-in allowance on back of seat to tuck-in allowance at inside back. Place cover back on chair. If you have checked every section as it was finished, your loose cover should fit perfectly (1088).

1088

Bottom-Edge Finishes

TUCK-UNDER FINISH WITHOUT SKIRT. A snugly fitted loose cover with this finish at the lower edge is difficult to tell from upholstery. Gripper snap tape attached to bottom of loose cover and chair hold the cover firmly in place (1089).

Tack one half of tape to inside edge of chair frame between legs on bottom of chair. Put loose cover on chair and pull down firmly on all sides.

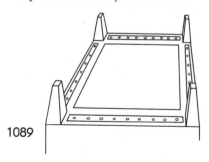

1089

You have left 2 inches of fabric below the lower edge of the chair frame on every side (1090). Mark the bottom edge of the chair on the fabric with chalk. This is the line where fabric will be tucked under. Extend line around chair legs.

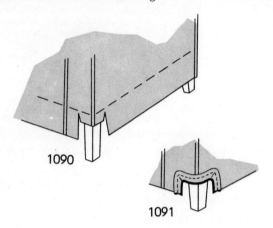

1090

1091

At chair legs, cut fabric away $^1/_2$ inch from chalk line. Apply facing of $1^1/_2$-inch bias strip to right side of loose cover around leg marking (1091). Stitch on chalk line. Clip seam allowance and turn facing to underside. Fold under edges of loose cover at bottom of chair and turn in raw edges in line with gripper snap tape tacked to chair frame (1092). Pin other half of gripper snap tape to this edge. Stitch all edges of tape securely in place. Tape makes it possible to remove cover easily for cleaning.

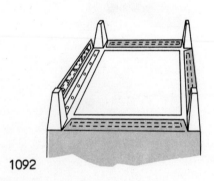

1092

SKIRT (tailored with 4-inch inverted pleat at each corner). Turn up bottom of chair cover at skirt line. Determine finished height of skirt from cover to floor. Add $^1/_2$ inch for seam and $1^1/_4$ inches for hem.

Cut four strips to this depth, on the crosswise grain of the fabric. Pin one strip to front of chair, centring design (1093). Mark corner edges. Take off chair. Add $8^1/_2$ inches from each corner marking. Cut away excess. Repeat for sides and back.

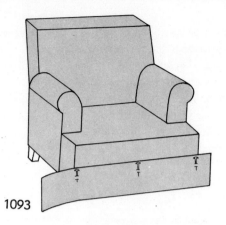

1093

Leave zipper corner open. Join strips for skirt at other three corners, with plain $^1/_2$-inch seams. Press seams open. Hem bottom of strip (1-inch hem and $^1/_4$-inch turn-under). Press.

At each joining seam, measure 8 inches away from the seam in both directions. Mark. Bring markings to meet at seam, on right side, forming pleats. Baste folds of pleat together. Press.

At edges left open for zipper, mark $^1/_2$-inch seam allowance. Measure 8 inches in from seam allowance and mark. Bring markings to seam allowance. Baste and press.

Stay-stitch around top of skirt, through pleats, $^1/_2$ inch from top edge. Stitch piping to right side of skirt on stay-stitching line (1094). Pin skirt to chair cover.

1094

Match corners and centres on each side first. Pin into place. Skirt is attached to cover by stitching to cording. Begin and end stitching at zipper opening (1095).

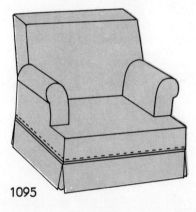

1095

Many variations are possible on the skirt section. Continuous box- or knife-pleated, group-pleated, or gathered skirts may be used. They are applied to the chair cover in the same manner as described above.

To hold cover firmly at bottom edge, attach a piece of cotton twill tape to the corner seams of chair cover, just above each chair leg (1096). Place free ends of tape around leg. Draw tapes tightly to inside edge of chair leg. Tie, or fasten with heavy-duty snaps.

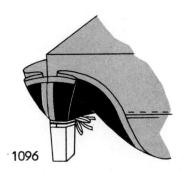

1096

Upholstery finish may also be used on cover with skirt. Allow 1-inch seam allowance on seam joining loose cover to skirt. Stitch one side of gripper snap tape to wide seam allowance and tack other side of gripper snap tape to chair frame as described on page 295. Snap loose cover to chair frame to hold cover securely in place (1097).

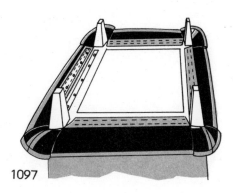

1097

Seat Cushion Cover

Place cushion on chair. Place fabric on cushion, centring design to produce best effect in relation to chair back. Pin from centre out to sides. Mark seam lines on outer edges of cushion (1098).

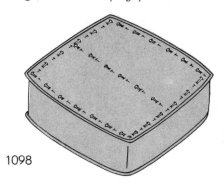

1098

Remove fabric from cushion. Cut away excess, leaving 1/2-inch seam allowance. Place cut section on fabric, right sides facing. Match design. Using cut piece as a pattern, cut the bottom of the chair cushion.

Place piping on right sides of both sections. Stitch 1/2 inch from edge. Piping should join on one side of the cushion, about 3 inches from the back corner.

BOXING:

Front. Measure depth of cushion. Add 1 inch for seam allowances (1/2 inch for each seam). Cut crosswise strip this depth, from selvage to selvage. Centre design on front of cushion. Pin across front, around corners and halfway back on each side.

Back. Cut another crosswise piece, the cushion depth, plus 3 inches (2 inches for zipper and 1/2 inch for each seam), and same length as front.

ZIPPER. The placket opening is in the middle of the back boxing. It must extend around at least one corner for the widest possible opening (1099).

Fold back boxing strip in half lengthwise, and press. Cut on fold entire length. Place strips with right sides facing and stitch together with 1-inch seam. Stitch 1½ inches with regular stitch and back-stitch. Then use machine-basting stitch for length of zipper, returning to regular stitch for balance of strip. Press seam open. Use lapped seam application for inserting zipper. Press the application and remove basting. Front and back sections are now the same width.

Pin back boxing to cushion back, meeting front boxing at centre of cushion sides. Mark seam lines. Remove from cushion. Stitch side seams of boxing with 1/2-inch seams. Press seams open.

Attach top and bottom to boxing. Pin top cover to boxing with right sides together and stitch on piping line. Open zipper. Pin bottom cover to boxing, right sides together, and stitch on piping line. Turn cover right side out through zipper opening and place on cushion.

1099

INDEX

INDEX

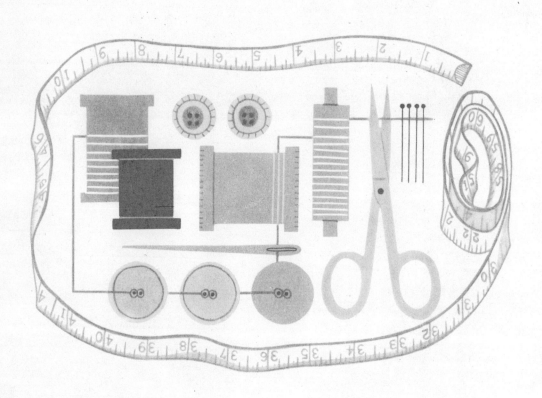